Mormonism

for

A Wiley Brand

Mormonism

2nd Edition

by Christopher Kimball Bigelow
and Jana Riess, PhD

Mormonism For Dummies®, 2nd Edition

Published by: **John Wiley & Sons, Inc.**, 111 River Street, Hoboken, NJ 07030-5774, www.wiley.com

For general information on our other products and services, please contact our Customer Care Department within the U.S. at 877-762-2974, outside the U.S. at 317-572-3993, or fax 317-572-4002. For technical support, please visit https://hub.wiley.com/community/support/dummies.

Wiley publishes in a variety of print and electronic formats and by print-on-demand. Some material included with standard print versions of this book may not be included in e-books or in print-on-demand. If this book refers to media that is not included in the version you purchased, you may download this material at http://booksupport.wiley.com. For more information about Wiley products, visit www.wiley.com.

Library of Congress Control Number: 2025933259

ISBN 978-1-394-31576-5 (pbk); ISBN 978-1-394-31578-9 (ebk); ISBN 978-1-394-31577-2 (ebk)

SKY10099738_031025

Contents at a Glance

Contents at a Glance

Table of Contents

Introduction

I f you're picking up this book, you may already know that Mormonism's largest denomination, The Church of Jesus Christ of Latter-day Saints, is one of the world's fastest-growing religions. The Church has about 7 million members in the United States and another 10 million people on the rolls around the world. Almost all this growth has happened in the last 50 years, making Mormonism a hot topic that many people want to understand better.

In this book, we focus on The Church of Jesus Christ of Latter-day Saints. You'll find the basics here for most everything you need to understand about the Church. We don't assume that you have any background. At the same time, even if you are a Latter-day Saint, you may find information in this book that helps you understand your religion more thoroughly and with a fresh perspective.

About This Book

Don't feel you have to read this book straight through from cover to cover. Each chapter is a self-contained unit designed to give you information about a particular topic. Where relevant, we also include cross-references to show you where to find more information. This way, you can find what you want quickly and skip over the stuff that seems less important to you.

One more thing: Although we're both practicing members of The Church of Jesus Christ of Latter-day Saints, the views you find in this book are unofficial and don't necessarily represent the opinions of the Church's leadership.

Furthermore, although we tried our best to capture the broadest cross-section possible and present a range of viewpoints, we certainly can't claim that every Latter-day Saint you meet will agree with everything we say. Throughout the book, we refer you to a few other books that the Church does produce and sanction, and we also point you to the Church's official website, www.churchof jesuschrist.org.

In addition, The Church of Jesus Christ of Latter-day Saints has some style preferences that we adopted for this book. You won't see the term *Mormon church* here because Mormon is a nickname, and the Church would rather have people use its official name. We do use *LDS church* for short, instead of spelling out the whole name each time, and we refer to Church members as *Latter-day Saints*. From time to time, you'll also see the word Mormon used as an adjective or a noun.

You may also notice a bit of fuss about the capitalization of *church*. Here's the deal: Whenever we're referring to other denominations or to churches in general, we use little c. But when we say "the Church" to mean the LDS church as a specific denomination, we use capital C. However, when we say "LDS church," we keep the c lower-case so it's clear that it's not an official name.

When it comes to the Bible, we stick with what Latter-day Saints still use: the good ol' King James Version (KJV for short). Because the Church's other scriptures are distinctively Mormon, they only come in one lingo — and it reads very much like the KJV. When we reference a particular verse or range of verses in any of the scriptures, we follow the standard: For example, in the Bible, Matthew 10:1 refers to Matthew as the book, 10 as the chapter number, and 1 as the verse.

Foolish Assumptions

While writing this book, we assumed that many of our readers aren't going to be Latter-day Saints, but some will be. Maybe you fit into one of these groups:

>> You've got friends, neighbors, relatives, or coworkers who are Latter-day Saints and you're naturally curious about their faith.

>> You've heard something or read an article about Mormonism, and it made you wonder what Latter-day Saints believe.

>> You're thinking of joining the LDS Church and want to know more about it.

>> You're a new Mormon convert trying to better understand what you've gotten yourself into.

>> You're an established Latter-day Saint, and you want to give this book to someone else who fits in one of the first four categories. Or maybe you like to read different perspectives on your own faith.

Icons Used in This Book

This book uses the following icons to help you find the information you need or to highlight ideas you may find particularly helpful.

TIP

This icon points to hands-on information to help you make sense of Mormon belief or practice.

REMEMBER

You find this icon next to significant information you'll want to remember.

SCRIPTURE

This icon appears next to most quotes from the Bible, Book of Mormon, Doctrine and Covenants, or Pearl of Great Price.

CONTROVERSY

This icon points to areas of disagreement within the Latter-day Saint community or among outsiders who have criticized the Mormon faith.

Beyond the Book

In addition to what you're reading right now, this product also comes with a free access-anywhere Cheat Sheet that provides even more information about Mormonism and the LDS church. To access this Cheat Sheet, simply go to www.dummies.com and search for "Mormonism For Dummies Cheat Sheet" in the Search box.

Where to Go from Here

Mormonism For Dummies is like a big Sunday buffet at Grandma's house. You can eat as many of the yeast rolls as you want, and you don't have to touch the peas if you don't want to. In other words, in this book, we bring a little bit of everything to the table: history, doctrine, fun facts, spiritual disciplines, culture, and scripture. You can go to any section and discover The Church of Jesus Christ of Latter-day Saints and its people, choosing what interests you the most.

If you're coming to this book with a specific question in mind, feel free to look up that topic in the index or table of contents and start with that section. Others may want to start with Chapter 1, which gives an overview of the whole Mormon topic. There's no wrong way to eat this buffet — just enjoy the meal.

1

What the Mormon Faith Is All About

IN THIS PART . . .

Here you find out the basics about what Mormons believe, including important stuff about God, Jesus Christ, the premortal life, the plan of salvation, and the afterlife. You also discover what happened in the 19th century when Joseph Smith was called as a prophet to restore the church of Jesus Christ and how the Mormon priesthood is organized and used today. Finally, you get to know more about the family: Why is the family such an important concept in Mormonism? Why do Mormons tend to have larger-than-usual families? Why are they so into genealogy?

IN THIS CHAPTER

» **Understanding the reasons for studying Mormonism**

» **Seeing life through Latter-day Saint eyes: The past, present, and future**

» **Discovering Mormonism from its beginnings**

» **Finding out what it's like to be a Latter-day Saint**

» **Exploring how Latter-day Saints are different from other Christians**

Chapter **1**

A New World Religion

Buddhism, Judaism, Islam, Hinduism, traditional branches of Christianity — and Mormonism? If you ask some demographers and sociologists, the idea of Mormonism emerging as the newest major world religion isn't far-fetched. In the Christian sector, although Protestantism grew out of Catholicism, Mormonism bills itself as a completely fresh start, with enough distinctive beliefs and practices to back up that claim.

Mormonism isn't the newest kid on the religious block, but its start during the 1820s seems relatively recent — in fact, compared to other world religions, Mormonism is a toddler, still maturing in terms of culture, identity, growth, government, and other aspects. As a blueprint for the rest of the book, this opening chapter gives an overview of what it means to be a Mormon.

Why Know about Mormonism?

If you ask Mormon missionaries why you should find out more about Mormonism, they'll tell you that The Church of Jesus Christ of Latter-day Saints, informally known as the LDS church, is the restoration of the Savior's true church, and he wants you to convert. However, we suspect this answer won't satisfy many of our non–Mormon readers, so here are some other reasons:

>> **It's the quintessential U.S. religion.** Increasingly, historians are acknowledging that Mormonism is perhaps the most successful, significant homegrown U.S. religion, founded just 54 years after the Declaration of Independence. In many ways, the story of Mormonism mirrors the story of the United States, and the faith reflects many American ideals and traits. In fact, Latter-day Saints believe God inspired the formation of the United States partly as a suitable homeland for the gospel's restoration. (For an overview of early Mormon history, see Chapters 4, 11, 12, and 13.)

>> **It's one of the fastest-growing religions.** Chances are that one or more of your friends, neighbors, or relatives has already joined the LDS church or soon will. Consider these statistics:

- As of December 31, 2023, the worldwide Church had 17,255,394 members; 31,490 congregations; 67,871 full-time teaching missionaries; and materials published in 188 languages. To illustrate typical Church growth, in 2023 the Church added 251,763 baptized converts and 93,594 children of record. (For more on missionary work and Church growth around the world, see Chapter 14.)

- The LDS church is consistently ranked among the five largest U.S. religious bodies, larger than mainline Protestant denominations such as Lutheran, Presbyterian, and Episcopalian. According to the National Council of Churches, the LDS church is the second-fastest-growing church in the United States.

>> **It teaches good principles and practices.** Even for those people who don't embrace Mormonism as a religion, the faith yields many useful ideas that you can adapt to fit any worldview. Following are some highlights:

- **Strengthening families:** Latter-day Saints are known for their large, tight-knit, super-functional families. One main reason is that Latter-day Saints believe families can be together forever (for more on this idea, see Chapter 5). Also, the LDS church teaches practical techniques for strengthening families, such as family home evening (for more information on this, see Chapter 17).

- **Providing for the needy:** Marshalling its organizational might, the LDS church has created one of the world's most admired systems for helping people provide for their own material needs. Church-owned farms, ranches, canneries, storehouses, and other enterprises provide not only essential goods but also employment. Increasingly, the Church shares its bounty with people outside the faith. (For more on the Church's welfare program and humanitarian efforts, see Chapter 8.)

- **Maintaining health:** When founding prophet Joseph Smith introduced Mormonism's health code, known as the *Word of Wisdom,* little did he know that science would validate many of these teachings more than 100 years later. Likewise, the Mormon law of chastity helps reduce a host of physical, emotional, social, and spiritual ills. Today, Latter-day Saints are known for enjoying some of the most favorable health rates of any demographic group. (For more on these teachings, see Chapter 16.)

The Mormon Worldview

REMEMBER

The following equation best sums up how Latter-day Saints understand the universe and the purpose of life: As humans are, God used to be; as God is, humans may become.

One main key to getting the gist of Mormonism is the belief that a person's existence doesn't begin with birth on this earth. Rather, Latter-day Saints believe that all people lived as spirits before coming here. For Latter-day Saints, this belief helps explain a whole lot about the conditions and purposes of this earthly life, which they view as God's test of his children. In addition, Latter-day Saints hold some unusual views about the afterlife, particularly regarding what human beings can become. (For a more detailed treatment of these beliefs, see Chapter 2.)

Life before mortal life

If life doesn't start with conception and birth, when does it start? For Latter-day Saints, it *never* really started because each person has an eternal essence that has always existed. However, Latter-day Saints believe that Heavenly Father and Heavenly Mother created spiritual bodies to house each person's eternal essence, so they are the spiritual parents of humankind. All human spirits were born before the earth was created.

Sitting at the knees of their Heavenly Parents, many spirit children expressed a desire to grow up and become like them (for more on the Heavenly Parents, see Chapter 3). So God set up the *plan of salvation,* which involved creating an earth where his children could gain physical bodies and go through a challenging test of faith and obedience. Those who pass the test with flying colors get the chance to eventually start an eternal family like God's.

In *premortality* or *the premortal life,* as Latter-day Saints interchangeably call this stage, two of the oldest spirit siblings made a big impression. The first spirit, named Jehovah, volunteered to help everyone overcome the sin and death they'd unavoidably encounter during the earthly test, and this brother was eventually born on earth as Jesus Christ (for more about him, see Chapter 3). Mormons believe he's their Savior and strive to be like him. The other spirit, named Lucifer, rebelled against God's plan of salvation, convincing a bunch of siblings to follow him and start a war. God banished Lucifer and his followers to the earth without bodies, and Mormons believe that these spirits are still trying to win humans to their side and thwart God's plan (for more about the devil, see Chapter 2).

Life on earth

Good news: In the Mormon view, everyone born on this earth chose to follow God's plan of salvation and come here. Even those who give in to evil during earthly life will still receive an eternal reward for making the correct choice during premortality. Latter-day Saints don't believe that humans are born carrying the stain of Adam's original sin, as Catholics and some Protestants do. But they do believe that each individual's circumstances in this life are at least partly influenced by what that person accomplished and became in premortality.

One of the most difficult aspects of this mortal test is that humans can't remember what happened in premortality, so they must rediscover their divine origins through faith. However, God sent Jesus Christ not only to overcome sin and death but also to establish the gospel, which serves as a road map back to God. Two kinds of messengers help people understand and follow this gospel: prophets and the *Holy Ghost,* a spiritual being who speaks directly to the human spirit (for more on him, see Chapter 3). By listening to these guides, people can figure out the puzzle of life. Unfortunately, the devil strives to fill the world with distractions, deceptions, and counterfeits.

Another hard aspect of the earthly test is that God generally won't interfere with people's freedom to act, even when they do terrible things to each other or fail miserably. In addition, God allows accidents, natural disasters, illnesses, and other difficulties to challenge his children and prompt them to seek him out. For Latter-day Saints, it helps to remember that these temporary trials represent a mere blink of the eye on an eternal scale, and they exercise faith that God will comfort and protect those who ask his help to endure suffering.

During mortality, Latter-day Saints believe that everyone needs to participate in certain rituals in order to live with the Heavenly Parents in the afterlife and become like them. Someone holding God's priesthood authority, which Latter-day

Saints believe currently comes only through the LDS church, must perform these rituals. If a person dies without receiving these ordinances, Latter-day Saints perform the rituals in temples on behalf of the deceased person, whose spirit then decides whether to accept (for more information, see Chapter 7). These ordinances include:

» Baptism (see Chapter 6)

» Confirmation and receiving the gift of the Holy Ghost (see Chapter 6)

» Priesthood ordination (for all worthy males; see Chapter 4)

» The two-part temple endowment (see Chapter 7)

» Sealing, including celestial marriage for those wedded on earth (see Chapter 7)

Life after mortal life

Latter-day Saints believe that when humans die, they slough off their physical bodies and return to the spiritual state. Some go to spirit paradise, and some go to spirit prison. Latter-day Saints believe that the spirits in paradise visit the spirits in prison and teach them the gospel, and some choose to accept it and cross over into paradise. Whether they're in paradise or prison, the stopover in the spirit world is only temporary because God has greater things in store.

Eventually, after God's spirit children have experienced their earthly tests and paid for their sins either by receiving the Savior's atonement or suffering themselves, he'll resurrect everyone with perfect physical bodies that will last forever. Then he'll sort people into three heavenly kingdoms:

» **Telestial kingdom:** Those who live in sin, die without repenting, and don't accept the Savior's atonement go here, after suffering for their own sins in spirit prison.

» **Terrestrial kingdom:** Those who live good lives but don't embrace the full gospel will inherit this kingdom. Jesus pays for their sins.

(Both the telestial kingdom and the terrestrial kingdom are glorious paradises, not hell or places of torture. For more on the three tiers of heaven, see Chapter 2.)

» **Celestial kingdom:** This highest kingdom is reserved for those who live the full gospel and receive the proper ordinances. This kingdom is where the Heavenly Parents live and where their children can become like them.

Joseph Smith and Mormonism's Beginnings

To Latter-day Saints, the term *gospel* means the "good news" that Christ died to save humanity and also refers to a very practical package of tools and instructions that the Savior provides for getting humans back home to God. That package includes doctrines, commandments, ordinances, continually updated revelations, and the priesthood authority to act in God's name (for more on the Mormon priesthood, see Chapter 4). Remember, Latter-day Saints believe that the Savior was God's first spirit child way back before the earth was formed, so he's been on deck to reveal his gospel to prophets from Adam onward.

In the Mormon view, the timeline goes like this: First the Savior gave his gospel to Adam, but Adam's descendants eventually lost it through disobedience and corruption. Then the Savior gave it to other prophets, such as Noah and Abraham, but their people gradually lost it, too. Finally, when the Savior was born on the earth to accomplish his mission of overcoming sin and death for all humankind, he reestablished his gospel. However, within a few decades after his resurrection, humans fumbled it away yet again.

During the 1,700-year religious dry spell that Latter-day Saints say started after the Savior's New Testament apostles died, he worked behind the scenes and prepared the earth to eventually receive his gospel again. In 1820, he began the process of restoring his gospel for the final time. When a teenager named Joseph Smith knelt in prayer to ask God which church he should join, God the Father and his son Jesus Christ appeared to Joseph and told him that none of the existing churches were fully true — in fact, according to Joseph, God used the words "abomination" and "corrupt" in describing them. Within ten years, Joseph Smith launched the Savior's restored gospel in the form of what people now know as the Latter-day Saint religion. (For a more detailed account of Mormonism's founding, see Chapter 4.)

Translating additional scriptures

After Joseph Smith's answer to prayer in 1820, which Latter-day Saints refer to as his *First Vision,* an angel began regularly appearing to prepare him for his prophetic calling. Finally, the time arrived for him to perform one of the most important steps in restoring the gospel: bringing forth additional scripture that helped restore correct principles and could serve as a witness and testament of the new faith.

As Latter-day Saints understand, something very special happened in the Western Hemisphere between 600 B.C. and A.D. 400. At the beginning of this 1,000-year time period, God instructed a prophet named Lehi to leave Jerusalem with some other families and move to the Western Hemisphere. Over the centuries, this little band grew into a major civilization that underwent continual cycles of faith and wickedness, prosperity and destruction. In his usual way, the Lord sent prophets to teach these people and call them to repentance.

SCRIPTURE

Soon after the Savior's resurrection, he dropped by to spend a few days with about 2,500 of his followers in the Western Hemisphere, ministering to his "other sheep" (John 10:16). Before the Savior ascended to heaven, he called 12 additional apostles to carry out his work in this part of the world. Under apostolic leadership, the people managed to hold onto the gospel for another 400 years after the Savior's momentous visit. Eventually, however, their lack of faith and charity led to their corruption and extermination, as recounted in the Book of Mormon, the LDS church's companion scripture to the Bible.

The Western Hemisphere prophets and apostles kept records on metal plates. A prophet named Mormon made a *For Dummies*-style compilation of the people's spiritual history — well, a shortened version, anyway — and his son Moroni buried it in a hillside. About 1,400 years later, Joseph Smith's family settled near this same hillside in upstate New York. With the help of God, who provided interpreting devices to go along with the metal plates, Joseph translated and published the ancient record, and today the LDS church distributes millions of copies each year in over 100 languages. If the proof of Mormonism is in the pudding, then the Book of Mormon *is* the pudding. (For more about the Book of Mormon, see Chapter 9.)

Establishing the Church

While translating the Book of Mormon, Joseph Smith and his helpers came across passages that prompted questions, such as how to properly baptize someone. The questions that Joseph asked Heavenly Father triggered the following key events:

>> In 1829, John the Baptist appeared to Joseph and his chief scribe to restore the *Aaronic Priesthood,* the preparatory priesthood authority necessary to perform basic ordinances, including baptism.

>> Soon after John the Baptist's visitation, the New Testament apostles Peter, James, and John appeared on earth to give Joseph the *Melchizedek Priesthood,* the full authority to act in God's name within the Church organization. (For more on the two Mormon priesthoods, see Chapter 4.)

>> In 1830, Joseph Smith officially organized the Church, which Latter-day Saints believe the Savior recognizes as his only "true and living" church.

>> Until Joseph's assassination in 1844, he received numerous additional revelations, scriptures, and ordinances that helped establish the new religion (for an overview of these additions, see Chapters 10 and 11).

Coming to terms with the M-word

As a prophet who lived somewhere in North or South America around A.D. 400, Mormon was just one of dozens of important figures in LDS history. Nevertheless, he's the man whose name became the nickname for this whole religious movement. Unfortunately, The Church of Jesus Christ of Latter-day Saints has recently expressed frustration with the nickname.

As we say earlier in this section, the prophet Mormon's claim to fame was compiling and abridging the ancient records that became the Book of Mormon, titled that way because of Mormon's central editorial role. After Joseph Smith translated and published the book, it didn't take long for detractors to start calling his followers *Mormonites*, because of their belief in the book. The "ite" part of the nickname dropped off, and eventually the term stuck and lost most of its negative connotations.

REMEMBER

Still, *Mormon* is just a nickname. What would Mormons rather be called? Although the Church hasn't completely ruled out the terms *Mormon* and *Mormonism* at the cultural level, it asks the media to use the Church's full name on first reference in a story — in other words, The Church of Jesus Christ of Latter-day Saints — and then say the generic-sounding "Church of Jesus Christ" on each subsequent reference. However, that somewhat clunky and vague lingo hasn't yet universally caught on.

At Church headquarters, use of the term *Mormon* has been phased out — even the Mormon Tabernacle Choir was renamed as the Tabernacle Choir at Temple Square (yeah, another clunky one). In public usage, what often takes the place of *Mormon* is the term *Latter-day Saint*, or *LDS* for short. The Church doesn't like being called the LDS church, but it's a heck of a lot better than *Mormon church*, which the leaders strongly discourage.

For this second edition of *Mormonism For Dummies*, the authors and editors seriously considered changing the title and terminology, but we felt it would be too confusing for the intended readership. Throughout this book, we use the terms *Mormon, LDS,* and *Latter-day Saint* interchangeably to refer to the doctrine, teachings, practices, and members of The Church of Jesus Christ of Latter-day Saints. Within the LDS culture, some hipsters — yes, Mormon hipsters do exist — have started using the word *Mo* to refer to things Mormon, but we won't go that far.

Day-to-Day Mormon Life

Viewing this mortal life as a time of testing, Latter-day Saints see their faith as the textbook for an A+, and they strive to live the religion 24 hours a day, 7 days a week. In fact, one of the primary virtues in Mormonism is obedience to the commandments and counsel of the prophets, as well as to the spiritual promptings of the Holy Ghost. The religion provides standards that Latter-day Saints believe will help them become pure and righteous enough to reenter the Heavenly Parents' presence, with the Savior's crucial help to overcome sin and death.

Following is an overview of what daily life is like for Latter-day Saints all over the world. Not everyone lives up to all these standards all the time, of course, but this is pretty much what practicing Latter-day Saints believe they ought to be trying to do:

>> **They follow a disciplined routine.** Each day, most Latter-day Saints pray individually, pray as families, and spend time reading the scriptures (for more on these practices, see Chapter 17). They may also devote time on one or more weekdays to fulfilling volunteer Church assignments, such as preparing a Sunday school lesson or helping clean the local meetinghouse (see Chapter 6).

>> **They embrace a G-rated lifestyle.** To avoid addictions and maintain spiritual purity, Latter-day Saints abstain from coffee, tea, tobacco, alcohol, and harmful drugs. In addition, they keep sex strictly within the bounds of heterosexual marriage and try to avoid anything "unholy or impure," including immodest clothes, pornography, profanity, and gambling. Some Mormons even refrain from R-rated movies. (See Chapter 16.)

>> **They seek a change of pace on Sunday.** On Sundays, Latter-day Saints spend the day resting and worshipping with their families, and they attend church for two hours at their local meetinghouse, which is open to the public. On the Sabbath, many Latter-day Saints avoid work, shopping, sports, and other worldly distractions. (See Chapters 6 and 17.)

>> **They kiss Monday-night football goodbye.** Latter-day Saints typically devote Monday evenings to spending time with their families, usually some mix of learning the gospel, enjoying wholesome recreation, and snarfing down unwholesome treats (see Chapters 5 and 17).

>> **They take part in rituals.** Latter-day Saints regularly attend the *temple,* a special building set aside for the faith's most sacred ordinances, such as celestial marriage. Temples aren't open on Sunday or to the public, and most of the ordinances performed there are on behalf of the dead. Latter-day Saints who've gone through the temple wear special undergarments each day

to remind them of their covenants with God and provide spiritual protection. (See Chapter 7.)

>> **They regularly fast and donate money.** Each month, Latter-day Saints fast for two meals (about 24 hours) to increase their spirituality, spending that time praying, reading the scriptures, attending church, and otherwise trying to get closer to God. They donate money saved from those meals — and more, if possible — to the Church's fund for helping the needy. In addition, Latter-day Saints tithe 10 percent of their income to the Church. (See Chapter 16.)

What Makes Mormonism Different?

Although Latter-day Saints share a lot in common with other Christian and non-Christian faiths, they hold several uncommon beliefs, especially when compared to Protestant Christianity. Here's a brief overview of some key points where Latter-day Saints differ from the norm:

>> **Premortality:** No other mainstream Christian denomination agrees with Latter-day Saints that the essence of each human has always existed and that humans were born spiritually to Heavenly Parents before being born physically on earth. Although people who believe in reincarnation can easily relate to the concept of a life before this life, Latter-day Saints believe that everyone gets only one shot at mortality. (See Chapter 2.)

>> **The Trinity:** Most Christians think of God as a universal spirit that manifests as Father, Son, and Holy Ghost (check out *Christianity For Dummies,* written by Richard Wagner and published by Wiley, for more on that idea). By contrast, Latter-day Saints see these deities as three separate, individual beings who are united in purpose. (See Chapter 3.)

>> **God's nature:** Latter-day Saints believe that their Heavenly Parents underwent a test much like this earthly one, which they argue doesn't deny their eternal nature because *all* individuals have always existed, in one form or another (see "Life before mortal life," earlier in this chapter). The Heavenly Parents now have glorified bodies of flesh and bones, and they possess all possible knowledge and power throughout the universe. (See Chapter 3.)

>> **The Savior:** Latter-day Saints believe that Jesus Christ was God's firstborn spirit child, which means he's the oldest spiritual sibling of all humans. However, Jesus is God's only *earthly* child, which means that he's the only perfect person who ever lived on this planet. Latter-day Saints believe that the name *Jehovah* in the Old Testament refers not to God but to his son, who's taken the lead role in saving humankind since before the earth was formed. (See Chapter 3.)

>> **The devil and hell:** Latter-day Saints believe that God didn't create evil but that each individual being has the ability to choose good or evil. The devil was God's most powerful spirit child to choose evil, and he tries to persuade others to do the same, but evil could still exist without him. As far as hell is concerned, Latter-day Saints believe that unrepentant wicked people will suffer consequences for their sins, but only those who personally know God and still rebel against him will go to an eternal hell, which Latter-day Saints call *outer darkness*. (See Chapter 2.)

>> **Adam and Eve:** In the Mormon view, Adam and Eve were heroes who consciously took the steps necessary to begin mortality. Latter-day Saints view mortality as an essential test for eternal progression. Without this physical experience in a fallen, isolated world, humans can't learn and grow enough to eventually become like their Heavenly Parents. (See Chapter 2.)

>> **Grace versus works:** Although many other Christians emphasize salvation solely by God's grace through faith, Latter-day Saints believe that people are saved by grace after they've done all they can to repent of their sins, obey God, and be righteous. Good works alone don't save people, but they do nourish people's faith and make them more open to receiving the grace that saves them. As far as bad works go, all sins require repentance before grace can kick in. (See Chapter 2.)

>> **The atonement:** Latter-day Saints believe that Jesus Christ paid for humankind's sins not just on the cross but also in the Garden of Gethsemane, where his pain was so great that he sweat blood. Christ paid the price of the sins of anyone who repents and obeys his gospel, but those who refuse will suffer for their own sins. Latter-day Saints generally don't use the sign of the cross, as some Christians do, but they believe that Christ broke the bonds of death through his resurrection. (See Chapter 3.)

>> **Salvation:** In contrast to many Protestant Christians, who believe you're either saved or you're not, Latter-day Saints believe all humans will be resurrected and will receive an eternal reward depending on individual worthiness. Although pretty much everyone will receive a measure of salvation in one of three eternal kingdoms, only those who accept the Savior's complete gospel — the one currently preached and practiced by Latter-day Saints — will receive *full* salvation, which means returning to live with God. In addition, Latter-day Saints use the term *exaltation* to refer to humankind's potential to become like our Heavenly Parents, which happens only for heterosexually married people who reach the highest level of the highest eternal kingdom. (See Chapter 2.)

>> **Priesthood:** In the Mormon view, the *priesthood* is the authority to act in God's name for the salvation of his children within the bounds of the LDS church organization. Instead of ordaining professionals who've completed special training, the Church ordains worthy and willing Mormon males from

age 11 on up, via the laying on of hands by someone already holding the priesthood. Any adult priesthood holder can perform ordinances such as baptism and healing or be called to lead a congregation. In contrast with the traditions of some other churches, Mormon priesthood holders don't get a nickel for their service. (See Chapter 4.)

>> **Ordinances:** In some Christian denominations, ordinances such as baptism are outward expressions of commitment, not requirements for salvation. Latter-day Saints, on the other hand, believe that each individual must receive certain physical ordinances in order to return to God's presence, and authorized priesthood holders must perform them. In addition, Latter-day Saints hold the unusual belief that if a person dies without receiving an essential ordinance, a living Latter-day Saint can perform it in a temple on the deceased person's behalf, and their spirit will decide whether to accept it. (See Chapters 6 and 7.)

>> **Apostles and prophets:** Latter-day Saints believe that the Savior issues revelations to whatever prophet is currently leading the LDS church. These revelations instruct how the leaders should administer the Church under current earthly conditions. In addition, Latter-day Saints believe that the Savior calls modern apostles to serve as his special witnesses, similar to the New Testament apostles, and they too serve as "prophets, seers, and revelators." (See Chapter 8.)

>> **Scriptures:** Most Christians believe the Bible is God's only authorized scripture. Although Latter-day Saints uphold the Bible and prayerfully study its teachings, they believe it contains some human translation errors and omissions. In addition, they believe that other civilizations recorded scriptures equally as valid as the Bible, most notably the Western Hemisphere civilizations that gave rise to the Book of Mormon. In fact, they believe that God is still revealing scriptures in this day and age. (See Chapters 9 and 10.)

>> **God's only true church:** Although most other Christians accept each other's churches as valid in God's sight, Latter-day Saints believe their own church is God's only fully "true and living" church currently on the earth. Latter-day Saints respectfully acknowledge that many religions contain elements of God's eternal truths, but they believe that only the LDS church possesses the full package of God's authorized priesthood, ordinances, and revelations. Latter-day Saints see the LDS church as the complete modern restoration of the same true religion that other groups have possessed throughout human history, particularly in New Testament times. (See Chapter 4.)

>> **Family and marriage:** Some people believe that earthly family relationships, including marriage, end at death. Latter-day Saints believe that specially ordained temple workers can seal earthly families together for eternity and that sealed couples can keep progressing together to eventually become Heavenly Parents. (See Chapters 2, 5, and 7.)

- » **Fulfilling the purpose of this mortal life**
- » **Reaching the intermediate spirit world after death**
- » **Going to an eternal heaven — or "outer darkness"**

Chapter 2

The Mormon Plan of Salvation

When it comes to pondering existence, each human being invariably faces three fundamental questions: Where did I come from? Why am I here? What show should I stream tonight? (Er, that last one should've been, Where am I going?)

As a religion, Mormonism provides some unique answers to all three of these eternal questions, answers that together are known as the *plan of salvation*. Latter-day Saints are Christians, but their beliefs about humankind's origin, purpose, and destiny differ considerably from those of Catholic or Protestant Christians. In a nutshell, the Mormon plan of salvation includes the following phases of existence:

- » **Premortal life:** Before this physical earth was created, the eternal essences of all people underwent spiritual development and preparation in God's presence.

- » **Mortal test:** Born into a physical body on earth and with their premortal memories veiled, humans face challenges and learn to exercise faith.

>> **Spirit world:** Depending on their earthly conduct and the desires of their hearts, spirits of the deceased wait in either paradise or prison for resurrection and the final judgment.

>> **Three degrees of glory:** Each resurrected person will spend eternity in one of three levels of heaven or — in rare cases — in "outer darkness."

In this chapter, we discuss each of these phases in detail (see Figure 2-1 for a quick graphic summary).

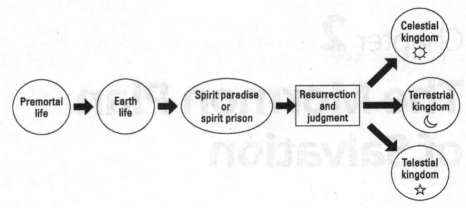

FIGURE 2-1:
An overview of the Mormon plan of salvation.

Mormon Karma: The Premortal Life

Every religion makes claims about the afterlife, but one of Mormonism's key concepts is the *before*-life. Latter-day Saints aren't the only ones who believe that humans are eternal beings, but Latter-day Saints are somewhat unusual — especially among other Christians — for believing that human eternity stretches in *both* directions, before and after mortality.

In Hinduism and Buddhism, a person's actions affect the nature of their next life, a process known as *karma.* Latter-day Saints don't believe in reincarnation, but they do believe that a person's actions in the premortal life can affect the nature and circumstances of their earthly life. It's not uncommon for a Mormon, when faced with some earthly trial, to half-jokingly mutter, "What did I do in the premortal life to deserve this?"

In the Mormon view, each human being arrives on this earth with subconscious baggage from the premortal life — and if you're here, it's because you *chose* to come. This section discusses what the concept of premortal life means to

Latter-day Saints and explains some significant historical premortal events, including the War in Heaven.

From intelligence to spirit

REMEMBER

Mormonism's founding prophet, Joseph Smith, taught that the essence of each human being has always existed, as opposed to being created. The Mormon term for an individual human essence is *intelligence*, but exactly what form an intelligence takes is a bit hazy. The important concept to understand, from the Mormon perspective, is that God didn't create our fundamental, individual existences out of nothing.

Instead, Latter-day Saints believe that, before this earth was formed, Heavenly Father and Heavenly Mother got together and procreated a spirit body to house each human intelligence. (For more on the infrequently discussed Heavenly Mother, see Chapters 3 and 15.) These spirit bodies resemble God's glorified physical body, but they don't yet have a physical presence. What the Heavenly Parents do for their spirit children is help them progress into increasingly advanced states of existence, potentially culminating in their becoming an eternal parent like the Heavenly Parents. After all, their spirit children carry their spiritual DNA.

But we're getting ahead of the story. Before the earth's creation, Mormon belief says that billions of spirit children lived and learned in the presence of their Heavenly Parents across eons of premortal time — and, in fact, those spirits who haven't yet been born on the earth are still dwelling in their presence. In this premortal spiritual state, future humans developed distinctive personality traits, attributes, and talents and interacted socially and politically with each other, preparing for the earthly test.

Why do the spirits want to come to earth? Just as an intelligence could progress only so far without a spirit body, a spirit can progress only so far without a physical body. Back before the earth was formed, the spirit children reached a point of maturity where they wanted to gain a perfect, glorified physical body like God's and become like him. Without a physical body, they couldn't do many of the things their Heavenly Parents could do, including procreate other beings.

Latter-day Saints believe that in order to enable his spirit children to become like him, God offered them the plan of salvation, which would allow them to test-drive a physical body on an earthly planet, prove how well they could exercise faith in God and follow his commandments, and strive to eventually return to God's presence. Through a mortal test like the one early Mormon leaders taught that God himself underwent innumerable eons ago, his children could start learning the godly attributes of disciplining physical appetites, shaping the elements, and loving and serving their offspring.

In addition, they could gain godly wisdom by encountering the opposing forces of good and evil, pain and pleasure, sickness and health, age and youth, sin and virtue, time and eternity, and death and immortality. If they learned these lessons well enough, the potential payoff could be huge: Eventually, they could become an eternal parent like their Heavenly Parents, perfect in love, justice, and mercy. Of course, they would still eternally respect and honor God as their father, even when having spirit children and creating planets of their own.

Relax, you've already passed the first test

Congratulations! As someone who lives here on earth, you've already passed the first test of choosing to follow God's plan of salvation. Due to what Latter-day Saints call the War in Heaven, it wasn't an easy choice to make. Allow us to explain.

As his spirit children considered the plan of salvation, God didn't hide the fact that the path would be fraught with danger, difficulty, and sacrifice. To facilitate effective testing conditions, he would place a veil over each spirit's memories of the premortal life. Each person would start over again as a baby and then age and die. God would allow evil to tempt people and chance to affect them for both good and bad. He would continue to absolutely respect human free will (Latter-day Saints call it *agency* or *free agency*), even when people chose to do terrible things to each other. In a kind of spiritual survival of the fittest — a process God would oversee with love and concern — only those who made enough progress in learning and obeying God's will would eventually be resurrected as heavenly parents; the rest would be resurrected to lesser degrees of glory, according to their efforts, desires, and faith.

Because all earthly mortals would sin and become unworthy to reenter God's presence, a sinless redeemer would be necessary to pay the price of sin so that those who repented could become clean again. In addition, beings with mortal flesh would need a way to overcome their physical death. Latter-day Saints believe that during a great council in heaven before the earth was formed, two of God's spirit children volunteered to serve as redeemer of humankind:

>> A high-ranking, widely influential spirit named Lucifer proposed to save everybody by forcing their obedience, and he would receive all the glory for himself. However, this plan didn't meet God's approval because true progress is impossible without *agency* and *accountability* — in other words, the freedom to choose and the obligation to face the consequences.

> ❯❯ The firstborn of all the spirits, named Jehovah, offered to pay the price for everybody's sins, guide those who were willing to follow him back to God, and overcome death through resurrection. In addition, Jehovah promised to obey God's will and give all the glory to God. God chose him as the redeemer, and he was later born on earth as Jesus Christ.

Unfortunately, Lucifer was a sore loser. Declaring war on God and Jehovah, he persuaded a third of the spirit children to take his side. Perhaps many of these followers of Lucifer feared they'd fail if left to make their own choices on earth, and they wanted someone to guarantee success. Eventually, God cast Lucifer and his followers out of heaven, denying them the opportunity to ever receive a physical body. Lucifer became the devil (also known as Satan) and his followers became demons, and the spiritual war that started in premortality continues here on earth. Lucifer hasn't admitted defeat, and he still lusts for power and tries to thwart God's purposes by usurping human freedom through whatever means possible. (See "Satan: A necessary evil" later in this chapter for more on Satan's role in Mormon theology.)

REMEMBER

If you're holding this book, Latter-day Saints believe that you took Jehovah's side in the War in Heaven and qualified yourself to be born onto this earth. So, kudos all around.

Premortality in the here and now

Premortality plays a central role in the Mormon religious imagination. However, the subject is also a troublesome area. Because the LDS scriptures don't give many specifics about premortality, some of the Mormon outlook results from informal or even folk teachings. Perhaps more than any other Mormon belief, the idea of premortality has been shaped by sentimentalized pop culture, especially the influential Mormon musical *Saturday's Warrior*, performed live for hundreds of thousands during the 1970s and still available on video. Even worse, Mormon folk beliefs related to premortality have contributed to some harmful attitudes, particularly concerning racial matters.

SCRIPTURE

By the way, although Latter-day Saints are unique among Christians for believing in premortality, they've spotted many glimpses of the concept in both the Old and New Testaments of the Bible, especially the following passages: Job 38:4–7, Proverbs 8:22–31, Jeremiah 1:5, John 9:1–3, Acts 17:28, Ephesians 1:4–5, 2 Timothy 1:9, Titus 1:1–2, Hebrews 12:9, Jude 1:6, and Revelation 12:7–9.

The following sections show premortality's effects, both positive and negative, in the here and now.

Effect on earthly circumstances

Latter-day Saints tend to wonder and speculate about how premortality affects conditions in mortality. You can imagine the questions. Was someone born into a prosperous Mormon household because they fought valiantly on Jehovah's side, or was it because this person was a spiritual weakling who needed a head start on earth? Was a person born into the slums of Calcutta because they only barely supported Jehovah, or was it because they were a particularly gifted spirit who needed an extra-challenging test? Although only God knows the reasons behind any particular individual's earthly situation, many Latter-day Saints find that premortality provides a comforting and reasonable explanation for the great variety of earthly circumstances, instead of attributing them all to randomness.

REMEMBER

Although Latter-day Saints don't believe in predestination, they do believe in *foreordination*, which means that God chose spirits with certain skills and capacities to fulfill special purposes during mortality, such as becoming a prophet. However, being given a particular foreordination doesn't necessarily mean the person will succeed in fulfilling it. In the Mormon view, someone who did well in premortality can mess up on earth, and someone who lagged in premortality can catch up here.

On the other hand, Latter-day Saints commonly believe that some spirits were so valiant in the premortal life that they simply needed to receive a physical body without being morally tested, which helps account for childhood deaths and people with mental limitations that make them unaccountable for their actions.

Effect on earthly attitudes

Following are some specific ways in which the Mormon belief in premortality affects earthly attitudes, for better or worse. Although widely prevalent, most of these beliefs aren't official Church doctrine.

>> **Dreams and déjà vu:** Although humans have no conscious memories of premortality, some Latter-day Saints believe that the subconscious retains ideas, plans, goals, instructions, warnings, and other impressions and impulses from the premortal days. For some, this belief helps explain some dreams, sensations of déjà vu, and perhaps even premonitions that seem to hold spiritual meaning or significance.

>> **Friendships and missionary work:** When a Latter-day Saint forms an unusually close bond with somebody and gets the feeling they've known each other forever, they will sometimes wonder if the friendship began in the premortal life. Some Latter-day Saints believe they promised certain individuals that they'd find them on earth and convert them to Mormonism — in fact, many Mormon missionaries keep such a possibility in mind while knocking on

endless doors. As missionaries contact people and try to teach them the LDS gospel, they hope that spiritually sensitive people will recognize the plan of salvation from premortality.

>> **The latter days:** As the Church's name indicates, Latter-day Saints believe that the period of earthly mortality is approaching its conclusion (for more on the return of Christ, see Chapter 3). Because this modern time is both the most advanced and most challenging era in the earth's history, with more temptations than ever before, Latter-day Saints believe that Heavenly Father reserved many of his brightest, strongest spirit children to be born in these latter days. Church leaders frequently repeat this message to the Church's teenage youth, which not only helps build spiritual egos but also gives Latter-day Saints a high standard to live up to — and yes, it can also increase guilt about shortcomings.

>> **Marriage and family:** Some Latter-day Saints believe that during premortality, they formed spiritual bonds with their future earthly spouses, parents, and children. It's not unusual to find a Mormon couple who believes they're meant to be together because of promises made during premortality. Likewise, some Mormon parents conceive another child because they feel a spirit is missing from their family.

>> **Race:** In an attempt to explain why certain people were born into what earlier Church leaders classed as supposedly inferior races, some leaders claimed that these people somehow performed inadequately during premortality. Although the LDS church no longer teaches these politically incorrect ideas, it hasn't fully apologized for those individual leaders' earlier racist teachings, and some Church members may continue to hold these beliefs. Other members, however, including some high-ranking leaders, suspect that many individuals of oppressed races may have been *more* valiant in the premortal life than their seemingly privileged counterparts, and thus are faced with a greater challenge here on earth. (For more on the racial controversies in Mormon theology, see Chapter 15.)

Acing the Test of Mortality

With the successful completion of Phase One — premortality — all those spirits who chose to side with Jehovah in the War in Heaven proceed to Phase Two, which is mortal life, sometimes called "the second estate." In Mormonism, everyone on earth is here because they chose to be, not by accident. That idea may give a spot of comfort when mortal life isn't a bed of roses.

Latter-day Saints regard mortality as both a blessing and a test. It offers the chance to come to know the Savior, Jesus Christ, and follow his teachings. Life's trials and triumphs can prepare humans to successfully return to their Heavenly Parents (see the section "The Afterlife: Eternal Progression," later in this chapter), provided they find and keep the faith and live worthily. If people want to spend eternity in a degree of heavenly glory, they have to go through this mortal life. There's no shortcut.

The basic principle of mortality is *agency*, or free will, and to understand that concept in Mormonism, you have to go way back. Back to a man, a woman, and a garden.

Adam and Eve: Heroes of humanity

In Catholic and Protestant Christianity, Adam and Eve sort of get a bad rap. If they hadn't eaten the fruit and screwed up everything for everyone else, the thinking goes, everyone would be happily cavorting in Eden. But Latter-day Saints don't see it that way at all.

SCRIPTURE

In the Mormon view, without Adam and Eve's heroic choice, no one but them would be on earth in the first place. Their decision to eat the forbidden fruit gave everyone the opportunity to experience a mortal life and have a crack at the celestial kingdom (see "Reaching the three degrees of glory . . . or outer darkness," later in this chapter). The Book of Mormon and the Pearl of Great Price (see Chapters 9 and 10 for an explanation of these LDS scriptures) both agree that Adam and Eve's choice wasn't a mistake or some great cosmic tragedy, but a necessary decision. As the Book of Mormon puts it, "Adam fell that men might be; and men are, that they might have joy" (2 Nephi 2:25). In other words, their decision brought the world potential joy as well as pain — both essential parts of being human. God wouldn't create a fallen world or force his children to inhabit one, but he would let them choose for themselves whether to usher in mortal conditions and undergo such a test, and Adam and Eve paved the way.

In the garden, God placed Adam and Eve in a state of innocence and gave them two seemingly contradictory commandments:

>> Be fruitful and multiply, replenishing the earth — in other words, have kids.

>> Don't eat from the tree of the knowledge of good and evil — in other words, don't lose your spiritual innocence, including about how to have kids.

No, God didn't make a mistake or succumb to a divine version of Alzheimer's by giving these apparently opposite pieces of instruction. It was a test of Adam and Eve's strength and determination. The decision to usher in mortality was so fraught with significance, difficulty, and danger that God had to make it crystal clear that they chose it for themselves and he didn't impose it upon them — in fact, he sternly warned them against it. Luckily, Adam and Eve passed this test with flying colors, due in no small part to Eve's particular understanding and vision. In so doing, they resolved two major problems for the human race:

>> One problem was that Adam and Eve had to eat the fruit before they could be fruitful, so to speak. The Book of Mormon explains that they couldn't have any "seed" (translation: kids) in their state of innocence. So, they needed to eat the fruit of the tree of knowledge of good and evil to lose their innocence and start procreating. If the earth's first children of God hadn't been able to start procreating, that would've been bad news for all the billions of spirits stuck in the waiting room of premortality, chomping at the bit for their shot at the mortal test.

>> A second problem with their situation in Eden was that Adam and Eve couldn't spiritually progress in their state of innocence. They were stuck, Peter Pan–like, in permanent immortality, which gave them nothing to lose or gain. To get the benefit of God's plan of salvation, they had to open their eyes to spiritual reality — good and evil — by eating the forbidden fruit. This caused the world to fall into the "lone and dreary" conditions of mortality, but it also gave them the opportunity to prove themselves and then die so they could return — with the Savior's necessary assistance — to God in heaven.

According to Latter-day Saints, Eve was the first to understand that she would have to disobey one commandment to obey the other. They consider her a heroine for making a difficult but correct moral choice, disobeying a lesser law and sacrificing her own peace and life of ease in the garden, where no one could age or die, in order to serve a higher law, enabling countless others to enter mortality and fulfill their earthly missions. By choosing death for herself, she gave the gift of life to all people, thus earning the name Eve, which means life, and the title "mother of all living." Latter-day Saints believe that God chose her for this mission in her premortal life and that she was one of the noble and great spirits mentioned in the Pearl of Great Price. In fact, modern LDS leaders have taught that Eve's premortal spirit even participated in the creation of the world.

REMEMBER

Although Latter-day Saints refer to Adam and Eve's decision as *the Fall*, they don't regard it as a failure, like some other denominations do. Catholics and some Protestants, for example, view the Fall as the moment that sin entered the world, and they believe that *original sin* — sin that is genetically passed from generation to generation at conception — is the direct result of the sin of Adam and Eve.

Latter-day Saints completely reject the idea of original sin; as the faith's second Article of Faith states, Latter-day Saints believe that people "will be punished for their own sins, and not for Adam's transgression." Note the use of the word *transgression:* Adam and Eve *transgressed* because their actions literally went beyond a boundary that God had set for them. But Latter-day Saints believe their actions weren't *sinful*, because their choice paved the way for the plan of salvation.

Satan: A necessary evil

SCRIPTURE

The Bible says that Eve made her choice in the garden following a proposal from a being who was, as Gollum in *The Lord of the Rings* might say, "very tricksy." Satan, disguised (perhaps figuratively) as a serpent, tried to trick Eve by telling her that the fruit would open her eyes and make her and Adam "as gods," with the intelligence to know good from evil — all true, according to Latter-day Saints. But one of Satan's techniques is to mix the truth with lies so that people become confused. He also told Eve (in the Bible, Genesis 3:5) that she wouldn't die if she ate the fruit, which was a lie. She knew he was wrong but chose to partake anyway and embrace mortality.

So who is this guy? Satan, known in the premortal life as Lucifer, and his demonic followers hold an interesting place in Mormon theology. They make life on earth quite a bit harder. Motivated by selfishness and hate, they declared war on God and everything God represents, and yet God allows them to play an important role in the plan of salvation. Latter-day Saints believe these beings entice humans with evil, making mortality a tough road, so people must consciously choose good in order to grow and progress.

In the Mormon view, demons can do only what God permits them to do, even though in their minds they're rebelling against him. God allows them spiritual access to tempt humans, because temptation puts pressure on humans to choose either good or evil, which is a main purpose of this earthly test. He allows these angels of evil to wreak havoc because that gives people a pressing need to seek out God. Eventually, Latter-day Saints believe, when the demons' usefulness in the plan of salvation has ended, God will permanently banish them to outer darkness, which we discuss at the end of this chapter.

SCRIPTURE

Because each being is free to choose right or wrong, evil would exist without Satan, but he certainly fans the flames. He and his followers are miserable on account of their own choices and want everyone else to make the same mistakes, too. Latter-day Saints believe that one of the key ways demons work is by counterfeiting love, religion, happiness, family, spirituality, and many other facets of life. For example, human beings are wired to crave spiritual experiences, so demons provide misleading ones through drugs, the occult, and other means. Satan can guess at most people's weaknesses, but God won't let him tempt people beyond what they can bear, if they exercise sufficient resistance and faith (see 1 Corinthians 10:13).

It ain't over till it's over: Enduring to the end

Adam and Eve's choice in the garden was risky but absolutely necessary. It was the first earthly instance of human beings exercising their agency, weighing their options between good and evil and determining how to navigate the best way forward in complex circumstances. As in the garden story, sometimes morally correct choices aren't always easy to discern; decisions don't come ready-made with a guaranteed Hallmark movie outcome. Of course, humans are going to make mistakes, but Christ's atonement paved the way for everyone to receive forgiveness for all their sins if they sincerely repent. For more on the atonement of Christ, stay tuned for Chapter 3.

REMEMBER

Latter-day Saints have a phrase for their stay-the-course philosophy: *enduring to the end*. This phrase is actually one of the main principles of the gospel: After faith, repentance, baptism, and receiving the Holy Ghost, all an individual must do to gain full salvation — in other words, return to live and work with their Heavenly Parents — is endure to the end in righteousness. These goals are easier said than done, however, because the journey is 24/7. Here are the basic expectations that Latter-day Saints consider to be part of hanging tough till the end:

» Exercise ongoing faith in the Savior, Jesus Christ.

» Repent and be baptized and confirmed.

» Do good works.

» Strive to keep the commandments and continually repent.

To bump salvation up a notch and achieve *exaltation*, which means becoming an eternal parent like God, enduring to the end includes making and keeping temple covenants, as discussed in Chapter 7.

What's interesting about this enduring cycle is how it feeds upon itself: Doing good works, obeying the commandments, and studying the scriptures spring from faith and simultaneously make people more open to deepening that faith. To Latter-day Saints, faith in Christ *is* what saves, but faith isn't a one-time event that you can check off a list. Rather, faith is an ongoing journey that takes people through this life and the next. Faith is always growing, and obeying commandments and doing good deeds play an important part in nurturing and expanding faith. This whole process is what it means to endure to the end.

SCRIPTURE

Sometimes it seems that mortal life is impossibly hard, and the paths people take are strewn with obstacles and suffering. Latter-day Saints take comfort from a revelation given to Joseph Smith when he was in jail, where the Lord told him that all the rotten things that had happened in his life — which up to that point included being tarred and feathered, falsely imprisoned, and driven from his home — would give him experience and would be for his ultimate gain (Doctrine and Covenants 122:7; for more on the D&C, see Chapter 10). Latter-day Saints believe that all life's ordeals and sufferings have the potential to bring people closer to God.

WHY DO BAD THINGS HAPPEN TO GOOD PEOPLE?

Every religion must answer the age-old question of why bad things happen in the world. Mormonism is different from traditional Christianity in its basic answer to that question. Traditional Christianity assumes that God is both entirely loving and entirely powerful, so it's very much an unresolved question why he doesn't intervene to save his children from things like famine, heartache, and untimely death. Mormonism also assumes that God is entirely loving but teaches that God limits his own power in order to grant human beings their agency and let them encounter hard realities that will help them grow in godly understanding.

Because free agency is such an important part of his plan of salvation, God won't typically intervene when people do bad things to each other, though Latter-day Saints believe he grieves deeply when his children hurt one another or themselves. In addition, God allows chance accidents and mishaps to occur. Latter-day Saints exercise faith that God will protect them and help orchestrate their lives, but even faithful people can't always be sure whether God will intervene to limit, prevent, or reverse something bad. However, God *always* supports and comforts his children in their sufferings, when they turn to him and ask for his loving care. Of course, those who do harmful things to others will eventually face the consequences.

While God may customize some trials to individual people as part of their earthly education, he generally seems to allow people and events to take their natural courses in this fallen world, occasionally tweaking things when people exercise enough faith and obedience in accordance with his will. It's a great comfort that God gives his children the spiritual tools to endure and overcome hardships and traumas. Latter-day Saints don't feel they know all the answers about why suffering exists, but they trust in God's goodness and strive to exercise their agency righteously so they don't cause unnecessary suffering to themselves or others.

Latter-day Saints also believe that this mortal journey can yield great joy, even though trusting that all life's twists and turns will work together for good isn't always easy. One Book of Mormon prophet, Nephi, told people who'd been baptized and were trying to stay on the right path to "press forward with a steadfastness in Christ, having a perfect brightness of hope, and a love of God and of all men" (2 Nephi 31:20). Latter-day Saints still cling to that advice more than 2,500 years later.

The Afterlife: Eternal Progression

The Mormon afterlife consists of two main phases. In the first phase, which human beings enter at the time of death, their disembodied spirits await resurrection. In the second phase, resurrected people dwell for eternity in one of several levels of heaven, as determined by the Lord's judgment of their worthiness and true desires.

A waiting room for spirits

Latter-day Saints aren't unusual for believing that when a human being dies, their eternal spirit leaves the body and goes to what Latter-day Saints term the *spirit world*. In this holding place, spirits temporarily await their resurrection and the final judgment, which won't occur until after all God's willing spirit children have had a chance to get a body and experience mortality.

When the physical body dies, a person's spirit presumably retains their personality, talents, habits, tastes, knowledge, attitudes, and so on. In the spirit world, people don't have tangible bodies but take a spiritual form that resembles their body in life. All spirits are in adult form, even if they died as mortal children, and the spirit body is perfect, with no defects or injuries. Mormon scriptures and prophets teach that the spirit world is divided into paradise for the righteous and prison for the unrepentant wicked. In addition, prophets have taught that the spirit world is located right here on earth, but mortals generally can't sense it.

Free parking: Spirit paradise

For those people who repented of their sins and strived to live righteously during mortality, Latter-day Saints believe their spirits go to a place of paradise, where they can rest from worldly pains and problems. As in premortality, these spirits enjoy relationships with each other and create social organizations. They can continue learning and progressing, and they can help further God's purposes, particularly by serving as missionaries to those in spirit prison.

Can these spirits observe mortals and influence us? Some Mormon prophets have taught that they can, although most angelic messengers to earth are former mortal prophets who have been resurrected (and no, they don't have wings). Latter-day Saints believe that occult efforts to speak with the dead actually summon demons, who masquerade as dead spirits to confuse mortals. Another interesting question is whether unborn premortal spirits can mingle with deceased postmortal spirits. The concept isn't an official doctrine, but some Latter-day Saints believe it happens.

Do not pass go: Spirit prison

SCRIPTURE

Latter-day Saints don't believe in the same concept of hell as most other Christians — in fact, Latter-day Saints don't even use the term *hell* very often. There are two places that Latter-day Saints think of when they imagine hell. We'll get to the second one, *outer darkness,* in just a moment. But first we discuss *spirit prison,* a temporary abode — although temporary may mean centuries or even millennia of earth time — where people's spirits go if they behaved wickedly on the earth, either because they didn't know or didn't accept the gospel message of Christ's atonement. Mormon scriptures say that spirit prison is for all people who "died in their sins" and still need the opportunity to repent of them (D&C 138:32–35).

Although spirit prison isn't staffed by pitchfork-wielding horned demons, the place probably isn't warm, happy, and relaxing, and the devil can still influence people there. One Book of Mormon passage says there's a lot of "weeping, and wailing, and gnashing of teeth" in spirit prison, probably because people recognize the harmful consequences of their choices on earth. Good news, though: In spirit prison, the possibility of parole *does* exist, and someone's sentence there can be cut short by a genuine change of heart and acceptance of Christ's gospel.

SCRIPTURE

Latter-day Saints believe that an impassable gulf used to exist between paradise and prison. Jesus Christ bridged this gulf when his spirit visited the spirits in prison during the time between his earthly death and resurrection (see 1 Peter 3:18–20 and 4:6 in the Bible). Ever since then, spirits from paradise have ministered to those in prison, teaching them the gospel and trying to convince them to accept Christ and repent.

For some spirits in prison, such as those who didn't get a fair chance to hear the gospel on the earth, learning the gospel and repenting may take a short time, and then they can cross over into paradise. Presumably, many people will become more eternally focused when they realize that their spirits have survived beyond death, and they'll accept the gospel and repent. For others, however, such as those who rejected the gospel or were grossly immoral on earth, repentance may be a long and painful process, far more difficult than it would've been during mortality. For the most stubborn spirits who never voluntarily accept the gospel and Christ as their Savior, they'll suffer for their own sins even as Christ already suffered on their behalf. However, even those souls eventually will be resurrected and assigned to the lowest degree of eternal glory; only a tiny percentage of people will spend eternity in *outer darkness* (see the next section).

Meanwhile, mortal Latter-day Saints continually perform crucial gospel ordinances, such as baptism, on behalf of dead people. If and when a dead person's spirit accepts the gospel in spirit prison, these ordinances allow him or her to potentially enjoy the gospel's full eternal benefits and, for those who qualify, eventually ascend to the highest tier of the celestial kingdom. Why can't a spirit perform its own ordinances? Because ordinances are physical and require a body. (For more on performing ordinances for the dead, see Chapters 5 and 7.)

Reaching the three degrees of glory . . . or outer darkness

One of the unusual features of LDS theology compared to other Christian denominations is that Latter-day Saints don't see heaven as a one-size-fits-all sort of place. Latter-day Saints believe that, as in life, where some people are more spiritually oriented and Christlike than others, heaven will feature considerable diversity as far as who receives what eternal reward. For those who earn the highest blessings, those blessings carry great responsibilities and expectations.

SCRIPTURE

In fact, for Latter-day Saints, the singular term *heaven* is a bit of a misnomer, because the afterlife will feature not one but three distinct *kingdoms,* or heavens. Latter-day Saints believe that the biblical apostle Paul was referring to this distinction in 2 Corinthians 12:2, when he spoke of having been taken up into "the third heaven" in a vision. In the Old Testament's original Hebrew, the word for *heaven* is always plural, and the Greek New Testament also often renders the term in plural form. So Latter-day Saints believe that the idea of a multitiered heaven is biblically based.

As is typical of the Mormon penchant for organization, each of the three kingdoms may have gradations *within* it. LDS leader James Talmage taught that because "innumerable degrees of merit" exist among all the people in the human race, it follows that God provides them with "an infinity of graded glories" in the afterlife.

Judging each person

After Christ returns and reigns on the earth for 1,000 years and all God's children — except the devil and his demons — have been resurrected, God's people and Satan will have one final battle (skip to Chapter 3 for more on the Second Coming and resurrection). If you're one of those who likes to read the end of a good mystery first, here's a clue: God's people win. Then all people will face Judgment Day and find out where they'll cool their heels for eternity.

Latter-day Saints believe that the Savior and his apostles from different time periods will carry out the final judgment. LDS scriptures say that a perfect record of all human deeds and thoughts — frighteningly enough! — has been made in heaven, and that people will get to see that record on Judgment Day. Some imagine themselves viewing their best and worst moments on a giant screen, like in the Albert Brooks–Meryl Streep movie *Defending Your Life.* Maybe a sympathetic Jesus Christ will stand with them, holding their hand as they cringe at the moments when they screamed at their children or smile at the times they selflessly helped someone in need. Hopefully, the worst scenes will have wound up on the cutting-room floor, forever forgotten because the person repented by asking the Savior's forgiveness and cleaning up their act.

SCRIPTURE

Whatever the case, Mormon belief is clear on the idea that people's actions in this life are terribly important in determining their status and opportunities in the life to come. Good deeds don't necessarily guarantee a place in heaven, but they're definitely not irrelevant, either. Latter-day Saints rely upon Christ's atonement for salvation, but good works are an important measure of faithfulness and make people more able to receive God's grace and understand his goodness (for more on the atonement, see Chapter 3). Latter-day Saints believe that when Christ spoke of the kingdom of heaven in the New Testament, he regarded it as hard-earned rather than easily understood or achieved. The kingdom of heaven, he said, is like the yeast that makes bread grow, or a pearl of great price that people may search for their entire lives, sacrificing everything in order to attain it (Matthew 13:33, 45–46). In other words, the covenant relationship with God established at baptism requires active human participation.

The challenging news about all this judgment business is that simply professing belief in Christ isn't enough; a person's actions must live up to the standard set by Christ's gospel, including repenting of sins. On the other hand, the good news is that Mormon theology doesn't send non-Christians to "hell" simply for not believing in Christ. In the Mormon view, the idea of a loving God sending whole cultures and peoples who never had the chance to hear of the Savior to eternal damnation makes no sense. Mormon theology teaches that good people of many different religious traditions will live and work in paradise conditions forever; they may even dwell in the highest of the three kingdoms and become like their Heavenly Parents, if they accept the gospel in the spirit world and so qualify.

The following sections provide a rundown of the three basic kingdoms of the Mormon afterlife. Think of each of these kingdoms as layers of a wedding cake.

The bottom layer: Telestial kingdom

The lowest and largest tier of the three-tiered heavenly wedding cake is the telestial kingdom, which is basically for the following kinds of people who died without repenting of their sins:

>> Adulterers

>> Liars

>> Murderers

>> Rapists

>> Those who "received not the gospel of Christ, neither the testimony of Jesus" (D&C 76:82)

You may think that such obvious violators of God's laws would be consigned to everlasting torment, but the telestial kingdom is actually a lovely paradise, once they finally get there after suffering for their own sins. So, what's the telestial kingdom like? LDS leaders have taught that even this lowest degree of glory is so marvelous that humans can't possibly understand it. The Holy Ghost will minister to this kingdom's inhabitants, and Satan will have no power to tempt or torment them anymore. However, their eternal progress will be curtailed — and in that sense, the word *damnation* applies to them. They will live singly forever, with no family bonds.

The middle layer: Terrestrial kingdom

This kingdom is even more glorious than the telestial, because terrestrial folks were basically decent and honorable during their time on the earth, although they didn't embrace the fullness of the gospel. The terrestrial kingdom is equivalent to the popular and mainstream Christian concepts of "heaven." This kingdom will include the following kinds of souls:

>> **Those confused or passive about religion:** When it came to spiritual matters, they weren't serious enough or were "blinded by the craftiness of men" (D&C 76:75) and didn't push through to find and embrace the full truth.

>> **Lukewarm Latter-day Saints:** They were members of the LDS church but "not valiant in the testimony of Jesus" (D&C 76:79).

>> **Those who waited too long:** They rejected the gospel during their mortal lives but later received it in the spirit world (D&C 76:73–74). This idea doesn't apply to those who never got the chance to accept or reject the gospel during their earthly lives.

At this point, you may be wondering why good people won't automatically inherit the most glorious celestial kingdom. Fundamentally, such is the case because they weren't willing to do everything the gospel requires, including participating in sacred ordinances. As the Mormon prophet Brigham Young put it, if people aren't prepared for or don't want the celestial kingdom's eternal responsibilities, then putting them there forever isn't kindness on God's part, because they would be uncomfortable.

For many people, even members of the Church, understanding the difference between the telestial and terrestrial kingdoms is tough, because both are paradises. Here's one key difference: Although the Holy Ghost will visit folks in the telestial kingdom, people in the terrestrial kingdom will also get to spend some time with Christ, whose atonement will have paid the price of their sins. Church leaders compare the difference between these degrees of glory to the relative brightness of the stars (telestial) and the moon (terrestrial). However, like the telestial people, those in the terrestrial kingdom are limited in their eternal progression and live singly forever, without family relationships.

The top layer: Celestial kingdom

At the top of the three-tiered metaphorical wedding cake is the celestial kingdom. Imagine this kingdom standing high above the others on little pillars, because the difference between its glory and that of the terrestrial kingdom is like the difference in brightness between the sun and the moon.

GETTING IN ON THE GROUND FLOOR

In the Mormon view, to cross the threshold into the celestial kingdom, where the Heavenly Parents themselves live, people must

>> Repent of their sins and accept Christ's atonement

>> Receive the saving ordinances of baptism and confirmation from an authorized priesthood holder in person or by proxy (for more on baptism for the dead, see Chapter 7)

>> Strive to keep God's commandments and continually repent

In addition, God has promised that the following two kinds of people will receive celestial glory:

>> "All who have died without a knowledge of this gospel, who would have received it . . . with all their hearts" (D&C 137:7–8)

>> "All children who die before they arrive at the years of accountability" (D&C 137:10), which Latter-day Saints believe is age 8

RISING TO THE HIGHEST LEVEL

SCRIPTURE

An entry-level spot living and working with God in the celestial kingdom is just the beginning. The celestial kingdom has three tiers of glory *within* it (as described in D&C 131:1–4), and Latter-day Saints strive to reach the pinnacle of celestial glory, where they can become eternal parents like their Heavenly Parents.

Picture a happy bride and groom on the very top of the wedding cake. This figurine is a good image to help people understand the highest tier of the celestial kingdom, because *it takes two to get there* — which makes sense, if they're going to become eternal parents. In Mormon belief, righteous husbands and wives who are sealed to one another for eternity in a holy temple can remain together forever in the celestial kingdom, and their children are also sealed to them. This pinnacle of success is known by several different names, including *exaltation* and *eternal life*. (For more on temples and celestial marriages, see Chapter 7.)

People in the highest level of the celestial kingdom can potentially get it all, including

>> Unlimited access to God the Father, Christ the Son, and the Holy Ghost

>> The joy of being with their families for all eternity

>> A perfected body capable of procreating spirit children

>> The right to continue in eternal progression, even to the point of divinity, although they'll always honor and respect Heavenly Father as their superior

But where much is given, much is also expected. The top level of the celestial kingdom won't be an eternal resting place like many Christians imagine heaven. This heaven is Mormon, after all, so there's always work to be done! Ultimately, that work entails the parenting of spirit children, who will then undergo the mortality process themselves on other yet-to-be-created earths. The Heavenly Parents are constantly progressing, which necessarily entails some suffering along the way, such as grieving when their offspring rebel and are eternally lost to them.

CONTROVERSY

Although the highest celestial level is reserved for heterosexually married people, LDS leaders assure righteous, unmarried Church members that they won't be denied any blessings they desire in the hereafter, including eternal marriage. In fact, early Mormons taught that *plural marriage* (polygamy — or, more accurately, polygyny) is a key feature of the highest celestial level. As in the earthly church, righteous women will outnumber righteous men in the top celestial level, and unmarried women can become plural wives there. Many modern-day LDS members feel a bit queasy about celestial plural marriage — see, for example, Carol Lynn Pearson's book *The Ghost of Eternal Polygamy: Haunting the Hearts and Heaven of Mormon Women and Men* — but the doctrine is still reflected in current Mormon scripture (see D&C 132) and the Church's temple-marriage policies (see Chapter 7).

ALL DOGS GO TO HEAVEN

Many people believe in heaven for animals or feel sure their pets will be waiting for them when they die. Mormonism may well be the only Western religion that directly addresses the eternal fate of Fido and Fluffy through prophetic revelation. Joseph Smith taught that animals have spirits and that after Judgment Day, they'll receive a resurrected body and enjoy eternal bliss through Christ's atonement. Like people, they had a premortal spiritual life, and like people, they'll continue to progress in knowledge throughout eternity — good news for those dogs who never quite succeeded in obedience school. According to Mormon teaching, they'll be able to praise God forever in a language that God understands.

The LDS church has no official doctrine about whether people will be reunited with their pets in heaven, though the concept is a popular folk belief for Latter-day Saints, as for many other Christians. After all, who will be happy in the celestial kingdom if Rover isn't there to frolic with all those spirit children on the front lawn?

SCRIPTURE

At the same time, the Church has said almost nothing about the other two celestial levels and who inherits them, except that those people will be "ministering servants" (D&C 132:16) to those in the highest level. The Church only focuses on preparing for the highest celestial level — anything less smacks of disappointment and failure, even though the other two levels are valid choices where Church members can realize the Mormon goals of living and working forever with their Heavenly Parents and earthly family members who likewise qualify. For more on these and other unresolved tensions in Mormonism, see Chapter 15.

If you're really, really, really bad: Outer darkness

Although Latter-day Saints believe that the vast majority of people will one day find themselves somewhere along the win-place-show spectrum of the three degrees of glory, that belief has one catch: outer darkness, which is one of the two "hells" of Mormon theology. (For more on the other, see the earlier section "Do not pass go: Spirit prison.") Because Latter-day Saints believe that even murderers, liars, and adulterers who died in their sins can inherit the telestial glory behind Door #3, it must follow that outer darkness is reserved for people who are worse than murderers. Those people include

>> The devil himself.

>> The one-third of spirits who — even while dwelling in God's presence in premortality — chose to follow Satan in the War in Heaven (refer to the

section "Relax, you've already passed the first test," earlier in this chapter). These rebellious spirits never received human bodies, so no one physically reading this book falls into this category.

>> The *sons of perdition* who *knowingly* and *willfully* turn against God, the Savior, and their plan of salvation. This doesn't apply to people who never heard the gospel, or who heard about it but didn't believe it was true, or who got baptized but then fell away, or who committed terrible sins. It's only for those who, during their lives, completely understood the gospel's truthfulness and received a spiritual witness from the Holy Ghost, but then deliberately chose to despise God and rebel against him. Latter-day Saints believe that when the Bible's New Testament speaks about blaspheming against the Holy Ghost as the "unpardonable sin," it refers to this extreme denial. Being a child of *perdition* — which means "loss" — is a one-way ticket to hell, and this time it's forever.

The best way to describe outer darkness is the complete absence of God's light and warmth. This place offers no forgiveness, no redemption, no progress, and no possibility of parole — in essence, outer darkness means permanent misery and perhaps even eventual dissolution. Thankfully, only a minuscule number of those who make it to mortality will inherit outer darkness, due to their fully realized hatred of God.

Chapter **3**

Heavenly Parents, Savior, and Holy Ghost

The Mormon God — whom they usually refer to as *Heavenly Father* — is quite different from the God most Christians worship. In fact, Latter-day Saints reject the traditional concept of the *Trinity*, the idea that the Father, Son, and Holy Ghost are different forms of one entity whose ethereal substance fills the entire universe. Rather, Latter-day Saints believe in a godhead staffed by three individual beings — Latter-day Saints also call them *personages* — who are one in mind and purpose:

» In the CEO position is God, a physically resurrected man who's achieved a glorified state of eternal *omnipotence* (meaning, he has all the power you could ever want and infinitely more). He's the literal father of human spirits and ruler of the universe.

» Second in command is God's son, Jesus Christ. He's a separate man whose spirit and physical body were literally procreated by God.

» Number three is a being whom Latter-day Saints commonly call the *Holy Ghost, Holy Spirit, Spirit of God,* or simply the *Spirit.* As a spiritual personage without a physical body, the Holy Ghost is able to directly communicate God's messages to the human spirit.

In addition, Latter-day Saints believe that God has a better half. He's eternally married to at least one glorified, deified woman who's known as *Heavenly Mother*, with whom he procreates spirit children. (Many Mormon leaders have taught that God has plural wives—see Chapters 13 and 15 for more on polygamy.) Most Latter-day Saints discuss their spiritual mother only rarely and briefly, but they believe that Heavenly Mother is equal to Heavenly Father in glory, perfection, compassion, wisdom, and holiness.

The Head Honcho: God the Father

To Latter-day Saints, God is the same species as humans, but he's infinitely more advanced. To make a comparison, if humans are like newly hatched tadpoles, then God has already progressed through the frog stage and become a handsome prince. In the Mormon view, God isn't so much a *creator* as an *organizer* of raw materials. As we discuss in this section, he's got a very specific purpose in mind for going to all this trouble to run the universe.

What if God were one of us?

Mormonism's founding prophet Joseph Smith taught, "If men do not comprehend the character of God, they do not comprehend themselves." More specifically, Joseph taught the following as life's great secret: "God himself was once as we are now, and is an exalted man, and sits enthroned in yonder heavens!" A later Mormon prophet put it this way: "As man now is, God once was: as God now is, man may be." (Don't worry — these 19th-century fellows were talking about women, too.)

To Latter-day Saints, these all-important concepts mean that God himself has gone through everything his human children have experienced, are now experiencing, and will yet experience. Nineteenth-century Mormon leaders taught that untold eons ago, God's eternal essence was born as a spirit to Heavenly Parents, just like human spirits would later be born to him. He received a physical, mortal body on an earthlike planet and passed his mortal test — evidently with flying colors. After his mortal body died and was resurrected, he advanced to his current position as supreme ruler of this universe. Of course, all this happened longer ago and via a more advanced process than any human can comprehend.

SCRIPTURE

Modern-day LDS leaders are more reticent about God's origins than those 19th-century freewheelers were, though they continue to emphasize that God has a glorified, resurrected physical body and our purpose is to eventually become like him, as Christ very clearly stated in the New Testament: "Be ye therefore perfect, even as your Father which is in heaven is perfect" (Matthew 5:48). The word *perfect* means not only flawless but also total and absolute. Not wanting us to feel overwhelmed as mortals, one current Mormon apostle added this perspective: "If we persevere, then somewhere in eternity our refinement will be finished and complete."

At some point after giving birth to their first spirit child (see this chapter's later section, "Second Mate: Christ the Son"), the Heavenly Parents had other spirit children as well — billions of them. To enable these children to start the cycle all over again by growing up and becoming like their own Heavenly Parents, God taught them the *plan of salvation*, which we describe in detail in Chapter 2. All humans who pass through this earth life are God's spirit children who agreed to undergo the most difficult phase of his plan: demonstrating their faith and obedience away from God's presence and thus determining their eternal pathway.

In the Mormon view, Heavenly Father is the source of everything good, and his attributes include the following:

>> **A glorified humanlike body:** When the scriptures say that people are created in God's image, Latter-day Saints take that claim literally — God looks like a man, with body, parts, and passions. Of course, he doesn't have any flaws or weaknesses, and he's so glorified that mortals would shrivel up in his presence if he didn't protect them. Mormon scripture reveals that he dwells near the universe's greatest star, Kolob, where one day equals 1,000 earth years.

>> **Omniscience and omnipotence:** God knows everything there is to know and has complete control of this universe, though he allows his children the freedom to choose their own actions and consequences. He perfectly comprehends, executes, and obeys all laws of nature and science — in fact, learning and obeying all those laws is basically *how* he became God. He administers the universe through an all-pervasive power called the *priesthood*, which he shares with his worthy children, as we explain in Chapter 4.

>> **Perfect love for all his children:** God is the ideal parent. Even when individuals don't comprehend or cooperate with his plan of salvation, God still loves them. Although people who are currently suffering — or watching others suffer — may not believe it, God is infinitely kind and compassionate and wants to help anyone who sincerely seeks him out. (For Mormon ways of connecting with God, see Chapter 17.) However, God practices tough love when it comes to upholding the terms of the plan of salvation, to which everyone agreed before being born on this earth. (To refresh your memory about these terms that Latter-day Saints claim you accepted, see Chapter 2.)

God the organizer

As we mention earlier in this chapter, Latter-day Saints see God as an organizer *of existing elements.* They don't believe he created anything out of nothing. However, even though they believe that all matter is eternal and can't be created out of nothing, members do still sometimes use the term *create* to describe what God does: He can manipulate existing matter any way he wants, whether he's forming comets or beetles. And he lets his children learn how to manipulate it, too.

REMEMBER

Latter-day Saints recognize two basic kinds of matter: spiritual and physical. Yes, spirit is considered matter, too, but this substance is more delicate and refined than physical matter and is kept veiled from the physical human senses. God first creates everything from raw spiritual material before he creates it physically, including animals, plants, and even planets themselves. In the case of humans, he and Heavenly Mother procreate their spirits from a mysterious raw material called *intelligence,* about which little is known beyond the belief that this material contains each individual's core essence, which is eternal.

Although God generally reserves initial spiritual creation for himself, he lets his children help in subsequent physical creation. Latter-day Saints believe that many of God's brightest spirit children, including Adam and Eve, fulfilled assignments to help form this physical earth under the direction of the Savior. (Kudos to whoever did the fjords in Norway and other cool spots.) Closer to home, God's children help create the initial mortal version of each other's physical bodies by conceiving and giving birth to babies, and God inspires mortals to make scientific discoveries about manipulating the elements. All this creation is practice for potentially becoming more like God himself.

Why does God go to all this trouble?

SCRIPTURE

The earth isn't merely God's hobby or a windup creation from which he has walked away. One of the most quoted scriptures in Mormonism reveals God's basic motivation for everything he does: "Behold, this is my work and my glory — to bring to pass the immortality and eternal life of man" (Moses 1:39; for more about this and other Pearl of Great Price scriptures, see Chapter 10). In other words, what gives God joy and satisfaction is helping his children become like himself. Whenever one of his children succeeds, God succeeds; human progress adds to God's eternal glory. In fact, Latter-day Saints believe that God has formed — and is still forming — numberless planets like this one, populated by broods of spirit children who are progressing through the plan of salvation.

Differences in beliefs about God

In some fundamental ways, Latter-day Saints differ from "traditional" Christians (such as Protestants and Catholics) who agree on the foundational creeds of historic Christianity: the Apostles' Creed, the Nicene Creed, and the Athanasian Creed. To help you understand, we created Table 3-1 to highlight some of the most important differences in beliefs about God. Even if you don't have time to read the whole chapter, you should be able to master the basic bones of contention from this table and Table 3-2 (later in this chapter), which outlines differences in beliefs about Jesus Christ.

TABLE 3-1 ## Mormon View of God versus Other Christian Views

Qualities of God	Mormon Christianity	Creedal Christianity
God the Creator	God organized all matter but didn't will it into being; matter has always existed.	God is the creator of the entire cosmos, including matter and everything that is not God.
God's substance	Heavenly Father was once human and is now a personage of glorified, perfected flesh and bone. He dwells in a specific location in space and time.	God's essence is indivisible, infinite, and eternal. He transcends space and time and is always present to his human creatures.
God's parenthood	Heavenly Father is eternally married to Heavenly Mother, and they populate planets with their human children, who have godly DNA and potential.	Humans are created in "God's image," implying not physical resemblance per se but Godlike capacity for love, creativity, reason, relationships, and moral responsibility. In this sense, God is the universal father of all humanity. Through faith in Jesus, humans enter a special familial relationship with God.
The Godhead	Heavenly Father, Jesus Christ, and the Holy Ghost were not always God but are now three separate divine beings who work together as one.	The Father, the Son, and the Holy Spirit are three distinct Persons who share one divine essence (substance) and purpose. The entire Godhead has always been God.
God's limitations	God is subject to certain moral and physical laws of the universe that existed before he became God.	God is the infinite source of all things, including the physical laws of the universe, and therefore has no limitations unless self-imposed.
God's goal for humanity	God wants people to return to him and become like him in work, glory, love, and joy.	God has promised to redeem the entire cosmos. All of creation will be resurrected, renewed, and redeemed, live in God's presence, and experience eternal peace, love, justice, and joy.

Second Mate: Christ the Son

Latter-day Saints view the New Testament as a mostly accurate account of Jesus's earthly ministry (for more on Mormon views regarding the Bible, see Chapter 9). However, additional revelations to Mormon prophets have clarified aspects of what Jesus did before, during, and after his short mortal life, as well as what he's expected to do in the future.

First and best

In Mormon theology, the being who would become known as Jesus Christ was born first among all the Heavenly Parents' billions of spirit children, and he was by far the brightest, strongest, and most advanced of them. In the premortal world, where human spirits dwelt with their Heavenly Parents and prepared for their earthly test, this eldest son took the primary leadership role and was known as *Jehovah*. Many people believe the names *Jehovah* and *the Lord* in the Old Testament refer to God the Father, but Latter-day Saints believe these names refer to the personage who would later be born as Jesus Christ.

As we mention earlier in the chapter, God instituted the plan of salvation so that his spirit children can progress to become like him. For this plan to work, a savior was required to help everybody recover from the sin and death they'd unavoidably encounter as part of the earthly test. Guess who volunteered?

Among God's oldest spirit children was another gifted and talented son, named Lucifer. As we discuss in more detail in Chapter 2, Lucifer developed the worst-ever case of sibling rivalry and rebelled against God and Jehovah/Jesus Christ, which got him and his followers kicked out of heaven. In the Mormon view, Jesus, the devil, and all humans everywhere are spiritual siblings.

Well before coming to earth to perform his saving mission, the Savior began serving as God's second in command. While God created the earth spiritually, the Savior took primary responsibility for the earth's physical creation. After mortals started wandering the planet with no memory of their premortal life, the Savior communicated with them through prophets and the Holy Ghost. On the rare occasion when God himself directly speaks to a human, it's generally to introduce his Son.

Both mortal and divine

In the Mormon view, God fathered everybody's spirit, but the Savior's *physical* body was the only one literally procreated by God, in partnership with the mortal Mary. (We could discuss what some early Latter-day Saints believed about the logistics of that situation, but we won't go there.) Possessing both eternal and mortal DNA, Jesus was able to die and then be resurrected in glorified immortality, thus opening the way for everyone to eventually be resurrected.

Equally as importantly, Jesus paid the price for all the sins of humanity. In the Mormon view, whenever a moral law is broken, justice must be satisfied, and the Savior accomplished that for humankind on a spiritual, eternal level. Having paid this bill that mortals couldn't pay for themselves, he forgives the debt for all people who sincerely repent of their sins and strive to live his gospel. Although many Christians believe that Jesus extends his grace to anyone who simply asks, Latter-day Saint Christians believe the Savior picks up the slack as a person makes their best effort to be good.

SCRIPTURE

An oft-quoted Book of Mormon scripture states, "It is by grace that we are saved, after all we can do" (2 Nephi 25:23). In contrast, the Bible states, "For by grace are ye saved through faith; and that not of yourselves: it is the gift of God" (Ephesians 2:8), which Latter-day Saints see as a true but incomplete assertion. For more on how faith and works go together in the Mormon mind, see Chapter 2; for more on Mormon feelings regarding the Bible, see Chapter 10.

WAS JESUS MARRIED?

Latter-day Saints view marriage as an eternal covenant that people must make in order to be *exalted*, or become like God (for more on Mormon marriage, see Chapter 7). In addition, Latter-day Saints believe that Jesus Christ set a perfect example in all things. According to this logic, the Savior must've gotten married at some point.

Some early Mormon leaders speculated that the marriage at Cana, where Jesus turned water into wine, was actually his own wedding, which would help explain why he was trying to be a good host. Additionally, some Latter-day Saints believe that Jesus married Mary Magdalene and had children, and they reject the notion that Magdalene was a reformed prostitute. However, modern Church leaders pretty much publicly avoid this subject altogether.

Together, the Savior's overcoming of death and sin is known as his *atonement*. Latter-day Saints believe that the hardest, most significant phase of the atonement occurred in the Garden of Gethsemane, during that long night when Jesus literally sweat drops of blood (as described in the Bible, Luke 22:44). Although crucifixion was a horrible way to die, numerous others died that same way. Consequently, Latter-day Saints don't place religious significance on the sign of the cross. To Latter-day Saints, the most important aspects of the story are that Christ's sacrifice atoned for people's sins and that he was resurrected.

The Savior's post-crucifixion checklist

After his mortal body died on the cross, the Savior immediately got busy with the following tasks:

>> **During the three days between Christ's death and resurrection, Latter-day Saints believe his spirit visited the realm of the dead.** Wanting to extend his atonement to every human who ever lived, the Savior organized the righteous spirits to start preaching the gospel to those who died without hearing or accepting it. Until then, an impassable gulf had lain between the righteous spirits and the wicked and ignorant spirits in the spirit world.

>> **Jesus transformed his physical body into a perfect, glorified, immortal vessel for his eternal spirit.** At the time of his resurrection, all the righteous people who'd died before him got resurrected too, all the way back to Adam. Most of the righteous who died after him will wait until his Second Coming to be resurrected. Many Latter-day Saints view the Savior's resurrection as the single most significant and miraculous event in human history.

>> **The resurrected Savior personally taught his New Testament apostles and called new apostles in the Western Hemisphere.** Latter-day Saints believe that the Western Hemisphere people were part of Christ's "other sheep" that the Bible's John 10:16 says he mentioned. Lasting several days, this visit is recounted as the centerpiece of the Book of Mormon, Joseph Smith's translation of the sacred account left behind by these people. (For more on the Book of Mormon, see Chapter 9.) Christ may also have visited additional people around the world, who presumably made their own sacred records that some Latter-day Saints believe may eventually become public like the Book of Mormon did.

>> **After the resurrected Savior ascended to heaven, he kept working behind the scenes among humans.** Latter-day Saints believe that, within a few decades after Christ left the earth, persecution and corruption ruined his church, as we discuss in Chapter 4. For about 1,700 years, the Savior didn't reestablish an official church or prophet on the earth, although he continued

blessing and inspiring worthy, faithful individuals, especially those who sought religious freedoms.

>> **Finally, when conditions were right for the restoration of the true religion, God and Jesus appeared to Joseph Smith in 1820.** During the subsequent 24 years, Jesus restored his church, his gospel, and God's priesthood through the Prophet Joseph Smith. Since then, Latter-day Saints believe the Savior has been actively leading the Church by inspiring whatever man is serving as the current prophet. One of the LDS church's main purposes is to prepare people for Christ's eventual Second Coming (see this chapter's next section, "When he comes again").

As Latter-day Saints strive to develop a personal relationship with Heavenly Father, they recognize that Jesus Christ is the middleman, the broker, and the gatekeeper — in theological terms, the mediator — between God and humanity. The only way back to God is through him. Latter-day Saints feel deep gratitude and love for the Savior and pledge total allegiance to him. When they pray to the Father or do anything else of a religious nature, they do it in Christ's name (for more on Mormon prayer, see Chapter 17). The Church is Christ's, the gospel is Christ's, and Christ administers God's priesthood among humans.

REMEMBER

Although everything centers on Christ, Latter-day Saints view him as a means to an end, not an end in himself. Latter-day Saints are sometimes accused of blasphemy for believing that humans can become like God. However, from a Mormon perspective, the idea that the Savior accomplished his incomprehensibly excruciating atonement for anything less seems almost blasphemous.

When he comes again

As the bumper sticker says, "Jesus is coming — everyone look busy." No one but God knows exactly when Jesus will return in glory to rule the earth for 1,000 years, but Latter-day Saints believe the time is approaching and people should prepare.

Signs of the times

Although the Church's restoration is one of the key signs that the Second Coming is near, Latter-day Saints believe they must still preach the gospel to all nations before Christ will return. Mormon missionaries have entered most countries, but places like Saudi Arabia and China still aren't open for evangelizing. Some Latter-day Saints semiseriously debate whether electronically transmitted missionary work suffices, or if missionaries must personally visit each nation. In addition, some still expect to build the New Jerusalem in the state of Missouri before the Savior returns, to serve as his headquarters. (Why Missouri? See Chapter 11.)

Unfortunately, many of the signs preceding the Second Coming don't sound like too much fun. Aware that time is running out, the devil is pulling out all the stops. The last century's wars and social ills — and those of the present day — are mere warm-ups for how much worse things will get. The earth will go increasingly haywire with natural calamities, including earthquakes, disease, storms, fires, and famine, and the wicked will run rampant. According to Mormon scripture, "All things shall be in commotion; and . . . fear shall come upon all people" (Doctrine and Covenants 88:91). Of course, the Lord has promised to comfort the righteous during these times of crisis, and many of them will survive in the flesh to welcome him back.

It's a bird! It's a plane!

At a crucial point during Armageddon, the world's final catastrophic war, Latter-day Saints believe the Savior will descend out of the sky to assume control of the earth and accomplish the following tasks:

» **Levitate the good people:** As the Savior comes down from the heavens, he'll resurrect the righteous dead, who'll be airlifted up to meet him, along with those righteous mortals who are still living. Together with those who were already resurrected at the time of Jesus's own resurrection, these people will eventually inherit the *celestial kingdom,* where they'll live and work with God and potentially become like him. (For more on Mormonism's three degrees of heavenly glory, see Chapter 2.)

» **Say goodbye to bad guys:** With the good people safe, the Savior will destroy the wicked mortals who are still living, imprison Satan, cleanse the earth with fire, and restore the earth to its Garden of Eden status, with no noxious weeds or predatory carnivores. All the unrepentant wicked spirits from throughout history will stay in timeout in spirit prison.

» **Start his own show:** The Savior will establish a perfectly fair, just, and peaceful worldwide government — run by both Church members and nonmembers — and launch the 1,000-year period of earthly paradise known as the *Millennium.* After the Millennium begins, he'll start resurrecting the medium-good people from throughout history, those who lived decent lives but didn't seek or fully embrace the gospel. These people will eventually inherit the *terrestrial kingdom.*

Peace on earth, goodwill toward men: The Millennium

During the Millennium, mortals will still dwell on the earth, having children and living out their lives. However, only people of celestial or terrestrial caliber will experience mortality during the Millennium, and Satan won't be able to tempt or confuse anybody. Even better, no one will have to deal with health insurance, because no one will suffer disease. Instead of experiencing death and burial, people will turn immortal "in the twinkling of an eye."

Not everyone living on the earth during the Millennium will be a member of the Savior's true church. People will still be free to believe and worship as they please, and some will hold onto mistaken beliefs and follow false religions — at least, until LDS missionaries can persuade them otherwise.

Two major religious efforts will continue through Christ's Millennium:

>> **Performing ordinances on behalf of the dead:** As discussed in Chapter 7, no one can be saved without receiving certain earthly physical ordinances, such as baptism. Latter-day Saints are currently trying to perform these ordinances on behalf of all dead people, who can then decide whether to accept or reject them. This effort will continue in the Millennium.

>> **Preaching and teaching:** In both the spirit world and on earth, missionaries will continue preaching the Savior's true gospel until they've reached all people, and eventually everyone will bend the knee and acknowledge Christ as their Savior.

During the Millennium, Jesus and other resurrected beings will visit the earth as needed to oversee the government and help Church members carry out ordinance work for the dead. At the conclusion of the Millennium, the spirits of the wicked from throughout history will finally finish their 1,000-year timeout and be resurrected, eventually to inherit the *telestial kingdom*.

As great as the Millennium sounds, it has a catch at the end. Satan will be unleashed for one last time, and he'll succeed in turning away more people from God. The armies of the righteous will defeat the armies of evil for the final time, and God will forever cast Satan and his followers into outer darkness. Then will come the final judgment, when all people receive their eternal reward in one of the three kingdoms of heaven.

Differences in beliefs about Jesus Christ

Table 3-2 illustrates how Latter-day Saints view Christ, compared to other Christians.

TABLE 3-2   # Mormon View of Christ versus Other Christian Views

Qualities of Christ	Mormon Christianity	Protestant and Catholic Christianity
Nature of Christ	Christ is the Messiah and the literal Son of God. He'll return someday and usher in 1,000 years of peace and glory on earth.	Christ is the Messiah, the Son of God, and also God the Father made flesh. He'll return someday, either just before or just after 1,000 years of peace and glory on earth.
Creation of Christ	Christ is the firstborn of Heavenly Father and the oldest brother of all human beings, spiritually speaking. He's the only one of Heavenly Father's children to be conceived in mortality by a human and God.	Christ is the only-begotten Son of God and is of one substance with the Father. He was "begotten" but not made or created.
Christ in the Godhead	Christ is a separate physical being from God the Father and the Holy Ghost. The three beings are united in purpose and love but not in substance. Christ is subordinate to the Father and does his will (John 14:28).	Christ is part of the Trinity, along with God the Father and the Holy Ghost, who all function as one being. God the Father was physically *incarnated,* or made flesh, in the person of Jesus of Nazareth. Christ is eternally coequal with God the Father.
Christ's activity on earth	Christ taught, healed, and performed miracles before his crucifixion. In the three days between his crucifixion and resurrection, he went to spirit paradise (see Chapter 2) to teach righteous spirits how to help those in spirit prison. After his resurrection, he taught his disciples in Jerusalem and the Nephites in the Western Hemisphere, and he may have taught "lost sheep" scattered in other places. After his ministry among the Nephites, he ascended into heaven.	Christ taught, healed, and performed miracles before his crucifixion and resurrection. After his resurrection, he spent 40 days teaching his disciples before ascending into heaven.
Christ's premortal résumé	Christ was chosen as Savior during the council in heaven (see Chapter 2), headed up the earth's physical creation, and functioned as Jehovah in the Bible's Old Testament.	Christ was spiritually present at creation, but his precise role is unknown.
Christ's atonement	In the Garden of Gethsemane and on the cross, Christ paid the price for our sins and offered himself as a sacrifice for all people.	On the cross, Christ paid the price for our sins and offered himself as a sacrifice for all people.

God's Whisperer: The Holy Ghost

Latter-day Saints are unusual in their belief that God the Father has a glorified physical body, like his Son Jesus Christ. The Holy Ghost, in contrast, is a spiritual being. In fact, Latter-day Saints often say *Holy Spirit* rather than *Holy Ghost,* using the two terms interchangeably. (*Ghost* was a term used in the 17th-century King James Version of the Bible to signify "spirit," and the name stuck, though it sounds a bit Halloween-y in modern times.)

Latter-day Saints believe the Holy Ghost is a witness to truth, a comforter, and a sanctifier. The purer and more obedient people are, the better they're able to feel the Holy Ghost's spiritual influence. Latter-day Saints strive to follow God's commandments so they can retain the Holy Ghost's companionship as much as possible, and they draw upon his guidance when discerning right from wrong, evaluating spiritual teachings, and pressing on toward eventual perfection. As the Spirit carries out the will of the Father, his influence can be felt everywhere in the world at the same time.

The Spirit who never got a body

The Holy Ghost is unique among the three personages in the Godhead because this member is the only one without a glorified physical body. Church leaders have taught that the Holy Ghost has a *spiritual* body, which is presumably a more advanced, deified version of the spirit body that Latter-day Saints believe everyone had in the premortal life.

CONTROVERSY

Mormon theology hasn't offered a definitive statement about the origins and identity of the Holy Ghost, focusing instead on this spirit personage's role in the Godhead and in people's lives. Some Latter-day Saints believe the Holy Ghost is one of God's spirit children who was called for this particular mission and will be the last spirit to be blessed with a physical body. Even more controversially, some Latter-day Saints would like to think the Holy Ghost is female, perhaps even Heavenly Mother herself — however, this is far from orthodox belief. As one Mormon apostle explained, God hasn't yet given revelation on the Spirit's origin or destiny, and debating it is "speculative and fruitless." In deference to current LDS church usage, in this book we refer to the Holy Ghost with male pronouns.

Latter-day Saints believe that as a spirit, the Holy Ghost can communicate intimately with every person's spirit, though the person needs to strive to live righteously so as not to repel the Holy Spirit. No unclean thing can sustain the presence of God, and the Holy Ghost literally imparts a bit of God's presence to humans in a tangible way. With this idea in mind, Latter-day Saints who've been baptized and have received the gift of the Holy Ghost (see the next section) are careful to remain worthy of that gift.

REMEMBER

Although no one knows everything about the Holy Ghost, the key thing to remember is that he quietly works wonders in the lives of believers. He may *seem* like a silent partner, but the Holy Ghost is actually a key mover and shaker in God's business on earth.

The gift of the Holy Ghost

Latter-day Saints believe that, from time to time and under special circumstances, such as while being taught by the missionaries, anyone can feel the Spirit's influence and confirmation of the truth of certain teachings. In addition, Mormon leaders have taught that great scientific discoveries and uplifting works of art are often influenced by the Holy Ghost's inspiration, whether or not their creators were members of the LDS church. (Latter-day Saints also believe that every person, Mormon or not, can have constant guidance from something called the *light of Christ*. This light comes from Christ's spirit and helps all accountable people discern between right and wrong.)

Having the Spirit all the time

Latter-day Saints believe that LDS church members can receive the *constant* gift of the Holy Ghost. After people are baptized — see Chapter 6 for more on baptism and its meaning for Latter-day Saints — the next ordinance they receive is confirmation, which includes the bestowal of the gift of the Holy Ghost. This happens through the laying on of hands by someone with the proper authority, meaning a Melchizedek Priesthood holder (see Chapter 4). After this ordinance, members can potentially experience the Spirit's influence ever after, not just on an occasional basis.

SCRIPTURE

During the confirmation ordinance, the priesthood holder simply blesses the individual to receive the Holy Ghost. Some Latter-day Saints believe that when this blessing takes place, it actually verifies the Holy Ghost's entry into that person's life and heart and imparts the Spirit's influence. Others feel that the ordinance establishes the person's *receptivity* and *willingness* to receive the Holy Ghost, but doesn't dictate where the Spirit goes and what he does. (As the Bible says in John 3:8, the Spirit's influence bloweth where it listeth, meaning it goes wherever the heck it wants to.) Whatever the case, receiving the gift of the Holy Ghost is essential to receiving full salvation.

Confirmation of membership and bestowal of the gift of the Holy Ghost can happen any time after baptism. In some cases, this ordinance is performed immediately following baptism, after the new member has changed into dry clothes. In other cases, particularly with adult converts, many wards hold the confirmation ordinance during sacrament meeting the Sunday after the baptism so the whole congregation can witness and welcome the new convert.

One thing you rarely see during these ordinances is something that's more common in Pentecostal services, where the person who's received the Holy Ghost dances, claps, whoops for joy, or falls down in the Spirit. Although Latter-day Saints in the 1830s engaged in ecstatic behaviors during worship, Latter-day Saints today are pretty sedate by contrast. The individual who's just received the gift may experience a warm and steady feeling of light or may shed tears of joy. Others report feeling nothing unusual at that time but then have deep spiritual experiences afterward. Latter-day Saints believe that understanding and using the gift of the Holy Ghost isn't a one-time affair but a lifelong experience that can grow in depth, frequency, and intensity.

Receiving specialized gifts of the Spirit

SCRIPTURE

Latter-day Saints believe that scripture promises some beautiful spiritual gifts that go along with receiving the Holy Ghost. Obviously, not all Church members possess every gift that Paul outlines in the New Testament or Joseph Smith and other prophets mention in modern revelations. As Paul put it, "There are diversities of gifts, but the same Spirit"; one person may be a healer and another an interpreter. Early Latter-day Saints wore their spiritual gifts on their sleeves a lot more than Latter-day Saints do today, but the fact is that Latter-day Saints still believe in miracles and seek them regularly. Some of the more common manifestations of spiritual gifts include the following:

>> **The gift of healing:** Today, many Mormon men who hold the Melchizedek Priesthood carry a small key-chain vial containing consecrated olive oil. At any time, in any kind of emergency, they're prepared to perform an anointing and blessing to heal someone. Although all priesthood holders possess the authority to administer to the sick, some Church leaders have taught that some individuals may have this gift to a greater degree than others. In addition, Mormon history is rife with stories of women and others who didn't hold the priesthood but who could heal through prayer and the gift of the Spirit.

>> **The gift of tongues:** Hearing spiritual gibberish in a Mormon chapel — other than a particularly long-winded talk in sacrament meeting — or seeing someone else rise up to interpret what's been said is unlikely nowadays. However, such *speaking in tongues* was common among Mormon men and women in the 19th century. Latter-day Saints believe that today's most common manifestation of this gift is missionaries quickly learning foreign languages.

>> **The gift of faith:** Latter-day Saints believe the Spirit witnesses about the truth of spiritual wisdom and increases faith. Again, some people seem to have the gift of faith more than others, while some have the gift of riding another person's coattails of strong, abiding faith.

» **The gift of prophecy:** Although the president of the Church is the only person who receives revelations from God that are binding for the entire Church, individual Latter-day Saints are entitled to revelations about their own lives, families, and Church duties.

» **The gift of casting out demons:** As with speaking in tongues, this spiritual gift was more visible in the 19th century than it is today, but Latter-day Saints still call upon the Holy Ghost to help them withstand temptation and repel Satan's influence. Such episodes may never be as dramatic as an *Exorcist* head spin, but this gift is nevertheless effective. If a Latter-day Saint senses the influence of a demon, they can verbally cast it out in the name of Jesus Christ.

REMEMBER

The most important thing to remember about these gifts is that they usually exist for the spiritual growth of the Church, not just the individual. Miracles should increase the faith and well-being of those who witness them; teaching should enlighten all who hear it. Doctrine and Covenants (D&C) 46 states several times in various ways that the gifts of the Spirit exist "that all might be benefited," so Church members are counseled to seek them for the right reasons, not for selfish ones.

Keeping the Spirit

The Holy Ghost is God's primary way of leading people to Christ, confirming spiritual truth, and helping them endure to the end in righteousness. When people have the Holy Ghost in their lives, they feel more connected to Heavenly Father through prayer and are more able to recognize the needs of people around them.

Latter-day Saints believe, however, that the trick is to keep the Spirit at all times. As people study the scriptures, pray regularly, and serve others, they can feel the influence of the Holy Ghost most clearly. But the Spirit won't stick around where he's not wanted. If people don't at least try to keep God's commandments, the Spirit will flee. Yet, he'll return after a person repents and tries again to live righteously.

Sometimes, even people who strive to obey God's commandments and do the right thing experience dry spells when the Spirit feels far away. Most Latter-day Saints can point to times in their lives when they felt very close to the Spirit and other times when they felt alone. Perhaps God uses these times to strengthen and test people — difficult times help us grow, and in the Mormon view, spiritual growth is a main reason we're here on earth. Even the mortal Christ, who was sinless and perfect, experienced loneliness when he felt that God had abandoned him (for more on that, check out Mark 15:34 in the Bible).

The Holy Ghost's many roles

So, what does the Holy Ghost *do*, exactly? While the Father organizes and sustains all things and the Son redeems people from mortality, the Holy Ghost kind of keeps the home fires burning. In fact, fire is one symbol of the Holy Ghost that frequently appears in scripture (see, for example, the apostles' experience with "tongues of fire" when they were baptized in the Spirit in the New Testament, recounted in Acts 2). The Holy Ghost performs several vital functions in the Godhead and in bringing people to Christ.

The witness of Christ

SCRIPTURE

Have you ever noticed that in scripture, the Holy Spirit seems to show up just when Christ makes an appearance? When Jesus is baptized in the New Testament, for example, the Spirit descends — perhaps figuratively — in the form of a dove just as Heavenly Father announces the coming of Christ: "This is my beloved Son" (Matthew 3:16–17). In John 15:26, Jesus promises that the Holy Ghost will *testify* of him. In other words, the Holy Ghost is a witness of Christ, pointing people to Christ's glory and truth.

In Mormonism, the *law of witnesses* dictates that more than one righteous person will confirm a true spiritual principle. This idea seems to be true of the Godhead as well: The Spirit is an additional witness of Christ. In the Savior's baptismal story, for example, God announces Christ's identity while the Spirit rests on Jesus. The other members of the Godhead testify to Christ's divine nature.

The comforter

Shortly before Christ was crucified, he promised his disciples that he wouldn't leave them comfortless but would send a comforter to help them in their path (John 16). This promised helper was the Holy Ghost.

The Holy Ghost exists as a comforter for each person and as an enabler of sorts: Latter-day Saints believe one primary way God answers prayers is through other people, and the Spirit is the still, small voice of God that keeps members in tune with the needs of others. Sometimes Latter-day Saints feel a little tug to pray for someone or do something to help someone they know. This urge may be as simple as a phone call to a particular friend, only to find out the friend had a rotten day and needed a boost at just that moment.

Sometimes, the Holy Ghost communicates comfort to an individual by showering that person with what the Bible calls the "peace that passeth all understanding" (Philippians 4:7). After prayer, a Latter-day Saint may feel an unexpected sense of calm about a difficult issue or problem and a knowledge of what to do. In addition, the Holy Ghost can provide the blessed assurance that a person's sins are truly forgiven.

The revealer of truth

SCRIPTURE

In John 16, Jesus says that he has many other things to teach his disciples, but they aren't ready for those additional truths. Jesus assures them the Holy Ghost will be their new teacher after his departure, guiding them into all truth as directed by the Father. Latter-day Saints believe that human beings learn spiritual truths "precept upon precept, line upon line" — in other words, slowly but surely (Isaiah 28:10 in the Old Testament and 2 Nephi 28:30 in the Book of Mormon). People don't learn truth in a vacuum because the Spirit is with them every step of the way, teaching them and helping them discern truth from error.

Latter-day Saints are prayerful people, and they often bring things to God in prayer that other folks may consider trivial (for more on Mormon prayer, see Chapter 17). They follow James 1:5, which says that if they lack wisdom, they should ask God, who gives to everyone liberally. With this idea in mind, Latter-day Saints pray for the answers to tough questions and for guidance in making all kinds of decisions, both major and minor. They believe the Holy Ghost often confirms the truth of something they've prayed about. Sometimes, they receive a tingling or warm sensation running through their bodies, or simply a peaceful sense of calm about a particular course of action. On the other hand, they believe they'll experience a "stupor of thought" if something isn't right.

SCRIPTURE

The end of the Book of Mormon contains an oft-quoted passage about praying to know the truth and receiving spiritual confirmation. Widely shared by Mormon missionaries, the passage is known as *Moroni's promise,* because the Book of Mormon prophet Moroni pledged that people who ask God sincerely in the name of Jesus Christ can receive confirmation of the truth by the power of the Holy Ghost (Moroni 10:3–5). The scripture further guarantees that by the power of the Holy Ghost, people can know the truth of all things.

The sanctifier and ratifier

The Holy Ghost plays an important role in helping members stay on the straight and narrow path. He *sanctifies,* or helps them become more holy. As we explain earlier in this section, the Holy Ghost is sometimes associated with fire, and fire is the ultimate refiner's tool. The Spirit's goal is to purify an individual. In addition, the Holy Ghost acts as "The Holy Spirit of Promise" by approving and ratifying the righteous acts of priesthood holders — such as sealing a couple in the temple (see Chapter 7) — so those acts are binding on earth and in heaven.

As we discuss in Chapter 2, one of the most important principles of Mormon life is what they call *enduring to the end.* Having faith in Christ, repenting, and being baptized are all wonderful, but those actions don't help people much in the long run if they backslide or fall away from the faith. Enter the Holy Ghost — the Spirit helps members stay in tune with the will of Heavenly Father and his Son, Jesus Christ. He keeps members honest — perhaps the Holy Ghost is even involved with the pricks of conscience that help keep members on the right path. The Holy Ghost grants people beautiful spiritual experiences, moments of great joy, and answers to prayer to help them stay on the journey and grow in grace.

The unforgivable sin

SCRIPTURE

Before you finish this chapter thinking everything about the Holy Ghost is warm and fuzzy, you should know one more thing: The Bible says that blaspheming the Holy Ghost is the one unpardonable sin (Matthew 12:31–32). As we discuss in Chapter 2, this kind of blasphemy is one of the few things that guarantee someone a room reservation in Hotel Outer Darkness.

Just what exactly does it mean to *blaspheme* the Holy Ghost? Well, Church leaders teach that a blasphemer needs to have experienced the full influence of the Spirit and then denied it by willfully, consciously turning away from God. Joseph Smith said that when a person knows all about the plan of salvation, receives a spiritual witness of its truth, and *then* denies Christ, they sin against the Holy Ghost. This idea makes sense because, as we explain earlier in this section, one of the Holy Ghost's primary functions is to testify of Christ. When we reject Christ's message, having previously fully understood and embraced it, we also shoot the messenger, the Holy Ghost.

Chapter 4

Restoring the Priesthood and the Church

Latter-day Saints respect people's right to worship as they please, and they acknowledge that many religions contain elements of truth. But members of The Church of Jesus Christ of Latter-day Saints believe their church is the only complete, "true and living" church that the Savior recognizes as fully his own. Other churches, in the Mormon view, can be excellent organizations, but they're human, not godly, institutions whose teachings reflect mostly human philosophies. Their scriptural interpretations and — according to Latter-day Saints — especially their priesthood authority come from human sources, not from God himself.

Looking back on human history, Latter-day Saints believe that, from time to time, different societies have received the Savior's true religion but then lost it due to the people's lack of righteousness. When the time and conditions are right, the Savior reinstitutes the true religion by calling a new prophet to restore the gospel principles and ordinances to a different group or generation of people. As we discuss in this chapter, Latter-day Saints claim that, most recently, the Savior restored his church and God's true priesthood through Joseph Smith, Mormonism's founding prophet.

In addition, we discuss the basic organization and purposes of the Mormon priesthood, which is the authority to act in God's name and can be held by any worthy Mormon male. To help explain the priesthood to their sons, some fathers even compare it to the Force from *Star Wars*.

Gospel Comings and Goings

Like some other folks, Latter-day Saints speak of gospel *dispensations* throughout history, or times when the full true religion, including God's authentic priesthood authority, exists somewhere on the earth. Each dispensation is usually tied to one special prophet, who receives revelations from God and leads the people back to him. For example, Adam, Noah, and Moses all led major gospel dispensations. However, those dispensations eventually fizzled out.

Why do gospel dispensations end? Often they end because the people are unwilling to follow the prophet and live the gospel. When the people start getting too rebellious, God lets his true religion pass away from the earth, usually because the last righteous leader dies without transmitting the *priesthood keys* (a term Latter-day Saints use for priesthood authority) to a successor. In time, God calls a new prophet to restore the gospel, and the cycle continues.

Before a young prophet named Joseph Smith performed the biggest, grandest gospel restoration of all in the early 1800s, roughly 1,700 years passed without an authorized prophet in the Eastern Hemisphere, perhaps the longest stretch in history. Latter-day Saints believe that within a few decades after Christ set up his New Testament church, all the apostles died without successors, due mainly to persecution. Some fragments of Christianity survived and evolved over the centuries. However, unauthorized men changed the doctrines and ordinances to suit their own purposes and interpretations. (Over in the Western Hemisphere, the last prophet didn't die until about A.D. 400, as recounted in the Book of Mormon — but that still leaves a span of roughly 1,400 years until Joseph Smith.)

SCRIPTURE

Latter-day Saints sometimes refer to this huge gospel gap as the *Great Apostasy*, the major falling away predicted by several biblical prophets (see Amos 8:11–12, Matthew 24:9–12, John 16:1–3, 2 Thessalonians 2:3–4, and 2 Peter 2:1). However, although the Savior didn't authorize any priesthood representatives during this long period of time, he did inspire certain people to help prepare the world for the eventual return of the fullness of his gospel. Latter-day Saints believe that movements ranging from the Renaissance to Protestantism and the establishment of religious freedom in the United States all opened the way for one key event: the Savior's final restoration of his gospel through Joseph Smith.

Beginning the Restoration

It's hard to imagine that many Americans have been as hated and beloved as Joseph Smith, the founder of Mormonism (see Figure 4-1 for a portrait). To Latter-day Saints, he was a prophet of God, chosen to restore the priesthood, the New Testament church, and a whole lot more, suffering persecution for his faith and dying a martyr's death. To some outsiders, he was a fraud who falsely claimed to have revelations and instituted the practice of polygamy not to obey God's commands but to satisfy his own carnal lusts.

FIGURE 4-1: Mormonism's founding prophet, Joseph Smith.

Everett Collection/Shutterstock

The debate about Joseph Smith continues today as fervently as it did when he was still alive. In this section, we take a quick look at the man and his spiritual claims.

Joseph Smith's early years

Very soon after America gained its freedom, Joseph Smith was born on December 23, 1805, in the small New England village of Sharon, Vermont. His story is pretty similar to that of many families in the early republic: His parents were hardworking farm folk who never seemed to catch a break, moving seven times in 14 years to find better land and more economic opportunities. With a large family to support — the Smiths would eventually have 11 children, with 9 surviving to adulthood — getting ahead was a constant struggle.

Religiously, the Smiths were good Christian people who knew the Bible well but weren't typically involved in any one particular church. Their lack of involvement was partly a result of moving around so much, but it also stemmed from their confusion and dissatisfaction about the many different religious sects of the day. The early 19th century was a time of great religious revival in northeastern states such as New York, where the Smiths moved when young Joseph was 10 years old.

Eventually, with the entire family doing odd jobs, the Smiths were able to afford a farm on the outskirts of Palmyra, New York, not far from Lake Erie. There, in 1816, they settled into the backbreaking work of clearing the land and harvesting crops until 1825, when a run of bad luck — including falling grain prices and the death of Joseph's beloved adult brother Alvin — forced them to sell the farm and live there as tenants. This change was a hard blow to Joseph's parents, who were then in their 50s.

To make ends meet, the Smith boys and their father hired themselves out for odd jobs in addition to working the land upon which they lived. They worked at haying, harvesting, clearing trees, digging wells — and searching for treasure. The Church has carefully downplayed this last point in its official history, but the fact is certainly true that, like many other Americans of this period, Joseph Smith was involved in treasure-seeking. Anti-Mormons are quick to emphasize this activity because they believe it casts doubt on Smith's later discovery of the ultimate treasure: golden plates that, when translated, became the Book of Mormon. (For more on the Book of Mormon, see Chapter 9.) In their minds, Smith's claim to have "discovered" the Book of Mormon through angelic intervention loses credibility if he already had a history of digging for buried treasure. Latter-day Saint apologists argue that the fact that Smith was occasionally drafted into treasure digging is hardly a stain on his name.

TRUE GRIT

Joseph's mother recorded in her memoir that he was a quiet child who was interested in spirituality from an early age. He seems to have been made of tough stuff; when he was about 7 years old, for example, he contracted typhoid fever and endured a horrible secondary infection that lodged itself in the bone marrow of his leg.

Mormon children today are regaled with the story of how Joseph bravely faced the surgeon's knife when the infection was being chipped out of his bone. Parents and teachers trot out the story to demonstrate more than just bravery: Little Joseph famously refused alcohol to help deaden the pain, making him a poster child for the later Mormon attitude toward tee-totalism. (For the skinny on why Latter-day Saints don't drink, see Chapter 16.)

Kneeling in the Sacred Grove

During the same period when the Smiths were experiencing such economic unrest, young Joseph was encountering serious religious turmoil. In the early 1820s, a series of religious revivals in upstate New York caused the teenage Joseph to feel some confusion about which church to join. Methodist, Presbyterian, and Baptist ministers were all vying for the souls of the locals. All these preachers seemed to speak some truth, and Joseph had trouble distinguishing which was right.

SCRIPTURE

What happened next is perhaps modern Mormonism's single most essential event. Although historians sometimes argue about how old Joseph was when he decided to ask God which church to join, the official LDS position is that he did so in the spring of 1820, when he was just 14. Around that time, he was wondering about spiritual questions when he happened upon James 1:5 in the Bible's New Testament: "If any of you lack wisdom, let him ask of God, that giveth to all men liberally, and upbraideth not; and it shall be given him." Joseph took from this that instead of just fretting about the problem and making his own decision, he should ask God for wisdom about choosing a religion.

Joseph couldn't find any privacy in his family's crowded cabin, so he headed into the woods to pray in solitude. He knelt in a nearby clearing — which Latter-day Saints now refer to as the *Sacred Grove* — and prayed to the Lord for guidance as to which denomination was right. He'd hardly finished talking when he felt some astonishing power seize him, making him feel as if his tongue had been bound, and he was surrounded by utter darkness. "It seemed to me for a time as if I were doomed to sudden destruction," he wrote later.

Latter-day Saints believe that Public Enemy Number One — Satan — attacked Joseph because he could see that something major was about to go down for the spiritual welfare of humankind and wanted to scare off Joseph before it could continue. Joseph felt himself sinking into despair but called upon God to deliver him out of the enemy's power. It was then that he saw a pillar of light appear directly above his head, shining even brighter than the sun. The light gradually descended, driving out all darkness from the grove.

After he adjusted to this shock, Joseph saw that the light was actually coming from two beings, Heavenly Father and Jesus Christ. (Talk about a dramatic answer to prayer.) One pointed to the other and said, "This is My Beloved Son. Hear Him!"

Now that he had their attention, Joseph asked the question that was in his heart: Which church should he join? Surprisingly, Heavenly Father and Jesus Christ told him to join none of them, because they were all established and run by humans and thus "corrupt." Considering how important the First Vision later became in the Mormon story, the fact that this is all Latter-day Saints know of the conversation is kind of surprising. Joseph said that Jesus Christ spoke of "many other things," but he either chose not to or was forbidden to tell about them.

After the vision

At some point, Joseph found himself lying alone on his back in the clearing, feeling spent and exhausted. He walked home and, in what may have been the understatement of the century, told his anxious mother he'd learned for himself that he wasn't supposed to join any of the existing churches.

Joseph, presumably quite flabbergasted by the unexpected divine visitation, seems to have kept pretty quiet about it, at least at first. He confided in a local Methodist preacher a few days after the vision but was disappointed by the minister's contempt. Given that God's revelation to Joseph almost entirely concerned the unfitness of existing churches and ministers, the fact that the minister loathed what Joseph had to say isn't too surprising. After a few more such encounters, Joseph learned to keep his mouth shut about his unusual experience for the time being.

CONTROVERSY

Joseph Smith's experience in the Sacred Grove is now canonized in Mormonism as the "First Vision," with his official account included in the LDS scripture known as the Pearl of Great Price (which we discuss in Chapter 10). At various times in his life, Joseph Smith also recorded three other versions of the First Vision in which some details are a little different. For a closer look at this slightly fuzzy situation, see Chapter 15.

According to the accepted official version, several more years elapsed before Joseph received another heavenly visitor. For more on the Angel Moroni and the coming forth of the Book of Mormon, see Chapter 9.

Bringing Back the Church Step by Step

After Joseph Smith's First Vision, about a decade passed before he officially organized the LDS church in 1830. Until he was martyred in 1844, 14 years later, he continued restoring gospel principles, translating ancient scriptures, and receiving new revelations. In this section, we provide a chronological overview of the major steps in the latter-day restoration of the Church of Jesus Christ and show how the modern Church relates back to earlier biblical versions.

It's worth noting that, at that time in United States history, lots of people were trying to set up churches that mirrored the original Christian church. These movements were known as "Christian primitivism" or "restorationism." So, this aspect of Mormonism's founding was at least partly a product of the times.

A parade of heavenly messengers

In order for Joseph to restore the Church, he had to receive the necessary priesthood keys from the men who'd last held them on the earth. Because those men were all long since dead, they returned to the earth as resurrected beings to make some special deliveries to Joseph and his associates.

>> Joseph Smith and his Book of Mormon translation scribe, Oliver Cowdery, said that the resurrected John the Baptist appeared to them in 1829 to restore the Aaronic Priesthood. (We explain this preparatory priesthood in more detail in the section "For boys: The Aaronic Priesthood.") They said that John laid his hands on their heads to confer this priesthood as they stood on the banks of Pennsylvania's Susquehanna River. John then instructed them to baptize each other in the river.

>> At some unspecified time after that, Joseph and Oliver said that the New Testament apostles Peter, James, and John appeared as resurrected beings to bestow the Melchizedek Priesthood on them. (For more about this priesthood, see the later section "For men: The Melchizedek Priesthood.") This event was a prerequisite to organizing and leading the Savior's authorized church, including performing ordinances and receiving revelations. Latter-day Saints believe that Peter served as prophet and president of the New Testament church after Jesus's resurrection, with James and John as his counselors.

>> On April 6, 1830, Joseph Smith convened a small meeting in a log farmhouse in upstate New York to officially organize the Church with six founding members. About two weeks prior to this, he'd published the first edition of the all-important Book of Mormon, his translation of ancient Western Hemisphere writings about Christ. Hot off the press, this book of scripture became the fledgling religion's calling card to the world. (For more on the Book of Mormon, see Chapter 9.)

>> Over the next several years, other resurrected prophets — including Moses, Elias, and Elijah — gave Joseph additional priesthood keys, such as the power to seal families for eternity and perform gospel ordinances on behalf of the dead. In addition, Joseph continued to expand and refine the Church's organizational structure, which Church leaders occasionally still tweak today. (For info on the Church's general worldwide leadership, see Chapter 8. For info on local congregational leadership, see Chapter 6.)

Continuing the gospel tradition

Latter-day Saints believe that the New Testament church was called the *Church of Christ;* today's restored church is called *The Church of Jesus Christ of Latter-day Saints.* To modern Latter-day Saints, the word *saint* simply means a person who strives to become like Christ. The early members of the LDS church knew that early Christians were called *saints*, so they took that name. The "latter-day" part of the Church's name signifies members' belief that they're living in the final gospel dispensation before Christ's Second Coming.

According to Latter-day Saints, the Savior's ancient and modern churches share the same priesthood authority, ordinances, and basic organization. Then and now, the Church is the kingdom of God on earth, and its main purpose is to enable all people, living and dead, to make eternal covenants with God by receiving ordinances, obeying commandments, and following Christ. When people hold up their end of the covenants they make at baptism (see Chapter 6) and in the Mormon temple (see Chapter 7), God provides blessings in return, the greatest of which is *exaltation*, or becoming an eternal parent like God.

In addition, Latter-day Saints believe that this new church launched by Joseph Smith includes, as predicted in the Bible, the "restitution of all things, which God hath spoken by the mouth of all his holy prophets since the world began" (Acts 3:21) — including, perhaps most challengingly, Old Testament polygamy. The gospel will never again disappear from the earth, in the Mormon view — in fact, another of the Church's main purposes is to prepare people to eventually welcome back the resurrected Christ, who will reign over the earth for 1,000 years before the final judgment (for more on these beliefs, see Chapter 3).

WHAT'S IN A NAME?

The Church of Jesus Christ of Latter-day Saints hasn't always gone by that name. In the 1830s, Joseph Smith tried out two other names before finally settling on the one that exists today (which was spelled a little differently during his lifetime, with no hyphen).

In April 1830, when the Church was first organized, it was called the Church of Christ. However, that name was already taken by a group led by Alexander Campbell, which similarly claimed it was the restored New Testament church, so Joseph Smith's followers needed to find some way to distinguish themselves in the public mind. In April 1834, Smith declared that the official name was the "Church of Latter Day Saints." In 1838, Smith put "Jesus Christ" into the name, making it the "Church of Jesus Christ of Latter Day Saints."

Today, the Church asks people to use its full name on first reference and the generic-sounding "Church of Jesus Christ" on subsequent references. However, many people outside the Church continue to use the nicknames "LDS church," which the Church tolerates, and "Mormon church," which Church authorities used to embrace but now actively discourage. (For more on where the nickname *Mormon* comes from, see Chapter 1.)

Understanding the Priesthood

In the Mormon view, the *priesthood* is nothing less than God's power and authority. God uses the priesthood to create worlds, keep the universe running smoothly, and perform other godly tasks. To give his children — who someday can become godlike — an opportunity to learn the ropes of the family business, God grants priesthood power and authority to all worthy male members of Christ's church. This way, they can help carry out God's purposes on the earth and perform ordinances that hold eternal weight. Of course, a mortal's priesthood power compared to God's is like a candle compared to the sun, but the type of power is basically the same, and it can keep increasing eternally. (If you're wondering what happened to the ladies, see the section, "What about women and the priesthood?")

The Mormon priesthood is divided into two levels. The Aaronic Priesthood used to be held by men who performed important adult functions, but today the Church has largely downscaled it into a "preparatory priesthood" to help Mormon teens get ready to become Jedi — er, to receive the higher Melchizedek Priesthood, which all worthy adult males can hold. (Don't worry; later in this section we explain where that *M* name comes from and how to pronounce it.)

REMEMBER

In Mormonism, the word *priesthood* usually refers to God's power and authority that he delegates to men, but sometimes people use the term to indicate male Latter-day Saints in general, as in "The priesthood will be responsible for setting up chairs before the meeting" — which sometimes feels like it's one of the chief priesthood duties, in addition to shoveling snow and helping families move.

For boys: The Aaronic Priesthood

Named after Moses' brother Aaron, the Aaronic Priesthood mainly performs the Church's outward ordinances of repentance, such as baptizing people and administering the sacramental bread and water to congregations. In biblical times, adult descendants of Aaron administered this priesthood. In the modern Church, all worthy teenage boys do, although they must be at least 16 to baptize someone.

This section outlines the three ranks of the Aaronic Priesthood, through which Mormon boys advance about every two years. Each time a boy advances, he can continue performing the duties of the lower ranks. Before advancing in the priesthood, a boy discusses his worthiness in an interview with his local congregational leader, who also holds an Aaronic Priesthood office. (In recent years, the Church has adopted a safer policy for youth interviews: "When a youth meets with a Church leader, a parent or another adult must be present. The youth may invite the adult to join the meeting or wait outside the room.")

By the way, when an adult male joins the Church, he's initially ordained to the Aaronic Priesthood, but he usually takes only a few months — rather than several years — to advance to the higher priesthood.

Step 1: Deacon

Turning 12 is a major milestone for a Mormon boy. He leaves the *Primary*, the Church's organization for children, and joins the *Young Men*, the program for boys ages 12 through 17. Even more significantly, if Church leaders deem him worthy, they make him part of the Aaronic Priesthood, starting with the office of deacon. (Most deacons actually start at age 11, because the Church ordains each year's crop of new deacons in January of the year they turn 12.)

The main duty of a deacon is to pass the sacramental bread and water to the congregation during *sacrament meeting*, Mormonism's main weekly congregational worship service (for more on sacrament meeting, see Chapter 6). In addition, deacons can serve as messengers for priesthood leaders, help take care of the meetinghouse, and in heavily Mormon areas may go house to house collecting *fast offerings* from members, although online donations have made this less common. (Once a month, Latter-day Saints skip two meals and donate what they would've spent on the food — plus more, if they're able — to the Church for helping the poor and needy. For more on Mormon fasting, see Chapter 16.)

Step 2: Teacher

At age 14, a Mormon boy can become a teacher in the Aaronic Priesthood. A teacher's main job is filling the sacramental trays with bread and water and setting them out to be blessed and passed. In addition, teachers can assist adult priesthood holders with *ministering*, the Church's program for assigning members to look after each other and keep in personal touch (for more on ministering, see Chapter 17).

Step 3: Priest

At age 16, LDS boys can become priests. The main job of Mormon priests is to bless the sacramental bread and water, saying the prayer exactly right or repeating it until they do. (Don't worry; they can use a cheat sheet.) In addition, priests can perform baptisms (see Chapter 6), ordain other males to Aaronic Priesthood offices, and conduct meetings when an adult priesthood holder is absent.

MELCHIZE-WHO?

Technically, the full name of Mormonism's higher priesthood is "the Holy Priesthood, after the Order of the Son of God." However, the Church generally refers to it as the Melchizedek Priesthood. Melchizedek was a high priest and king in Old Testament times of whom the Book of Mormon says: "There were many before him, and also there were many afterwards, but none were greater" (Alma 13:19).

The name *Melchizedek* is a combination of two Hebrew words meaning "king" and "righteous"; the Roman Catholic Church also has a Melchizedek Priesthood order. The key to pronouncing *Melchizedek* is to treat the "ch" as a "k" sound. Other than that, the pronunciation is pretty much phonetic: Mel-*kih*-zeh-dek.

The bishop

Okay, this section is a little confusing, so bear with us. The leader of a full-sized Mormon congregation, or *ward*, is called the bishop (his counterpart in a smaller congregation, or *branch*, is called a branch president). Why do we list that role here, under the Aaronic Priesthood? Because, technically, the office of bishop is part of the Aaronic Priesthood. The bishop directly oversees the boys who hold the Aaronic Priesthood, and he uses that priesthood to perform some of his duties, such as handling finances and helping the poor.

However, the bishop of a ward is also a high priest in the Melchizedek Priesthood (see the next section), which gives him authority to act as CEO of the ward and conduct its spiritual affairs. In addition to overseeing the efforts of all the volunteers who typically staff a ward (see Chapter 6), the bishop spends a lot of time interviewing individual members for a variety of reasons, such as issuing temple recommends (see Chapter 7). Bishops act as judges in God's earthly kingdom, and Latter-day Saints believe they can receive revelation about how to run the ward, including discerning the needs of individuals.

For men: The Melchizedek Priesthood

Given to all worthy adult Mormon males, the Melchizedek Priesthood provides men with the power and authority to lead the Church and preside in their own families, including receiving revelations directly from God to help them carry out those stewardships. From the prophet on down, all men hold the same priesthood, but they have different offices within that priesthood, including apostle, seventy, patriarch, high priest, and elder.

The Church's prophet and president is the only single man who can exercise or delegate all the keys of authority. Latter-day Saints believe God recognizes the actions of priesthood holders only when they're in complete harmony with the chain of command, so a priesthood holder can't go off and start his own church. (However, plenty of people have launched offshoots of Mormonism, all of which the LDS church regards as illegitimate — especially ones involving that old bugaboo, polygamy.)

Elders

As early as age 18, any worthy Mormon man can hold the Melchizedek Priesthood office of elder. This rank allows them to teach and administer in the Church, bestow the gift of the Holy Ghost, do missionary work, attend the temple, and perform a variety of blessings and other ordinances. Elders preside in meetings when no high priest is available.

High Priests

In order to hold a high-ranking leadership position, such as bishop or *stake president* (leader of a grouping of congregations), a man is first ordained a high priest. A younger man can become a high priest if the Church has called him to a senior leadership position, but most high priests are middle-aged or retired.

Patriarchs

Usually retirement-aged, patriarchs are fairly rare in the LDS church, with many *stakes* (groups of congregations) having only one. Typically during the teen years, a Latter-day Saint goes to a patriarch to receive a *patriarchal blessing*. This one-time blessing tells the receiver which tribe of Israel they belong to and includes personal advice and revelations that Latter-day Saints consider important enough to transcribe and keep handy for lifelong reference. Adult converts to the Church can receive a patriarchal blessing, too. (For more on patriarchal blessings, see Chapter 5.)

Seventies and Apostles

The relatively few men who hold the offices of *seventy* (several hundred men) and *apostle* (only 15 men) typically serve the Church full time, and together they're known as *General Authorities*. Usually based at Church headquarters in Salt Lake City, Utah, they're assigned to oversee Church functions and departments and to rotate among positions governing the Church in defined areas of the world. We discuss General Authorities in more detail in Chapter 8.

Performing priesthood ordinances

Holders of the Melchizedek Priesthood bring the Savior into people's lives by performing ordinances. Many of these ordinances include *blessings*, which are free-style words of counsel and promise, as inspired by the Holy Ghost in accordance with God's will. For most of these ordinances, the recipient typically sits down in a chair, and the priesthood holder stands behind the chair and places his hands on the person's head, acting as proxy for the Lord himself. If additional priesthood holders participate, they too place their hands on the recipient's head. Some men like to dress up in Sunday clothes before administering an ordinance even at home, and some like to say a personal prayer first to get themselves spiritually in tune.

Many priesthood ordinances, such as healing the sick or injured and giving blessings of comfort, can be performed at will by any worthy priesthood holder. Others, such as baptism, confirmation, and priesthood ordinations, must be authorized by local priesthood leaders. Following are the main ordinances that holders of the Melchizedek Priesthood perform:

>> **Blessings of comfort:** Anyone — Church member or not — can ask a priesthood holder for a blessing of comfort in times of difficulty or decision making. Often the blessing recipient requests a family member or local leader who's familiar with their situation. The priesthood holder simply lays his hands on the person's head, starts the blessing, and offers whatever words he feels inspired to say.

>> **Confirmation and bestowing the gift of the Holy Ghost:** For new members of the Church, this ordinance takes place soon after baptism. We discuss it in detail in Chapter 6.

>> **Dedications:** In a manner similar to blessings but without the laying on of hands, priesthood holders can dedicate a building or gravesite as a place of spiritual sanctuary and protection. Upon moving into a new house or apartment, many Mormon priesthood holders dedicate it for their families, and some Latter-day Saints even dedicate their businesses to the Lord. The dedication process is quite simple, not much different from a normal prayer. In a more formal manner, senior Church officials dedicate new or remodeled meetinghouses and temples, and they can dedicate entire nations for the preaching of the gospel.

>> **Fathers' and husbands' blessings:** The Church encourages Mormon dads to give regular priesthood blessings to their children, and wives can ask their husbands for blessings. For example, many fathers bless their children at the beginning of a new school year, as they're getting ready to face new challenges and opportunities. In addition, fathers of newborns perform a special blessing ceremony for infants; however, unlike in other faiths, this baby blessing is not a crucial saving ordinance (find out more in Chapter 6).

>> **Healing the sick or injured:** Two or more priesthood holders usually perform this two-step ordinance, although one can perform both steps if others aren't available. One priesthood holder dabs a drop of *consecrated* olive oil (meaning it's been previously blessed for such use) onto the head of the recipient, lays his hands on the person's head, and says a short prayer of anointing. Another priesthood holder "seals" the anointing and offers a blessing of healing, comfort, and counsel. (A priesthood holder can buy pure olive oil at the grocery store and consecrate it with a special prayer, and many Mormon men carry a small vial of this oil at all times.)

Latter-day Saints believe that unless a person is appointed by God to die, a healing blessing can save the person's life. Sometimes priesthood holders feel inspired to use extra-powerful wording, such as rebuking an illness or commanding a body to be healed. At the same time, a priesthood holder can't force a healing against God's will. Latter-day Saints are encouraged to seek out appropriate medical treatment, as well as priesthood blessings, when they are ill. Coauthor Chris Bigelow believes he was healed of Hodgkin's lymphoma via a priesthood blessing, although he still underwent chemotherapy and radiation because modern medicine is also a blessing of God.

>> **Priesthood ordinations:** The priesthood is transmitted from person to person by the laying on of hands. Whenever a boy or man advances in the priesthood, another priesthood holder ordains him to the new office. After stating the details of the ordination, most priesthood holders include a blessing of advice about exercising the priesthood. Some Mormon men carry a wallet-sized card outlining their priesthood *line of authority* — or genealogy — all the way back to Christ. (Yes, a big-time gap lies between the apostle Peter and Joseph Smith.)

>> **Starting a new Church job:** Whenever anyone accepts a calling to perform a job or fulfill a leadership position in the Church, that person is usually "set apart" for the calling by a priesthood leader. After laying hands on the person's head and stating the facts of the calling, most leaders also include a blessing of guidance and encouragement. For more about volunteer Church callings, see Chapter 6.

What about women and the priesthood?

In the Mormon view, men and women are equally vital, though different, halves of a whole, and neither can achieve *exaltation* — becoming like the Heavenly Parents — without the other. At the same time, Mormonism is adamantly, unapologetically patriarchal. Without exception, men preside in the Church and their families, and, ideally, they're the sole breadwinners, freeing women to bear and rear children. However, lots of Mormon women work outside the home, and Church authorities frequently remind Mormon men that they must respect their wives and the women of the Church as equal partners and consult them in making decisions. Many LDS women express gratitude for having a priesthood holder in the house who can perform ordinances, receive revelations for the family unit, and unscrew jar lids.

SCRIPTURE

One oft-quoted scripture in Mormonism warns priesthood holders against misusing the priesthood. If someone tries to dominate his wife (or anyone else) or gratify selfish desires through the priesthood, "the heavens withdraw themselves; the Spirit of the Lord is grieved; and when it is withdrawn, Amen to the priesthood or the authority of that man" (from the Doctrine and Covenants 121:37; for more on the D&C, see Chapter 10). In other words, that man's priesthood authority goes kaput unless and until he repents of any abuse or toxic behavior. Rather, men must use the priesthood "by persuasion, by long-suffering, by gentleness and meekness, and by love unfeigned" (D&C 121:41). In other words, they need to be kind and use the priesthood to serve others.

CONTROVERSY

In recent years, the Church has taken steps to make female leaders more visible and involve them more in decision-making processes. However, Mormon attitudes and policies regarding the patriarchal priesthood and gender roles still cause controversy, even within the Church — for more about the kerfuffle, see Chapter 15.

Chapter 5

Together Forever: The Eternal Importance of Family

Upon hearing that Latter-day Saints believe families can be together forever, some people think the idea sounds more like hell than heaven, depending on the state of their own family relationships. Nevertheless, Latter-day Saints preach that people reach the highest level of heaven as families, not as individuals. Known for marrying younger, divorcing less often, and having more children than today's average couple, devout Latter-day Saints who are sealed to one another in the temple believe they can accomplish nothing greater than building a strong, successful family that will continue throughout eternity.

In addition, Latter-day Saints think that discovering their ancestors and taking certain steps to eternally bind together their extended families, all the way back to Adam and Eve, is extremely important. Also, Latter-day Saints believe that all humans can become part of God's eternal family by making covenants with God and thereby becoming adopted into the *house of Israel*, which is what God calls his covenant people.

The Eternal Family Unit

In the Mormon view, all human beings are the spirit children of Heavenly Parents and can grow up to become like them (we discuss this core concept in more detail in Chapter 2). So that humans can learn how to become parents, God commands them to form family units on this earth, which serve as miniature models of God's own eternal family organization. Latter-day Saints have faith that, through the gospel, their earthly families can eventually become like God's eternal family.

Why families are so important

Latter-day Saints currently teach that the traditional nuclear family is part of God's plan and must remain the basic unit of society. In addition, they believe that the LDS church's main role is to help families gain eternal blessings together, through Jesus Christ.

In the Mormon view, all men and women are commanded to "multiply and replenish the earth" — in other words, have children. As we discuss in Chapter 2, God wants all his spirit children to come to this earth, gain a physical body, and go through a human test, and this can happen only if people make babies. Latter-day Saints insist that all children deserve to be born to a married husband and wife. Although the Church expresses compassion for those people who can't find a partner or bear children, it discourages self-imposed celibacy — unless you're gay (see Chapter 15) — and has zero tolerance for sexual activity outside marriage (for more on Mormon views regarding chastity, see Chapter 16).

One of the most repeated sayings in Mormonism is "No other success can compensate for failure in the home," which has given pause to many a career-oriented Mormon. In a one-page document titled "The Family: A Proclamation to the World," which many Latter-day Saints keep framed on their living-room walls, LDS prophets and apostles declare: "We warn that the disintegration of the family will bring upon individuals, communities, and nations the calamities foretold by ancient and modern prophets." This proclamation hasn't yet been canonized in the Doctrine and Covenants (for more on this modern-day scripture and on the family proclamation, see Chapter 10), but many members expect that will happen eventually.

Because heterosexual nuclear families are so central and important to their faith, Latter-day Saints believe this family model is one of the devil's main targets. That's why Latter-day Saints get so alarmed about divorce, adultery, premarital sex, and gay marriage, which they view as sinful trends that move society away from traditional families. (Some observers find the Church's opposition to gay marriage ironic because its objections resemble those raised about polygamy in the 19th century, when the Church was on the other side of the table — for more on gay marriage, see Chapter 15.) Even the 1970s women's liberation movement threw some Latter-day Saints into a tizzy because they believe that a woman's main role should be nurturing children in the home.

"Till never do you part": Eternal sealing

Although many successful couples and families instinctively feel they'll always be together, Latter-day Saints believe that love isn't enough to preserve relationships past death. Rather, an eternal *sealing* ordinance is necessary to join husbands, wives, and their children together forever.

How and where

SCRIPTURE

Someone holding the proper authority from God must perform an eternal family sealing, and Latter-day Saints believe their specially ordained sealers are the only ones who currently hold that authority. This authority is what Jesus gave to Peter, the senior apostle: "And I will give unto thee the keys of the kingdom of heaven: and whatsoever thou shalt bind on earth shall be bound in heaven: and whatsoever thou shalt loose on earth shall be loosed in heaven" (Matthew 16:19). Latter-day Saints believe that this authority was lost from the earth due to corruption and apostasy but was later restored through Mormonism's founding prophet, Joseph Smith (for more details, see Chapter 4).

All eternal sealings occur in a sacred building called a *temple* (we discuss temples in detail in Chapter 7, including an overview of what goes on inside them). After a Mormon couple is sealed, any children they bear after that point are automatically sealed to them at birth. If a couple adopts a child or doesn't get sealed until after children are born, those children participate in a temple sealing ordinance with their parents. However, getting sealed doesn't guarantee that every family member will make it to the eternal reunion — the sin in an unrepentant person's life overrides the sealing ordinance for him or her.

To offer the blessings of eternal families to everyone who's ever lived, Latter-day Saints are in the process of performing sealings by proxy in the temple for all husbands, wives, and children throughout history, especially their own ancestors. In the afterlife, these people can decide whether to accept the sealing — but there's a catch: The sealing is available only as a package deal that includes allegiance to Christ and his gospel. For more on this idea, see this chapter's section on family history work, as well as Chapter 7.

The eternal payoff

For Latter-day Saints, eternal marriage offers several benefits:

>> Knowing that marriage can last forever adds a deeper dimension to a relationship and gives couples an important goal to work toward together. When a spouse dies, Latter-day Saints find it reassuring to look forward to resuming the relationship in the afterlife.

>> Parenthood becomes more meaningful when parents focus on the belief that their relationship with their children can be eternal. Motivation increases for parents to teach their children well and build stronger, happier homes.

>> Although someone can be *saved* to live with God in the afterlife without being sealed to a spouse, Latter-day Saints believe that only those with an opposite-sex marriage partner can be *exalted* to become like God. Latter-day Saints don't often mention Heavenly Mother, but they believe God himself is married — which stands to reason if he's going to produce spiritual offspring, which is what we humans are. (For more on the Heavenly Parents, see Chapters 2 and 3.)

Breadwinning and homemaking

To keep families strong, Latter-day Saints uphold traditional gender roles — at least on paper. Ideally, men earn the money so women can stay home with the kids. However, U.S. demographics show that Mormon women work outside the home just as much as non-Mormon women do. LDS church authorities still sometimes preach the ideal, but they allow for the fact that some women want careers outside the home and that some families require two incomes to make ends meet. However, authorities warn against women working just so the family can enjoy more luxuries.

In Mormonism, men are expected to preside over their homes and families by exercising their priesthood authority in love and righteousness, not with bossiness or intimidation (for more on the Mormon priesthood, see Chapter 4). Mormon men are frequently reminded to treat their wives as equals and consult with them in making decisions. Although "househusbands" aren't unheard of in Mormonism, the idea makes most Latter-day Saints uncomfortable because the Church teaches men to provide for their families to the best of their ability.

In addition to encouraging offspring and traditional gender roles, Mormonism elevates marital sex and romance to near-religious status. Church leaders encourage men and women to continue courting each other throughout their marriage, including spending an evening alone together on a weekly basis, if possible. Sex is not just for procreation but also to bless and unite married couples. Mormon spouses recognize the obligation to do their best to help keep their partners happy.

Populating the earth

When it comes to having children and raising them, Latter-day Saints go for both quantity and quality. Church members aren't prohibited from using birth control, but they're still known for having large families (see Chapter 16 for more on Mormon views regarding birth control). For example, coauthor Chris Bigelow is the oldest of ten children, which his parents spaced out about every two years. Although Mormon birth rates typically follow the general trend, which means that Latter-day Saints in developed nations are having fewer children nowadays, they still have more kids on average than their non-Mormon contemporaries.

Why do Latter-day Saints have so many kids? Beyond simply valuing family life and parenthood, several possible reasons exist.

>> **To make sure they're not leaving anyone out:** As we discuss in Chapter 2, Latter-day Saints believe that everybody's spirits lived together and formed relationships before coming to earth. Mormon parents sometimes have more children because they sense that another spirit who belongs in their family is still waiting to be born, although this widespread belief isn't official doctrine.

>> **To give premortal spirits the opportunity of a lifetime:** Latter-day Saints want to give as many people as possible the opportunity to come to earth and be raised in a Mormon home, where they can learn the gospel and receive the necessary ordinances for salvation, such as baptism.

>> **To extend their boundaries:** Latter-day Saints believe they'll progress together through eternity as families, and having lots of children is good preparation for that. In heaven, exalted couples — see Chapter 2 for more about exaltation — will produce endless spirit children and organize numberless planets over which they'll preside, like God the Father presides over this world and numberless others. This belief has led evangelical Protestants and other Christians who oppose Mormonism to charge that Latter-day Saints believe in many gods, but Latter-day Saints point out that they never stop honoring and obeying their own Heavenly Father, even after becoming like him. He remains the only God to them throughout eternity.

Latter-day Saints view parenting children as perhaps the most critical aspect of this earthly test. According to the LDS document "The Family: A Proclamation to the World," parents are under solemn obligation to "rear their children in love and righteousness, to provide for their physical and spiritual needs, to teach them to love and serve one another, to observe the commandments of God, and to be law-abiding citizens wherever they live." Latter-day Saints believe that parents who fail in these duties will be held accountable before God. (For more on the Proclamation, see Chapter 10.)

As a family-centered organization, the LDS church teaches members several ways to strengthen their families:

>> **Family home evening:** Latter-day Saints reserve Monday evenings (or another evening, if their schedule requires) to gather as families and study the gospel, discuss plans and problems, and enjoy a fun activity together. This evening is so sacred that all Church buildings are closed, and Latter-day Saints consider even telephoning another Mormon family on Monday evening to be bad form. (We discuss family home evening in more detail in Chapter 17.)

>> **Family prayer:** Every morning and night, the ideal Mormon family kneels and says a prayer together. Also, Mormon families say a prayer before each meal.

>> **Family council:** On a regular basis and especially when a family faces a significant decision or challenge, the LDS church encourages parents to hold a family meeting so each person can express their insights and opinions.

>> **Family scripture study:** The Church urges its members to spend time each day reading from the scriptures together, especially the Book of Mormon. Many families do this in the morning, before school. Mormon children *never* doze through it. (Yeah, right.) The Church provides manuals, video clips, and other tools to help with family study.

>> **Family work:** Mormon families are generally big on assigning chores and organizing family projects to help children learn to work and cooperate. One common project is a family vegetable garden, and some Mormon families do service projects for widows or other needy people.

>> **Family recreation:** Mormon families place a high priority on taking time to play games and sports together and go on outings and vacations. In addition, many LDS fathers make a point of regularly spending time alone with each child, whether doing something fun together or in a more formal personal priesthood interview (PPI), a one-on-one conversation that is also employed in other aspects of Church administration.

>> **Extended family relations:** Latter-day Saints are typically very big on extended family gatherings, reunions, cousin sleepovers, newsletters, and other traditions. In multigenerational Mormon families, the first cousins alone often number in the dozens, which can really be a ton of fun.

Shaking the Family Tree: Family History Work

Southeast of Salt Lake City, Utah, the white-topped peaks of the Wasatch Mountains beckon with the promise of powdery snow, great skiing, and . . . millions of rolls of microfilm? Yes, you read that right. The LDS church, long known for its obsession with eternal families, considers genealogy (more commonly called "family history") to be so important that it has buried the world's largest collection of genealogical records 700 feet deep in the cool, solid earth underneath a granite mountain.

Since 1894, Church volunteers have been gathering copies of public documents — including records of births, marriages, deaths, probates and wills, land ownership, military service, and censuses — from more than 100 countries. More recently, the emphasis has been on digitizing and databasing these records. Master copies go into the Church's Granite Mountain Records Vault for safekeeping.

The vault's giant doors are made to withstand a nuclear blast. (Sure, it may seem like overkill, but the site was built at the height of the Cold War.) For six decades, this site — off-limits to anyone who's not a Church employee — has protected billions of genealogical images on microfilm, microfiche, and digital media, keeping them at a constant temperature of 60 degrees Fahrenheit, preserved for the ages and ready for people to access worldwide through the Church's expansive FamilySearch organization.

The reason for the fuss

In 2004, a tropical cyclone devastated the island of Niue in the South Pacific. In the village of Alofi, 180-mph winds swept away homes, businesses, and all the village's vital records of births, deaths, immigrations, and marriages. However, only the original records were lost because the LDS church had already microfilmed all the records a decade before. The Church presented a copy of the microfilms to the local government so that Alofi's people wouldn't lose their knowledge of their ancestors.

As wonderful as stories like that are, Latter-day Saints have an even more cosmically important reason for doing family history work. The LDS church urges all its members to contribute their time, energy, and prayer to the eventual salvation of all people, and doing family history work is part of that. You can thumb back to Chapter 2 for the full scoop on the Mormon plan of salvation, but here's the nutshell version: Every person can be reunited with God in heaven after living faithfully and receiving certain ordinances, including baptism (see Chapters 6 and 7) and the temple endowment (see Chapter 7). This opportunity is available not only to those who've lived since the restoration of the gospel in Joseph Smith's time but also to everyone who's ever existed on earth, from Adam and Eve on down through the entire human race.

Latter-day Saints believe that *proxies* (substitutes) can perform the essential ordinances on behalf of people who didn't have the chance in this mortal life to be baptized and attend the temple. In acting as proxies, Latter-day Saints give those spirits the chance to embrace or reject the gospel in its fullness in the spirit world. (For more on the spirit world and the decisions that spirits there can make, see Chapter 2.)

Family history is the key to making temple ordinances such as eternal family sealing possible for the dead, because family history work provides the names and essential data for people who still need their ordinance work done. Latter-day Saints research their genealogy carefully because they want to be with their own families forever. They also want to give other families that same blessing and extend the opportunity for exaltation to anyone who's ever lived. So, the Church does family history research in all parts of the world.

CONTROVERSY

Some cultures have readily accepted the Mormon practice of proxy baptism, especially parts of Asia, where paying reverence to ancestors is considered a sacred duty. However, others have criticized it, saying that a posthumous baptism or temple ordinance makes a person a Mormon against their will. For example, Mormon leaders have told Church members to refrain from performing baptisms on behalf of Holocaust victims, because some Jewish groups felt that baptizing those who were killed due to their affiliation with Judaism was insulting.

Latter-day Saints are a bit puzzled by the hullabaloo because proxy baptism doesn't *make* the baptized person Mormon or force a spirit-world conversion — it just provides deceased spirits with the *choice*. As we explain in Chapter 2, *agency* (free will) is one of the most important principles of LDS theology. No ordinance or ritual can take away a person's right to choose their own path.

The cloud of this controversy does have a silver lining: Although Jewish advocacy groups have criticized the practice of proxy baptism, they've also praised Mormon genealogists' efforts to use knowledge of Jewish family history in order to regain property lost in the Holocaust.

Using FamilySearch — whether you're Mormon or not

The LDS church believes family history knowledge can enrich and improve everyone's life, so it makes its family-history resources publicly available at no charge. It does this through FamilySearch, a Church-owned nonprofit organization that provides genealogical records, training, software, local research centers, and a robust, user-friendly website. As of 2024, the FamilySearch system contains over 13 billion searchable names, over 5 billion digital images, and over 600,000 digital books.

Many people find they can experience all the family history they want at the FamilySearch website (www.familysearch.org). A great place to start is with Family Tree, billed as "a global, unified family tree for mankind." You just input your parents and grandparents, and the automated tree builder populates your tree with ancestors identified by other users and gathered from historical records around the world by volunteers. Each deceased person has a single public profile that can include photos, documents, audio clips, and other files, so you can really get to know your ancestors. The site fosters connection and collaboration while also protecting privacy.

The main FamilySearch Library

Located in downtown Salt Lake City, Utah, amidst other LDS church headquarter buildings, the FamilySearch Library is the world's largest genealogical library. Open to the public, this mothership library is known for providing lots of personal, hands-on assistance, interactive tools, learning resources, and even self-serve equipment so you can digitize your tapes, photos, slides, books, film, and other family-history media.

TIP

The FamilySearch Library provides a ton of onsite genealogical materials, including millions of microfilms and microfiches and hundreds of thousands of books, serials, periodicals, and other formats. It also provides thousands of electronic resources, including subscriptions to other major genealogical websites.

Local FamilySearch Centers

All over the world, the Church has more than 6,400 FamilySearch Centers that are open to the public. No matter where you are in your family-history efforts — just starting out or working on a tricky research problem — the volunteers in these centers can help you. FamilySearch Centers are often located in local LDS meetinghouses, but if you're not a Church member, don't let that scare you — many patrons are members of other faiths or no faith.

FamilySearch Centers function as branches of the main FamilySearch Library in Salt Lake City. As you can imagine, individual centers vary in size, volunteer staffing, and resources, so feel free to contact your local center to learn more. To find a FamilySearch Center near you, visit https://locations.familysearch.org.

RootsTech: A "family discovery event"

Held each year in Salt Lake City, FamilySearch's RootsTech conference features hundreds of classes, speakers, exhibitors, and other in-person family-history experiences. Attendees can chat with experts, test-drive the latest technology and products, and learn family-history skills and storytelling. Many sessions are accessible online for free. For more information, visit www.familysearch.org/rootstech.

TIP

Coauthor Jana Riess, who volunteered for several years as a family history consultant in her former congregation, has a word of advice for people who are thinking about starting their family history: Don't wait. She found that most people who participated in family history were retired; they had the time to spend doing the research, and they also were more aware of their own mortality and the need for keeping records. But many of these people said they would've given anything just to have their mother or grandmother with them for an hour to answer questions about family history. The moral of this story is . . . don't wait until all the previous generations are gone before you begin making a record. Start it now.

God's People: The Family of Israel

The Mormon concept of family begins with the nuclear family — Mom, Dad, and the pitter-patter of (quite a few, ideally) little feet. Beyond that is the extended family — ancestors and descendants who become sealed forever along patriarchal lines through family history and temple work. But hold your horses: The Mormon concept of family has a third level that binds Latter-day Saints together with lots of people who aren't even their blood relatives.

One of the distinguishing factors of Mormonism compared to other forms of Christianity is its emphasis on the role of Israel in God's plan for the world. By *Israel*, Latter-day Saints don't mean the modern-day nation-state of Israel, but all the many people in the world who are heirs to particular promises God made in the Bible's Old Testament. Latter-day Saints believe that anyone can become part of the *house of Israel* — the chosen people of God — whether or not they're genetic descendants of the ancient Israelites. What's more, one of the LDS Articles of

Faith states that Latter-day Saints believe in the "literal gathering of Israel and in the restoration of the Ten Tribes" — something that isn't a core belief of other Christian denominations.

Why is the house of Israel so important? The story begins with a guy called Abraham.

Abraham and God shake on it

SCRIPTURE

In the Bible's book of Genesis, God made a *covenant,* or two-way agreement, with Abraham. Basically, God told Abraham that if he and his descendants would be God's people, then he would be their God. In return for love, obedience, and faithfulness, God promised Abraham two basic things:

» A bountiful land where he and his descendants could reside
» Descendants without number

For Abraham, an old nomad, both promises were basically laughable. He was rich in everything *but* land and children — and by the time he was 99 years old, neither had materialized. But God made good on his promise with the birth of Isaac, and today Abraham's descendants number as the stars in the sky, as God told him they would.

But according to Latter-day Saints, Abraham's descendants aren't just his literal biological offspring, the Jewish people. In fact, they believe that the *Abrahamic covenant* — God's promises to Abraham — extends to all people who are worthy to be *grafted in* to the house of Israel. (That term is a spiritual one and not something painful, like a skin graft.) So, each and every person has the potential to enter the Abrahamic covenant. How does a person get grafted into the house of Israel? By joining the LDS church.

The house of Israel in Mormon scriptures

The concept of Israel as a factor in community identification shows up not just in the Bible, but in distinctively Mormon scriptures as well. The plight of Israel's scattering and promised regathering is one of the major themes of the Book of Mormon, in which the term *house of Israel* appears no fewer than 107 times.

In fact, when the newly resurrected Savior appears to the Nephites as recorded in 3 Nephi 10, the very first thing he does is to greet them as "descendants of Jacob . . . who are of the house of Israel." To Latter-day Saints, the fact that Christ got right to the point about the Nephites' lineage is significant: The Book of Mormon is about people who were Abraham's descendants.

In the Book of Mormon's opening chapters, the prophet Lehi receives a vision in which he sees the destruction of Jerusalem and the scattering of Israel, so he and his family flee Jerusalem. Six hundred years later, the promised Messiah visits their descendants over in the New World to gather them, as the Savior put it, as a hen gathers her chickens. In other words, the people were restored to their rightful heritage. (For more on the Book of Mormon, see Chapter 9.)

Gathering God's children

SCRIPTURE

The prophets of old and modern-day Mormon prophets have stated that in the latter days prior to the Savior's Second Coming, the house of Israel will be gathered once again, with the remnant being assembled from among the nations of the earth (Jeremiah 23:3).

What does it mean to be gathered? The LDS church teaches that Israel's gathering will happen in two stages:

>> First, Israel will be *spiritually* gathered into the LDS church. This stage is already happening as people all over the world embrace the gospel and come to understand themselves as part of God's great work.

>> Second will be the *physical* gathering of Israel, which won't be completed until the Savior's Second Coming, although it has already gotten underway. This gathering will involve an actual, bodily migration as the different tribes of Israel move back to biblical and Book of Mormon lands to reclaim their heritage. (Even the ten "lost" tribes recounted in the Old Testament will be restored to their lands, as directed by the descendants of Ephraim. For more on Ephraim, skip ahead to the section on patriarchal blessings.)

Becoming adopted into Israel

Presumably, hundreds of millions of people walking the earth today have some genetic link, however faint, to the 12 tribes of ancient Israel. Because bloodlines have been diluted through the centuries and the Jewish Diaspora was so geographically extensive and prolonged, there's no easy way of telling who has Israelite heritage and who doesn't. However, it doesn't matter, because those who aren't born into the Abrahamic covenant can become adopted into Israel through LDS baptism.

Personal Prophecy: Patriarchal Blessings

Latter-day Saints can discover their personal lineage in the house of Israel through an ordinance called a *patriarchal blessing*, which is also an opportunity to receive some personalized prophecy regarding their individual lives. Many Latter-day Saints refer to the typed transcript of their patriarchal blessing throughout life, prayerfully consulting it for insights into personal circumstances and future events.

Unlike other priesthood blessings in the Church, a patriarchal blessing is a once-in-a-lifetime experience, never to be repeated. What's more, not just any Melchizedek Priesthood holder can offer it. Only a *stake patriarch* who's specifically ordained to that role and gifted with the insights of the Holy Ghost can give this blessing. (For more about priesthood blessings, see Chapter 4. To understand what a *stake* is, flip ahead to Chapter 6.)

Each stake usually has only one patriarch, though very large stakes may have two. As the title implies, patriarchs are typically advanced in age, often of retirement age. Until very recently, the Quorum of the Twelve Apostles in Salt Lake City individually chose and ordained all patriarchs. Now, with so many stakes around the world, the stake president submits a recommendation to the Twelve, who must approve the proposed patriarch before the stake president ordains him.

Discovering personal lineage

One of the most important aspects of every patriarchal blessing is the declaration of a person's lineage in the house of Israel. Drawing upon the inspiration of the Holy Spirit, the patriarch indicates which *tribe* the individual belongs to. Remember that in the book of Genesis, Abraham's grandson Jacob had 12 sons who became the 12 tribes of Israel.

SCRIPTURE

Most, though not all, Latter-day Saints are declared to be of the tribe of Ephraim — an interesting lineage, because in Genesis 48, this tribe receives a special blessing to be great and to be the source of many nations. Having such a noble lineage is a privilege and responsibility, one that Latter-day Saints take seriously. Latter-day Saints believe that it doesn't matter whether they became part of the tribe by adoption or by blood; the important thing is to participate in the vital work that the tribe of Ephraim must complete to restore the whole people of Israel.

Other aspects of a patriarchal blessing

Latter-day Saints rarely show their patriarchal blessing transcripts to people outside their own families. To them, blessings are sacred; in addition, Church leaders don't want people to covet one another's promised gifts, talents, or destinies. For example, if some teens compared their blessings, one young man may feel pangs of jealousy that his best friend's blessing contains specific information about the woman he'll someday marry. Or a young woman may realize that all her buddies' blessings contain promises of missions they'll serve and worry why hers doesn't.

However, Latter-day Saints sometimes mention the promises of their patriarchal blessings when they're relevant to a church discussion or in private conversations. In addition to the declaration of lineage discussed in the preceding section, most patriarchal blessings contain some, though by no means all, of the following aspects. These aren't prepared or researched by the stake patriarch beforehand but come to him through prayer during the blessing, as directed by the Spirit:

>> **Discussion of the person's premortal existence:** Often, this statement is simple and general, saying that the person fought valiantly in the War in Heaven. (For more on that topic, see Chapter 2.) But some patriarchal blessings are quite specific about what people did and whom they knew before coming to earth.

>> **A statement about the person's earthly family:** Some patriarchal blessings make general mention about a person's family situation ("You've been raised by loving parents who've taught you gospel principles," and so on). Others are quite particular about unique circumstances in the person's family life or make predictions about the recipient's future spouse or children.

>> **Reference to individual strengths and weaknesses:** Some blessings are very personal, as the Spirit inspires the patriarch to talk about the individual's personality traits, spiritual assets, and potential flaws.

>> **Mention of a full-time mission:** Some blessings for young people mention serving a full-time mission for the Church. (To understand what missionary work means to Latter-day Saints, see Chapter 14.) For example, in the mid-1980s, one young man's patriarchal blessing said that he would one day serve a mission to Russia. The Cold War still prevailed, and the Soviet Union didn't exactly welcome the evangelistic efforts of Mormon missionaries, so he rightly wondered if the patriarch had gotten soft in the head. However, by the time this fellow was 19, the Church had just opened its first mission in post-Soviet Russia, and he was among the charter group of missionaries sent to preach the gospel there. (At the same time, some pioneer-era patriarchal blessings contains statements that did not come to pass, such as that the recipient would live to see the Second Coming or visit another planet.)

>> **Message from Heavenly Mother:** Heavenly Mother has been known to make an occasional appearance in patriarchal blessings, especially for young women. In these blessings, the message from Heavenly Father is supplemented by words that Heavenly Mother specifically wants the person to hear:

that the individual is dearly loved, has a divine nature, and possesses special and unique qualities (which may or may not be spelled out). The recipients, who don't hear much about Heavenly Mother in church, often cherish these words.

» **Predictions of events the individual will personally witness:** Some patriarchal blessings make statements about things the person will someday see, whether they be Church growth or signs of the last days before Christ's Second Coming.

» **Specific blessings related to career or Church service:** Patriarchal blessings can vary dramatically in this regard. One coauthor of this book was stunned to receive very detailed guidance about education and individual talents through a patriarchal blessing, despite having never met the stake patriarch before the blessing.

» **Loving reminders to live worthily:** Most patriarchal blessings contain counsel to follow the promptings of the Holy Ghost and remain worthy to keep his constant companionship (see Chapter 3). Many also urge the individual to be a good influence in the family, at work, in the community, and in all other circumstances.

» **A final promise to be sealed and protected against the dark side:** Many patriarchal blessings close with a benediction for protection against Satan and his minions.

Understanding a patriarchal blessing

Most Church members are grateful for their patriarchal blessings, which they believe are tailor-made for them and reflect the guidance of the Holy Ghost. However, these blessings are not always easy to understand.

One of the most interesting aspects of a patriarchal blessing is the high emphasis the Church places on its individuality. If a member has questions about the content of a blessing, the patriarch, bishop, and other Church leaders are explicitly told *not* to interpret the blessing for the member. Church members can, through prayer, bring all their questions directly to Heavenly Father.

The LDS church encourages members to remember that although patriarchal blessings come from the Holy Ghost, they aren't necessarily road maps for life and should not be viewed like fortunes from a soothsayer. Some elements of a patriarchal blessing may not be realized until late in mortal life, or even in the afterlife. (For example, someone who was told that he'd see peace established on the earth may eventually view that transition from the spirit world, not this one.)

OBTAINING A PATRIARCHAL BLESSING

To get a patriarchal blessing, you must be a Mormon in good standing and be considered worthy by your bishop. This worthiness interview isn't as set in stone as an interview for a temple recommend (for more on that process, see Chapter 7), but it's important for the bishop to determine whether you're ready. (The LDS church doesn't set a fixed age for a person to receive a patriarchal blessing, so Latter-day Saints who grow up in the Church don't have absolute guidance about when to seek it, although most do it during their mid-to-late teens.) By interviewing you, your bishop can figure out whether you're spiritually mature and responsible enough, or if you should wait a little longer. If you're a recent convert, he can see whether you're established enough in the gospel to be ready for the blessing. Unlike the temple, which a new convert must wait a full year to enter, there's no preset waiting period for getting a patriarchal blessing after baptism.

If your interview with the bishop goes swimmingly, you make an appointment with the patriarch. Unless you have a family member who's an ordained stake patriarch, you can't cross stake lines to have the patriarch of another stake perform the blessing. Some patriarchs allow you to bring one or two loved ones to hear the blessing — parents, a spouse, or a good friend.

At the appointed time, you all sit down for a few minutes with the patriarch, usually in his home. Many patriarchs ask questions that will help them pray about and personalize the blessing. When the time comes for the blessing to begin, the patriarch stands behind you and places his hands on your head. Every blessing is recorded on audio and then transcribed, often by the patriarch's wife or another family member, so don't worry if you don't catch every word. One copy of the transcript is sent to Church headquarters, and another is mailed to you to consult throughout your life. You can also view your own blessing transcript online through your personal Church account.

Eternal Rituals and Endless Meetings

We look at the Church from the bottom up, so to speak. We start with the *ward* (local congregation) and *stake* (regional gathering of wards) and reveal everything that goes on from day to day and week to week. You find out what to expect if someone invites you to attend a Mormon *sacrament meeting* (Sunday service), baptism, or funeral, and you get the scoop on all the different activities and organizations at the ward and stake levels.

Then you take a trip inside a Mormon temple and see why Mormons feel that temples are so important for the spiritual health of the living — and the dead. Finally, you go on a quick tour of Church headquarters in Salt Lake City, meeting the General Authorities and learning about the semiannual televised meeting led by Church leaders and the welfare and Humanitarian Relief programs that help poor people all over the world.

Chapter **6**

Welcome to the Meetinghouse!

When imagining Latter-day Saint life, many non-Mormons immediately picture an eye-popping LDS temple, one of the religion's most instantly recognizable symbols. And though these Magic Kingdom–ish buildings house some of the most sacred rituals of the Mormon faith — see Chapter 7 for the skinny on that — you need to spend some time in the public meetinghouse of the local *ward*, or congregation, in order to understand the heart of what it means to be a Latter-day Saint.

The ward is the second-most-important unit of Mormon life and culture after the nuclear family. In fact, wards are a lot like a family, with members addressing each other as Brother or Sister, followed by the surname — collectively, the men are called "brethren" and women "sisters" (or "sistren" by the occasional wag). Led by a bishop, a ward usually encompasses all the Latter-day Saints within certain geographic boundaries, which can sometimes lead to either bland homogeneity or interesting diversity in a congregation.

Also in this chapter, we offer a sneak peek into a Mormon sacrament meeting, which is the main Sunday service, and tell you what to expect if you find yourself a guest at a Mormon baptism, wedding, or funeral. We take a look at the classes and auxiliary organizations that meet on Sundays and explain the Church's system of volunteer service, which is one of the most distinctive elements of Mormon spiritual life; because Latter-day Saints have no paid clergy, Church members all have assignments, or *callings*, to fulfill. Finally, we talk about the *stake* (a grouping of several wards led by a stake president) and what stake conferences and activities entail.

What's a Ward?

In plain English, a *ward* is simply a local Mormon congregation. Wards usually have about 300 to 350 members who meet for two hours on Sundays and enjoy other events and activities together. On Sundays, the first hour is usually the *sacrament meeting,* during which everyone gathers in the chapel to partake of the sacramental bread and water, sing hymns, and listen to *talks* — short informal sermons — given by fellow ward members (including teens and children). After a 10-minute break, everyone attends one of several 50-minute classes, depending on the week. Some wards might choose to start their Sunday services with the classes and then hold the sacrament meeting. (We describe these classes later in this chapter in "Other Sunday meetings.")

Unlike most other Christian denominations, The Church of Jesus Christ of Latter-day Saints is a geographically based organization. Ordinarily, the Church doesn't want members to choose the ward in which they want to participate; instead, the Church expects members to become involved with whatever ward encompasses the neighborhood or area where they live. Not only does this ideal avoid the phenomenon of church hopping, but Latter-day Saints also believe that part of the genius of the ward concept is that it can put all kinds of people into communion with each other — people who may not otherwise make a connection. Latter-day Saints of all races and socioeconomic backgrounds attend church together and feel more blessed because of it.

The geography of a ward can change when the congregation gets too large for every member to have a *calling* (see "Get to work! Every member has a job," later in this chapter) or otherwise becomes unwieldy. When a ward gets too large, the leaders may split it or create three wards out of two. Sometimes the opposite happens, with two or more shrinking wards getting combined into one. Latter-day Saints are accustomed to the fact that the Church's rapid growth often causes ward boundaries to change, putting members in a new ward with people they don't know very well. That fact is all part of the adventure.

Specialty wards

Most wards are multigenerational and cater to all ages, including children. But the Church designs some wards to meet certain individual needs, including the following:

>> **Singles wards:** Single members are always welcome to attend their regular family ward based on geographical location, but areas with lots of singles can set up singles-only wards. Of course, one hope for these wards is that marriages will naturally result (some cynics call these wards "meat markets"). But singles wards mainly operate under the premise that young people and college students enjoy one another's company and learn the gospel best when they're serving as moral and spiritual examples for one another. Separate singles wards serve members ages 18 to 35 and 36 to 45, and, if population warrants, the younger wards can be further split into ages 18 to 25 and 26 to 35.

>> **Language wards:** As we explain in Chapter 14, the LDS church has been growing at a phenomenal rate and now includes members of many different nationalities and ethnic groups. Sometimes, the Church operates ethnic wards and *branches* (see the following section) in languages other than the one dominant in the nation where they're located. In the United States today, you can find Spanish, Portuguese, Korean, Chinese, Vietnamese, and Tongan wards, as well as other languages. Numerous sign-language congregations for the deaf are also in operation.

Wards in the making: Branches

Wards don't just spring up full-blown in an area shortly after the missionaries first set foot there to convert new members. In the beginning, only a few converts and the missionaries themselves might meet in members' homes or in a rented building. This would-be ward is called a *branch*, and it can consist of as few as two Mormon families if at least one priesthood holder is available to administer the Sunday *sacrament* (communion of bread and water; see the section "What to do when you're in the pew: Sacrament meetings"). The leader of a branch is called a *branch president.*

As branches grow in membership, they gradually add classes and programs until they become a fully functioning ward. When we say *ward* and *bishop* in this book, we generally mean branches and branch presidents, too.

Participating in the Ward

In contrast to the architectural appeal of many LDS temples, most LDS meeting-houses appear, um, *functional*. Older wards were a bit fancier and sported different architectural styles, but newer ones are fairly bland and usually very much the same architecturally (see Figure 6-1).

desertsolitaire/Adobe Stock Photos

Some visitors who come to church for the first time wonder aloud at the near-total absence of stained-glass windows, altars, candles, murals, and statues. A few older ward houses sport beautiful murals inside, but for the most part meet-inghouse artwork is mass-produced. Various portraits and scenes from the scrip-tures and LDS church history often adorn the buildings' halls and classrooms but are never inside the chapels themselves. Services involve no incense, no priest who changes into different brilliantly colored stoles with the passing of the litur-gical seasons, and no objects with cool names like *mitre* and *orb*. You won't see any crucifixes; Latter-day Saints prefer to focus on the Savior's resurrection, not his death. Visitors who are used to a more visually stimulating atmosphere — all the "smells and bells," as Catholics may say — are often a little disconcerted at the apparent starkness of Mormon ward buildings and services.

Looks can be deceiving, however, because the life that teems underneath the bland meetinghouse surface is something to behold. Participating in a ward community is a vital and exciting part of being Mormon, plain and simple.

Get to work! Every member has a job

In some other Christian churches, laypersons attend Sunday-morning services as spectators of sorts, while professional clergy deliver prepared sermons and teach classes. Churches may have paid staff members who corral the teens, teach the children, counsel members who are grieving, and play the organ. The advantage of such a system is that the sermons are often well conceived and capably delivered, the music holds to the highest standards of excellence, and the congregants receive professional-quality counseling. The disadvantage, from the LDS point of view, is that little may be expected of rank-and-file people, and therefore, they don't grow as much spiritually.

In Mormonism, only *General Authorities* (such as the prophet, apostles, and seventies; see Chapter 8) and mission presidents (see Chapter 14) receive a living-expense allowance to facilitate their full-time church work. In addition, the Church has a few thousand full-time employees worldwide who work in administrative functions or teach in the Church Educational System (see Chapter 8). Everyone else, including every person you see teaching or leading at the ward level, is a part-time volunteer who has accepted a calling.

Ward members have all kinds of callings: They may teach the *Sunbeams* (three-year-olds), keep the financial records, or plan youth activities. Others help people research their genealogy or direct the ward choir. Bishops and other high-level local leaders are also volunteers, often juggling church service with demanding careers and the needs of a large family. (For more on bishop duties, see Chapter 4.) Even meetinghouse cleaning is generally the responsibility of members.

Ward callings are extended by the bishop or one of his two counselors (together known as the bishopric), who pray collectively to God for guidance about where to assign various individuals. Some people stay in the same calling for years and years, while others receive temporary assignments (like being the youth summer camp director) or move around every couple of years. In less-populated wards, one person might hold two or more callings at the same time. Latter-day Saints can be very busy folks!

With so many volunteers working together, wards have lots of special coordinating meetings and committees. Perhaps the most important is the *ward council meeting*, a weekly get-together attended by the bishopric, ward clerk, ward executive secretary, and presidents of the elders quorum, Relief Society, Young Women, Primary, and Sunday School (all of which we discuss in this chapter). The bishop can also invite other ward workers, like the mission leader, temple and family history leader, leaders of the ward's young single adult committee, music coordinator, and even the local full-time missionaries. In these hour-long meetings, the attendees not only coordinate ward doings but also discuss how the ward can better support specific families and individuals.

The LDS church encourages members to accept whatever calling their bishop offers them and to regard it as coming directly from the Lord. However, in some circumstances, an individual might refuse a calling because of family issues, personal problems, or severe time constraints. Mormon adults are expected to consult with their spouses (especially if their spouse isn't a member) about a proposed calling from the bishop.

MAGNIFYING YOUR CALLING

Most Latter-day Saints have received a calling for which they felt unprepared, and when they accepted the assignment in faith, they said that they found themselves richly blessed by the experience. In the Church, a popular saying is that the Lord doesn't call people who are already qualified; he qualifies those who are called. In other words, Latter-day Saints believe that if they pour themselves into church service, the Lord will help them in their efforts and increase their effectiveness.

Another popular saying is "magnify your calling," whatever it may be. This statement means that if your assignment is to stack chairs after an activity, do it cheerfully and well. If your assignment is to be the stake president, do it cheerfully and well. If you were formerly a ward leader but now you're called simply to teach the 11-year-olds on Sunday, you do it cheerfully and well. All such service contributes to God's kingdom and helps the individual become more spiritual and Christ-centered.

What to do when you're in the pew: Sacrament meetings

Mormon chapels are open to visitors, and stopping in is a great way to get a glimpse of Mormon life and practice. Here's a quick rundown of what to expect in a Mormon sacrament meeting.

What to wear

Although many churches and denominations have accepted the casual dress movement, Mormon services are generally still pretty formal. Men typically wear a suit or jacket and a tie — if you dress like Mormon missionaries, you won't go wrong. In addition, men and boys often choose to wear white shirts, especially if they're participating in rituals like passing the sacrament. Women generally wear a dress, a suit, or a blouse and skirt with hemlines usually below the knee. A few women have started wearing dressy slacks to church.

Where to sit

Seating in Mormon sacrament meetings is on a first-come, first-served basis. Visitors can sit anywhere they want except on the *stand*, an elevated area in front where the pulpit and organ are located. This part of the chapel is reserved for the day's speakers, the choir, and the *bishopric* (the bishop and his two counselors). Also, the front two rows of the chapel on the left or right side are generally reserved for the young men who pass the sacrament.

What about the kids?

Mormon services differ from those of many other Christian denominations in that children stay with their parents during the entire sacrament service. A nursery and classes are available for children during the second hour of church, but sacrament meeting is for everyone, from Baby to Grandma and Grandpa. If you have children, bringing quiet games, coloring books, and simple snacks to entertain them during sacrament meeting is perfectly acceptable. Cheerios are a great favorite among the Mormon preschool set (and their parents).

Visitors are sometimes delighted, sometimes dismayed by the din during sacrament meeting in wards with lots of children. Latter-day Saints try to be reverent during sacrament meeting, but sometimes sitting still and keeping completely hushed is tough when families are large and the gang's all together. The best advice we can give you is to just bear with the situation, even if a toddler is screaming in the next pew.

How the service proceeds

With the exception of the monthly fast and testimony meeting (see the next section), most sacrament meetings follow the same basic order. They're predictable to a fault, which is good news if you're a visitor and don't yet know the score. Many wards provide a bulletin or program that volunteers hand out at the chapel entrance, making it much easier to follow along. Here's the rundown:

>> **Prelude music:** In many wards, for 10 to 15 minutes before the sacrament meeting officially begins, a pianist, organist, or other musician will provide background music to set a reverent tone as people arrive, take their seats, and chat — hopefully quietly — with friends.

>> **Announcements:** The meeting opens with the bishop or one of his counselors making announcements about upcoming activities and meetings in the ward and stake.

>> **Opening hymn:** Hymn singing is important in Mormon services, and the sacrament meeting usually features three or four hymns. The opening hymn is a time to get into the groove of preparing for worship; Latter-day Saints use this time to settle their hearts into a more reflective and spiritual mode. Many of the hymns in the LDS hymnbook are recognizable, especially to visitors from a Protestant tradition; others are unique to Mormonism. Unlike most Protestants, however, Latter-day Saints usually remain seated while singing hymns. Visitors are always welcome to pick up a hymnbook and join in the singing, although some visitors comment that the slow tempos and serious nature of Mormon hymns are very different from the rollicking hymns of other denominations.

>> **Opening prayer:** Mormon meetings always begin and end with a prayer. Latter-day Saints bow their heads and fold their arms as they remain seated in the pews. One member of the ward, chosen in advance, comes to the front pulpit and offers a short invocation. In English-speaking wards, prayer language is formal, using "thee" and "thou" to address God; other languages may or may not follow similar customs. Every Mormon prayer ends with some variation of the phrase, "In the name of Jesus Christ, amen." If you feel comfortable, you're welcome to join the congregation as they respond by saying "Amen" — however, that's the *only* time Mormon congregants say anything out loud during the sacrament meeting. For more on prayer in Mormon life, see Chapter 17.

>> **Ward business:** At this point, the bishopric member conducting the meeting announces new callings that members have accepted, and the congregation *sustains* them on cue by raising their right hands in support. (Members also have the right to raise their hands in opposition to a calling, but most members go through their entire lives without ever seeing that happen.) If any baby blessings or baptismal confirmations are scheduled to take place on a particular Sunday, they occur at this point in the program (we describe these events later in this chapter).

>> **The sacrament:** Partaking of the *sacrament* (bread and water that members of the priesthood have blessed) is the main reason everyone gathers. After ward business, the congregation sings a special hymn to remind everyone of Christ's sacrifice and Atonement, which is what they commemorate by taking the sacrament. Then teenage boys who hold the Aaronic Priesthood (see Chapter 4) bless the sacrament and pass it to the congregation (adult men can fill these roles if needed).

According to Latter-day Saints, the bread and water don't *become* the body and blood of Christ (a theological concept known as *transubstantiation*), as members of the Catholic faith believe they do. Rather, these elements are symbols that remind Latter-day Saints of the Savior's sacrifice and their own willingness to love and serve him. If you listen carefully to the words of the sacrament prayer — which is one of the few prayers in Mormonism that priesthood holders must recite absolutely the same every time — you'll hear the word *remember* a couple of times. Basically, Latter-day Saints believe that taking the sacrament of bread and water in a spirit of repentance helps them remember Christ's love, renew their baptismal covenants, and become more worthy of his Atonement.

TIP

If you decide to take the sacrament, take a single little piece of bread and put it in your mouth before passing the tray along and then go ahead and chew; Latter-day Saints don't wait to partake until the whole congregation is served. When the water is passed, take one of the tiny cups, chug it down — ironically,

people often use the same motion as someone gulping a shot of alcohol —
and drop the empty cup in the tray's waste receptacle before passing the tray
to the next person. Latter-day Saints give their kids the sacrament, so you may
be amused by a toddler grabbing a whole handful of bread or crying, "I'm still
thirsty," as the tray moves down the row.

REMEMBER

The sacrament is the holiest part of what goes on in a Mormon service; now
isn't the best time to take little Timmy to the potty. Latecomers who arrive
during the sacrament's passing aren't seated until after it's finished. Latter-day
Saints try especially hard to keep their children quiet and to preserve a spirit
of dignity and reverence during the sacrament. You may see people meditat-
ing with their eyes closed or reading their scriptures, trying to turn their minds
to the Savior and repent of their sins.

>> **Talks:** The longest portion of a Mormon sacrament meeting consists of talks
given by three or four members of the congregation, assigned in advance.
Teens generally speak for less than five minutes, while adults generally take
10–15 minutes. These short sermons mingle doctrine and scripture verses
with self-help advice, personal experiences, and anecdotes — not all of which
may seem relevant to the topic at hand. Occasionally, the last speaker is a
representative of the stake high council (see the section "Participating in the
stake," later in this chapter), who addresses a topic assigned by the stake
president. (Because these talks are sometimes longish and a bit dull, Latter-
day Saints often joke that the speaker is a member of the *dry* council.)

>> **Intermediary hymn:** At some point between talks, many LDS wards will have
a congregational hymn or a musical number performed by a choir, vocal or
instrumental soloist, or small group.

>> **Closing hymn and closing prayer:** The congregation sings a final hymn, and
after the closing prayer that follows, the organist or pianist usually plays some
postlude music as people get up and start chatting and moving to the foyer.
This marks the end of the service.

Step up to the mike: Fast and testimony meeting

The first Sunday of each month is usually the fast and testimony meeting, which
differs from the ordinary pattern in two key ways. First, members come to the
sacrament meeting in the midst of *fasting* (abstaining from food and drink) for
two meals, or about 24 hours. (For more on fasting, see Chapters 16 and 17.) Second, after the sacrament has been passed, an open mic is provided for members to
spontaneously "bear their testimonies," if they desire. Even the smallest of the
small fries can choose to take a turn at the microphone, sometimes with a parent
at their shoulder whispering the words.

WHO'S ALLOWED TO PARTAKE OF THE SACRAMENT?

For visitors to an LDS sacrament meeting, a common question is whether they should partake of the sacrament when it's passed. In Mormonism, congregants remain seated while teenage boys bring the bread and water to everyone in little trays, so you're expected to pass the tray down your pew whether you take the elements or not.

In the LDS church, the only people who are forbidden from taking the sacrament are individuals who have had their Church membership restricted or withdrawn due to serious sin. Obviously, if you're a first-time visitor, this doesn't apply to you. At the same time, partaking in the sacrament isn't a good idea if you know you have major, unresolved sins in your life or you don't believe in God and his Son, Jesus Christ. Otherwise, feel free to partake if you feel prompted by the Spirit to do so — in other words, if you have a good, warm feeling about it.

Although the other Sundays of the month feature assigned speakers who come prepared to address the congregation, testimonies are almost never prepared in advance. Members speak when they feel the Spirit move them. Testimonies give members a chance to express gratitude to the Lord for help in difficult times, bear witness of the Savior's love, explain why they believe the gospel, thank family and ward members for their love and support, and talk about inspiring experiences or struggles they've been facing.

Testimony meetings are fascinating because, although a testimony has a certain basic formula ("I know the Church is true," "I know the Book of Mormon is true," and so on), the meeting is one of the most unscripted events in Mormon life. Some meetings are so full of people bursting to share their feelings that there's not enough time to accommodate them all. Other meetings suffer awkward pauses between testimonies. Some testimonies are so beautiful and honest that they bring the congregation to tears, but sometimes people ramble, go off on tangents, or say something that makes listeners uncomfortable. On rare occasions, a bishop may turn off the microphone or stand up to gently escort a problematic testifier back to their seat.

If you're visiting during testimony meeting and find some members' testimonies to be a little loopy, be generous and attribute it to the fact that they're likely fasting and may not be thinking very clearly.

Special sacrament meetings

A few times a year, Latter-day Saints devote the sacrament meeting to a particular theme or purpose.

HIGHLIGHTING WARD GROUPS

One sacrament meeting each year is typically devoted to a children's program, during which they sing Primary songs and wow their parents with brief — ideally memorized — scriptures, gospel messages, or personal expressions. In addition, representatives of the Young Women, priesthood quorums, and Relief Society may occasionally speak or perform music during the sacrament meeting, as directed by the bishopric (we discuss these groups in the section "Other Sunday meetings," later in this chapter).

HOLIDAY THEMES

On occasions such as Mother's Day, Father's Day, or a patriotic holiday, speakers during a sacrament meeting often address those topics. At Christmas and Easter, many wards offer lovely programs that feature more music than usual. Don't look for those majestic trumpets that you find in other Christian Easter services, however. In LDS meetings, you're not likely to hear anything but piano, organ, and occasionally some classical woodwinds or stringed instruments.

WARD CONFERENCE

One Sunday a year, each ward typically holds a *ward conference* during which stake leaders come to check out the ward and offer support, feedback, and instruction. On this day, the stake president plans the ward's sacrament meeting program, during which he and the ward's bishop typically speak to the congregation. In addition, stake leaders may attend some of the ward's other classes and meetings, and the stake presidency meets with the bishopric to "review the progress of God's work of salvation and exaltation in the ward."

Getting dunked

LDS baptisms generally take place in the local meetinghouse — unless someone is already dead, in which case Latter-day Saints can perform baptism by proxy on that person's behalf in a temple, and their spirit-self can decide whether to accept it (see Chapter 7). For Latter-day Saints, getting baptized — and yes, they do it by full immersion — signifies many important concepts:

> » It marks the beginning of a person's official membership in the Church.

> » It washes away sins, an effect that a person can renew each week by partaking of the sacrament (see the section "What to do when you're in the pew: Sacrament meetings," earlier in this chapter).

> » It represents a covenant with God to keep his commandments, stand as his witness, and love and serve fellow Church members.

- >> It prepares a person to receive the constant companionship of the Holy Ghost (as we discuss in the section "Confirmation: Installing a direct line to God," later in this chapter).

- >> It obeys the example that Jesus set in the New Testament.

- >> It symbolizes being buried and then resurrected (being lowered into the water and then lifted out).

- >> It qualifies a person to receive salvation in the *celestial kingdom,* the highest level of heaven where God himself lives (see Chapter 2).

Preparing for baptism

The earliest someone can receive Mormon baptism is at age 8, which Latter-day Saints view as the *age of accountability* — when a person is spiritually mature enough to discern right from wrong. (People with mental disabilities that prevent accountability don't need baptism — they're automatically saved. It's the same for children who die before age 8.) Latter-day Saints don't recognize baptisms performed in other religions, so anyone who wants to join the LDS church must receive Mormon baptism, even if they were already baptized in another Christian church. (Why don't Latter-day Saints recognize other baptisms? See Chapter 4.) At the same time, some other Christian churches don't recognize Mormon baptism, either.

Following are several ways in which baptismal candidates prepare for baptism. These steps don't necessarily happen in the order that we list them, and they often overlap. In fact, ideally a Latter-day Saint keeps cycling through these steps for the rest of their life.

- >> **Learn the gospel:** Children raised as Latter-day Saints learn the gospel by attending regular Sunday classes and being taught at home. People who've grown up outside the faith take a series of special lessons prior to baptism, usually from the local full-time missionaries. In addition, they study the scriptures and other sources on their own. (For more on missionaries, see Chapter 14.)

- >> **Exercise faith:** Preparing for baptism includes developing an abiding faith in Heavenly Father, Jesus Christ, the divine mission of the founding prophet Joseph Smith, and the truthfulness of the Book of Mormon, other scriptures, and the LDS church itself. Faith begins with the *desire* to believe, and it grows as a person experiences good results from studying, praying, repenting, and living the gospel. (For more on faith, see Chapter 17.)

- >> **Repent of sins:** Everyone makes mistakes due to ignorance, weakness, or disobedience. To gain freedom and forgiveness from sins through the Savior, a person feels remorse about their sins, asks the Savior's forgiveness in prayer, stops the sinful behavior (with professional help, if needed, such as therapy or rehab), confesses and makes restitution to others as necessary, forgives others, and renews their commitment to keep the commandments.

>> **Gain a testimony:** Latter-day Saints believe that real, lasting conversion comes through a personal experience with the Holy Ghost. As a person puts effort into learning the gospel, exercising faith, and repenting of sins, they can pray for confirmation that Mormonism is true. Latter-day Saints say that, often in private, prayerful moments, God's answers arrive through unmistakable spiritual impressions from the Holy Ghost, often accompanied by warmth, tingles, or other sensations (Mormon scripture calls it "burning in the bosom").

>> **Talk with a Church leader:** Before a person receives clearance for baptism, they undergo a private interview with a local priesthood leader to discuss their readiness. Even 8-year-old children and their parents meet with a leader. The leader asks questions to find out whether the person understands basic gospel principles, has developed sufficient faith, and is committed to living the gospel. Although the leader doesn't typically need to hear a confession of past sins, he makes sure the candidate isn't still committing significant sins, such as having sex outside of marriage. (For an overview of Mormon behavioral standards, see the temple-recommend questions that we summarize in Chapter 7.)

Going through the baptism process

For 8-year-olds reared in the LDS church, group baptismal services often take place once a month at a larger meetinghouse called a *stake center* (see the section "Participating in the Stake," later in this chapter). For converts, a ward often holds a special individual service. Baptisms can take place any day of the week, and they can occur in any suitable body of water, although meetinghouse fonts are preferred. Here's how the event typically plays out:

>> Upon arrival at the meetinghouse, the baptismal candidate changes into plain, white clothing in a small dressing room adjacent to the baptismal font. Most congregations keep some baptismal clothes on hand, or the candidate can arrange to borrow some. *Tip:* White clothes become see-through when wet, so try to wear thicker fabrics, if available, and don't wear colored underwear. Also, bring a plastic bag for the wet clothes, in addition to a towel and hair implements.

>> Baptismal services generally take place either in the main chapel or in the auxiliary room where the font is actually located. White-clothed and shoeless, the baptismal candidate sits at the front with the baptizer, a priesthood holder who's also dressed in white. The meeting begins and ends with a hymn and prayer, and assigned members give inspirational talks, usually on faith,

repentance, baptism, and the gift of the Holy Ghost. At some point, a congregational leader usually offers words of advice and welcome.

>> When it comes time for the actual baptism, the candidate and baptizer enter the font via steps descending from the dressing room. (In the best-case scenario, the water will be bathtub warm.) If young children are present, they typically cram along the font's front edge for the best view.

>> After the baptizer gets the candidate situated in the font, he raises his right arm, calls the person by their full name, utters a short, scripted baptismal prayer, and then lowers the person back into the water. Two witnesses standing at either side of the font make sure everything goes under — if even a big toe pops out, the baptizer does the ordinance over again. Most baptizers hold the candidate's wrist in such a way that the candidate can reach up and pinch shut their nose. After the quick immersion, the baptizer pulls the candidate back up into the standing position.

>> Confirmation and bestowal of the gift of the Holy Ghost (which we explain in the next section) can happen at the conclusion of the baptismal service or — especially for new adult converts — during sacrament meeting the following Sunday.

Confirmation: Installing a direct line to God

Many religions believe that any human being who's pure and sincere can feel the influence of the Holy Ghost on an extraordinary occasion, such as when praying to know whether a spiritual concept is true. However, Latter-day Saints believe that Church members can enjoy the *constant* companionship of the Holy Ghost if they're trying to live worthily. A priesthood holder bestows this gift during an ordinance commonly referred to as *confirmation*. The confirmation ceremony goes something like this:

>> The recently baptized person sits in a chair. The priesthood holder who will act as voice places both hands on the person's head. Other invited priesthood holders can circle around and lay their hands on the new member's head.

>> The priesthood holder calls the person by their full name, confirms them as a member of the Church, and confers the gift of the Holy Ghost, usually using the phrase "I say unto you, receive the Holy Ghost." These words don't have to be exact, as in the case of the baptismal and sacramental prayers.

>> The priesthood holder blesses the person with some words of encouragement and advice as the Holy Ghost inspires him.

>> Afterward, the person traditionally shakes hands with or hugs everyone in the circle.

REMEMBER

Latter-day Saints believe that receiving the gift of the Holy Ghost is essential to full salvation because no one can make it back into God's presence without guidance and purification from the Holy Ghost. However, even with this gift, recognizing the Holy Ghost's promptings still takes effort. To invite his influence, members strive to obey the commandments and keep their thoughts and actions pure. We talk about the Holy Ghost in detail in Chapter 3, but here's an overview of what the Holy Ghost does:

» Provides spiritual strength and protection

» Subtly whispers knowledge, peace, and guidance to a person's heart and mind

» Sanctifies a person's soul in what Latter-day Saints refer to as the "baptism of fire"

Baby blessings: Welcoming a new lamb into the flock

Within a few months after birth, new Mormon babies typically receive a blessing in front of the whole congregation during the sacrament meeting.

» The father and other invited priesthood holders (typically family members) stand together in a circle, which turns into an oval if too many men are present. (If the baby's father isn't a member or isn't in good standing with the Church, the family can ask another priesthood holder to perform the blessing.)

» The father holds the baby securely in both arms, and each man puts his left hand on the shoulder of the man in front of him and his right hand under the baby, helping gently bounce the baby to prevent crying (which doesn't always work). The baby usually wears something white.

» Using a microphone, the father calls on Heavenly Father in prayer, declares the baby's full name, and then directly addresses the baby with advice and promises about its future. Typical utterances include telling the baby to always obey its parents and stay close to the Church and promising the baby that they will meet the right person to marry at the right time. If the baby's a boy, the blessing almost always includes a mention about serving a full-time mission (see Chapter 14).

» After the blessing, traditionally the father briefly holds up the baby for the congregation to admire. The mother typically stays seated in the congregation during the blessing, but some members feel that mothers should be able to hold the baby during the blessing (for more about controversies related to women and the priesthood, see Chapter 15).

Although Latter-day Saints don't believe that a baby blessing is necessary for salvation, it does trigger the official listing of the baby as a *child of record* in the Church, and the parents receive a blessing certificate. Babies aren't yet technically members of the Church because they haven't been baptized, but they're counted in the Church's membership total. During 2023, the Church added 93,594 children of record worldwide.

Funerals: Saying farewell, for now

Usually held in the deceased person's home meetinghouse, Mormon funerals tend to be relatively upbeat, personalized affairs, celebrating the person's progress to the next step as much as mourning their departure. Before the funeral, there's usually a preliminary viewing. Adult Latter-day Saints who've been endowed in the temple are typically dressed for burial or cremation in their ceremonial temple clothes (for more on temples, see Chapter 7). The funeral service mainly consists of family members and friends giving talks and performing musical numbers. The talks tend toward specific personal remembrances of the deceased person, often sprinkled with humorous anecdotes. At least one talk typically addresses how the Savior's resurrection opens the way for everybody to eventually be resurrected.

After the funeral, a short graveside service usually takes place, during which a priesthood holder dedicates the gravesite as a place of shelter for the remains until the day of resurrection. Back at the meetinghouse, Relief Society sisters (see the next section) typically serve the extended family a luncheon. In Utah and other places, this meal so frequently includes a certain cheesy potato casserole that many Latter-day Saints refer to this dish as "funeral potatoes" no matter when it's served. Latter-day Saints in other countries add a gospel spin to their own funeral customs.

Meetinghouse weddings: For time only

Most Mormon weddings take place inside a temple, not a meetinghouse (see Chapter 7). When solemnized inside a temple, a marriage is both legally valid (in most countries) and eternally valid. When held in a meetinghouse, a civil marriage lasts only until death. For doctrinal reasons, the Church doesn't perform or recognize same-sex marriages (see Chapter 15 for more on that).

If a couple isn't yet worthy of temple marriage — such as in the case of a shotgun wedding — the bishop can marry them civilly in the meetinghouse, in a ceremony much like that of other faiths. As soon as the couple demonstrates repentance and worthiness for a temple recommend, they can get eternally sealed together in the temple.

Meetinghouse weddings can occur on other occasions, too. If a woman is married to someone in the temple and becomes a widow, she can remarry "for time only" in a meetinghouse ceremony. (However, a widower can be married in the temple to both his first and second wives if the second wife wasn't previously sealed to someone — a lingering echo of 19th-century plural marriage.) If a couple doesn't live near a temple, they can wed in a meetinghouse and get sealed later when they're able to visit a temple.

If a couple wants non-Mormon family members to witness their wedding, they can hold a civil marriage in an LDS meetinghouse or elsewhere and then also immediately get sealed in a temple, which only qualified Latter-day Saints can enter.

Other Sunday meetings

On a typical Sunday, a good place to see Mormonism's calling system in action is during the 50-minute breakout classes and meetings. For a visitor, the variety of classroom options can be confusing; probably the easiest thing to do is approach someone who looks official, say you're visiting, and let them point you in the right direction.

Which class you attend depends on which Sunday of the month it is, as follows:

>> **First and third Sundays:** Sunday school (men and women attend class together, teen boys and girls attend together in classes determined by age)

>> **Second and fourth Sundays:** Priesthood quorum meetings for men and teen boys, Relief Society meetings for women, or Young Women meetings for teen girls

>> **Fifth Sundays (4 to 5 times a year):** The bishopric chooses a special topic, assigns teachers, and decides whether youth, adults, males, and females meet separately or all together

>> **All Sundays:** Primary and nursery for children ages 11 and younger, with classes determined by age group

Sunday school

For teens and adults, Sunday school classes on the first and third Sundays are taught on a four-year cycle, with individual years spent on the Old Testament, the New Testament, the Book of Mormon, and the Doctrine and Covenants (for more on these LDS scriptures, see Chapters 9 and 10). Sunday school is intended to supplement the home gospel study that the Church encourages all members to regularly do. Each year, the church puts out a lesson manual designed for church, family, and personal use.

Teen girls and boys meet for Sunday school in classes determined by age. Depending on a ward's adult population, men and women ages 18 and older meet in one or more *Gospel Doctrine* classes, which have different teachers but cover the same material.

In addition, some wards offer a Sunday-school class called *Gospel Principles* for new converts and investigators (those who are meeting with the missionaries and thinking about joining the Church). You'll probably attend this class if you're visiting for the first time unless the class isn't currently taught in that ward. The goal of the class is to help new members build their testimonies and understand the core teachings of the LDS church.

Other special-focus classes (such as a teacher-preparation class or a class on conducting genealogical research) may be held during Sunday school time.

For the men: Elders quorum

On the second and fourth Sundays, adult men and women divide into separate meetings. All the men (18 on up) attend *elders quorum*, including both *elders* and *high priests* (for more on Melchizedek Priesthood offices, see Chapter 4). Also included are *prospective elders*, men who haven't yet received the Melchizedek Priesthood but are either at least age 19 or are already married at a younger age. Technically, the high priests have their own quorum at the stake level, but they meet with the elders on Sundays.

After a prayer, the men spend a few minutes discussing how the quorum can assist with specific challenges, needs, and opportunities in the ward. They spend the rest of the time discussing one or more talks given by General Authorities during the most recent General Conference at Church headquarters in Salt Lake City (for more on these "generalities," see Chapter 8).

From time to time, elders quorums organize activities or service projects during the week for their members.

For the women: Relief Society

The Relief Society, founded in 1842, is one of the oldest women's organizations in the world — and with several million members, it's also one of the largest. All adult Mormon women ages 18 and over are automatic members of Relief Society, whose motto, "Charity never faileth," reveals one of the organization's main purposes: to provide relief to the poor and needy.

Throughout its history, the Relief Society has founded hospitals, provided many of the resources to begin the Church's welfare program, and assisted untold numbers of needy families. Although the Relief Society no longer builds hospitals, its members devote countless hours to compassionate service on an individual level, which involves fixing meals for families in need, driving sick people to the doctor, and other kind acts.

On the second and fourth Sundays, Relief Society meetings generally begin with a group discussion about local needs and issues, followed by a lesson taught by one of the sisters, usually based on one or more recent General Conference talks. Relief Society sisters also sometimes get together outside of church for activities and service projects.

For the teens: Aaronic Priesthood quorums and Young Women

Being a Mormon youth (ages 12 to 17) can be tough, especially when you live in an area where you may be one of the only LDS students at your high school. Sundays offer a chance for Mormon youths to gather with others who have the same G-rated lifestyles.

On the second and fourth Sundays, Mormon youths meet separately as boys and girls. As boys advance by age through the three offices of the Aaronic Priesthood — deacon, teacher, and priest — they attend quorum meetings with others who hold those offices (for more about Aaronic Priesthood, see Chapter 4). Similarly, the girls meet by age group in Young Women classes.

In Sunday classes, the youth generally have lessons from the same scripture-focused Church manual used in other classes and at home, and they also frequently use a slim, Church-issued book called *For the Strength of Youth: A Guide for Making Choices*, which is easy to read online if you're interested. In addition to adult leaders and advisors, each class has its own youth-staffed presidency so the youth can learn how to lead, serve, and organize like good Latter-day Saints.

As you'd expect, the youth enjoy lots of activities and service projects beyond Sunday classes, sometimes separately as boys and girls and sometimes together. They get together midweek almost every week, and during the year they have special camps, conferences, and other events.

SHARING A BUILDING

One unusual aspect of Mormonism is that two or more congregations may share the same meetinghouse. One ward may start its Sunday meetings at 9:00 a.m. and then another ward at 11:00 a.m. and another at 1:00 p.m. These wards also juggle a host of weeknight events, which can be tricky at times.

Wards that share a building usually bend over backwards to ensure that the arrangements are fair, and they rotate their meeting times each January to give all members a turn to enjoy their most-preferred Sunday meeting time (some members like mornings, some afternoons). In addition, the wards take turns cleaning the building, shoveling snow, and doing other chores.

For the kids: Primary

Kiddies love Primary, the Church's organization for children ages 3 to 11. (In addition, there's a nursery for children from 18 months to 3 years, where they can play with toys, have short lessons, and eat yummy snacks.) During Primary every Sunday, Mormon boys and girls gather as a group for about 20 minutes to hear short talks by other kids, learn scripture verses, and sing songs with great enthusiasm. In addition, they break up into small classes by age for 20-minute lessons. Beyond Sunday, the older Primary kids enjoy midweek activities a couple of times a month and, in some wards, attend an annual day camp.

Weekday events

Mormonism isn't just a Sunday religion, and if you drive by the parking lot of a local meetinghouse you may find it busy anytime except Monday evening, which is *family home evening* (for more on that, see Chapter 17). The other times are fair game for activities, classes, meetings, book clubs, sports, holiday parties, wedding receptions, funerals, and the like.

Participating in the Stake

SCRIPTURE

If a ward is the equivalent of a Catholic parish, then a *stake* is like a diocese, a gathering of 5 to 12 adjacent wards that a stake president oversees. The word *stake* comes from the Old Testament prophet Isaiah's prophecies comparing the latter-day Church to a tent held fast by stakes (see Isaiah 33:20 and 54:2).

Each LDS stake usually has about 3,000 members. In heavily Mormon areas such as Utah, this quota can be met in a matter of blocks. In other parts of the country and the world, traveling from one end of the stake to another can take several hours — a difficult consideration for unpaid stake leaders who regularly visit all the wards within their jurisdiction. With many specialized committees and leaders, stakes provide a lot of behind-the-scenes support and resources to their wards, and they interface with Church-wide departments and administrators.

TIP

Here's a note on one bit of Mormon jargon that may be confusing: Each stake president appoints two *counselors* to assist him in his duties, just as each ward bishop appoints two Melchizedek Priesthood holders to be his counselors. Stake presidents also choose 12 *councilors* — pronounced the same, but spelled differently — to serve on the *stake high council.* These 12 men travel to all the wards in the stake and carry out specific assignments in supervising various stake programs.

Unless they have a stake calling, such as stake high councilor or stake Relief Society president, most Latter-day Saints don't experience quite the same weekly connection with their stakes as they do with their wards. Their participation usually happens during the semiannual stake conference and in occasional stake activities.

Twice a year: Stake conference

Four Sundays each year, Latter-day Saints don't meet with their normal ward. They spend two of those Sundays (every April and October) watching *General Conference,* a Churchwide broadcast that we discuss in Chapter 8. They spend the other two Sundays attending their local *stake conference.*

Stake conferences usually feature several sessions and meetings within the same weekend. At the general two-hour session on Sunday, members of all ages hear from any General Authority who may be visiting, the stake president, and other male and female leaders and members. Members also listen to special music and hear about stake business, including the appointment and release of stake officers. In addition, many stakes hold a Saturday evening session for adults and special leadership training sessions.

Finding Grandpa's grandpa: Stake family history centers

Most stake centers in the United States, and many abroad, house a family history center where anybody, Mormon or not, can research their genealogy. As we explain in Chapter 5, Latter-day Saints are avid researchers of family history, and each stake family history center is a branch library of the FamilySearch Library, the world's largest family history library, located in Salt Lake City, Utah. Some ward buildings also house small libraries.

You usually don't need an appointment to use a stake family history center, but you should phone ahead to find out when the center is open. They're staffed by volunteers and are often open only during evenings and weekends. If you bring information about your ancestors, a consultant can help you figure out the next step. Some centers offer periodic classes on how to get started in doing family history research.

Stake 'n' shake: Stake activities

The Church encourages members to get together in fun, recreational ways, particularly for the benefit of the teens. Many of these opportunities are organized at the stake level, including sports and cultural arts. Sometimes, several stakes join forces for programs and activities, in which case you'll hear terms like *multistake*, *regional*, or *area*.

In the United States and elsewhere, basketball is so popular among Latter-day Saints that nearly every meetinghouse has basketball standards installed in the large, multipurpose room adjacent to the chapel, a gym-like room still known in old-fashioned terms as the *cultural hall*. (In addition, the Church uses this room for overflow seating, dinners and parties, and other activities, and members can arrange to hold wedding receptions there.) Many stakes also run softball, volleyball, and other sports programs.

For teens and older singles, stakes typically hold dances that feature actual worldly pop music as long as the lyrics aren't blatantly crude. Immodest clothing is discouraged, and the tongue-in-cheek standard is that couples must dance far enough apart that you could slide a copy of the Book of Mormon between them.

IN THIS CHAPTER

» Knowing the difference between temples and meetinghouses

» Summarizing what goes on inside a temple

» Getting ready for temple service

» Being initiated into the temple

» Becoming a forever family

Chapter **7**

Sacred, Not Secret: Inside Mormon Temples

Like Charlie in *Charlie and the Chocolate Factory*, Latter-day Saint children grow up wondering just what goes on inside a certain mysterious building. Ideally at least monthly, their parents dress in Sunday best, retrieve small suitcases from the closet, give last-minute instructions to the sitter, and disappear into the local temple for an hour or two. Although Latter-day Saint children learn the general purposes of temples, for all they know Oompa Loompas serenade those who go inside. Many non-Latter-day Saint observers are equally mystified about what goes on inside temples.

To Latter-day Saints, temples symbolize God's entire plan of salvation and provide a safe, private place for performing the faith's most sacred ordinances (for more details about the plan of salvation, see Chapter 2). In this Internet age, the goings-on inside Mormon temples aren't secret to anyone who can use an internet search engine. However, Latter-day Saints still revere temple work as too sacred to discuss in detail outside the temple itself. This chapter unfolds the Mormon temple experience in as much detail as practicing Latter-day Saints can reasonably discuss without breaking vows of sanctity. As Latter-day Saints often say, "It's *sacred*, not *secret*."

Distinguishing the Temple from the Meetinghouse

Although the LDS church has built thousands of cookie-cutter public meeting-houses globally, as of 2024 the Church has erected only about 190 temples world-wide, with another 160 temples in various stages of planning, construction, or renovation. Some of these temples are magnificent multimillion-dollar whoppers (see Figure 7-1 for an example), but many of the newer temples are smaller than earlier temples, although still ornately plush. Public meetinghouses always sport plain steeples, while temple steeples are sometimes topped with a gold-leafed statue of the Angel Moroni, the Book-of-Mormon prophet who buried the golden plates and, as a resurrected angel, led Joseph Smith to them (for more on the Book of Mormon, check out Chapter 9).

FIGURE 7-1: The Washington, D.C. Temple is one of the LDS church's largest.

jonbilous/Adobe Stock Photos

In short, the LDS church puts more intricate detail and care into these temples than it does into meetinghouses because Latter-day Saints consider the temples to be the literal house of the Lord, a place of maximum beauty and reverence where they would feel comfortable hosting the resurrected Savior himself. Latter-day Saints use the meetinghouses, on the other hand, for day-to-day worship, instruction, and recreation.

The higher-quality construction and, often, larger size of Mormon temples aren't all that distinguish them from the more common meetinghouses, though. Here are a few of the major differences:

Meetinghouses	Temples
Open on the Sabbath (Sunday).	Closed on Sundays.
Visitors are welcome.	Only members who meet certain requirements are allowed to enter, and they must have an entry card called a *temple recommend*.
Businesslike, no-frills style of worship.	More elaborate rituals; too sacred to discuss in detail outside the temple.
Latter-day Saints teach each other gospel lessons, perform simple ordinances, and socialize.	Temple rituals follow scripts, with very little free-style preaching, praying, or socializing.
Used for both worship and recreation, with casual dress okay on some occasions.	Used strictly for worship, and participants wear white temple clothes. Only whispering is allowed in most areas.
Children of all ages welcome.	Adults only; teens and children allowed entry only in certain circumstances.

Temple Ordinances — Why Latter-day Saints Go to the Temple

Simply put, temples are where adults — and, to a limited degree, children and teens — perform a variety of eternally vital *ordinances*, or hands-on ceremonies, both for themselves and for people who've died. These ordinances are collectively known as *temple work*.

Understanding the essential ordinances

To appreciate what goes on inside a temple, you first have to familiarize yourself with the basic Mormon ordinances considered necessary for full salvation and exaltation.

In Mormonism, full *salvation* means returning to live with God, and *exaltation* means becoming an eternal parent like God (for more on these concepts, see Chapter 2). To gain full salvation, a person needs to be baptized, be confirmed, and receive the gift of the Holy Ghost, which happens during confirmation. To qualify for exaltation, a person must receive several additional ordinances: priesthood ordination (if male), a two-part *endowment* (described as "a sacred gift whereby we are clothed with blessings from God"), and celestial marriage.

Following is a more detailed overview of these essential ordinances, in the order in which they occur. For living people, the first three ordinances occur in a public meetinghouse, and the last two occur in a private temple. On behalf of the deceased, Latter-day Saints perform all the ordinances inside a temple, which is why we include a summary of them all in this chapter.

>> **Baptism:** Full immersion to wash away sins, make covenants with God, and commence Church membership (see Chapter 6).

>> **Confirmation:** Laying on of hands to confirm Church membership and bestow the right to spiritual guidance by the Holy Ghost (see Chapters 3 and 6).

>> **Priesthood ordination for all worthy males:** Laying on of hands to confer priesthood power and authority (see Chapter 4).

>> **Endowment:** Involves two parts — individual initiatory ordinances for spiritual cleansing and empowerment, followed by group instruction about the plan of salvation and making covenants with God (see "Becoming endowed," later in this chapter).

>> **Sealing:** A temple ordinance to bind spouses to each other and children to parents for eternity (flip ahead to "Sealing Families for Eternity," later in this chapter).

Why perform ordinances for the dead?

Before we discuss temple work for the dead, we must clarify one point: Latter-day Saints don't dig up decayed corpses and haul them into the temple Igor-style. Rather, genealogical researchers comb through records to extract names and essential data about people who've died all over the world — theoretically, anyone who's ever lived could appear on the list. (For more on family history work, see Chapter 5.) Latter-day Saints who visit the temple perform ordinances as *proxies* (substitutes) on behalf of dead people, whose spirits choose whether to accept the ordinances. Why do Latter-day Saints do this? Well, allow us to try to explain.

Latter-day Saints believe that missionary spirits in the afterlife preach the gospel to all spirits who didn't receive a sufficient opportunity to hear the gospel while alive, thus allowing them to accept the gospel after death. (Head back over to Chapter 2 for more about Mormon beliefs regarding the afterlife.) Latter-day Saints feel that during many historical eras, most notably in the Eastern Hemisphere during the 1,700 or so years between the New Testament apostles and Joseph Smith, no one held God's true *priesthood authority* (the power to act in God's name; see Chapter 4). In the Mormon view, without the true priesthood the true church doesn't exist, and, as a result, they believe that billions of people died without receiving a fair chance to accept or reject the gospel. Since the time the LDS church began in 1830, billions more have died before Latter-day Saint missionaries could reach them.

LDS theology says that disembodied spirits can't perform the physical ordinances that are essential for full salvation and exaltation. Consequently, earthly beings must do it for them. And because Latter-day Saints don't know who will accept the gospel and who will reject it in the afterlife, they aim to perform the necessary gospel ordinances for every person who ever lived so that those spirits potentially may be saved and exalted. After a living person has done temple work for a spirit, that spirit has the option of saying, "Thanks a lot, but no thanks," or of accepting the gospel message. If the spirits accept, they still await the final judgment before receiving their eternal reward (for more details, see Chapter 2).

Beginning in childhood, Latter-day Saints are taught about the sacred obligation to perform temple ordinances for the dead, starting with their own ancestors. In fact, the Church teaches that temple work is urgent, because many departed spirits who've already accepted the gospel in the afterlife are anxiously waiting for somebody on Earth to complete the ordinances on their behalf. Latter-day Saint folklore includes stories about a baptismal proxy seeing a queue of patiently waiting spirits; as the proxy performs each spirit's baptism, that spirit disappears from the line.

Yes, Latter-day Saints have undertaken a big job. Completing all the temple ordinances on behalf of one dead person requires a couple of hours of combined labor, and Latter-day Saints have already completed the work for well over 100 million deceased people. To identify every human being who ever lived, Latter-day Saints spend considerable time and money on genealogical research (see Chapter 5 for a more detailed discussion of family history work). Having only just scratched the surface, the Church doesn't expect to complete this project until sometime during the 1,000-year Millennium that they believe will follow the Second Coming of Jesus Christ. (Scratching your noggin? Go to Chapter 3 to find out about the Millennium and the Second Coming.)

REMEMBER

By providing the living with the opportunity to serve the dead in this manner, the temple helps draw together the entire family of God. Many have commented on the Christ-like nature of temple service: Just as mortals could never pay for their own sins and must rely on Jesus Christ, spirits can't perform their own ordinances and must rely on living disciples of Jesus Christ. In addition, the repeated visits to the temple help members better understand and remember the ordinances, particularly the jam-packed endowment.

A LITTLE TEMPLE HISTORY

Latter-day Saints believe that God always commands his people to build temples, from Old Testament times onward. Here's the lowdown on a few temples that are noteworthy because of their influence in the LDS church:

- The early Latter-day Saints built their first temple in Kirtland, Ohio, in 1836. Many spiritual manifestations and heavenly visitations occurred in this temple. Persecution by local settlers led to its abandonment just a few years after its completion, but it still stands today and is open for public historical tours.

- The Latter-day Saints completed an even grander temple in Nauvoo, Illinois, in 1846. Early versions of most of the ordinances and ceremonies that Latter-day Saints perform in today's temples originated during this Nauvoo period. Destroyed by arson and tornado soon after local persecution drove the Latter-day Saints from Nauvoo, this temple was rebuilt in 2002 and is now used for temple work, meaning it's open only to Church members in good standing.

- In Utah, the Latter-day Saints completed three temples before finally finishing the flagship Salt Lake Temple in 1893, after 40 years of construction.

- During the first half of the 20th century, temples began to expand outside Utah, first appearing in Hawaii, Arizona, Idaho, and Alberta, Canada.

- The Church built its first temple outside the United States and Canada in Switzerland in 1955. By 1980, it had completed temples in New Zealand, England, Japan, and Brazil.

- The vast majority of the world's temples have been built since 1995, and temples are now operating or underway in 39 states and more than 70 countries on six continents.

Becoming Eligible for Temple Ordinances

Entering the temple to receive your own endowment requires careful planning and preparation on both the spiritual and practical levels. You have to be at least 18 and no longer attending high school, and you must have been a baptized Church member for at least a year. In addition, you attend a special temple preparation class, buy or rent some special temple clothes, and allow local Church leaders to evaluate your personal worthiness.

However, before qualifying to receive their own endowment, teenagers and converts who haven't yet reached their one-year baptismal anniversary can get their toes wet — figuratively and literally — by being baptized and receiving the gift of the Holy Ghost on behalf of dead people. Performing these two simple ordinances for the dead in the temple doesn't require as much preparation and provides a good warm-up for the full temple experience.

Getting a temple recommend

The Church strives to make sure that only sufficiently pure, worthy individuals (according to the standards set by Latter-day Saint prophets) enter the temple. The way the Church safeguards the temple's sanctity is by issuing a special card called a *temple recommend*, which a person must show at the front desk for entry into the temple.

To get a temple recommend for the first time, a member sits down in two private, confidential, one-on-one appointments with local church leaders and candidly answers pointed questions about personal righteousness. Initially, the *bishop* interviews the member, and within a few days, the *stake president* interviews the member. (In Mormonism, a *ward* is a single congregation and a *stake* is a grouping of adjacent wards. A bishop oversees a ward, and a stake president oversees a stake. See Chapter 6.)

If you're simply performing baptisms for the dead, only your bishop interviews you, and the questions are simpler than those in the bulleted list that follows. In this case, the recommend you receive is called a *limited-use recommend*, because it allows you access only to the temple baptistry area.

A temple-recommend interview usually takes about ten minutes, unless you want to discuss additional matters with the leader. The leader asks whether you obey

Church standards in several areas, including the following (not necessarily listed in order of importance):

>> Attendance of Church meetings

>> Abstinence from coffee, tea, alcohol, tobacco, and harmful drugs

>> Avoidance of any form of family-member abuse

>> Avoidance of apostate beliefs and groups

>> Belief in God, Jesus Christ, the Holy Ghost, and other points of Mormon doctrine

>> Chastity outside of marriage and fidelity within marriage

>> For divorced parents, payment of any court-ordered support

>> Honesty

>> Loyalty to general and local church leaders

>> Payment of *tithe* (10 percent of income)

Latter-day Saints renew their temple recommends every two years by going through the same two interviews, which in the case of renewals can be conducted by the bishop and stake president's counselors.

REMEMBER

Qualifying for a temple recommend gives members a practical, specific goal for religious discipline. While ever mindful of not being perfect, members take pride in staying current as literal card-carrying Latter-day Saints. If any serious sins come to light in a temple-recommend interview, the leader helps the member work out a plan for repentance and may possibly withhold the recommend for a time or initiate disciplinary action, which we discuss in Chapter 16.

Performing baptisms for the dead

Remember, living Latter-day Saints don't receive their own baptism, confirmation, and priesthood ordination inside a temple — rather, temple-goers perform these ordinances only for the dead. However, living Latter-day Saints do perform their own endowment and celestial marriage inside the temple, in addition to performing these ordinances on behalf of the dead. We discuss baptism for the dead here because, like we said earlier, it's a good optional introduction to the temple for teens and new converts before they qualify to receive their own endowment.

In the temple baptistry dressing room, baptismal proxies change into white baptismal clothing that they brought or the temple provided. After they're dressed, proxies gather at the temple baptismal font, which sits atop statues of 12 oxen that represent the 12 tribes of Israel (see Figure 7-2). After saying the brief baptismal prayer, a temple worker fully immerses the proxy on behalf of a dead person, repeating the process for several dead people in rapid succession.

FIGURE 7-2:
Temple baptismal fonts are patterned after Old Testament fonts.

In addition, baptismal proxies can receive the gift of the Holy Ghost on behalf of deceased people. To complete this ordinance, which is generally known as *confirmation*, priesthood holders (see Chapter 4) lay hands upon the proxy's head, confirm him or her as a member of the Church on behalf of a deceased person, and, most important, bestow the gift of the Holy Ghost.

SCRIPTURE

Regarding baptism for the dead, much has been made of the Apostle Paul's comment in 1 Corinthians 15:29, which is the only biblical mention of the practice: "Else what shall they do which are baptized for the dead, if the dead rise not at all? Why are they then baptized for the dead?" (In other words, why would anyone bother getting baptized for the dead unless our souls continue living after death?) Latter-day Saints emphasize this surviving fragment as proof that the practice has ancient validation, while opponents argue that Paul's comment means that he did *not* endorse baptisms for the dead as a Christian practice.

A preparation checklist

As soon as Latter-day Saints finish attending high school or reach their one-year baptismal anniversary, they can qualify for full temple privileges and receive their own endowment. Many young Latter-day Saints "go through the temple," in the common phrasing, a few weeks before leaving on a mission to preach the gospel full time, at as early as age 18 for men and age 19 for women. For those who don't serve missions, a common time to go through the temple is prior to getting married in the temple.

The following checklist outlines the tasks that members complete before they arrive at the temple to receive their own endowment. These items are roughly in chronological order:

>> **Temple preparation class:** Most local congregations provide a temple preparation class for those anticipating going through the temple for their own ordinances. This class typically meets once a week for several weeks.

>> **Temple recommend:** You must have a *temple recommend,* a small card that you show to gain entry into the temple. We discuss the temple recommend in more detail in an earlier section, "Getting a temple recommend."

>> **Temple clothing:** The Church encourages members to purchase their own set of white temple clothing, worn to symbolize purity and equality. However, some larger temples rent out temple clothing for a nominal fee. Temple clothing includes a basic white outfit and some ceremonial accessories.

- You can purchase the components of the basic all-white outfit at any store, including Church clothing distribution centers. Women wear a long-sleeve or three-quarter-sleeve dress (or skirt and blouse), socks or hosiery, and shoes or slippers. Men wear a long-sleeve shirt, necktie or bow tie, pants, socks, and shoes or slippers. All these items must be true white, not off-white or cream.

- During some temple ordinances, members put on additional ceremonial clothing over their basic white clothing, including a robe, hat or veil, apron, and sash. If you hold a temple recommend, you can purchase these special accessories through one of the Church's clothing distribution centers, including via phone or the Internet.

>> **Temple garment:** As part of the temple ordinances, a Latter-day Saint is authorized to start wearing a special garment that becomes their underwear style for the rest of mortality (see the section "Receiving part one of the endowment," later in this chapter). Garments are sold only to current temple-recommend holders through Church clothing distribution centers, and local leaders can answer any questions about buying and wearing them.

>> **Special appointment:** Prior to attending the temple for the first time, a member should contact the temple to make a special appointment and receive some additional preparatory instructions. Keep in mind that all temples are closed on Sundays, to encourage Sabbath meetinghouse attendance and home family worship. In addition, temples are closed on Monday evenings for family home evening, which we discuss in Chapter 17.

>> **Escort:** Oftentimes, Latter-day Saints invite a few close friends and family members to accompany them on their first temple visit, including one individual of the same gender who's designated as the newbie's escort.

GETTING A SNEAK PEEK DURING A TEMPLE OPEN HOUSE

The only time people can enter a temple without a temple recommend is during the open house held upon completion of a temple's construction or remodeling. Before the prophet or an apostle consecrates a temple for sacred use by saying a prayer of dedication, the building is open to the public for a short period of time, usually between a few days and a month. During this time, visitors of all faiths (or no faith) can tour the temple and learn a bit more about the worship services that occur there.

If you want to attend a temple open house, here are some things you should know:

- **You sometimes need a ticket.** The tickets are free, but they can go quickly. If you want to attend an open house, go online to www.churchofjesuschrist.org/temples, scroll to "News and Events," and click on "Temple Open Houses and Dedications." Of course, if you don't have a ticket and there's room for you to join a tour, you're not going to be turned away.

- **Dress appropriately.** Some visitors wear Sunday best to show respect for the temple's sacred nature, but it's not required.

- **It's movie time.** Before the tour, you usually watch a short film about Latter-day Saint beliefs, and you may walk through an informational exhibit as you wait in line.

- **Cover those kickers.** On the tour, you'll probably need to cover your shoes to show respect and avoid tracking dirt into the new temple. Visitors usually receive disposable booties to pull over their street shoes before they walk through the temple.

Feel free to ask questions of your tour guide. However, please understand that Latter-day Saints consider the temple ordinances sacred and won't discuss them in much detail.

Finally! Receiving Your Own Endowment

Some Latter-day Saints compare receiving the temple endowment to trying to catch the output of a fire hose in a teacup; you're faced with so much new information that it's hard to absorb much on your first time through. However, Church leaders encourage you to keep returning to perform the same ordinances on behalf of dead people so you can gradually digest the experience.

After checking your temple recommend at the front desk, where you leave behind any cameras or recorders, temple workers process your first-timer paperwork and then escort you to the dressing room. To maintain modesty, all patrons are assigned private changing booths.

REMEMBER

The first endowment you receive is for yourself. For every endowment you attend after that, you perform it on behalf of a deceased person, whose name and details you have on a slip of paper that you printed from your home computer or, if you didn't bring one, that a temple worker gives you.

When an adult receives their own temple ordinances, both parts of the endowment take place during the same visit, while marriage sealings may take place on another day. When people perform work for the dead, they can choose whether to do part one of the endowment, part two, or marriage and family sealings.

Receiving part one of the endowment (the initiatory)

Part one of the endowment involves individual, ceremonial washing and anointing, which takes place in what's called the *initiatory area*, which is adjacent to the dressing room. Wearing basic white temple clothes, the recipient moves through a series of small, white-curtained booths, sitting in each booth for a few minutes while a white-suited temple worker touches the recipient's head with a dab of water or olive oil and pronounces blessings of purity, health, and eternal potential.

The short initiatory process concludes with authorization and instructions for wearing the white temple undergarment, which the recipient will have privately donned for the first time shortly before the initiatory. This garment then becomes the member's underwear style for life, available for purchase from the Church in a variety of fabrics and styles.

TEMPLE GARMENT WASH AND WEAR INSTRUCTIONS

One of the temple-recommend questions asks whether members properly wear and care for the garment. The Church gives some instructions and rules regarding garments, encouraging members to seek the guidance of the Holy Spirit in their personal habits and attitudes related to the garment. Following are several expectations for day-to-day life with garments:

- Latter-day Saints wear both pieces of the garment 24 hours a day, removing them only for such activities as showering, swimming, or sex, and putting them back on again as soon as reasonably possible. Some Latter-day Saints wear them during exercise, and some don't.

- Latter-day Saints don't wear clothing that reveals any portion of the garment, which rules out tank tops, shorts that rise above the knee, midriff-baring tops, and so on.

- Latter-day Saints aren't supposed to remove the garment top during yard work, roll up the garment legs to accommodate a favorite pair of shorts, or otherwise "cheat."

- Latter-day Saints avoid exposing the garment to non-Latter-day Saints. For some members, that means changing into regular underwear before visiting the doctor or the gym. Others, however, just try to be discreet.

- Latter-day Saints launder garments normally with other clothing. Some members avoid casually letting them touch the floor.

- Latter-day Saints are asked to keep garments in good repair. When a piece wears out, they destroy it before disposal.

According to the official Church handbook, "When you put on your garment, you put on a sacred symbol of Jesus Christ. Wearing it is an outward expression of your inner commitment to follow Him. The garment is also a reminder of your temple covenants." Further, "As you keep your covenants, including the sacred privilege to wear the garment as instructed in the initiatory ordinances, you will have greater access to the Savior's mercy, protection, strength, and power."

In addition to spiritual protection, some members feel that the garment can provide miraculous physical protection. Mormon folklore includes stories about a member suffering a catastrophic accident but not sustaining any injuries on areas covered by the garment.

In earlier times, the garment was a one-piece affair that reached to the ankles and wrists. Today's most-worn garment style comes in two pieces, with the bottom reaching to the knee and the top covering the shoulders and scooping down almost to the bottom of the breastbone. Garments are available in a variety of comfortable, lightweight fabrics, but wearing them still limits one's clothing style choices, especially in hot weather. Latter-day Saints can sometimes recognize a fellow endowed member at first glance by the garment outline visible through some clothing fabrics.

Receiving part two of the endowment

Clothed in your basic temple whites, you sit quietly in a temple chapel until summoned for the next endowment session. Then you walk to a theater-style ordinance room, carrying the packet that holds some clothing accessories you'll put on during the session. (In smaller temples, there's no waiting chapel and you go straight to the ordinance room.)

For part two of the endowment, you sit with other temple patrons in a session that takes about an hour. It's not a social time, however — everyone stays quiet and focuses on the presentation. In some larger temples, temple workers will guide patrons to walk into adjacent ordinance rooms as the endowment proceeds, lending an additional sense of progression through God's plan of salvation.

In a nutshell, part two dramatizes the entire plan of salvation, from the Earth's creation to humankind's falling away from God and redemption through the Savior (for more about the plan of salvation, see Chapter 2). After an overview of the creation stages, the endowment video portrays the story of Adam and Eve, who represent everyone in the human dilemma.

At various points, participants receive instructions and, in unison, perform brief rituals, covenanting with God to follow five laws:

>> **Law of Obedience:** Striving to keep God's commandments.

>> **Law of Sacrifice:** Supporting the Savior's work and continually repenting of sins.

>> **Law of the Gospel:** Following the Savior's example and teachings, as provided during his earthly ministry.

>> **Law of Chastity:** Enjoying sexual activity only with a partner legally wedded "according to God's law" (in other words, not a same-sex partner — for more on Church views on gay marriage, see Chapter 15).

> **» Law of Consecration:** Dedicating time, talents, and "everything with which the Lord has blessed us" to furthering The Church of Jesus Christ of Latter-day Saints.

So, what's God's side of the bargain? According to the Church, "All covenants with God are intended to be binding. When you keep your covenants and repent of your imperfections, your relationship with Him is strengthened and He will bless you more fully. Your relationship with the Savior also becomes closer and more meaningful. Covenant keepers gain greater access to the power of God and to lasting love, peace, comfort, and joy. God promises that those who keep their covenants will have the opportunity to return to live with Him forever."

Both symbolically and literally, the temple teaches members how to successfully pass the earthly test and reenter God's presence, where Latter-day Saints believe humans can eventually become eternal parents like God. According to the prophet Brigham Young, the gestures and phrases learned during the endowment "are necessary for you, after you have departed this life, to enable you to walk back to the presence of the Father, passing the angels who stand as sentinels."

At the conclusion of the endowment, a temple worker reveals a gauzy white curtain known as the *veil*. After ritualistically passing through this veil, patrons enter the beautifully furnished *celestial room* — in Mormonism, the word *celestial* refers to the highest degree of heaven, where God the Father resides. This symbolic room provides plush, elegant chairs and couches for those who want to ponder and pray before returning to the dressing room.

ANOTHER BRICK IN THE WALL: THE MASONRY CONNECTION

Masonry is an ancient fraternal order that its members believe existed when King Solomon built his temple, as recorded in the Old Testament. Some people claim that early Mormons, many of whom were Masons, borrowed elements of the secret Masonic rituals for the Mormon endowment ceremony, including aspects of the temple clothing.

According to the *Encyclopedia of Latter-day Saint History*, "Latter-day Saints, including Joseph Smith, believed that the Masonic ceremony and the temple endowment had a common origin — ancient temple ceremonies — and this accounted for any similarities between the two rituals." Others point out that the meaning and symbolism of the rituals differ vastly, with any similarities largely cosmetic.

Sealing Families for Eternity

In the Mormon faith, the highest earthly ordinance is celestial marriage, also known as eternal marriage, temple marriage, or "getting sealed." This ordinance is necessary for exaltation, or becoming an eternal parent like the Heavenly Parents. Thanks to the sealing authority restored to Joseph Smith by the resurrected prophet Elijah and handed down since then from prophet to prophet, Latter-day Saints believe that marriages performed in the temple don't dissolve at death, but last forever.

In addition, Latter-day Saints believe that the sealing power eternally binds children to parents, linking each Latter-day Saint in a massive eternal family that could conceivably include each person's entire progeny and ancestry, all the way back to Adam and ultimately to God himself. Children who are physically born to a sealed couple are automatically sealed to them, which is known as being "born in the covenant." In all other cases, including adoption, the child is sealed to their parents during a special temple ceremony.

SCRIPTURE

From the Mormon viewpoint, the Bible's most significant mention of the sealing power appears in Matthew 16:19, where the Savior says the following to Peter, the senior apostle: "And I will give unto thee the keys of the kingdom of heaven: and whatsoever thou shalt bind on earth shall be bound in heaven: and whatsoever thou shalt loose on earth shall be loosed in heaven." Latter-day Saints equate the word *bind* with *seal*. It's possible for sealings to be canceled or revoked — "loosed" — under certain circumstances, which we address in this chapter's later section "When the going gets tough: Sealing complexities."

We don't go into detail in this chapter about all the theological ideas behind eternal families, but you can find a complete discussion on the topic in Chapter 5. Here, we zone in on the ceremony.

Temple sealings for the living

Temple work for the dead includes performing sealings for all husbands, wives, and children who ever lived. In this section, however, we focus on two of Mormonism's most anticipated, celebrated events for the living: temple marriages and, when required, the sealing of children to parents. Children born to already-sealed parents are "born in the covenant," meaning they're automatically sealed to those parents. But if you adopted a child or got sealed to your spouse after you already had kids, your family gets to enjoy a special sealing experience inside the temple. Bring a hanky!

Before a woman and man can get married in a temple, each must first have received all the other essential ordinances, including the endowment. Depending on their personal situation, newly marrying Latter-day Saint couples can choose between two options:

>> **Two birds with one stone:** Get civilly married and eternally sealed at the same time inside a temple. In the United States and some other countries, temple sealings are recognized as legal marriages.

>> **One-two punch:** Get civilly married outside the temple and then get eternally sealed inside the temple, even on the same day if desired.

Why the two options? It's to help newly marrying couples whose parents or immediate family aren't Church members. Only temple-recommend holders can attend a temple ceremony, and some couples — quite understandably — want their non-LDS family members to witness their civil marriage, which can take place in a public Church meetinghouse or wherever else the couple prefers. This is a recent improvement — prior to 2019, the Church pressured couples to marry only in the temple even if their family couldn't attend, discouraging civil marriage by making couples wait a full year before they could get sealed.

If you and your opposite-sex spouse are already civilly married when you convert or rejoin the Church, you can get sealed as a couple as soon as you both receive a *temple recommend* (discussed earlier in "Getting a temple recommend"). If a frisky couple can't get married in the temple due to premarital sex — yes, Latter-day Saints have shotgun weddings too — a Church bishop can perform a regular "till death do you part" wedding in a public meetinghouse. When the couple qualifies — or requalifies — for a temple recommend, they can get sealed in a temple and have any children sealed to them.

Eternal marriages and sealings of children to parents take place in special sealing rooms located near a temple's endowment rooms. Sealings for living people differ from other temple ordinances in several ways:

>> **The family can invite a few adult guests who hold temple recommends to witness the sealing.** These guests don't typically dress in white, but they do remove their shoes in a special waiting area.

>> **Not only can children enter the temple to be sealed to their own parents, but they can also witness the sealing of a sibling.** These are the only occasions when children under age 12 can enter the temple. Temple workers typically take care of the children in another room until they're needed.

>> **Sealings for the living are generally preceded by a freestyle sermon.** The sealer, who is usually advanced in years, typically offers some practical family advice combined with eternal perspective, oftentimes sprinkled with reverent humor.

Here's how a temple sealing ceremony goes down: Kneeling on opposite sides of a cushiony altar and grasping hands, a couple is sealed together for eternity by one of the church's relatively few priesthood holders who hold the sealing power, given to him by the Church's prophet or an apostle. The brief ceremony is the same whether the couple is getting married for the first time or sealing their previous civil marriage. When children are being sealed, they gather around the altar to participate in a similar ceremony.

MY BIG FAT MORMON WEDDING

Whether a couple is getting married for their first time in the temple or eternalizing their previous civil marriage, Latter-day Saints celebrate the occasion in the following ways:

- The bride can wear a white wedding dress in the temple. However, several style limitations and requirements apply, in order to make the dress suitable for the temple. The dress can't be sleeveless or backless, for example.

- Right after the ceremony, the couple usually kisses over the altar.

- The couple doesn't exchange rings as part of the sealing ceremony. However, they can step away from the altar and informally slip rings onto each other's fingers. Some Latter-day Saint couples have a public ring-exchange ceremony later, often as part of the wedding reception.

- Many sealing rooms are furnished with large mirrors facing each other from opposite walls. A couple can gaze together into these endlessly reflecting mirrors and witness their image perpetuated into infinity.

- Afterward, many families gather in the beautiful temple grounds for photos. Some arrange for a professional photographer to meet them there.

- If they want to save money, families can hold a reception or open house for free in the local Latter-day Saint meetinghouse's *cultural hall*, a gym-like room used for sports, parties, and overflow seating. (Just ignore those basketball standards overhead.)

- Latter-day Saints follow most other local marriage customs, from bridal showers to honeymoons. Cleaned-up versions of bachelor and bachelorette parties aren't unheard of, either.

When sealing relationships get complicated

Eternal sealings can bring up some complex family situations, and sometimes a person must exercise faith that Heavenly Father will eventually work out everything to everyone's satisfaction and fill in any gaps.

The Church stopped practicing earthly polygamy more than 100 years ago, but some hints of heavenly plural marriage remain in the Church's sealing policies (for more on polygamy, see Chapters 13 and 15). A living man can technically be sealed to several women at once, but a living woman can be sealed only to one husband at a time. After she dies, however, sealings can be performed with all her husbands from life — presumably, only one of these sealings will actually take effect in the afterlife, depending on what the parties choose.

Here's how some tricky sealing situations play out:

» **Death of a spouse:** If a widower who was sealed to his first wife marries a new wife who isn't already sealed to a husband, the widower can be eternally sealed to both wives. However, a widow who was sealed to her deceased husband has to get that sealing canceled before she can be sealed to a new husband.

» **Divorced couple:** If a sealed Latter-day Saint couple divorces in civil court — which, of course, the Church discourages — the man can receive clearance to get sealed to a new wife, but the woman must get the first sealing canceled before she can be sealed to a new husband.

» **Divorced parents:** An official Church youth magazine states that if your sealed parents divorce, you are still sealed to both. "This is true even if your parents' temple sealing to each other is canceled. The important thing to remember is that Heavenly Father loves all of you and wants the best for you, both now and in eternity. If you keep your covenants, your relationships in the next life will be fair and right. You can seek peace in these matters by praying and, if you feel you need extra support, by counseling with your bishop."

» **Divorced couple, both passed away:** Interestingly, if a deceased couple was divorced before death and never sealed, their children can arrange for the parents to be sealed by proxy in the temple (see the previous section "Why perform ordinances for the dead?") so that the children can then be sealed to them. Even if the parents don't accept the ordinances in the afterlife, the children still reap the full benefits of being sealed into God's eternal family.

» **Parents not Mormon:** Adult converts to Mormonism can perform temple work for their own parents after the parents die, eternalizing their parents' marriage and then getting sealed to their parents. Even if the parents don't accept the ordinances, Latter-day Saints believe that the convert will receive the full sealing benefits.

>> **Spouse who leaves the Church:** If someone gets excommunicated from the Church or officially resigns by requesting removal of their name from Church records, that person's sealings are revoked. However, the spouse and children of that person don't lose their sealing blessings if they remain faithful.

>> **Spouse who doesn't join the Church:** What if two members of another faith (or no faith) get married, and only one of them later converts to Mormonism? Because the nonmember spouse won't qualify to be sealed, what happens to the Latter-day Saint spouse's eternal prospects? If the quandary is never resolved during the couple's lifetime, the sealing can be performed posthumously in the hopes that the nonmember spouse will finally convert in the afterlife. Otherwise, the Latter-day Saint spouse simply trusts in Heavenly Father to eventually work things out to everyone's wishes and best advantage.

>> **Cohabitation:** If a couple lived together in a permanent relationship and fulfilled marital and parental responsibilities but never got legally married, they can be sealed after one or both partners are deceased.

>> **Adultery:** If a person who commits adultery while sealed to a spouse later marries the partner in the adultery, the new couple can apply to be sealed after demonstrating temple worthiness and marital stability for at least five years.

>> **Never married:** For those who don't have the opportunity to marry during their earthly lifetime through no choice or fault of their own, Latter-day Saints believe they can still qualify to receive all eternal blessings. Many believe that those who die single and worthy will be provided with an eternal spouse at a future time, if they so desire.

Occasional complexities notwithstanding, sealings can imbue earthly family relationships with greater meaning and purpose. When you know you're building something that can last forever, you'll likely put more effort into it and value it more. Without a doubt, temples are one of the key ways in which Mormonism strives to strengthen families.

Chapter **8**

In and Around Church Headquarters

I n the heart of Salt Lake City, Utah, the LDS church makes its headquarters on a sprawling campus of sturdy, staid buildings, many of them made of gray granite. From this headquarters, the prophet (the one man who serves as president and worldwide spiritual leader of the Church), the apostles, and other high-level leaders (collectively known as *General Authorities*), plus several thousand bureaucratic employees, run the affairs of Mormonism worldwide. In addition, female leaders oversee the Church's programs for women, teenage girls, and children.

Twice a year, during an important worldwide event called *General Conference,* the spotlight focuses on Church headquarters and the General Authorities, with about ten hours of general proceedings broadcast around the world via satellite and the Internet. In addition, members can get acquainted with General Authorities when these leaders travel to local areas to speak at large-scale regional gatherings and conduct Church business.

Although many Church headquarters functions are what you'd expect for a multinational religious corporation — finances, membership records, curriculum development, property management, public affairs, and so on — in this chapter, we look more closely at some unique worldwide programs administered from Church headquarters: the welfare and humanitarian efforts and the Church Educational System. (How does the Church pay for all this? Mainly through donated tithing funds. For more on that topic, see Chapter 16.)

A Tour of Church Headquarters

Visible from afar, two prominent landmarks show where the Church headquarters is located in downtown Salt Lake City. The 28-story, cream-colored Church Office Building is one of the city's tallest high-rises, and the gray, six-spire Salt Lake Temple sports a golden statue of the Angel Moroni (see Chapter 9 for an overview of who Moroni is).

One of the most visited U.S. tourist destinations, Temple Square was originally a single walled city block, but the term now covers a five-block headquarters campus where the following buildings are located:

>> **Assembly Hall:** This ornate, Gothic Revival–style building is used for lectures, recitals, free concerts featuring international artists, and overflow seating during General Conference (see the section "A Two-Day Marathon: General Conference," later in this chapter).

>> **Church Administrative Building:** This bank-like granite structure houses the offices of the Church's president, 12 apostles, and many other General Authorities. Unlike most Church headquarters buildings, it's not open to the public.

>> **Church History Library:** This archive contains many unique sources by and about the LDS church, not all of which are endorsed by today's Church. The library is open to the public, but you can only view most of the materials in the library's tightly monitored reading room. The best place to start a research project is online at https://catalog.churchofjesuschrist.org.

>> **Church History Museum:** Historical exhibits highlight the past and present LDS church, and art exhibits reflect a wide variety of media and worldwide cultures. The museum provides immersive and interactive experiences and holds international art competitions.

>> **Church Office Building:** Visitors can ride an elevator past all the bureaucratic departments to this skyscraper's top floor, which provides a panoramic view of the Salt Lake Valley.

>> **Conference Center:** Filling an entire city block, this gigantic auditorium is where General Conference occurs twice a year, as well as other occasional events. It's worth touring for the artwork, displays, and extensive rooftop gardens.

>> **FamilySearch Library:** Known for providing lots of hands-on assistance to visitors, this library contains the world's most extensive collection of genealogical records (for more on family history, see Chapter 5).

>> **Joseph Smith Memorial Building:** Formerly Salt Lake City's grandest hotel, this elegant building now houses Church offices, restaurants, meeting areas, and entertainment facilities. It's a popular place for wedding banquets and receptions.

>> **Lion and Beehive Houses:** Originally built by Brigham Young to house many of his wives and children, these restored homes are now used for historical tours and entertaining. (FYI, the cafeteria-style Lion House Pantry is the premier place to go for Mormon comfort food.)

>> **Relief Society Building:** Here, the Church's female general officers oversee its worldwide programs for women, young women, and children (for more information on these programs, see Chapter 6).

>> **Salt Lake Tabernacle:** With its distinctive domed roof and massive pipe organ, this building is home base for the world-famous Tabernacle Choir at Temple Square (formerly known as the Mormon Tabernacle Choir, back when the Church was cool with the M-word).

>> **Salt Lake Temple:** Although only worthy Church members can go inside, this iconic temple is fascinating to view and learn about (for more on temples, see Chapter 7).

Governing the Church: General Authorities

Latter-day Saints believe that Jesus Christ directly governs their church, making his will known through revelation to 15 men who together function as the earthly heads of the Church. The most senior apostle — by date of apostleship, not date of birth — is set apart as the prophet and president of the Church, and he selects two other apostles as his counselors to constitute the three-man *First Presidency*. The two counselors work closely with the president, and they're highly visible and respected leaders in the Church.

The remaining 12 leaders constitute the *Quorum of the Twelve Apostles.* Although the president is the only individual who holds all the Church's priesthood *keys* (meaning the authority to perform or delegate priesthood roles and ordinances) and the only one officially known as the prophet, the 15 men are all considered prophets, seers, and revelators who act as "special witnesses of the name of Christ in all the world" (Doctrine and Covenants 107:23; for more on the D&C, see Chapter 10). All 15 of these men generally govern together as an executive board, not taking any significant action without unanimity. Their average age is probably well over 70.

In addition, the Church calls men to serve as *seventies,* a New Testament term referring to the original number of such leaders (see Luke 10). Today's LDS church has far more than just 70 seventies; organized into several quorums, they function under the apostles and are like vice-presidents in a corporation. (In fact, one prominent scholar refers to them as "ecclesiastical middle management.") Many seventies are middle aged rather than retirement aged, and although the president and apostles serve for life, seventies can eventually be given emeritus status or released.

Rounding out the Church's top government is the *Presiding Bishopric* (a bishopric is a three-man supervisory board, consisting of a bishop and two counselors — the Church also uses the terms *bishop* and *bishopric* for the leaders of local congregations). This Church-wide bishopric leads the Aaronic Priesthood (described in Chapter 4) and oversees the faith's temporal concerns, such as building meetinghouses and collecting tithes. Together, the president, apostles, seventies, and Presiding Bishopric are known as General Authorities, because they preside over the whole Church. Often referred to informally as *GAs,* they're also known as the *Brethren,* with a capital B.

General Authorities receive no professional training specifically to lead the Church. Before being called as full-time GAs, most of these men establish successful careers in professions such as business, law, education, and medicine, which helps explain why the LDS church feels so corporate in personality. Undoubtedly, all the General Authorities previously served the Church in many important, demanding volunteer leadership positions, which helped prepare them and bring them to the attention of Church headquarters. As General Authorities, they don't receive salaries, although the Church does provide them with a living allowance.

Following the prophet

Latter-day Saints believe that the man who leads them possesses prophetic powers every bit as real and potent as those of Adam, Noah, Moses, or any other biblical prophet. The prophet's job is to bring people to Christ in preparation both for the Savior's eventual return to earth (which we discuss in Chapter 3) and for humankind's existence with him in eternity (which we discuss in Chapter 2).

WHO'S THE CURRENT PROPHET?

At this writing, the LDS church's prophet and president is 100-year-old Russell M. Nelson. A former heart surgeon who didn't become prophet until age 93, President Nelson has nonetheless made numerous dynamic changes in the Church, which *Atlantic* staff writer McKay Coppins summarizes like this: "Worldwide travels that took him to every continent (save for Antarctica), a historic partnership with the NAACP, greater gender equity in temple rituals, the reversal of a controversial policy regarding same-sex couples, two-hour weekly church services, a slate of relaxed rules for missionaries, and an unprecedented wave of temple building."

During his time as prophet, President Nelson has emphasized making and keeping covenants with God, spiritually hearing the Lord, letting God prevail in your life, being a peacemaker, and "thinking celestial" — in other words, always striving to be worthy of heaven's highest degree of glory (for more on that, see Chapter 2).

The apostle next in line to become Mormon prophet is Dallin H. Oaks, who at this writing was serving as President Nelson's first counselor. Before his call as an apostle, President Oaks practiced and taught law in Chicago, served as president of Brigham Young University, and served as a Utah Supreme Court justice.

According to Latter-day Saints, today's prophet received his prophetic authority through a chain of prophets leading back to founding prophet Joseph Smith, who received it at the hands of resurrected prophets from biblical times. The person chosen to receive this ultimate authority is the apostle with the most seniority in the quorum. The last man that Latter-day Saints believe carried the prophetic mantle before Joseph Smith was the New Testament apostle Peter, who led the early Christian church after Christ's resurrection, with James and John as his counselors (for more about Mormon views on priesthood succession, see Chapter 4).

Although Church leaders admit that no one is perfect except the Savior himself, members generally feel tremendous respect and affection for the prophet. Some members believe that Heavenly Father would never allow the prophet to lead the Church astray, so they can pretty much assume that everything the prophet says is the will of God. At the same time, however, they believe that God's will in one era isn't necessarily his will in another, because human conditions and needs change. Therefore, the living prophet's teachings outweigh those of deceased prophets.

What the prophet does

As leader of the Church, the prophet clarifies and interprets the Church's doc-trines, policies, and organization; introduces new programs and initiatives; warns members and the world at large about sinful trends; and oversees numerous other aspects of Church administration. Each prophet's personality makes a unique impact on the Church as he communicates the ideas and instructions that are most important to Christ's people at any particular time.

As God's spokesman to Church members around the world (and anyone else who will listen), the prophet unifies the whole Church, including making international visits. During his journeys, the prophet dedicates new temples for sacred use, meets with secular officials and dignitaries, speaks to large congregations, and conducts other Church business. When the prophet enters or exits a congrega-tional gathering, everyone typically stands up, and the Latter-day Saints often serenade him with a hymn entitled "We Thank Thee O God for a Prophet."

OPINION VERSUS REVELATION

Undoubtedly, prophets sometimes speak more from their own understanding and opinion than from direct revelation, but most Latter-day Saints give the prophet all possible benefit of the doubt and strive to obey his teachings. For example, during a speech one previous prophet expressed distaste for body piercing beyond a single pair of earrings for women. On the spot, some listeners reached up and removed their extra earrings, and the comment triggered similar reactions throughout the Church. Although not on the level of a commandment, this kind of *counsel* — as such prophetic admoni-tions are commonly called — can fast become a new cultural standard among conform-ist Mormons, of which there are many (especially in Utah).

Does God himself disapprove of, say, body piercing? If an individual wants personal confirmation that what a prophet says is God's will, Church leaders urge them to pray about the matter and receive an answer from the Holy Ghost. Some Latter-day Saints feel that simply demonstrating *obedience* to the prophet's counsel is as important as the particulars of the counsel, if not more so. Others emphasize the role of individual agency and personal spiritual confirmation when questions arise. Most Latter-day Saints are somewhere in the middle of this spectrum, considering the prophet's counsel together with scripture and personal revelation when making any major decision (or even a relatively minor one, like body piercing).

REMEMBER

For the prophet's teachings to become an official commandment, doctrine, or scripture of the Church — something that happens extremely rarely these days — the other 14 top apostolic leaders all need to agree to the elevated status, and the teachings go through an official process, often including presentation to the body of the Church for a sustaining vote during General Conference. (No, the Church isn't a democracy by any stretch of the imagination, but members get the opportunity to demonstrate their acceptance of official actions by raising their right hands when called upon to do so.) The best overview of the Church's *commandments* — as opposed to *counsel* — is the temple-recommend interview, which we explain and summarize in Chapter 7.

Hotline to heaven

How exactly does a modern prophet receive revelation from God? Does the Church Administration Building have a special satellite dish through which God beams down instructions? Um, no. Unlike the early days of Mormonism, there's nothing too dramatic about Mormon revelation anymore. By all appearances, the days when resurrected beings — including the Savior himself — regularly appeared to Mormon leaders are long gone, and today's leaders don't use prophetic devices like Joseph Smith did, such as a *seer stone* or *Urim and Thummim*. (If visions and angelic visitations *are* still happening, leaders generally don't talk about them. In today's media-saturated culture, you can understand why they wouldn't.)

Judging by what the prophet and other General Authorities say in public, revelation comes to them in much the same way it comes to individuals: through strong, unmistakable impressions inside the mind and heart from God's messenger, the Holy Ghost (for more about the Holy Ghost, see Chapter 3). What's more, revelations seem to come in response to direct, prayerful appeal by leaders on a particular issue; God doesn't just randomly zap the prophet with lightning to make a point. Thus the difference between prophetic and personal revelation is in scope, not method of delivery. Individuals can receive revelation for themselves, their families, and their immediate assignments within the Church, and so can the prophet — but his responsibility includes the *whole* Church, if not the whole world.

Apostles and seventies and bishops — Oh my!

From the First Presidency, the Church hierarchy filters down to the apostles, and then to the Presiding Bishopric and the seventies, and then to the Church's hundreds of thousand local leaders, whom we discuss in Chapter 6.

Apostles

With 12 apostles, most every Church member can find at least one or two with whom they especially relate — and one or two with whom they *don't*. Because all 12 apostles give sermons in General Conference every six months and travel widely around the Church, most members get to know their distinctive personalities and gospel outlooks pretty well. Their attributes run the gamut: Some are business-like, some eloquent, some intellectual, some intensely spiritual, and some folksy.

The First Presidency appoints new apostles to replace those who pass away, presenting their names during General Conference to the whole Church for the symbolic gesture of a sustaining "vote." Through the laying on of hands by the First Presidency and the other apostles, each new apostle receives the same *priesthood keys* (meaning authority to perform certain duties and ordinances) that the Savior gave to the apostles in the New Testament. These keys include the authority to preach the gospel worldwide and to perform eternal sealing ordinances, such as celestial marriage (for more on sealing ordinances, see Chapter 7).

Under the direction of the First Presidency, each apostle receives assignments to oversee administrative departments and geographical areas of the Church. Apostles negotiate with national governments to allow the Church to preach the gospel and establish congregations there. In addition, they supervise the Church's *stakes*, or local groups of 5 to 12 congregations, and direct the work of the seventies.

Seventies

At the beck and call of the apostles, the seventies work to spread the gospel around the world and help manage the Church. Some fulfill assignments at Church head-quarters in Salt Lake City, and others move abroad to head up the Church's area offices in foreign lands.

Seventies are organized into several different quorums, and some receive lifelong assignments while others serve for a period of five years. Another layer or two of middle management lies between seventies and local *stake presidents*, who keep an eye on clusters of adjacent congregations, but the Church reorganizes those layers fairly often, so it's hard to keep track of exactly what the org chart looks like.

Presiding Bishopric

The three men in the Presiding Bishopric govern the Church's temporal affairs, or things related more to the physical than the spiritual, such as building meeting-houses. In addition, they preside over the Aaronic Priesthood, also known as the preparatory priesthood (see Chapter 4).

For most members, the term *bishop* brings to mind their local congregational leader, not a member of the Church's Presiding Bishopric. Although nearly all experienced members can name each of the 12 apostles, most probably can't name all three men who serve in the Presiding Bishopric, even though some of these Brethren usually speak at General Conference, too.

Female auxiliary leaders

Nine women hold leadership positions at Church headquarters under the supervision of the General Authorities. Like the General Authorities, they oversee their areas of assignment on a worldwide scale, speak in General Conference and at other Church-wide or regional meetings, and travel around the world. A presidency of three women — a president and two counselors — leads each of the following three Church auxiliaries:

>> **Relief Society:** The Church's worldwide organization for women

>> **Young Women:** The program for girls ages 12 to 17

>> **Primary:** The program for all children ages 3 to 11

In addition, each auxiliary also has a general board with a flexible number of members. For more information about these auxiliaries, see Chapter 6.

A Two-Day Marathon: General Conference

Twice a year, Latter-day Saints get to see and hear their worldwide leaders during General Conference on the first weekends of April and October, with three two-hour sessions on Saturday and two on Sunday. Thanks to today's broadcast and streaming capabilities, members can choose to watch General Conference at their local meetinghouse or anywhere else they find convenient, including at home in their pajamas while enjoying cinnamon rolls, a traditional conference-weekend treat for some Mormons.

To outsiders, nothing much seems to happen at these meetings beyond preaching. This event isn't like the General Conference of the United Methodist Church, for example, during which delegates vote on controversial issues and their disagreements often make the national news. LDS General Conference is staid by contrast, and leaders don't make key decisions at this time, although they sometimes announce decisions there. General Conference is a time to reaffirm the core teachings of the Church, emphasize the importance of faith and family, and marvel anew at the gospel's reach into many cultures and nations.

ONE OF THE LARGEST RELIGIOUS AUDITORIUMS

Until the year 2000, Latter-day Saints almost always held their General Conferences in the Salt Lake Tabernacle. In the late 1990s, the Church built the Conference Center, which is more than 40 times the tabernacle's size. This vast and stately granite building seats around 21,000 people. Amazingly, the cavernous interior has no visible pillars, so there's no such thing as a bad seat.

One of the most beloved Mormon stories about the building centers around the pulpit, which was constructed from an old walnut tree that Gordon B. Hinckley, the LDS prophet at that time, planted in his backyard in the 1960s. He seemed touched and pleased as he told Church members during General Conference that he was speaking to them from the wood of the same tree his children had played under.

The Conference Center is also used for concerts, special events, and other large meetings and activities. Additionally, the building has a state-of-the-art, 850-seat theater for plays, shows, and other theatrical events. The entire building is topped by a 4-acre meadow — yes, a meadow — with gardens of wildflowers and native grasses.

During the conference sessions, members hear from the prophet and other leaders and listen to inspirational music from the Tabernacle Choir at Temple Square and other choirs. Two-hour breaks between meetings ensure that members have time to eat and rest a bit before continuing.

Conference talks — Latter-day Saints don't call them sermons — are relatively brief and almost never spontaneous. In this age of simultaneous broadcast in many different languages and cultures, General Authorities submit their talks in advance so they can be translated for the live broadcast. Transcripts of the talks appear in the May and November issues of the *Liahona*, the official magazine of the LDS church, and audio, video, and text versions are available at www.churchofjesuschrist.org. In fact, some members focus more on studying the talks over several months than on trying to watch and absorb them all in just one weekend.

For kids, General Conference can be — yes, we're going to say it — a little boring. In fact, an entire cottage industry has arisen to help parents keep children busy during the marathon with games such as "General Conference Bingo" and "Apostle Flashcards." These flashcards may be the *only* flashy aspect of General Conference. However, most adult members find that each conference produces at least one gem of a talk that seems to speak directly to them. So, although this conference is long, Latter-day Saints don't see it as an ordeal but as an opportunity for spiritual insight and growth.

LDS Welfare and Humanitarian Relief

Joseph Smith taught that each Christian has a responsibility "to feed the hungry, to clothe the naked, to provide for the widow, to dry up the tear of the orphan, [and] to comfort the afflicted, whether in this church, or in any other, or in no church at all, wherever he finds them." Latter-day Saints take this recommendation very seriously. They believe that because they're followers of Jesus Christ, they're supposed to try to be like him, which includes ministering to the poor.

The Church has two basic programs for combating poverty, ignorance, and disease:

>> *Welfare services* help primarily Church members become more self-reliant and assist them if they're unemployed or facing financial hardship.

>> *Humanitarian services* send aid all over the world, primarily to people who aren't members of the Church.

Taking care of their own: The Church's welfare program

In 1936, alarmed by the global depression that had left millions in poverty, LDS President Heber J. Grant and his counselors started a coordinated Church welfare plan that gave food and clothing to Church members who were willing to volunteer their time and work in exchange for the assistance. This plan was far-reaching in its intent to help fellow Latter-day Saints and get them off "the dole" — government programs that Church leaders believed encouraged a cycle of idleness and poverty. In fact, the LDS welfare program was actually one of the first workfare programs in the United States, because members had to contribute their time and talents if they wanted to receive material help.

The funding for the welfare program comes from Latter-day Saints all around the world. Generally, on the first Sunday of every month, Latter-day Saints everywhere fast for two meals and donate the money they would've spent on their own food to the program — plus more, if possible — in order to share their material blessings with others. (For more on fasting and other Mormon sacrifices, see Chapter 16.)

Although some Latter-day Saints may imagine they'll never be among "the poor and needy," the fact is that many members fall on hard times at some point in their lives. A parent may experience a job layoff, or an illness or injury may prevent a family from making ends meet. After the family's resources have been exhausted and the extended family has assisted all they can, the Church can help get a family back on its feet. Many Latter-day Saints see government help as a last resort and would rather receive Church assistance than government welfare.

Staffed mainly by volunteers and service missionaries, the Church's welfare program includes the following components:

>> *Bishops' storehouses*, where needy people authorized by *bishops* (local congregation leaders) can get groceries, household supplies, and clothing at no cost.

>> *Canneries* and other facilities, where volunteers of any faith can help process food for use in the welfare program or their own home storage (see Chapter 18 for more about food storage and other principles of self-reliance).

>> *Farms*, where grains, vegetables, and livestock are raised for use in the welfare program.

>> *Employment resource centers*, where volunteers help people find and train for new jobs.

>> *Deseret Industries* thrift stores, where the public can buy donated clothing and household items.

Many of the people who work at the Church's canneries, thrift stores, farms, and other welfare facilities are the same people getting free food and clothing from the Church.

SCRIPTURE

The welfare program not only meets the physical needs of poorer Church members, but it also meets a spiritual need of *all* Church members: to be of service. The Book of Mormon says, "When ye are in the service of your fellow beings ye are only in the service of your God" (Mosiah 2:17). In other words, when Latter-day Saints serve other people — whether those people are Mormon or not — they feel blessed because they're also serving God.

Taking care of others: LDS humanitarian relief

Responding to a major famine in Ethiopia, in 1985, the Latter-day Saints held a special 24-hour fast in addition to their regular monthly fast (see Chapter 16 for more on fasting). Donating the money they would've spent on food and additional funds as able, Church members raised $6 million in one day to aid famine-stricken people in Ethiopia. Thus, the Church's Humanitarian Relief program was born.

In addition to giving financial assistance to established relief organizations such as the Red Cross, the LDS church runs its own extensive international program to help with famines, natural disasters, and refugee needs. With the Church's vast wealth now increasingly under scrutiny, its humanitarian program has been growing by leaps and bounds, although many would like to see it grow even faster. See the stats for just one year in Table 8-1.

TABLE 8-1

LDS Humanitarian Aid in 2023

Humanitarian projects	4,119
Hours volunteered	6.2 million
Expenditures	$1.36 billion
Countries and territories served	191

At the Church's Humanitarian Center in Salt Lake City, clothing, quilts, and hygiene and school kits are sorted, assembled, and sent all over the world to assist people in crisis, regardless of their religion. In addition to preparing and shipping emergency supplies, the center serves as a training ground to help people — many of whom are refugees and immigrants — develop employable skills and learn self-reliance.

During the holidays each year, the LDS church sets up "Light the World Giving Machines" in shopping centers and elsewhere. These distinctive red vending machines allow generous passersby to swipe their credit card and choose whether to donate food, shelter, clothing, medical services, school supplies, or livestock to needy people worldwide. In 2024, the Church's "kiosks of kindness" popped up in 106 cities, 13 countries, and five continents.

Survival of the Smartest: Latter-day Saint Education

SCRIPTURE

Both secular and religious education are vital to Latter-day Saints — in fact, they believe that separating the two is unnatural, and Latter-day Saints avidly pursue all legitimate branches of knowledge. Mormon scripture makes frequent reference to learning and intelligence, including: "Whatever principle of intelligence we attain unto in this life, it will rise with us in the resurrection. And if a person gains more knowledge and intelligence in this life through his diligence and obedience than another, he will have so much the advantage in the world to come" (Doctrine and Covenants 130:18–19). In other words, you *can* take it with you if you stow it away inside your brain before you die.

SCRIPTURE

When it comes to education versus religion, Latter-day Saints buck the trend. American sociologists say that, in most cases, more education results in less religiosity. However, the more education a Latter-day Saint receives, the more devoted their religious observance becomes, on average. Perhaps this tendency is because the Church provides so many opportunities for combining secular and spiritual education, reflecting the perspective expressed in a Book of Mormon passage: "To be learned is good if they hearken unto the counsels of God" (2 Nephi 9:29).

In this section, we look at the Church's international *seminary* and *institute* programs for providing every Latter-day Saint high school and college student with religious instruction to complement their worldly studies. In addition, we take a gander at Brigham Young University. Together, these programs and schools fall under the umbrella of the *Church Educational System*, or CES for short. (The Church also runs the career-focused Ensign College in Salt Lake City and high schools in several Pacific Islands, but we won't delve into those.)

THE PERPETUAL EDUCATION FUND

Because Latter-day Saints value education so much, the Church helps its impoverished members in underprivileged countries pay for college or vocational tuition so they can get better jobs. Funded by donations from Latter-day Saints all over the world, this program loans money to LDS students who qualify based on need, and they pay it back after they get jobs, replenishing the fund for future students.

Called the *Perpetual Education Fund,* this program is modeled on the Church's 19th-century emigration program that helped needy pioneers pay for their trip to Utah, back when all Latter-day Saints gathered there (see Chapter 12). The Perpetual Education Fund had helped more than 90,000 students in needy countries since its start in 2001, with loan recipients often tripling or quadrupling their earning potential.

A daily dose of the gospel

For Mormon students, a spoonful of spirituality helps the secularism go down. Designed to add an eternal Mormon perspective to mainstream education, the religious instruction program for high-school students is called *seminary*; for college students, it's *institute*. Both programs are open to members of other faiths.

Seminary: Instead of sleep

The idea that teenagers love to sleep is a universally acknowledged truth. However, if you were a Mormon high-school student growing up outside the heavily LDS areas of the United States Intermountain West, you likely wouldn't get much sleep during the week. Why? Because every school morning, you'd rise at an ungodly hour to attend seminary before school — well, perhaps that would make it a *godly* hour. No, you wouldn't be in special training to become a priest or minister — every Mormon teen is expected to take seminary, which is available around the world.

Some would say that the kids living in heavily Mormon areas are spoiled because the Church builds seminary buildings near most public high schools, and the kids can register to attend seminary like any other class during the day. This idea of mixing church and state has caused some court cases, which succeeded in preventing the awarding of high-school credit for such religious classes.

Each of the four years of seminary (which correspond with U.S. grades 9 through 12) covers one of the main books of Mormon scripture: the Old Testament, the New Testament, the Book of Mormon, and the Doctrine and Covenants, or D&C (for more on Mormon scriptures, see Chapters 9 and 10). In places where not enough Latter-day Saints live close enough together to warrant early-morning classes, the Church provides an individual home-study program.

Institute: Giving the gospel the old college try

The full name of the Church's worldwide college-level education program is *institutes of religion*, but most people just call it *institute*. The instructors often hold advanced degrees, and they generally address the subject matter with at least some academic rigor. Most institutes offer a variety of classes covering scriptures, history, and doctrine, as well as topics such as marriage and missionary preparation. The institute program serves Latter-day Saint students attending thousands of postsecondary schools around the world.

The Church has constructed institute buildings near many colleges and universities in the United States. In other places, classes are held in regular meetinghouses or rented facilities, often on campus — however, these classes usually happen in the evening, rather than early in the morning. For many Mormon college students, institute becomes not only a place for religious education but also a social and recreational hub. Many members agree that the institute manuals are some of the best educational books published by the Church; these manuals are available at https://store.churchofjesuschrist.org.

Stone-cold sober: Brigham Young University

When the BYU football team won the national championship in 1984, many people around the country asked, "BY-*who*?" However, BYU's Provo, Utah, campus is one of the largest privately owned educational institutions in the United States, with a bigger enrollment — nearly 30,000 — than many public universities. The university also has smaller campuses in Idaho and Hawaii, and it offers inexpensive "spiritually based" online degrees at www.byupathway.edu, which annually serves more than 65,000 students in over 180 countries.

While BYU football doesn't crack the national top-25 rankings every year, the school does consistently rank atop national college surveys in such categories as "Most Religious" and "Most Stone-Cold Sober." And BYU has joined the ranks of top U.S. universities — in 2024, it was 20th overall in the Best Colleges in America rankings from *The Wall Street Journal* and College Pulse.

Not so academically free

BYU's mission is to combine the highest-quality secular teaching with religious education to produce eternally well-rounded graduates. Although most of the secular classes are like those at any other university, many professors bring prayer or spiritual perspective into the classroom. LDS religion classes are part of the general education requirements for all students.

The Church keeps a close eye on BYU and occasionally clamps down on perceived troublemakers. LDS professors must hold a current *temple recommend* (explained in Chapter 7), and the handful of non-Mormon faculty must abide by similarly high moral standards. From time to time, BYU declines tenure to faculty members not because of inadequate scholarship but because their expressions aren't in harmony with official Church teachings. As a result, professional agencies have criticized BYU for its lack of academic freedom.

Cracking the code

BYU's strictly enforced student honor code gives the school a wholesome 1950s aura. Like its sponsoring church, it doesn't allow premarital sex, smoking, alcohol, coffee, recreational drugs, gay dating and marriage, or pornography. Dorms have curfews and rules limiting gender interaction. Students can now buy caffeinated soda on campus, but for some reason men still can't grow beards unless they have a medical waiver (such as for a skin condition). Men's hair can't cover their ears or touch their collar. Women can't wear sleeveless or backless clothes or bare their midriffs. For both sexes, shorts must extend to the knees, and extreme or grubby styles aren't allowed.

Non-Mormon students are welcome to attend the university if they abide by the same standards, and a few hundred actually do. One reason is that BYU charges relatively low tuition for its level of quality. Non-Mormon students pay half again as much tuition as Mormon students, whose families presumably help support the school by paying tithing, but it's still a bargain by national standards.

3
Holy Books and Sacred History

IN THIS PART . . .

We show you a thumbnail sketch of the plot and teachings of the Book of Mormon and give you a rundown of what Mormons believe about the Bible. You also get a taste of the other major books that Mormons regard as scripture: the Doctrine and Covenants and the Pearl of Great Price. Then we go on a whirlwind tour of LDS Church history, from the early days in Ohio, Missouri, and Illinois to the great pioneer trek that led the Mormons to Utah. We also lift the veil on the history of polygamy, which Latter-day Saints no longer practice, and highlight Mormon trends in the 20th century.

Chapter **9**

The Bible and the Book of Mormon

When people hear *The Book of Mormon*, some may think first of the 2011 musical comedy that won nine Tony Awards and is now approaching $1 billion in gross revenues. While the musical sends up Mormon missionaries in a (mostly) affectionate way, it's not actually about what happens in the Book of Mormon. Surprisingly, the Church's response to the irreverent, raunchy show has been more chill than chilly: "The production may attempt to entertain audiences for an evening, but the Book of Mormon as a volume of scripture will change people's lives forever by bringing them closer to Christ." The Church has even purchased ads in the musical's playbill with taglines like "The book is always better" and "You've seen the play, now read the book."

So, now let's talk about the real Book of Mormon, the signature scripture of the LDS church. Latter-day Saints believe that both the Bible and the Book of Mormon are the word of God and that people need to study both books frequently and prayerfully. Latter-day Saints also hold up two other books, the Doctrine and Covenants and the Pearl of Great Price, as scripture; we discuss them in the next chapter. Together, these four books of scripture are known as Mormonism's *standard works*.

Like the Bible, the Book of Mormon is a hodgepodge of sacred texts written over the course of many centuries by many different people. Like the Bible, it traces God's dealings with particular groups of people — especially the Nephites — and their trials and triumphs in a promised land. Unlike the Bible, which was translated by hundreds of people (and continues to be translated in new versions today), the Book of Mormon had only one modern-day translator, Joseph Smith.

However, when Latter-day Saints say *translate* in connection with Joseph Smith, they generally don't mean using human linguistic skills to turn a text originally written in another language into English. Rather, they believe Joseph translated by receiving holy text from God via revelatory devices such as a seer stone or the Urim and Thummim, a prophetic instrument mentioned several times in the Bible. (We discuss this idea more in the section "Seer stones and scribes: Translating the golden plates.")

The Bible: True, with a Few Tweaks

Latter-day Saints see their church as the restoration of the religion whose evolution is chronicled in the Old and New Testaments. So, of course, the Bible is extremely important to Latter-day Saints, and they put a high emphasis on studying it and quoting from it. According to Mormonism's eighth Article of Faith, "We believe the Bible to be the word of God as far as it is translated correctly" (for more on the Articles of Faith, see Chapter 10). However, the ninth Article of Faith states that Latter-day Saints believe in continuing revelation — in other words, scripture is open to addition. The other three standard books of scripture work together with the Bible to establish Mormon belief and practice.

Thus saith the King James Version

Latter-day Saints recognize the *King James Version* (KJV) as their official Bible. They publish their own edition of the KJV, which stays true to the original text and is also jampacked with LDS-specific supplements and reader aids. For a sampling of Bible teachings that are significant to Latter-day Saints, see Table 9-1.

TABLE 9-1

Significant Bible Teachings for Latter-day Saints

Doctrinal Point	Biblical Support
Human spirits lived with God before earthly birth (for the modern Mormon outlook on this topic, see Chapter 2).	Job 38:4–7, Proverbs 8:22–31, Jeremiah 1:5, John 9:1–3, Acts 17:28, Ephesians 1:4–5, 2 Timothy 1:9, Titus 1:1–2, Hebrews 12:9, Jude 1:6, and Revelation 12:7–9
God speaks to humans through prophets (see Chapters 4 and 6).	Amos 3:7, Ephesians 2:20, and Ephesians 4:11
God enters into two-way promises with worthy individuals, who are collectively known as his *covenant people* (see Chapters 5 and 7).	Genesis, Exodus, Deuteronomy, and Hebrews (especially 8–10)
God gives his people standards of conduct, including a health code (see Chapter 16).	Leviticus
God leads his chosen people to a Promised Land (see Chapters 11–13).	Exodus
God assigns people to tribes in the house of Israel, either through blood or adoption (see Chapter 5).	Genesis, Matthew 3:9, Luke 3:8, Romans 8:15–17, Galatians 4:5–7, and Ephesians 1:5
God will prepare the earth for the Savior's Second Coming (see Chapter 3); members must pay a tithe (see Chapter 16); people will seek out their ancestors (see Chapters 5 and 7).	Malachi 3 and 4
The basic principles of Christ's gospel include faith, repentance, baptism, and receiving the gift of the Holy Ghost (see Chapter 6).	Isaiah 1:18, Matthew 3:13–17, John 14:26, Acts 19:1–6, Romans 6:4, 2 Corinthians 7:9–10, and Hebrews 11
Christ's church is organized and administered through certain priesthood offices, such as prophet, apostle, seventy, elder, bishop, and others (see Chapters 4 and 8).	Luke 6:13 and 10:1, Acts 14:23, Ephesians 2:20 and 4:11, and Philippians 1:1
God's priesthood must be transmitted through ordination by one possessing authority from God (see Chapter 4).	Hebrews 5:4 (see also Exodus 28:1 and 40:13–15, Matthew 10, Acts 1:21–26)
God's people should perform ordinances, such as baptism, on behalf of those who died without receiving the ordinances (see Chapter 7).	1 Corinthians 15:29
The Church possesses God's priesthood authority to seal families together for eternity (see Chapters 5 and 7).	Matthew 16:19
After Christ's death, his full gospel was absent from the earth for a long time (see Chapter 4).	Amos 8:11–12, Matthew 24:9–12, John 16:1–3, 2 Thessalonians 2:3–4, and 2 Peter 2:1

Why do Latter-day Saints stick with the old-fashioned King James Version, even though so many more-accessible Bible versions are available? The main reason is that the KJV is the Bible version that founding prophet Joseph Smith used, as did most people in his time. Many of Joseph's revelations and translations appearing in the other standard works dovetail with KJV passages and style. All the Mormon prophets since Joseph Smith have used the KJV, and apparently, no modern versions have impressed Mormon authorities enough to switch.

Not enough by itself

Although Latter-day Saints are traditional in sticking with the KJV, they're radical in accepting additional scriptures beyond the Bible. Complaining about this element of Mormonism, many mainstream Christians quote the following passage from Revelation: "For I testify unto every man that heareth the words of the prophecy of this book, If any man shall add unto these things, God shall add unto him the plagues that are written in this book" (22:18). Latter-day Saints point out that John was talking only about the *book of Revelation*, not the whole *Bible*, which hadn't yet been compiled. And he was talking about humans adding to God's word, not God revealing new and additional information. Latter-day Saints also point out that a similar warning appears in Deuteronomy 4:2, but no one argues that the Bible should stop at that point.

SCRIPTURE

In fact, one of the Book of Mormon's most pointed passages concerns attitudes regarding the Bible. The prophet Nephi predicted that "many of the Gentiles shall say: A Bible! A Bible! We have got a Bible, and there cannot be any more Bible." To which the Lord replies: "Because that ye have a Bible ye need not suppose that it contains all my words; neither need ye suppose that I have not caused more to be written" (2 Nephi 29:3,10) — in other words, the Bible isn't God's final word, and exhibit A is, of course, the Book of Mormon itself.

Joseph Smith's corrections to the Bible

With so many people having translated — by traditional means, not like Joseph Smith — and rewritten the Bible over the centuries, Latter-day Saints believe that inaccuracies and omissions have crept into it. Joseph Smith said, "I believe the Bible as it read when it came from the pen of the original writers. Ignorant translators, careless transcribers, or designing and corrupt priests have committed many errors." Even though Joseph didn't possess the original Bible manuscripts, Latter-day Saints believe he could identify biblical trouble spots through God's inspiration.

In the Mormon view, many of the Bible's skewed or missing teachings have been amended or restored by other scriptural records, particularly the Book of Mormon. In addition, Joseph Smith received a divine commission to make a "new translation" of the King James Version itself. (Remember, for Latter-day Saints the concept of *translation* carries a different meaning when applied to Joseph Smith: He prophetically received text from God, instead of using scholarly skills to rewrite original non-English text into English.)

In carrying out this project, Joseph worked on more than 3,400 individual verses, sometimes tweaking just a few words and other times adding whole new chapters. This translation contains too many significant changes and nuances to summarize in this book, but see Table 9-2 for a few representative tidbits.

TABLE 9-2   **A Sampling of Joseph Smith's Bible Revisions**

Original KJV Passage	Joseph Smith's Revised Passage (Differences Noted in Italics)
In the time of Noah, "It repented the Lord that he had made man on the earth, and it grieved him at his heart" (Genesis 6:6).	"It repented *Noah, and his heart was pained,* that *the Lord* had made man on the earth."
When 12-year-old Jesus taught in the temple, he was "sitting in the midst of the doctors, both hearing them, and asking them questions" (Luke 2:46).	"*. . . they were* hearing *him,* and asking *him* questions."
"Jesus was led up of the Spirit, into the wilderness, to be tempted of the devil. And when he had fasted forty days and forty nights, he was afterward an hungred" (Matthew 4:1–2).	"Jesus was led up of the Spirit, into the wilderness, to be *with God.* And when he had fasted forty days and forty nights, *and had communed with God,* he was afterwards an hungred, *and was left to be tempted of the devil.*"
Regarding the performance of baptisms, "Jesus himself baptized not, but his disciples" (John 4:2).	"*He* himself baptized not *so many as* his disciples; *for he suffered them for an example, preferring one another.*"
Paul wrote, "It is a shame for women to speak in the church" (1 Corinthians 14:35).	"It is a shame for women to *rule* in the church."

So, where are Joseph's corrections?

After Joseph's 1844 martyrdom, his widow Emma gave his unpublished Bible manuscript to the Reorganized Church of Jesus Christ of Latter Day Saints (RLDS), which is known today as the Community of Christ (see Chapter 12). This denomination has published several editions of the Bible that reflect Joseph's translations, but the LDS church never has. However, the LDS church has inserted large portions of the *Joseph Smith Translation,* as Latter-day Saints call it — or *JST* for short — in various locations inside the LDS scriptures, including footnotes throughout the Old and New Testaments, a 17-page appendix to the Bible, and two books within the Pearl of Great Price (which we discuss in greater detail in Chapter 10).

Confused yet? So are many Latter-day Saints, many of whom rarely encounter the JST directly, at least in the somewhat inconvenient Bible footnotes and appendix. One has to ask, "Why doesn't the LDS church just go ahead and publish an edition of the Bible that fully incorporates Joseph Smith's corrections?" Perhaps one answer lies in the area of missionary work. In sharing the Mormon gospel, missionaries make connections with other Christians through the Bible. If the missionaries used a version of the Bible rewritten by Joseph Smith, mainstream Christians would be quicker to dismiss it.

REMEMBER

Although the JST provides many doctrinal insights and clarifications, one of its most valuable roles was immersing Joseph Smith more deeply in the Bible. As he studied and translated it, he asked many questions of God, which led to new revelations, several of which are recorded in the Doctrine and Covenants (see Chapter 10).

Getting Acquainted with the Book of Mormon

The Book of Mormon isn't just a simple batch of sermons or a book of prophetic sayings. The volume is a family saga that stretches over more than 1,000 years of history (roughly 600 B.C. to A.D. 421) and mixes visions, religious symbolism, and prophecies about the Messiah with records of migrations, civil wars, and the difficulties of governing a remote New World society. This book is long — it has about 270,000 words — with a complex, involved story. It features 15 parts, generally called *books*, and these parts are divided into chapters and verses, much like the Bible. The parts are in chronological order except for the 14th part, called the Book of Ether, which covers events that happened *before* the rest of the Book of Mormon.

Hitting the highlights

The Book of Mormon has the feel of a Cecil B. DeMille production from the 1950s, complete with an enormous cast of extras and pumped-up manly men. (Not surprising, considering that Arnold Friberg, one of the chief artists for missionary editions of the Book of Mormon, was also the costume designer and assistant art director for DeMille's classic movie *The Ten Commandments*.) The bulk of the Book of Mormon takes up the centuries-long civil war between the sometimes-righteous Nephites and their often-rebellious cousins, the Lamanites, a war of smoldering hatred that eventually spells doom for the Nephites. One of the key points to remember is that all the good guys die by the end of the book, mostly violently. Table 9-3 highlights a basic timeline of the book's happenings.

TABLE 9-3   ## A Beginner's Book of Mormon Timeline

Approximate Year	Event	Book of Mormon Reference
600 B.C.	Warned of Jerusalem's impending destruction, the prophet Lehi and his family flee into the wilderness.	1 Nephi 1–7
590 B.C.	Lehi's family builds a ship and sails to the Americas (exact location unknown), where they form a new society.	1 Nephi 18–19
580–150 B.C.	After Lehi's death, his sons split into two factions. The Nephites (descendants of the prophet Nephi) are usually righteous, but their pride occasionally leads them away from God. The Lamanites (descendants of Nephi's rebellious older brothers) are generally barbaric, but some convert to the true religion.	2 Nephi 1–5, books of 2 Nephi, Jacob, Omni, and Mosiah
100 B.C.	Alma the Younger, one of the great prophets of the Book of Mormon, is converted and preaches to the Lamanites for 14 years.	Mosiah 27–28
92 B.C.	The prophet Mosiah translates the records of a separate Israelite civilization that lived earlier in the Western Hemisphere. This relatively short account appears as the Book of Ether, near the end of the Book of Mormon.	Mosiah 21 and 28; Ether
90–1 B.C.	More wars and political treachery, with one of the most inspiring victories won by a Nephite army of 2,000 righteous young men.	Alma 53–62
6 B.C.	Samuel, a righteous Lamanite, prophesies to the Nephites about signs that will attend the coming birth of Christ.	Helaman 13–15
A.D. 1	People in the Americas experience a night with no darkness and see a new star in the sky, as Samuel had predicted, so the Nephites know that Christ has been born.	3 Nephi 1

(continued)

TABLE 9-3 (continued)

Approximate Year	Event	Book of Mormon Reference
34	After the Nephite society has almost disintegrated due to wickedness, great calamities visit the earth upon Christ's death and destroy the unrighteous people. Then the resurrected Savior appears and teaches the gospel to about 2,500 survivors.	3 Nephi 8–28
35–231	All the people live together in righteous harmony and hold property in common.	4 Nephi 1
231–380	War resumes between the Nephites and the Lamanites. As the Nephites drift away from God, the Lamanites gradually get the upper hand.	Mormon 1–5
380–385	The Lamanites launch a devastating attack and wipe out the Nephites, who have become "ripened in iniquity."	Mormon 6
421	Moroni, the lone Nephite survivor, buries the 1,000-year record that he and his father Mormon compiled, abridged, and supplemented with their own writings.	Moroni
1823–1830	Moroni, now a resurrected angel, teaches Joseph Smith about the buried record, which Smith eventually retrieves, translates, and publishes.	Joseph Smith History 1:27–54 (in the Pearl of Great Price)

What a long, strange trip: Lehi's journey to the New World

The Book of Mormon opens with the record of an Israelite man named Lehi who lived around 600 B.C. Lehi had a vision that foretold the destruction of Jerusalem (which actually happened around 587 B.C., when Babylonian invaders destroyed the temple there), so he started urging people to leave the city while they still had time. As you can imagine, most people thought Lehi was a nutcase. They didn't want to follow his counsel and began to threaten his life, so Lehi obeyed a directive from the Lord to gather his family together and escape. The family was fairly wealthy, and several family members were reluctant to leave their comfortable home and social position in Jerusalem. Lehi's oldest sons, Laman and Lemuel, openly rebelled.

The son who obeyed without quibbling was Nephi, a righteous young man who prayed to God for his own confirmation of the spiritual vision his father received. He got that confirmation and more, so he threw himself into his father's work. After several unpleasant years of wandering in the wilderness (probably the

Arabian Desert), Nephi and other members of the family constructed a boat —
according to a unique design that Nephi said he received by revelation — to take
them to what would later become known as the Americas.

The journey by sea was no picnic. Laman and Lemuel resented the fact that Nephi,
their younger brother, was their father's favorite and had taken to preaching at
them a good deal. They tried to kill him several times, both en route and after
arriving in the New World. (We don't know exactly where they lived, though some
individual Latter-day Saints have identified Central America as a likely place. See
Chapter 15 for more on Book of Mormon controversies.) Nephi was brokenhearted
about his brothers' treachery, resulting in the "Psalm of Nephi," an achingly honest plea Nephi makes to God in 2 Nephi 4. Although he was sick about it, Nephi
knew that he had to separate his followers from his wicked brothers and try to
build a just society on his own.

Can't we all just get along? The Nephites and the Lamanites

The majority of the Book of Mormon is taken up with the plots and perils of the
Nephites (including the descendants of Nephi) and the *Lamanites* (including the
descendants of Laman and Lemuel, who sometimes devolved into savagery
because of their wickedness). The Lamanites outnumber the Nephites throughout
the Book of Mormon, causing some scholars to think that they intermarried with
natives already in the Americas.

Although good and evil may seem cut and dried in the Book of Mormon, with the
Nephites always righteous and the Lamanites always sinful, the plot just isn't that
simple. At numerous times, they switch roles. Dramatizing one of history's worst
cases of *Groundhog Day*, the Book of Mormon tells about the same chain of events —
some Mormons call it "the pride cycle" — happening over and over again to the
Nephites throughout the centuries:

>> The Nephites love God and take care of their neighbors.

>> Because of this righteousness, they prosper.

>> They get obsessed with their own wealth, loving money and becoming corrupt
   and immoral.

>> The Lord somehow humbles them, often by allowing the Lamanites to defeat
   them in battle or bring them into submission via slavery or heavy taxes.

> » When the Nephites are humble again and repent of their sins, they resume doing what the Lord wants them to do: Worship him and deal justly with one another.

> » Sadly, before long, the whole pride-prosperity-greed-war-repentance cycle starts again with a vengeance.

Throughout Nephite history, numerous missionaries risk their lives to preach the gospel to their own people and to the Lamanites, with some success. At one point, the Lamanite king converts, and many of his people follow suit.

Having been saved from their sins, the Lamanite converts decide to bury their swords rather than risk murdering again. In battle, they fall face down before their fellow Lamanites who've come to kill them for adopting the Nephite religion. The result is a horrific massacre, but the sight of so many Lamanites going willingly to the slaughter makes such a deep spiritual impact that some of their countrymen also convert.

Despite occasional alliances or truces between the Nephites and Lamanites, no real or lasting peace exists between them until Christ comes.

The crowning event: Christ's appearance

SCRIPTURE

The Book of Mormon is a very consciously Christ-centered book, featuring prophets hundreds of years before Jesus's birth who look forward to the event and declare Jesus Christ as the Messiah by name. For example, 600 years before Christ came, Nephi wrote, "And we talk of Christ, we rejoice in Christ, we preach of Christ, we prophesy of Christ, and we write according to our prophecies, that our children may know to what source they may look for a remission of their sins" (2 Nephi 25:26). In other words, Christ is the hero of the Book of Mormon, the one to whom all the people through the ages look for atonement for their sins. (For more on the Mormon concept of atonement, see Chapter 3.)

REMEMBER

The Book of Mormon teaches that Christ visited the Nephites after his resurrection and before he ascended into heaven, preaching among them, healing their sick, and calling 12 Western Hemisphere disciples (or apostles). The LDS church considers Jesus' visit to the Nephites as the "crowning event" of the Book of Mormon. But much more happens in the 400 years or so after this visit, including the final destruction of the Nephites. Mormons consider this climactic event as a warning to modern-day inhabitants of the Americas about what can go wrong when societies turn away from God.

Some anti-Mormons claim that the fact that Jesus's teachings in the Book of Mormon are so similar to those in the New Testament proves that Joseph Smith wrote the Book of Mormon himself, copying key passages from the Bible to supplement his own story. Latter-day Saints counter that it makes perfect sense that Christ's teachings in Jerusalem would be the same as those in the Americas and elsewhere, because the core of the gospel is the same in all times and places. They see the Book of Mormon account as a second witness of these key teachings, fulfilling the Bible's promise that "in the mouth of two or three witnesses every word may be established" (Matthew 18:16).

Among the familiar teachings of Christ in the Book of Mormon, you'll find

>> The Lord's Prayer ("Our Father, who art in heaven . . .")

>> Teachings on faith, repentance, baptism, and the Holy Ghost

>> The Beatitudes ("Blessed are the poor," and so on)

>> Discussion of the last days and the restoration of Israel

Near the end of his visit to the Nephites, Christ promises 9 of his 12 disciples that they'll be with him in his kingdom immediately after they die. He allows the three other disciples, however, to remain on earth as long as they desire, establishing the gospel and helping God's people. As far as Latter-day Saints know, they're still ministering on the earth today. These immortal fellows are called the *three Nephites*, and they occupy a delightful place in Mormon folklore. Through the years, Latter-day Saints have told stories around the campfire about possible sightings of one or more of the three Nephites, who've reportedly helped people in danger, plowed fields when a person was too sick to do it, and even changed a car tire when someone got a flat while on a mission of mercy.

Biting the dust: The end of the Nephites

After Christ's brief visit to the New World, the people put aside their old divisions, including the terms *Nephite* and *Lamanite*. Now sharing the same religion, they founded a church based on the principles Christ taught them. They held their wealth in common, so no one was rich or poor. They healed the sick and worked mighty miracles. The Book of Mormon reports that during this peaceful time, crime and conflict didn't exist, and the people were united in love.

As in any tragedy worth its salt, the peace, love, and understanding couldn't possibly last. About 200 years after Christ's visit, this utopian society gave in to the same old story: The people prospered and then became full of pride. Class divisions between rich and poor again became a big problem. False religions arose, their leaders persecuted the Church, and the old lines between Nephite and Lamanite were redrawn in the sand. War became inevitable.

As the situation worsened, the Lamanites began to slaughter any Nephite who wouldn't deny Jesus Christ. Most of the Nephites, in turn, became as wicked as the Lamanites or even more so. Seeing that their end was near, two faithful Nephite prophets named Mormon and his son Moroni set about creating a condensed *Reader's Digest* version of their people's records from Lehi on down, also adding some of their own words of wisdom. In addition, they included a historical summary of an earlier civilization called the *Jaredites*, some Israelites who'd journeyed to the New World hundreds of years before Lehi and his family.

Mormon and Moroni engraved their abridgment onto golden tablets — which Latter-day Saints commonly call *plates* — and Moroni buried them in the ground for safekeeping, until that day some 1,400 years later when the time would be right to make them known to the world. Because Mormon did most of the editorial work on the book, it was named the Book of Mormon. Moroni did some of the writing and abridging too, but his reward was to serve as the angel who helped Joseph Smith discover the record.

ABINADI? RAMEUMPTOM? A BOOK OF MORMON PRONUNCIATION GUIDE

Newcomers to the Book of Mormon often trip and stumble over the funkier names in the book. Heck, even lifers sometimes get tongue-tied at such monikers as Irreantum, Ammonihahite, and our personal favorite, Gidgiddonah. That last one makes us downright giddy.

Here are three basic tips to make your reading a bit less challenging:

- If it ends in the letter *i*, you typically pronounce it as a long vowel. Abinadi is pronounced uh-*bin*-uh-dye; Moroni (the angel you see atop most Mormon temples) is pronounced moh-*roh*-nye. (If you say something that sounds like *moron* here, you're on the wrong track.) Nephi, one of the principal figures in the Book of Mormon, is pronounced *nee*-fye.

- The next-to-last syllable is often (but not always) the one that you accent. Limhi is *lim*-hye; Moriantum is mor-ee-*an*-tum. However, in plenty of circumstances this rule isn't true, so your best bet is in the next bullet.

- Check out the one-stop-shopping pronunciation guide at the end of the Book of Mormon. However, this guide doesn't appear in some non-English editions, so Spanish-speaking Latter-day Saints, for example, pronounce Nephi as *neff*-ee.

How the Book of Mormon Came to Be

When Latter-day Saints give their testimonies at fast and testimony meeting on the first Sunday of the month (see Chapter 6), they frequently mention that they know the Book of Mormon is true. What they generally mean by this claim isn't simply that the *teachings* of the book are true but that it came into being the way Joseph Smith claimed: by a miracle.

In this section, you find out how the Book of Mormon appeared — it didn't exactly fall from the sky, but it was a pretty astonishing event — and what it teaches about sin, repentance, family, and social justice.

An angel in the night

Joseph Smith, as we discuss in Chapter 4, had his first major spiritual experience when he was a young teen. This event, known as the *First Vision* to Latter-day Saints, was a direct answer to Joseph's prayer about which church to join. That incident opened the floodgates of Joseph's prophetic calling.

The second major event happened in September 1823, and again it was the direct result of prayer. Seventeen-year-old Joseph was praying for forgiveness of his sins (which apparently included *levity*, or lightheartedness) when a glorious being appeared in his room. The man was dressed in a loose white robe, and his feet didn't touch the floor. His whole body seemed to be luminous, almost glowing white. He called Joseph by name and said that he was named Moroni, sent from God to tell Joseph about the work he was called to do.

As you see in the earlier section "Getting Acquainted with the Book of Mormon," Moroni wasn't just a glow-in-the-dark angelic messenger but a resurrected inhabitant of the Americas who, as a mortal, helped edit and write the ancient record that became the Book of Mormon. Hovering there in Joseph's bedroom, Moroni discussed the set of golden plates that he had buried in the ground some 1,400 years earlier and told Joseph how to find it. He also gave Joseph directions for using the *Urim and Thummim*, a biblical device that helped him translate this ancient record. In addition, Moroni instructed Joseph in biblical prophecy.

One of the most unusual features of this story — as if it weren't odd enough! — is that just after Moroni finished his little speech and zoomed back into heaven, leaving Joseph in bed to wonder about it all, the angel reappeared and proceeded to tell Joseph the same information again. And then he came a third time, repeating exactly the same stuff and adding a caution that Satan might try to tempt

Joseph to get rich from the Book of Mormon plates, given the poverty of the Smith family. (No, Joseph probably didn't get a very good sleep that night.)

The next day, Joseph found the golden plates buried on the hillside where Moroni had indicated, but the angel wouldn't let him remove them yet. Every September 23 for the next four years, Joseph went to the same spot for instruction. From Joseph's own account, Moroni seems to have been pretty severe with him, repeatedly lecturing him about not losing the plates and not making a profit from them. Finally, in September 1827, Joseph was allowed to take the plates and figure out how to translate them.

Seer stones and scribes: Translating the golden plates

Because word leaked out about the golden plates and many people wanted to see and handle them — something the Lord had forbidden except in special circumstances — Joseph temporarily moved to Pennsylvania with his new wife, Emma. There, with the assistance of several scribes, the translation went forward in earnest during 1829. (See Figure 9-1 for an illustration of what the plates may have looked like.)

FIGURE 9-1:
An artist's rendition of what the golden plates may have looked like.

Eyewitnesses to the translation process reported that Joseph dictated the Book of Mormon while looking at a seer stone in his hat, which blocked the light so he could see each character as it appeared on the seer stone. The plates themselves weren't even always necessary to the translation, as they were usually still covered by a cloth.

Latter-day Saints believe that the Lord gave Joseph the translation by revelation, which explains why no one revised or rewrote this complicated narrative during the translation process. When Joseph or his scribe needed a break, they resumed work precisely where they left off, because Joseph didn't need to look at the previous dictation to refresh his memory or remind himself where they were. He simply picked up where they stopped before the interruption.

After the long wait to get the plates, the actual translation took only three months. With this 588-page book, Joseph made an impressive achievement, one that Latter-day Saints believe couldn't have happened by human means. The book displays remarkable self-consistency, especially considering that Joseph wasn't referring back to the English longhand dictation during the process. If the book were of his own creation, Latter-day Saints note, he would've had to remember hundreds of character and place names, master a dizzying timeline, be familiar with the history and geography of the ancient Middle East and Nephite lands, and be able to write in many different voices.

"You believe what?!" Reactions to the book

In the spring of 1830, 5,000 copies of the Book of Mormon were printed in Palmyra, New York, and missionaries started selling them to the public. However, as with many self-published books, this one wasn't an overnight sensation. (Joseph and his printer may have the last laugh, though: Today, a first edition of the Book of Mormon in fine condition can top $100,000.)

CONTROVERSY

As news spread throughout New York State of the "golden Bible" that Joseph Smith had translated, reactions were mixed. Polarized, even. Some professed an immediate recognition that the book was of divine origin. (You can read about Brigham Young's initial reaction in Chapter 12, for example.) Others were horrified that anyone would dare add to the Bible and attempted to discredit both the book and Joseph Smith, the man they presumed had written it. They came up with many different explanations for how the book came into existence: It was the product of Smith's fertile imagination, or Smith plagiarized it from someone else. (For more on some current controversies regarding the Book of Mormon, see Chapter 15.)

What happened to the plates?

According to Joseph Smith, shortly after the translation was finished, he gave the plates back to the angel Moroni. Skeptics see this claim as a convenient excuse for why the LDS church can't produce the plates or submit them to scientific inquiry. Certainly, the skeptics have a good point. The plates are no longer available, so all we have is Joseph Smith's word on the matter.

Or is it? In the opening pages of every edition of the Book of Mormon, you see the testimony of 11 different witnesses who claimed that they saw the plates and believed Smith had translated them by the gift and power of God. Although several of the key witnesses later left the Church over personal or institutional disagreements, they never denied their belief that Smith translated the Book of Mormon from the plates by divine inspiration.

Interestingly, Joseph translated only a portion of the plates, and not everything he translated got published. He couldn't access the majority of the plates because metal bands kept them locked tight, but Latter-day Saints believe that this sealed portion will one day be translated and published if Moroni would be so kind as to return the plates. In addition, Joseph loaned the first 116 pages of his translation of the manuscript to the Book of Mormon's chief financer, Martin Harris, who lost them. This episode was one of Joseph's most difficult learning experiences as a prophet, and he said the Lord wouldn't allow him to retranslate those pages.

The Book of Mormon in Mormon Life

Mormon missionaries today are instantly recognizable by their appearance (see Chapter 14), but also because they offer a unique product: the Book of Mormon. This dark-blue book with distinctive gold lettering has become a familiar sight around the world. As of December 2023, 200 million copies have been printed, and the book is now available in 113 languages (92 full translations and 21 partial).

Non-Mormons sometimes have a difficult time understanding the tremendous love and respect that Latter-day Saints have for this book. To some outsiders, it reads like a string of "and-it-came-to-pass" segments with a few exciting battle scenes thrown in. To Latter-day Saints, the book is a guide to life, a story about righteousness and courage against overwhelming odds. The Church subtitles the Book of Mormon as "Another Testament of Jesus Christ." Like the Bible, the Book of Mormon is a witness of Christ and his atonement for all people.

Latter-day Saints look to the Book of Mormon for some distinctly Mormon teachings, such as the spiritual innocence of children, who don't need to be baptized until age 8. However, the bulk of its messages are similar to those you find in the Bible, if slightly more detailed in some cases. Many people are surprised to discover that some of Mormonism's most distinctive teachings, such as the premortal existence (see Chapter 2), eternal marriage (see Chapter 7), and humanity's potential to become like God (see Chapter 2), don't really even crop up in the Book of Mormon. (In fact, the book specifically condemns polygamy, because God didn't command it for those people at that time like he did for the 19th-century Latter-day Saints, as we discuss in Chapter 13.)

Avoiding the sin of pride

As you see in the section "Can't we all just get along? The Nephites and the Lamanites," pride is the source of most of the heartache in the Book of Mormon. (You know the people are in trouble every time the text says they started wearing "costly apparel." It's all downhill from there.) Pride is the most destructive force in Nephite society, a cancer that consumes the culture from the inside. At the end of the book, the prophet Moroni concludes unhappily that pride was the root of his people's destruction.

Because Latter-day Saints believe that the Book of Mormon was custom edited to suit the needs of 19th-century readers and later, this constant harping on the sin of pride raises an obvious question about the modern era: Will pride be the Latter-day Saints' downfall, too? In 1989, LDS prophet Ezra Taft Benson warned of pride being the Church's "great stumbling block" and admonished the Latter-day Saints to become humbler and more teachable. This warning is one of the modern Church's most famous talks, and people still quote it in LDS meetings.

Taking care of the poor

Along with pride, another major cautionary theme in the Book of Mormon is the failure of the proud Nephites to care for the poor among them. In the Book of Mormon, the quest for a just society included the goal to have no poor and to share their wealth, as the people did during the 200-year golden age that followed the Savior's visit.

Repeatedly throughout the Book of Mormon, prophets urge the people to

» Feed the hungry

» Visit the sick

» Clothe the naked

The Book of Mormon prophet Alma, for example, encourages people to "impart their substance" to each other.

Teaching the children

The Book of Mormon pays a lot of subtle attention to teaching children right from wrong and showing the essence of true religion. You see numerous examples of righteous parents who raise wayward kids — Lehi worrying over Laman and Lemuel, or Alma coping with his rebellious son Corianton, who gets a stern lecture on sexual immorality. In the Book of Mormon as in Mormon life today, children can exercise their *agency* (free will; see Chapter 2) and choose to reject godly teachings, much to the sorrow of those who try to teach them the correct way. However, you also see cases of children (almost exclusively sons, unfortunately, because the Book of Mormon mentions only a handful of women by name) who follow their parents' righteous examples.

SCRIPTURE

Mosiah 4:14 encourages parents to "teach them to walk in the ways of truth and soberness . . . teach them to love one another, and to serve one another." Mormon parents take such admonitions very seriously. (For more on the importance of the family in Mormonism, see Chapter 5.)

Repenting of sins and receiving forgiveness

Another recurring theme in the Book of Mormon is repentance. In fact, one of the *antichrists* (false teachers) who appears in the book is so dastardly and dangerous precisely because he teaches that repentance is unnecessary. The Book of Mormon makes it clear that repentance is absolutely crucial — the Savior's followers must feel a clear sorrow for sin and develop the desire to never repeat it. (For more on repentance, see the section on baptism in Chapter 6.)

SCRIPTURE

Prophets in the Book of Mormon speak often about how, through repentance, all people can receive forgiveness for their sins through Christ's Atonement. "It is expedient that there should be . . . an infinite and eternal sacrifice," Amulek taught in Alma 34. "There can be nothing which is short of an infinite atonement which will suffice for the sins of the world." (For more on the Savior's Atonement, see Chapter 3.)

Finding answers to spiritual questions

Table 9-4 lists some of the spiritual questions for which people can find answers as they read and study the Book of Mormon.

TABLE 9-4   ## Spiritual Questions Answered by the Book of Mormon

Question	Answer
Do babies need to be baptized?	No. According to Moroni 8:22, little children are "alive in Christ" and don't sin. (Any parent of a strong-willed toddler may disagree, of course.)
What happens to my body after I die?	Good news. At their appointed time of resurrection, all people will be restored to perfection, with bodies and spirits reunited (Alma 40:23).
What's the purpose of my life?	To attain eternal joy, plain and simple (see 2 Nephi 2:25). Also, life is "a probationary state; a time to prepare to meet God; a time to prepare for that endless state . . . after the resurrection of the dead" (Alma 12:24).
How can I be happy?	By obeying God's commandments. "If there be no righteousness, there be no happiness" (2 Nephi 2:13). Even more pointedly, "wickedness never was happiness" (Alma 41:10).
Do I have free will, or is everything predestined?	God gives people free will — generally called *agency* — and permits them to choose and act for themselves (Helaman 14:30–31).
How can my desire to believe be transformed into faith and eventually knowledge?	By experimenting on God's word through putting it into practice and observing its effects on our spiritual feelings (Alma 32).

Chapter **10**

Mormonism's Other Scriptures

I n addition to the Bible and the Book of Mormon, Latter-day Saints recognize two more books of scripture: the *Doctrine and Covenants (D&C)* and *Pearl of Great Price,* which we discuss in this chapter. Together, these four books of scripture are called the *standard works,* and the LDS church publishes an official edition with all four standard works cross-referenced in one fat volume or two paired volumes. The Church provides these scriptures through its Gospel Library app, but some Latter-day Saints still lug dead-tree scriptures to church each Sunday, often zippered inside a protective carrier. (For more about why and how Latter-day Saints study the scriptures, see Chapter 17.)

If the Bible is the spiritual history of God's people in the Middle East until shortly after the time of Christ, and the Book of Mormon is the spiritual history of God's people living in the Western Hemisphere from about 600 B.C. to A.D. 400, then you can consider the Doctrine and Covenants to be the spiritual history of God's people — er, the Latter-day Saints — living in modern times from about 1830 onward, though nearly all of the D&C's revelations occurred in America during the earliest days of the Church. And the Pearl of Great Price is a grab bag of scriptural odds and ends, both ancient and modern.

A Scriptural Hodgepodge: The Pearl of Great Price

Although the Pearl of Great Price contains much essential doctrine, it also sometimes seems like the stepchild among Mormon scriptures for several reasons:

» At only about 60 pages, this text is considerably shorter than the other three Mormon standard works.

» The book is a jumble of several different eras and writing styles.

» It creates more than its fair share of ongoing controversy, especially with regard to some of the material's origins (see Chapter 15 for more on that).

» This scripture is the only one of the four standard works that Church members don't study for a full year in the four-year teaching cycle, which goes through the Old Testament, New Testament, Book of Mormon, and Doctrine and Covenants. However, teachers touch upon aspects of the Pearl of Great Price in various classes.

» Its pages include three funky, Egyptian-looking facsimiles (more on those pictures later in this section).

SCRIPTURE

This book of scripture takes its name from a New Testament passage: "A merchant man, seeking goodly pearls . . . when he had found one pearl of great price, went and sold all that he had, and bought it" (Matthew 13:45–46). The Pearl of Great Price began as a collection of scripture published in England in 1851 by a Mormon apostle, but the Church didn't canonize it as a standard work until 1880. Over the decades, several components have been added or removed, such as in 1979, when Church authorities moved a couple of modern revelations into the Doctrine and Covenants, where all such other revelations were already collected (yes, scriptural change moves at a glacial pace).

Revisiting Moses

As we discuss in Chapter 9, Mormonism's founding prophet Joseph Smith received a divine commission to make a new translation of the Bible's King James Version (KJV). Pondering Genesis, which Latter-day Saints believe Moses wrote, Joseph wrote an inspired expansion of certain sections, parts of which now appear as "Selections from the Book of Moses" in the Pearl of Great Price.

The eight-chapter book of Moses covers the following territory:

» **Details of a vision that Moses experienced but didn't discuss anywhere in his biblical writings:** During this vision, which happened after the burning bush incident but before the parting of the Red Sea, Moses is transported to "an exceedingly high mountain," where he meets the premortal Jesus Christ, who was then a spirit personage known as Jehovah, and learns more about the nature of God (for more on the Mormon concept of God, see Chapter 3). In addition, Moses encounters Satan and learns more about the devil's goals, motivations, and methods (for more on the devil, see Chapter 2).

» **A recounting of the earth's creation and Adam and Eve's experience, with more particulars than the Genesis account:** For instance, Latter-day Saints learn from these chapters that God first created everything spiritually before creating it physically. (When Latter-day Saints use the word *create*, they generally mean "form" or "organize," because they believe all spiritual and physical matter is eternal, not created.) In addition, these chapters touch on many aspects of God's plan of salvation and the uniquely positive Mormon outlook regarding the role of Adam and Eve (for more on these topics, see Chapter 2).

» **New perspective on Adam's children and descendants:** Although Genesis only briefly mentions the prophet Enoch, the book of Moses provides several pages worth of Enoch's experiences and prophecies, which play an important role in Mormon doctrine, including what will happen in connection with the Savior's Second Coming (for more on that topic, see Chapter 3). According to this section, Enoch led his people in such great righteousness that their entire city was taken up into heaven. This part also includes some additional chilling detail about Adam's bad seed, Cain.

Mummy dearest: Uncovering the writings of Abraham

In 1835, a traveling exhibit of Egyptian mummies and papyri passed through Kirtland, Ohio, where Joseph Smith was then living (see Chapter 11). After the Church purchased the papyri (in a package deal that included the mummies too), Joseph concluded that one papyrus contained writings of the Old Testament prophet Abraham, who lived about 2,000 years before Christ.

CONTROVERSY

In the mid-1960s, a University of Utah professor discovered portions of Joseph Smith's Egyptian papyri in New York City's Metropolitan Museum of Art. Experts dated them as originating between 100 B.C. and A.D. 100, and translators found no resemblance to Joseph Smith's claimed translation. However, defenders point out that the papyri found in the museum may not have included the one containing Abraham's writings. Whatever the case, most Latter-day Saints continue exercising faith that divine revelation played a role in Joseph's translation of this document. (See Chapter 15 for more on this controversy.)

The five-chapter Book of Abraham covers the following territory:

>> **The skinny on Abraham's origins and experiences:** The early chapters go into greater detail than the Bible, including Abraham's ordination to the priesthood and his narrow escape from being sacrificed to pagan gods.

>> **The Abrahamic covenant:** This covenant includes God's guarantee of a Promised Land, numberless descendants, priesthood authority, and eternal exaltation. Latter-day Saints believe that anyone can enter into Abraham's covenant by joining the LDS church, which Latter-day Saints view as the modern continuation of the same faith that Abraham practiced. (For more on why God's covenant with Abraham is important to Latter-day Saints, see Chapter 5.)

>> **Details about sacred astronomy, an account of humankind's premortal existence, and a description of the earth's creation:** Abraham taught that the earth was formed from existing materials, not created out of nothing. (This scripture is one of the main reasons why Latter-day Saints reject the common Christian notion of creation out of nothing.) In addition, he calls the creative steps *times* rather than *days,* suggesting that the earth's creation took longer than six earthly days.

>> **Three distinctively Egyptian images:** In 1842, Joseph Smith asked one of his followers to make woodcuts of some drawings from the papyri so he could print these images along with the translation. The pictures depict symbolic figures allegedly related to Abraham's experiences and his understanding of astronomy as discussed in the text, and it's not entirely clear to most Latter-day Saints why Joseph included these images. Still, during long meetings it's fun to puzzle over these *facsimiles,* as they're called.

Expanding Matthew

During Joseph Smith's prophetic revision — Latter-day Saints call it *retranslation* — of the KJV Bible (see Chapter 9), he made a particularly large number of changes to Matthew 24. This revised chapter now appears in the Pearl of Great Price as "Joseph Smith — Matthew." The original KJV chapter contains 1,050 words, but Joseph's version contains about 1,500 words.

In Matthew 24, the Savior gives several prophecies about two future times of trouble and destruction, including what would happen to Jerusalem soon after his death and what would happen before his Second Coming. As the KJV presents them, the chronology of these prophecies is hard to understand. Joseph's translation clarifies Jesus's distinction between the two time periods, which are separated by at least a couple thousand years.

Chronicling Joseph Smith

While the first two sections in the Pearl of Great Price are from Old Testament times, and the third section is from the New Testament era, the fourth section is an autobiographical account of Joseph Smith's early experiences as a prophet, which was first published in 1838. It covers events that occurred during the decade between 1820 and 1830. Titled "Joseph Smith — History," this part relates the following:

SCRIPTURE

>> **Religious upheaval:** In upstate New York during Joseph's boyhood, many churches were vying for members. Joseph writes that he felt it was vitally important to choose the right one.

>> **Joseph's First Vision:** A Bible verse informed Joseph how to solve his dilemma: "If any of you lack wisdom, let him ask of God, that giveth to all men liberally, and upbraideth not; and it shall be given him" (James 1:5). In 1820, Joseph found a private grove of trees and knelt to put James's promise to the test. Heavenly Father and Jesus Christ appeared to Joseph and told him not to join any of the existing churches. (For more on the First Vision, thumb back to Chapter 4.)

>> **The visitations of Moroni:** Over the next several years, Joseph was instructed several times by a resurrected being named Moroni, who in A.D. 421 buried the golden plates from which Joseph would translate the Book of Mormon. (See Chapter 9 for more about the coming forth of the Book of Mormon.)

>> **More angelic visitors:** In 1829, after reading about baptism during the translation of the Book of Mormon, Joseph Smith and his scribe prayed to learn more. In response, the resurrected John the Baptist appeared to them, ordained them to the lower of Mormonism's two priesthoods and instructed them to baptize each other. Soon after, the resurrected apostles Peter, James, and John ordained them to the higher priesthood. (See Chapter 4 for more about the restoration of the priesthood.)

Here, Joseph's Pearl of Great Price narration ends. Within another year or so, he published the Book of Mormon and formally organized what would subsequently become named The Church of Jesus Christ of Latter-day Saints. Further revelations and events dating from later in Joseph Smith's life are partially chronicled throughout the Doctrine and Covenants, described later in this chapter.

CONTROVERSY

In writing and speaking on different occasions about his early experiences, Joseph apparently made some inconsistent statements about what happened to him and when (see Chapter 15). Anti-Mormons seize on these inconsistencies as proof that Joseph isn't a true prophet, while Church members attribute any flaws to normal human limitations of memory and communication. After all, the Bible itself contains some inconsistencies among the Gospels and gives conflicting accounts of Paul's vision on the road to Damascus.

Lining up the Articles of Faith

In 1842, two years before his martyrdom, Joseph Smith wrote a letter in response to some questions about Mormonism from a Chicago newspaper editor. Included in this letter were 13 statements of Mormon belief that later became canonized as Mormonism's Articles of Faith. This section occupies only two pages of the Pearl of Great Price, and the individual articles are often the first scriptures that Mormon children memorize.

REMEMBER

Although the Articles of Faith touch on several important aspects of Mormonism, they aren't a comprehensive summary of Mormon beliefs. For instance, they don't say anything about humankind's premortal existence, the performance of gospel ordinances for the dead, eternal marriage, or humankind's potential to become like their Heavenly Parents (for more on these topics, see Chapters 2 and 7). Rather, the Articles of Faith seem to function more as an introductory calling card to the faith, a way of establishing common ground with other Christians while also introducing a few unique Mormon beliefs.

The complete text of the Articles of Faith appears on the Cheat Sheet at the beginning of this book. Several of the points aren't that different from what you'll find in any other Christian denomination, but the following are highlights of some of the more distinctively Mormon elements:

>> Humans will be punished for their own sins, not for Adam's transgression (for more on this idea, see Chapter 2).

>> Proper priesthood authority and organization are required in God's true church (see Chapter 4).

>> Latter-day Saints believe the Bible insofar as it's "translated correctly," meaning that some parts contain errors or omissions, and they believe in additional scriptures (see Chapter 9).

>> Latter-day Saints believe that God still reveals his will to humankind through a living prophet (see Chapter 8 and the following section).

>> Latter-day Saints believe in the gathering of Israel (see Chapter 5) and that they'll build a New Jerusalem — also known as the City of Zion — before the Savior's Second Coming (see Chapters 3 and 11).

So, if the Articles of Faith aren't comprehensive, does a single source exist for an official overview of Mormon beliefs and doctrine? The Church doesn't like creeds, having rejected all historic Christian creeds, but it does publish a comprehensive manual titled *Gospel Principles.* Commonly used in Sunday-school classes for new converts, this source provides a thorough but simple overview of LDS beliefs and doctrine.

Modern-Day Revelations in the D&C

As the ninth Article of Faith makes clear, Latter-day Saints don't see the canon as closed; they believe other scriptures are yet to come. Latter-day Saints trust that Heavenly Father is still revealing, and has yet to reveal, many "great and important things pertaining to the kingdom of God."

In this sense Mormonism is a bit of a conundrum. On the one hand, Latter-day Saints claim to have a complete fullness of truth, with the restored gospel and Church organization as established by Christ himself. On the other hand, they know that God hasn't yet spoken the last word on every subject, and they remain open to new revelations through the current prophet. At a minimum, Latter-day Saints realize that the Church's structure and programs continue to evolve to meet new needs and challenges.

In this section, we look at the Doctrine and Covenants, a canonized book of Mormon scripture that contains modern revelations, mostly from the 19th century.

But wait, there's more: God's revelations to Joseph Smith and others

Every president of the LDS church is considered a *prophet, seer,* and *revelator,* which basically means that he has the spiritual authority to lead and guide the Church as God directs. Although any Church member can receive revelations pertaining to their own family, Church calling, and spiritual life, Latter-day Saints believe that the prophet is the only one who can receive revelations from God for the whole Church. (For more on the role of the LDS prophet, see Chapter 8.) Many of the Church's early revelations — and a handful of more recent prophetic statements — find their home in the Doctrine and Covenants, which Latter-day Saints affectionately call "the D&C."

Getting revelations

Almost all the revelations in the D&C came about because a prophet — usually Joseph Smith — had a question and prayed about it. The revelations are God's answers to specific questions, which is why so many of them open with the phrase "thus saith the Lord." For example, D&C 91 begins, "Verily, thus saith the Lord unto you concerning the Apocrypha." (The *Apocrypha* is the collection of ancient books that Catholics have as part of their biblical canon, but Protestants don't.) Joseph Smith was curious about the role of the Apocrypha when he retranslated portions of the Old Testament, so he asked God whether he should translate the Apocrypha, too. (Short answer: Translating it wasn't necessary, but it would be beneficial to study.)

By far, the Mormon leader who received the most revelations is Joseph Smith, the religion's founder. Poor Brigham Young has just one revelation in the entire D&C, and even that was basically how-to advice on organizing the Mormon pioneers for the trek west. (For more on that advice and Young's genius as a manager, see Chapter 12.) The other prophets represented in the D&C include John Taylor, Wilford Woodruff, Joseph F. Smith (a son of Joseph's brother Hyrum), and Spencer W. Kimball. Most Mormon prophets haven't added any revelations to the D&C, showing how rarely new scripture surfaces.

Some sections of the D&C deal with issues that are no longer applicable to most Latter-day Saints. For instance, D&C 49, which was recorded in 1831, commanded three Mormon men to go and preach the gospel to the Shakers, a celibate religious group that was popular in the 19th century. Because fewer than a dozen Shakers remain in the world today, this revelation doesn't light a fire under many Latter-day Saints in the 21st century. However, it does address some timeless spiritual issues as well as concrete historical ones, including the need for missionary work, the importance of marriage, and the Second Coming of Christ, so it remains relevant for Latter-day Saints today.

Tracing the evolution of the D&C

The D&C has gone through many different editions since the early 1830s, when the Church first published it under the title *A Book of Commandments.* Through the years, the Church has made changes to the collection's organization, removing some revelations, adding others, and combining others together. The book now contains 138 sections, plus a couple of official declarations (see "Wrapping up: Official declarations," later in this chapter).

The earliest editions contained the *Lectures on Faith,* unsigned discourses on faith that Sidney Rigdon (see Chapter 11) or Joseph Smith may have written. Although Latter-day Saints still occasionally quote from these seven lectures, they haven't been part of the D&C since 1921.

How does the Church choose which revelations to include? The First Presidency and Quorum of the Twelve Apostles make this decision, with the consent of Church members who affirm it in General Conference. However, it's unusual nowadays for changes to be made to the D&C, and it hasn't happened in more than 40 years.

TIP

If you're new to Mormon culture, you may be surprised to find that Latter-day Saints don't use the same chapter and verse system for the D&C that they do for the other standard works. Each revelation is its own *section*, which is then subdivided into verses. So, a Mormon vegetarian might draw on section 89, verse 13 of the D&C to try to persuade a meat-eating Mormon that there's a scriptural precedent for abstaining from meat. Then the meat-eater would quote section 49, verse 19, which seems pretty clear that eating meat is okay in certain circumstances.

Key LDS scriptures in the D&C

Here you take a look at some of the most significant revelations of the D&C and find the origins of some of Mormonism's most distinctive teachings.

Understanding the power of the priesthood

In D&C 121, God says that the rights of priesthood (see Chapter 4) are inseparably connected with the powers of heaven. In other words, Latter-day Saints believe that all worthy men who hold the Melchizedek Priesthood have the very power of God at their disposal. Think this power could lead to some serious abuses? Not so fast. The rest of the section details all the many ways a man can lose his heavenly priesthood power: If he's selfish, proud, controlling, ruthlessly ambitious, or unrighteous, the Spirit departs. The scripture says that if a man ever tries to lord his priesthood over someone, he's exercising "unrighteous dominion," and his priesthood power goes bye-bye.

Keeping the Mormon version of kosher

In Chapter 16, we take a thorough look at the Word of Wisdom, or the Mormon dietary laws. There, we walk you through what's allowed, what's forbidden, and what falls into a gray area. In the meantime, the basic rules to remember are as follows: no coffee, tea, alcohol, tobacco, or harmful drugs.

The whole idea of the Mormon diet comes from D&C 89, which is commonly called the *Word of Wisdom*. In 1833 Joseph Smith received this revelation when he asked God if the guys were in the clear to use tobacco in their meetings. Joseph's wife, Emma, had already made a stink about it. (She had to clean the floor afterward and didn't appreciate scrubbing up their tobacco-laden spit.) Apparently, God agreed with Emma, because the revelation clarifies that tobacco "is not for the body." What's more, it was only one of several items identified as forbidden fruit — showing that you should always be careful what you pray for. This revelation didn't become a full-fledged, rigidly enforced commandment for Latter-day Saints until nearly 100 years later.

Marrying for eternity

Several revelations in the D&C speak about marriage, which Latter-day Saints believe can be an everlasting covenant. As you discover in Chapters 5 and 7, Latter-day Saints don't want to just marry "till death do us part" but for eternity. D&C 131 and 132 speak of celestial, or eternal, marriage, which is necessary for both men and women if they want to reach the highest level of the celestial kingdom, where they can become eternal parents.

When these revelations were given in the 1840s, Mormon leaders were practicing polygamy, and section 132 explains the theological justification and biblical basis for having multiple wives. This section of the D&C is still printed in its entirety today, indicating that Mormon doctrine still includes plural marriage as an eternal principle, even though Latter-day Saints don't practice earthly polygamy anymore. (See Chapters 13 and 15 for more on that ever-fascinating topic.)

Distinguishing the three degrees of glory

D&C 88:20–32 offers a pretty comprehensive overview of the Mormon belief regarding a three-tiered heaven, with celestial, terrestrial, and telestial kingdoms. (See Chapter 2 for more on these *three degrees of glory*.) The Lord makes it clear in this revelation that the arrangement is designed so that people will wind up spending eternity in a place that's right for them.

Baptizing by immersion

Many of the revelations in the D&C concern Church organization and rituals. Joseph Smith was trying to build a new religious organization without much experience to guide him, so the fact that he often consulted the Lord with rather nit-picky questions about how he should do it isn't surprising. D&C 13 — which is only one verse long — explains that baptism is an ordinance of the Aaronic Priesthood (see Chapter 4) and immersion is the only way to go. In other words, no sprinkling allowed.

Meeting together often

D&C 20 contains important details about such things as how to conduct Church meetings and who's responsible for what in the Church. (Yes, we know it sounds boring, but now you know that Latter-day Saints aren't kidding when they say God set up every jot and tittle of the Church's organization.)

Other revelations deal with organizational matters such as General Conference (see Chapter 8) and Church disciplinary actions (see Chapter 16).

Paying an honest tithe

As we discuss in Chapter 16, Latter-day Saints are well known for donating 10 percent of their income to the Church. In D&C 119, the Lord lays down the law of tithing, which supports the Church's building efforts, missionary work, and other activities.

Understanding humanity's divine nature

Some Latter-day Saints cite section 93 as their favorite part of the D&C, because it beautifully sets forth the divine nature of the soul, discusses the relationship between being faithful and receiving wisdom from God, and promises that those who keep the commandments can find "all truth."

Living in the spirit world

The last full section of the D&C is 138, a fairly trippy and fascinating account of visions seen in October 1918 by President Joseph F. Smith, founding prophet Joseph Smith's nephew, who served as prophet from 1901 until his death in November 1918, just six weeks after the visions. He saw that Christ had spent time in the spirit world in the brief period between his crucifixion and resurrection, preaching liberty for the captive spirits. (For a crash course on the Mormon notion of the afterlife, refer to Chapter 2.)

Although Christ's visit to the spirit world was just a brief weekend stopover, it was a successful little tour. Christ didn't personally visit the rebellious folks in spirit prison ("unto the wicked he did not go"), but he did organize a missionary force in typical Mormon fashion to carry the gospel there too.

One key element of this revelation is the role of temple work in freeing the spirits of the dead and helping them prepare for their eventual reward in one of the three heavenly kingdoms. In order for them to obtain full celestial glory, Latter-day Saints here on earth must do their temple work for them, and they must accept those ordinances and otherwise qualify. (For more on temples and their meaning to Latter-day Saints, see Chapter 7.)

Wrapping up: Official declarations

The closing pages of the Doctrine and Covenants feature two official declarations that represent a different mode of prophetic communication than the preceding 138 sections. Both of these declarations demonstrate that Mormonism is an evolving, dynamic religion in which belief in continuing revelation can cause 180-degree turns in direction, as the Spirit guides.

Making polygamy a no-no

The first of these official declarations is unusual in that it doesn't seem to come directly from the mouth of God. You may even consider it to be more of a press release than a revelation because it begins with the bureaucratic wording, "Press dispatches having been sent for political purposes. . . ." Dated October 6, 1890, and read aloud to the members at General Conference, the statement basically bans the continued practice of plural marriage because of congressional laws forbidding it. (For more about governmental pressure to stop polygamy in the late 19th century, see Chapter 13.)

Now known as the *Woodruff Manifesto* because LDS President Wilford Woodruff wrote it, the document was widely circulated to smooth the Mormons' strained relations with the federal government and pave the way for Utah's statehood, which Congress finally approved in 1896.

Immediately after President Woodruff's declaration, a few members continued quietly entering plural marriage. President Woodruff warned in late 1891 that the Lord had shown him through a vision the trouble the Mormons would face if they didn't abandon polygamy. (An excerpt from this talk is included at the end of the D&C in teeny-tiny type.) In 1904, the Church issued a clearer statement that absolutely prohibited new plural marriages and promised excommunication for anyone who disobeyed. That statement, or *Second Manifesto*, isn't in the D&C, but it's binding on all Latter-day Saints. (For more on why Latter-day Saints believe such a flip-flop on polygamy, for example, is okay, head to "Day-to-day wisdom from the prophet," later in this chapter.)

Extending the priesthood to all races

The other official declaration in the D&C is from June 1978, when the Church extended the priesthood to "all worthy male members" regardless of race. Before that time, the priesthood was denied to any man of African ancestry, and Blacks could not receive a temple endowment or sealing (for more on these ordinances, see Chapter 7). Of course, by 1978 many members and nonmembers alike were offended by this policy.

In the declaration, President Spencer W. Kimball speaks of the many hours he'd spent in the upper room of the temple, begging the Lord for guidance. He was apparently heartbroken over the idea that faithful converts from many nations who were joining the Church in ever-increasing numbers couldn't hold the priesthood or enter the temple. Pleading on their behalf, President Kimball received the answer that the time had finally come to offer those blessings to all, without consideration of race or color. (For more on the controversial history of race in Mormonism, see Chapter 15.)

The Beat Goes On: Recent Revelations Not Found in the D&C

Just because a prophetic teaching isn't contained in the four standard works of Mormonism doesn't mean that it doesn't carry the weight of scripture for most Latter-day Saints. In addition to the canonized revelations that appear in the D&C, recent prophets have made other statements that are widely regarded as modern additions to scripture. In fact, any time a prophet speaks in the capacity of his holy office, Latter-day Saints consider his words to be a form of scripture.

Picturing the ideal family

In 1995, the *First Presidency* (the prophet and his two counselors) and Quorum of the Twelve Apostles released a statement that has since assumed the status of gospel in the Church. Its official name is "The Family: A Proclamation to the World," but most Latter-day Saints just call it the family proclamation. We wouldn't be surprised to see it appear in future editions of LDS scriptures. In the meantime, many members hang a framed version of the family proclamation in their homes.

Basically, the proclamation sets forth the Church's position on gender and family responsibilities more specifically than ever before, putting it all in theological perspective. Although the language is usually gentle, the message is clear: Latter-day Saints believe in traditional gender roles and the sacred nature of the nuclear family. The family proclamation explains that

>> **"Gender is an essential characteristic of individual premortal, mortal, and eternal identity and purpose."** The current orthodox interpretation of this passage is that our gender here on earth is the gender we had in the premortal world and that we will retain this gender in the hereafter.

>> **Marriage is between a man and a woman.** Not only does this proclamation apparently slam the door shut on gay marriage, but it also confirms the prohibition on earthly marriage between one man and several women, as 19th-century Mormons once practiced and some fundamentalist Mormon-adjacent offshoots still practice.

» **Children deserve to be raised in a home where parents honor their marriage vows completely.** The proclamation affirms that sex is a gift from God that people should enjoy only within the bond of heterosexual marriage (for more on Mormon views regarding chastity, see Chapter 16). What's more, the proclamation clarifies that sexual fidelity alone is not enough to guarantee a happy marriage; husbands and wives also need to practice forgiveness, compassion, and mutual respect.

» **The primary duty of fathers is to preside over their families and provide for their material needs, while the first responsibility of mothers is to nurture their children.** Husband and wife are expected to honor one another as equal partners in the fulfillment of these responsibilities. Although the proclamation doesn't pronounce dire punishments on women who work outside the home and even makes allowances for special circumstances, the general ideal is clear. (For more on the roles of Mormon men and women, see Chapter 5.)

The proclamation closes with specific warnings against domestic abuse, adultery, and other moral failures, saying that people who engage in such behaviors will be held accountable before God. This proclamation is unusual in that it's worded as a warning to the whole world, not just Latter-day Saints. For more about hot-button "LDS vs. LGBTQ+" issues related to gender and marriage, see Chapter 15.

Day-to-day wisdom from the prophet

In addition to the "Proclamation on the Family" and additional proclamations, any guidance that the General Authorities give during General Conference assumes the status of *de facto* scripture for Latter-day Saints. When the prophet speaks, people listen; in one popular LDS hymn, Latter-day Saints sing about how thankful they are for a prophet to guide them in these latter days. They *expect* him to give them guidance about spiritual issues, doctrine, family matters, and the like. What's more, they love him for it.

However, any Mormon who reads history knows that what some prophets (and other Church leaders) spoke in the past isn't necessarily Church doctrine today. The primary example of this situation is, of course, polygamy; most 19th-century LDS leaders practiced it and preached glowing sermons about it from the pulpit. Obviously, though, Latter-day Saints don't feel this way today, and no prophet of the Church has sanctioned polygamy in over a century.

REMEMBER

So what happens when the teachings of LDS prophets seem to collide? The basic rule is that according to the doctrine of continuing revelation, the Lord continues to reveal more light and knowledge on various subjects as people are ready for it. In other words, *a living prophet always trumps a dead prophet*. Latter-day Saints expect that some Church rules and programs will change as society evolves and the Lord offers new revelations. Sometimes a lower law is replaced by a higher law, such as in the Bible when Jehovah gave the Mosaic Law and later, after he was born to the earth as Jesus Christ, upgraded it with his gospel. But sometimes the reverse happens as well when people can't live up to the higher law, such as the early LDS church's *united order*, in which LDS communities attempted to share property, goods, and profits — now, members everywhere just pay tithing and voluntary donations directly to the Church (see Chapter 16).

Hearing an LDS leader publicly challenge the statements of a dead or past leader is highly unusual, though it has happened — in the late 1970s, for example, one apostle told Church members to forget everything that Brigham Young or any other 19th-century leader ever said about race. (Brigham Young made some racist remarks about Blacks being inferior to whites, which is certainly *not* taught by the Church today — see Chapter 15 for more on this issue.) More often, a former teaching slowly fades into obscurity because Church leaders no longer mention it, such as prohibitions on birth control.

Some people feel that "continuing revelation" means that the Mormon God waffles on important truths. Latter-day Saints, on the other hand, believe that *of course* a dynamic God who's interested in people in all times and places offers revelations that pertain to their circumstances, and he'll fine-tune things as their circumstances change, just as he did in biblical times. God may be the same yesterday, today, and forever, but the human world isn't, and God helps Latter-day Saints find ways to live in it.

Chapter 11

Searching for a Home

To understand today's Mormon culture and mindset, you have to understand what happened during the faith's earliest days, especially the period between Joseph Smith's organization of the Church in 1830 and his martyrdom in 1844. The Church devotes considerable instruction time to early Latter-day Saint history, and most Latter-day Saints are quite familiar with what happened during the 1830s and 1840s. In contrast to some other religious groups today, Latter-day Saints often can not only name the Church's earliest converts but also provide details about those early Mormons' lives, sufferings, and contributions. Especially for U.S. Latter-day Saints, history *is* theology, so they can't take it lightly.

Mormonism has changed a great deal since the early decades, including spreading so broadly that more members now live outside the United States than inside. To many, the spiritual fervor and extreme persecutions of early Mormonism seem downright otherworldly compared to today's stable, wealthy, corporate-style Church. At the same time, some argue that the early persecutions continue to motivate U.S. Latter-day Saints to blend in with mainstream society so that they don't have to endure the same violent fate. In fact, some even say that U.S. Latter-day Saints still have a persecution complex.

This chapter traces Joseph Smith's attempts to settle his people in Ohio, Missouri, and Illinois and analyzes what happened when Mormonism collided with the local populations. In addition, we look at the origins of many ins and outs of Mormonism today.

A Significant Pit Stop: Kirtland, Ohio

Just a few months after officially organizing the Church in upper New York State (see Chapter 4), Joseph Smith sent missionaries to the far-off Missouri territory to teach the Native Americans about this restored gospel. In November 1830, led by leading Book of Mormon scribe Oliver Cowdery, the missionaries took a break from their 1,500-mile journey and preached in the area of Kirtland, Ohio, not far from Cleveland. Little did they know their efforts would be so successful that, because of persecution, Joseph Smith would soon move the fledgling Church's headquarters there from New York State.

One of the missionaries wanted to reconnect with a Kirtland-area man who he'd studied religion with a few years before discovering Mormonism. This man, a Campbellite minister named Sidney Rigdon, was actively seeking a return to New Testament Christianity — not unlike what the Mormons were trying to do. Sidney allowed the Mormons to preach to his congregation, and impressed by the Book of Mormon, he converted. Within a month, more than a hundred others were baptized into the Mormon faith.

Soon after his conversion, Sidney visited Joseph Smith in New York State, and the Prophet received a revelation to move to the Kirtland area. A powerful speaker but also somewhat eccentric and temperamental, Sidney played a central role in Mormon leadership for more than a decade until parting ways with the faith after Joseph was murdered in 1844.

Receiving new revelations and doctrines

During Joseph Smith's Ohio residence of nearly seven years (February 1831 to January 1838), a whole lot happened:

>> **The Church grew like a weed.** With missionaries traveling from the Kirtland hub into Canada and England, as well as throughout the United States, worldwide Church membership grew from 280 to more than 16,000.

>> **People packed up and moved in.** Announcing Kirtland as its official gathering place, the Church encouraged converts to move there, which many did despite severe economic hardships.

>> **The temple went up.** At great cost and sacrifice, the Church built its first temple, which boosted the people's spirituality and helped the Church's progress.

>> **Joseph began putting his revelations in writing.** During this Ohio phase, Joseph Smith received nearly half of the total revelations contained in the

Doctrine and Covenants, one of Mormonism's four main books of scripture (for more on the D&C, as it's commonly called, see Chapter 10). These revelations include

- **The Word of Wisdom,** Mormonism's well-known health code against addictive, intoxicating substances (see Chapter 16).

- **The three degrees of glory,** Mormonism's three-tiered heaven that symbolizes humankind's potential eternal rewards (see Chapter 2).

- **Plural marriage,** which would remain confidential until years later. Joseph probably entered into his first polygamous marriage in 1835, with a young neighbor (see Chapters 13 and 15).

» **Joseph uncovered scriptural pearls.** Several of Joseph's Kirtland-era scriptural translations were later gathered, along with additional material, into the Pearl of Great Price, the smallest and perhaps most unusual collection of Mormon scripture (see Chapter 10). These key Kirtland writings include

- Portions of the Bible's King James Version, which Joseph "retranslated" to correct errors he said had been introduced by earlier translators (see Chapter 9). In particular, Joseph received additional revelations by Moses.

- Revelations of the Old Testament prophet Abraham, which Joseph Smith claimed he "translated" from ancient Egyptian papyri (see Chapter 15 for more on this controversy).

» **The Mormons adopted a what's-mine-is-yours philosophy.** Joseph Smith introduced the concept of "consecration of properties," which led to Mormon ideals of caring for the poor, maintaining self-sufficiency, and sharing common resources. Driven by his concern for poor Church members, Smith created a community storehouse that would meet their needs by pooling the extra stuff of more fortunate Saints. (Although these attempts at communal living — often called *united orders* — had fizzled out by the end of the 19th century, their legacy lives on in the Church welfare program, which we discuss in Chapter 8.)

» **The Church figured out its org chart.** Its main governors include the *First Presidency,* consisting of the prophet and his two counselors; the Quorum of the Twelve Apostles; and other general and local priesthood offices. (For more about the Church's priesthood organization, see Chapters 4, 6, and 8.)

» **Education became the new wave.** Joseph Smith, Sidney Rigdon, and others pioneered the Mormon emphasis on education by teaching classes that mingled religious instruction with secular subjects such as literature, history, and philosophy. Today, Brigham Young University and other LDS schools maintain a similar balance, and the Church provides weekday religion classes all over the world to supplement the secular curriculum of Latter-day Saints in high school and college. (For more on Mormon education, see Chapter 8.)

Building the Kirtland Temple

When it came time to start putting up the first temple in 1833, Joseph Smith unveiled unique plans for its construction, which he said he received via revelation from God. This sacred structure featured large meeting rooms on the first and second floors, each with multilevel pulpits at either end for use by priesthood officials. Mormon women donated china and glassware to be ground up for sparkle in the temple's exterior glaze. Because persecution was constant in the early days of Mormonism, people guarded the temple day and night against vandals, both during construction and afterward. Take a peek at this temple yourself — see Figure 11-1.

FIGURE 11-1: The Kirtland Temple, dedicated in 1836, is now a popular tourist destination.

WesternCowgirlDesign/Adobe Stock Photos

Before, during, and after the Kirtland Temple's dedication in 1836, many Mormons reported visions, visitations, and other spiritual manifestations. Joseph Smith said that the resurrected Savior himself appeared and accepted the temple. Then several resurrected biblical prophets came and restored vital priesthood keys to Church leaders, including Moses, Elias, and Elijah (for more on the Mormon priesthood, see Chapter 4).

Joseph Smith didn't reveal most of the key temple ceremonies to Mormons until the later Nauvoo period, so the Kirtland Temple was more of a glorified meetinghouse than a place to perform rituals and ordinances, like today's temples (for more details on Mormon temples, see Chapter 7). However, one ordinance introduced in the Kirtland Temple was the washing and anointing of feet, similar to what Jesus did in the Bible's New Testament. Versions of this practice continue in Mormon temples today.

Empty pockets and loaded threats: Good times come to an end

Unfortunately, the temple added to the Church's large debt burden, which in turn led to financial chaos that ultimately helped trigger Joseph Smith's flight from Kirtland. Joseph decided to fix the situation by forming a bank-like organization to issue currency notes. However, people cashed in the notes for real coins faster than the organization could handle, and a national banking panic in 1837 sealed the financial doom. People became upset both inside and outside the Church, contributing to increased persecution and hundreds of excommunications, including 4 of Joseph Smith's handpicked 12 apostles. Clutching pistols and knives, one group of *apostates* (former Mormons who rebelled against the faith) even tried to take over the temple.

In January 1838, fleeing from lawsuits, arrest warrants, and assassination plots, Joseph Smith moved his family to Missouri, effectively ending Kirtland's role as Church headquarters. With mobs rising against them, hundreds of Mormons followed him.

Kirtland here and now

The Kirtland days remain a controversial period in Mormon history. Some historians argue that Church leaders caused many of their own problems by participating in land speculation and using credit unwisely. Others say Joseph Smith was blameless and did the best he could, considering the new religion's complex challenges and needs. Despite the controversy, one point is true: The Church learned valuable lessons in Kirtland, and the difficulties revealed who was faithful and who wasn't.

Still standing in excellent condition, the Kirtland Temple isn't used for sacred ordinances as other Mormon temples are, and the building is open for tours. In addition, the LDS church has rebuilt a nearby village of stores, homes, and other buildings where important events in Mormon history took place.

Seeking Zion in Missouri

Many people think Utah is the promised land for Mormons, but in the minds of many Latter-day Saints today, that arid, mountainous state is just a temporary refuge — with *temporary* measured in centuries — until the promised return to Missouri, home of cherished, significant geographical locations that some Latter-day Saints believe could be critical to the faith in the future.

The early Mormons sought to establish *Zion* somewhere on earth, a place where they could practice their religion freely and commune with each other. Zion would be the location where the righteous took refuge when the wicked brought chaos into the world, a site identified in the Book of Mormon as the New Jerusalem. In 1831, Joseph Smith received a revelation directing him to travel from Ohio to Missouri, where God would reveal the location for a permanent Latter-day Saint homeland that would last through the Millennium (see Chapter 3 for more on Christ's Second Coming and the Millennium).

While visiting the rough-hewn frontier outpost of Independence in Jackson County, Missouri, Joseph Smith declared that the town would become the center place of Zion and the site for the New Jerusalem, and he identified the spot where the Latter-day Saints would build a temple. (In addition, many Latter-day Saints believe that Jackson County was the original site of the Garden of Eden.) While Joseph didn't actually move to Missouri for another seven years, saying God wanted him to finish his work in Ohio, many of his followers immediately started settling there to stake the Church's claim. Unfortunately, their best shot at Zion lasted only two years.

REMEMBER

While early Mormons used the word *Zion* to refer to Jackson County, today's Latter-day Saints generally use it to mean "the pure in heart," wherever they may live. On the other hand, some Latter-day Saints believe the "city of Zion" is not so much a location or mindset as an ecologically and economically sustainable community pattern (see, for example, https://newvistas.com). As Joseph Smith detailed in his 1833 "Plat of the City of Zion," this community pattern is designed to "fill up the world in these last days" for people of all faiths.

Getting booted out of Zion

For the early Mormons, *Missouri* could well have been spelled *m-i-s-e-r-y*. Although many significant hopes and plans arose there, Missouri was also where the early Mormons suffered some of their worst persecutions. In the Mormon mind, that equation makes perfect spiritual sense: the greater the potential good, the greater Satan's opposition.

Persecution starts again

With about 1,200 Mormons living in Jackson County by the summer of 1833 (almost a third of the total local population), other settlers began to worry — and not without good reason — that the Mormons would soon overtake them politically, economically, and culturally. Encouraged by local government officials, a large mob formed in July 1833 to force the Mormons out of Jackson County. They destroyed the Mormon printing office, tarred and feathered leaders, and burned down homes and businesses. Even after the Mormons signed an agreement to leave within several months, daily harassment and violence continued. When appeals to the state government didn't do a lick of good, the Missouri Mormons started arming themselves against the mob, and soon the state militia was called out.

In November 1833, after a second attack in which over 200 Mormon cabins were robbed or burned, the Mormons left Jackson County months earlier than originally agreed. Many of them lost everything they owned. Crossing the Missouri River, they found temporary winter shelter among friendlier settlers in Clay County. Church leaders took their complaints and pleas not only to the Missouri governor but also all the way to the U.S. president, Andrew Jackson. However, fearful of open warfare, the government and courts didn't intervene. Thus, the early Mormons lost their all-important Zion homeland — for the time being, anyway.

Trying to stay in Missouri

If the Mormons couldn't live in Zion, at least they could put down temporary roots nearby while they kept petitioning the government to reclaim their rightful Jackson County properties. For over a year, the local settlers across the river in Clay County allowed the Mormons to live peaceably among them. New converts kept arriving, and Mormons started buying up property. Disregarding a prophetic warning from Joseph Smith, individuals openly spoke of taking over the area. By 1836, the locals again began to resent the Mormons.

Clay County locals, however, took a more civilized, diplomatic approach to ridding themselves of the Mormons than did their Jackson County counterparts, refraining from violence and negotiating comparatively reasonable agreements. When Mormon explorers found some sparsely populated land in northern Missouri, Church leaders asked the government to set aside territory for the Mormons to call their own. In December 1836 the state created Caldwell County just for the Mormons.

With a temporary homeland secured, the Mormons started building a new city called Far West and establishing other settlements in the area. Despite the promising new arrangements, however, hostilities started festering again. When some

Mormons threatened violence against a handful of internal troublemakers living in Far West, these rebels fled, triggering anti-Mormon feelings in nearby communities. An underground gang known as the *Danites* arose, falsely claiming that Church leaders authorized them to use extreme measures — including robbery and murder — against Mormonism's enemies.

Although the Church didn't sanction the Danites' activities, the words of some Mormon leaders seemed to justify such actions. On Independence Day in 1838, Sidney Rigdon delivered a no-tolerance pledge against any future persecutors. Although the Mormons had repeatedly taken the abuse without fighting back, Rigdon declared that they wouldn't do so anymore. Unfortunately, copies of this speech circulated widely in pamphlet form.

Going to war

Tensions continued to increase between the Mormons and their non-Mormon neighbors. After a brawl broke out when residents of a nearby county tried to stop some Mormons from voting, anti-Mormon agitation swept throughout Missouri. Joseph Smith, who had recently moved from Ohio to Missouri, submitted to arrest on false charges, but this didn't diffuse the hostility. Soon both sides began forming militias, capturing prisoners, and robbing each other. Mob militias invaded settlements, destroyed property, and tortured Mormons, many of whom fled to Far West.

Believing exaggerated reports of Mormon "outrages," Missouri governor Lilburn W. Boggs signed an infamous extermination order in October 1838 stating that the Mormons must either be killed or driven entirely from the state, an order that wasn't officially repealed until 1976.

During the Mormon War, most of the Mormon deaths occurred at the small settlement of Haun's Mill. On the afternoon of October 30, 1838, a mob of over 200 men attacked the settlement, shooting at Mormon men, women, and children alike. In a blacksmith shop, a concealed 7-year-old boy watched the invaders kill his father and 10-year-old brother. Later justifying the boy's murder, the triggerman said, "Nits will make lice, and if he'd lived he would have become a Mormon."

At least 17 Mormons died in the massacre, with another 13 wounded. Only three Missourians were injured. Joseph Smith lamented that the slain Saints would've been spared if they'd followed his direction and fled earlier to the Far West. About 20 years later, a desire to avenge Haun's Mill was one factor that helped motivate some Mormons to commit a much worse massacre against some Missourians; for more on that, see Chapter 13.

At the end of October 1838, approximately 2,000 mob soldiers surrounded the barricaded Far West, outnumbering the Mormon soldiers five to one. Apostle Parley P. Pratt recorded that many in the mob disguised themselves as Indians and made a racket like "bloodhounds let loose upon their prey." A Mormon military commander made a secret deal to end the standoff, putting Joseph Smith and other Church leaders into the hands of the mob.

Meanwhile, the again-impoverished Latter-day Saints crossed the Mississippi River eastward into Illinois (see Figure 11-2 for a map of their journey). For many, it was their fifth forced exodus in less than a decade. When Missouri officials eventually decided they couldn't convict Joseph on charges of murder and treason, they allowed him to escape in April 1839 and rejoin his exiled people in Illinois. Before long, the Mormons built a beautiful city that, by 1846, rivaled Chicago in population.

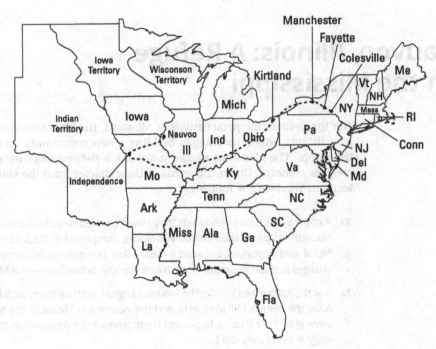

FIGURE 11-2:
Map of the Mormon migrations from New York to Ohio, Missouri, and Illinois.

Missouri here and now

Many Latter-day Saints still believe that they'll eventually reclaim Jackson County as the center of Zion. In the meantime, they believe that Zion exists in the hearts and minds of the righteous, as well as wherever a stake of the Church exists. (The term *stake* is Mormonism's equivalent of *diocese*, meaning a grouping of local congregations; see Chapter 6.) As odd as it may sound to outsiders, some members believe that Latter-day Saints will someday build the New Jerusalem at Independence, Missouri, which is now a suburb of Kansas City. This long-prophesied city would serve as Jesus Christ's headquarters during the Millennium, the 1,000-year period of paradise ushered in by his Second Coming (see Chapter 3).

Today, three competing Mormon groups own portions of the Independence land where Joseph Smith identified that a temple should be built. A small offshoot known as the *Church of Christ (Temple Lot)* controls the spot where Joseph actually stood. The *Community of Christ,* a modern version of the second-largest Mormon denomination that formed after Joseph Smith's 1844 martyrdom (see Chapter 12), has built two significant structures at the site, a tabernacle and a beautiful temple that is open to the public and bears almost no functional resemblance to the temples of the Utah-based Church. In addition, the LDS church built a visitors' center at the site.

Nauvoo, Illinois: A Refuge on the Mississippi

After the devastating persecutions of Missouri, the Mormons welcomed the shelter of Illinois, where they began building a new community on the banks of the Mississippi. The Mormons named it *Nauvoo,* a Hebrew word meaning "beautiful, lovely, or comely." Under the terms of their charter from the state of Illinois, the Mormons received the following:

>> A court system through which they could be tried by judges elected by the Nauvoo residents themselves, with juries composed of Nauvoo residents. This factor was important because it meant that no court could come up with false charges just to persecute — or, more literally, prosecute — the Mormons.

>> A state-authorized militia, the Nauvoo Legion, with as many as 5,000 men. After the Haun's Mill Massacre and the violence in Missouri, the Mormons were glad for a chance to protect themselves if the need arose. (Not surprisingly, it eventually did.)

>> A liberal amount of land and great opportunities for economic prosperity through the profitable Mississippi River trade.

COME ON OVER!

The Nauvoo period marked the first significant migration of Mormon converts from England and continental Europe. In 1840, Brigham Young noted that even if he and other missionaries had tried to prevent the British Latter-day Saints from emigrating, they wouldn't have been able to stop them. Part of the appeal was certainly religious — in Nauvoo, they could live among other Latter-day Saints, meet the prophet Joseph Smith, and enjoy the blessings of the temple under construction. But the reasons were economic as well; many of the European converts were poor or working class, and America offered them cheap land and much more opportunity for economic advancement.

Between 1840 and 1846, approximately 4,800 British converts made the voyage, braving the Atlantic Ocean in passenger ships and then taking steamboats up the Mississippi to Nauvoo.

Building a community

When winter turned to spring and the Mormons set about building their new community in earnest, they got some good news: Joseph Smith was freed by his Missouri jailers and permitted to join the Latter-day Saints in Nauvoo. With Smith to lead them, the Mormons were confident that they could make the city flourish.

However, the reality was that they'd settled in a mosquito-infested swamp. Many of the already-weakened Saints got malaria, and Joseph and Emma Smith filled every bed in their home with ill Church members, moving their own family to a tent in the yard. Eventually Joseph and other members of his family became ill as well.

Latter-day Saints are known as planners, and the early days of the religion were no exception. Despite the hurried purchase of the land and the onset of disease when the Mormons settled there, the city was carefully planned to the last detail. Because Nauvoo was intended to be as self-sufficient as possible, individual family lots were large: each city block was 4 acres, divided into 1-acre plots. Here, the Mormons could raise livestock and crops to help sustain themselves. As the city grew, they divided many of those 1-acre lots into quarter-acres to accommodate the newcomers.

Constructing the Nauvoo Temple

In April 1841, the Latter-day Saints laid the cornerstones for what would become the Nauvoo Temple, an enormous limestone structure to house their most sacred rituals. With almost 50,000 square feet of interior space, it was the largest building the Saints had ever attempted — three times the size of the Kirtland Temple. Construction of the Nauvoo Temple was an arduous five-year process, and tragically, the Prophet was killed before he could see its completion.

The temple funding came from the *tithe* of the Latter-day Saints — defined as 10 percent of their "increase," whether in cash, quilts, chickens, jewelry, food, or other items. Many of Nauvoo's men gave a tithe of their time, working every tenth day to build the temple rather than doing their usual jobs. The women of the community sewed shirts for the construction workers, and the Church asked each sister to donate a penny each week — a significant sum for the time — to purchase supplies.

SCRIPTURE

One of the most distinctive features of the Nauvoo Temple was the symbolism of the sun, moon, and stars carved into its limestone exterior. (For an example of a sunstone, see Figure 11-3.) This symbolism may be a reference to the third chapter of the Book of Abraham, part of the Pearl of Great Price (see Chapter 10). This scripture refers to the sun, moon, and stars and their proximity to God. Another possible explanation is that the symbols represent the three degrees of glory in the afterlife: the stars for the *telestial* kingdom, the moon for the *terrestrial*, and the sun for the *celestial* kingdom, the highest tier of heaven. For more on the three degrees, see Chapter 2.

FIGURE 11-3:
Nauvoo
Temple sunstone.

Although the Kirtland Temple had served primarily as an assembly hall or chapel and housed many kinds of functions, the Nauvoo Temple represented a whole new order. Or rather, a whole *old* order, as the Latter-day Saints believed that the rituals Joseph Smith taught them in the 1840s were part of the Lord's restoration of ancient elements, including some that had been safeguarded over the centuries in Freemasonry. Although Mormons used the middle floors of the temple for public meetings, they reserved the top and bottom floors for these ordinances, including baptism for the dead, endowment, and celestial marriage. (For more info on these and other temple ordinances, refer to Chapter 7.)

Trouble in Nauvoo

In 1844, anti-Mormon sentiment spilled over once again. Some of the reasons this time were familiar from the Ohio and Missouri days: The Mormons became very powerful, with a population of more than 20,000 people, making Nauvoo the largest town in Illinois at the time. They were prosperous, and people considered their doctrines strange.

But there were other reasons as well, and the Mormons weren't entirely blameless victims of persecution. Many people in Illinois and elsewhere worried that Joseph Smith had accumulated too much power. He was mayor of the city, leader of the Church, and the lieutenant general of Illinois's largest militia force. He also ran for President of the United States in 1844.

After several key Mormons left the Church in 1842 and 1843, they publicized the Prophet's then-secret teaching of plural marriage, which had been the reason for their leaving. They challenged polygamy and claimed it was an insult to Christian morality (to better understand the Mormon rationale, see Chapter 13). In June 1844, the protesters printed a rival newspaper, the *Nauvoo Expositor*, in which they publicly exposed polygamy and claimed that Joseph Smith was a fraud. They demanded the repeal of the Nauvoo Charter, saying that the Mormons had violated its provisions by merging church and state too closely.

Joseph Smith, as mayor of Nauvoo, called his city council together and deliberated with them. In the end, they decided that the press was a public nuisance and that its printers were disturbers of the peace. But instead of closing it down, which would've been legal, Smith instructed the city marshal to "destroy the printing press, scatter the type in the street, and burn all remaining copies of the newspaper and its advertising handbills," as one LDS historian summarized. In doing so the Prophet may have overstepped his legal bounds and verified the charges against him: that he inappropriately meshed religion and government.

Arrest and martyrdom

Joseph Smith's mistake in handling the *Expositor* debacle had fatal consequences. All over the state, anti-Mormon sentiment was stirred into a frenzy, and agitators often urged citizens to act against the Mormons. Reacting to such attitudes — and undoubtedly remembering the violent persecutions of Missouri — Smith used the Nauvoo Charter and encouraged all Mormon men to prepare to defend Nauvoo if an attack should come. He held a full-regalia militia rally during which he told the men not to initiate an attack but to defend their families if necessary.

The governor of Illinois traveled up to Carthage, the county seat, to hear evidence on both sides of the matter. He ruled that Smith and the city council had violated the protesters' constitutional rights by unlawfully taking and destroying their property and by not heeding the law and allowing a jury trial.

The Prophet fled Nauvoo in an attempt to draw public hostility away from the city and its people. However, after hearing that the governor intended to bring him to trial and had pledged full protection for him, Smith returned to Nauvoo and surrendered. He also laid down the state-owned weapons used by the Nauvoo Legion, hoping along with the governor to avoid an armed conflict.

Accompanied by his brother Hyrum and several other men, Joseph Smith was arrested and put in a small second-floor jail in Carthage, Illinois. In the early evening of June 27, 1844, a mob of about 200 armed men surrounded the building, their faces painted brown or black. Some rushed into the building and up the stairs, where the Smiths and their companions tried to hold the door and fire their own pistols at the intruders. Joseph's beloved older brother Hyrum was killed instantly in the fray. When members of the mob glimpsed Joseph looking through a second-story window, reportedly lifting his arms in the Masonic signal of distress, they shot him. Smith fell through the window to the ground below, where the mob shot him several more times and then stabbed him with a bayonet.

The Mormons were horrified by the news that Joseph and his brother Hyrum had been killed. However, contrary to the expectations of many of their Illinois neighbors, the Mormons didn't react violently to the martyrdom. But their troubles weren't over; within two years, the people of Illinois were again gunning for the Mormons and made it clear that they had to leave the state or face consequences — continued violence, robbery, and maybe even death. The Mormons decided to pack up and head out; see the next chapter for more on their famous trek west to what later became Salt Lake City. They were heartbroken to leave their beautiful city and temple, but they looked forward to a place of refuge in the West.

Although nine men were tried for the murders of Joseph and Hyrum, they were all acquitted. In 2004, the Illinois legislature formally expressed regret for the assassinations and for the later expulsion of Mormons from Nauvoo.

Nauvoo here and now

For almost a century after the Mormons abandoned Nauvoo, the area saw little development or progress. The temple was gutted by arson not long after the Mormons left the city, and a tornado finished the destruction in 1850.

Gradually, however, the Mormon presence returned. In the 1930s, the LDS church regained the land where the Nauvoo Temple stood before its destruction. In the 1950s, Dr. J. LeRoy Kimball — grandfather of coauthor Christopher Kimball Bigelow — acquired and started restoring the still-standing redbrick home of Dr. Kimball's great-grandfather, Heber C. Kimball, who served as a right-hand apostle to both Joseph Smith and Brigham Young (another main man in Mormon history, who we discuss in Chapter 12). Dr. Kimball originally intended the home for private family use, but people wanted to tour the house. Within a few years, Dr. Kimball was spearheading the restoration of 1840s-era Mormon buildings throughout old Nauvoo, with LDS church financing and oversight.

Today, Nauvoo is one of the world's most visited Mormon locations, and it has been called the "Colonial Williamsburg of the Midwest." Although the town has only about 1,500 permanent residents, it attracts hundreds of thousands of tourists each year, which isn't always a source of joy to all the locals. In 2002, the LDS church built a fully functioning replica of the Nauvoo Temple on the original site, prompting reverent celebration throughout the faith. (Check out Chapter 20 for a picture of this temple.)

IN THIS CHAPTER

» Regrouping after the death of Joseph Smith

» Following Brigham Young

» Surviving the pioneer trek

Chapter **12**

Moving on to Utah with Brigham Young

T he Mormons in Nauvoo, Illinois, were devastated by the 1844 martyrdoms of Joseph Smith and his brother Hyrum in the neighboring town of Carthage. But soon enough, they found that they could survive and even thrive without their beloved founding prophet. In this chapter, we talk about the critical period after Joseph Smith's death, a time when several competing groups fought for leadership of the Mormon movement and angry Illinois neighbors drove the Latter-day Saints out of Nauvoo.

We also introduce you to Brigham Young, who led the majority of Latter-day Saints west in one of the greatest mass migrations in American history. After their ill-fated stints in New York, Ohio, Missouri, and finally Illinois, this group of Mormons headed for Utah, which was then outside the borders of the United States. They hoped that this time, their settlement would be for keeps.

A Crisis of Leadership

In today's Utah-based LDS church, when a Church president dies, a whole system is in place to make sure that the transition to the next president is smooth and uneventful. The most senior member of the Quorum of the Twelve Apostles almost immediately becomes the next prophet and president. When Joseph Smith was killed in 1844, however, the Church hadn't devised an orderly succession process, and Church members weren't sure at the outset how to fill Joseph's shoes. Several people seemed to have legitimate claims to leadership, including the following:

>> Joseph's young son, Joseph Smith III, who received a blessing in the spring of 1844 from his father, which some Mormons believed indicated that one day he'd become prophet.

>> Sidney Rigdon, Joseph's mentor and counselor in the First Presidency.

>> Joseph's older brother Samuel, who was the candidate that the Smith family favored most, at least until Joseph III could come of age. However, Samuel died in July 1844, only a month after his brothers Joseph and Hyrum.

>> Brigham Young, the president of the Quorum of the Twelve.

>> James J. Strang, a recent convert from Wisconsin, who came to Nauvoo announcing that he'd received a revelation in which God directed him to lead the Church.

Church members cooled their heels and didn't make their decision immediately. Shortly after Joseph was killed, they voted unanimously to keep the whole Quorum of the Twelve as a sort of interim presidency. As the quorum's president, Brigham consolidated some (but by no means all) of the various LDS-affiliated groups and, under pressure from local mobs, planned a mass exodus to the Rocky Mountains.

The Lion of the Lord: Brigham Young

Many Latter-day Saints have called Brigham Young the "lion of the Lord" because of his fierce loyalty to the Mormon cause. He was also a lion in longevity, serving the Church for roughly 30 years — longer than any other LDS president. So who was Brigham Young, and how did he come to lead the Latter-day Saints? In this section, we look at this capable and colorful commander-in-chief, describing his personal life as well as his ability to lead the Church in turbulent times. For a peek at what he looked like, see Figure 12-1.

FIGURE 12-1:
A portrait of
Brigham Young,
an effective
leader in
difficult times.

Mannaggia/Adobe Stock Photos

Another unschooled boy from Vermont

As you can see from the following table, Brigham shared some interesting parallels in heritage and upbringing with Joseph Smith, the first prophet and president of the LDS church.

Joseph Smith	Brigham Young
Born in 1805	Born in 1801
From rural Vermont	From rural Vermont
5th of 11 children	9th of 11 children
Poor, hardworking farm family	Poor, hardworking farm family
Very little formal schooling	Only 11 days of formal schooling
Moved to upstate New York as a boy	Moved to upstate New York as a boy

Both boys grew up in large families and faced some difficult times. Sadly, Brigham lost his mother to tuberculosis when he was just 14. He left home a couple years later to make his way as a carpenter, painter, and glazer. A hard worker, Brigham spent his 20s as a skilled craftsman, constructing houses and making furniture. These practical skills served him well when the time came to plan and build the new settlement of Salt Lake City, Utah (for more on settling in the West, see Chapter 13).

Becoming a leader in the Church

Brigham and his young wife, Miriam, discovered the Book of Mormon in 1830 when they received a copy from a family member. When some missionaries came to talk about the book, Brigham asked them to give Miriam a blessing because she was ill. The missionaries expressed their testimonies, and Brigham said that hearing their words "was like a fire in my bones . . . it was light, intelligence, power, and truth." He and Miriam joined the LDS church in April 1832, using their own millpond in Mendon, New York, for baptisms. Brigham's father, brother, and sisters were also baptized, and all remained Latter-day Saints for the rest of their lives.

After he lost Miriam to tuberculosis later that year, Brigham threw himself with characteristic determination into the fledgling religious movement. He became a trusted friend of the Prophet Joseph Smith and swiftly rose in the ranks of the organization. Here's a quick rundown:

» Brigham gained the Latter-day Saints' confidence when he took charge of their flight from Missouri back across the Mississippi River to Illinois in 1838.

» He went on several preaching missions, including one to England from 1840 to 1841.

» He was instrumental in organizing the emigration of many British converts to Nauvoo and in establishing the LDS church in the British Isles.

» At the time of Joseph Smith's death in June 1844, Brigham was the president of the Quorum of the Twelve.

Before his martyrdom, Joseph Smith was campaigning to become president of the United States. At the time Brigham heard the sad news about his friend's death, he was in the eastern United States combining preaching and political campaigning to make converts to Mormonism who would vote for the Prophet to head the nation.

With a heavy heart, Brigham returned to Nauvoo, where he found the Church in disarray. He and the other 11 apostles quickly asserted their leadership. In a famous episode in Mormon history, Brigham spoke at an outdoor prayer meeting and seemed, at least to some of his hearers, to supernaturally take on the voice and appearance of the dead Prophet Joseph Smith. Years later, one audience member, Benjamin Johnson, said, "As soon as he spoke I jumped upon my feet, for in every possible degree it was Joseph's voice, and his person, in look, attitude, dress, and appearance. . . . I knew in a moment the spirit and mantle of Joseph was upon him." For many Latter-day Saints, this event seemed like a miracle and an answer to prayer: God was making it clear to them that Brigham should be their new boss.

Because of the difficulties of the westward trek, Brigham wasn't officially sustained as president of the Church until December 1847, three and a half years after he spoke in the Nauvoo meeting. But the time in between only further proved his determination to lead the Church through one of its toughest periods.

Famous leader and down-to-earth family man

One thing you can say about Brigham Young is that he lived large, both in his public life and behind the scenes. Although Brigham originally resisted when he learned of the doctrine of *polygamy*, or plural marriage (see Chapter 13), he married again after Miriam's death . . . a couple dozen times (including getting hitched to two daughters of Nahum Bigelow, another of coauthor Christopher Bigelow's great-great-great-grandfathers). Brigham was the father of 56 children by 16 of his wives and was by most accounts a loving and involved parent. His personality was firm and steadfast, yet affectionate. He was a man of deep loyalty and constant practicality. He preached economy, frugality, moral behavior, and hard work.

Brigham's leadership style differed a great deal from the first prophet; Joseph was the dreamer, but Brigham was the builder of the kingdom. American history is full of prophets and charismatic founding religious leaders, but what distinguished Mormonism as a successful religious sect wasn't just the quality of its founder, but the quality of his successor. Most other movements failed because no one who survived the founder was capable of carrying out their vision.

Today, you'd call Brigham a micromanager because delegating responsibility doesn't seem to have been his strong suit. Most Mormons feel that this quality was one main reason why they needed his leadership at this point in their history. Without Brigham's intense interest in and keen attention to all the aspects of building the kingdom, the movement may not have thrived. He was methodical and detail oriented, with apparently inexhaustible energy.

Brigham served as president of the Church and governor of the territory of Utah for many years simultaneously, sitting on the board of trustees of numerous businesses and utility companies all the while. (This apparent mixing of religion, government, and commerce made some people uncomfortable, but Brigham felt that having centralized leadership in Utah was important. Today, high Church leaders rarely hold both ecclesiastical and governmental offices.)

A legacy to build on

Brigham Young died in 1877 of a ruptured appendix, having served as president and prophet for nearly 30 years. He's famous for many reasons, from his numerous wives (inquiring minds everywhere debate about how many he actually had, by the way) to his unflagging commitment to Mormon independence. Here are a few of his main accomplishments:

>> **He welcomed Latter-day Saints of many different nations to Utah, making Salt Lake City a melting pot of Euro-American peoples.** On the other hand, Brigham was primarily responsible for establishing the legacy of 19th-century racism that prohibited anyone of African descent from holding the priesthood until 1978; see Chapter 15 for more about that scar on Mormon history.

>> **He furthered Joseph Smith's insistence on Mormon independence, saying that the Latter-day Saints should be self-sufficient in every possible way.** To this day, you can trace back to Brigham's presidency the programs that Mormons use to stay out of debt, store food and supplies for emergencies, and help one another. Claiming to be "America's first department store," the *Zion Cooperative Mercantile Institution (ZCMI),* was founded under his direction to help the Latter-day Saints keep their economic dealings under their own control. (The Church didn't sell off ZCMI until 1999, and today it's part of the Macy's chain.)

>> **Although he was unschooled himself, he believed strongly in the value of education.** He founded three colleges, including the institutions that became Brigham Young University (see Chapter 8) and the University of Utah, which today are sports archrivals. He also sent many Latter-day Saint men and women to the East Coast in the late 19th century for their educations. Under Brigham's initiative, Mormon women were among the first women in America to become physicians.

>> **He instilled in the Latter-day Saints a respect for hard work.** He reveled in work and expected his fellow Mormons to toe the line too. "I have the grit in me," he once said, "and I will do my duty anyhow."

>> **He has many descendants who are visible participants in Mormon life today.** One such descendant is the NFL's former Most Valuable Player, quarterback Steve Young.

Westward Ho! The Pioneer Experience

In the summer of 1997, thousands of Latter-day Saints participated in a three-month reenactment of the 1846 to 1847 pioneer trek that Brigham led. Beginning in Nauvoo, Illinois, and ending triumphantly in the Salt Lake Valley, these modern-day pioneers endured mosquito invasions, torrential rain, and bloody foot blisters in their quest to understand their ancestors' sacrifices. Some participated for the whole three months, while others popped in for just a few days to get a taste of the experience. Some less-hardy folks followed along in air-conditioned RVs.

Why did they undertake this reenactment? For Latter-day Saints, the pioneers aren't just long-dead people who baked corn bread, sang hymns all day, and wore ankle-length dresses. Latter-day Saints today hold up the pioneers' example as the ideal for what modern Church members should be: patient in suffering and willing to sacrifice everything for the Savior and his church. And this indoctrination starts early, with LDS kids learning a song called "Pioneer Children Were Quick to Obey."

REMEMBER

When Mormons speak of the *pioneer trek,* they're not talking about one journey, but many. From 1846 until the railroad reached Salt Lake City in 1869, an estimated 70,000 Mormons made the journey to Utah on foot or in wagons. About 3,000 of them lost their lives on the way, mainly due to disease. In this section, you find out about the pioneers and their courage in difficult circumstances.

Packing up and leaving Illinois

Mormons today know a great deal about their ancestors' mass exodus to the Rocky Mountains. Although Brigham Young led the migration, it was actually Joseph Smith's idea; while he was still alive, Joseph proposed sending scouts west to investigate the possibility of a new home for the Latter-day Saints. The plan to go west sped up as a result of the ill feeling in Illinois toward the Mormons, who were ordered out of the state in 1846 (see Chapter 11). Mobs burned the homes of Mormon families and poisoned their wells (including the well of coauthor Chris Bigelow's ancestor Nahum Bigelow, who suffered a slow death from mob poison). With heavy hearts, the Mormons reconciled themselves to the idea that they would have to leave their beautiful city of Nauvoo.

Of course, not all the early Mormons left Illinois or trekked to Utah. After the death of Joseph Smith, several Mormon groups and denominations went their own way instead of following Brigham Young. The largest and best-known of these churches is today called the Community of Christ (formerly the RLDS church), which now has more in common with mainstream Protestant Christianity than with Mormonism. Interestingly, none of Joseph Smith's immediate family members went west with Brigham Young.

PIONEER DAY TRADITIONS

A calico-clad woman carries a wriggling toddler in one arm and a cellphone in the other. Brass bands strike up patriotic songs in the town square while young men compete against each other in a log-splitting contest. A parade marches down the main street, featuring folks dressed in sunbonnets and string ties but riding on flatbed trucks. Is this fiesta a time-travel experiment gone horribly awry?

Not quite; it's a Pioneer Day celebration. On July 24, many Latter-day Saints — especially in the U.S. Intermountain West — commemorate the sacrifices and courage of the pioneers. In Utah, the day is actually a state holiday. Even though the original pioneers specifically wanted to get *away* from United States influence, Pioneer Day is now a patriotic holiday for some, with a repeat of the Fourth of July's fireworks, barbecues, parades, and other traditions.

As Mormonism has spread outside the United States and become a world religion, Pioneer Day celebrations have multiplied as well, though nowadays, Latter-day Saints in other countries are likely to use the occasion to remember their own nations' Mormon pioneers and early converts.

The first company

When the Mormons began fleeing Nauvoo early in 1846, Brigham led a group across the frozen Mississippi River to Iowa to rest and figure out their route for the rest of the way. Although the cold was a real hardship for the shivering Mormons, Brigham believed that the river froze as a result of God's provision, allowing them to flee tough times in Illinois just as the ancient Israelites escaped from Egypt through the miraculous parting of the Red Sea (check out Exodus 14 in the Bible). This move was to be a new exodus, another example of God leading people from oppression to a promised land.

However, just as the Israelites experienced a rough time in the wilderness, the Latter-day Saints' journey was no picnic. They encountered hunger and disease and sometimes challenged their leaders, wondering aloud whether God had abandoned them. But they also enjoyed a few miracles along the way. In October 1846, for example, some hungry Mormons on the trek experienced what they called "the miracle of the quail" — the sudden landing of flocks of quail in the Mormon camp. The people scooped up the birds, praising God and likening this unexpected bounty to the time when God provided quail to the Israelites in the wilderness (see Exodus 16).

One feature of this first pioneer trek was its strict organization according to the pattern the Israelites followed under Moses' leadership. Brigham divided the company into groups of 10, 50, and 100. This chain of command helped ensure that everyone was accounted for and that they'd help each other if someone's oxen became sick or a wagon wheel got stuck in the mud. Some of the highlights (and lowlights) of this first group included

» **Composition of the hymn "Come, Come Ye Saints," by English convert William Clayton:** Mormons still sing this song to remember the pioneers. Because this song is one of the signature numbers of the world-famous Tabernacle Choir (see Chapter 18), many people outside the faith are familiar with it.

» **Recruitment of 500 Mormon men to serve as United States soldiers in the Mexican War:** Despite the fact that they were defending the same government that allowed its citizens to drive them from their homes, Mormon soldiers dutifully marched 2,000 miles to San Diego — one of the longest infantry treks in American history.

» **Terrible months at Winter Quarters, a temporary settlement on the border between Iowa and Nebraska:** Hundreds died from starvation and exposure during the cruel winter of 1846–1847.

» **Preparation along the way for future groups of pioneers:** Because the first company knew they'd be followed by many other groups of Mormons, they planted crops and prepared the land so later Mormon emigrants would have food to eat during the journey.

» **Triumphant arrival in the Salt Lake Valley on July 24, 1847:** Most of the first group actually arrived on July 23, but an ill Brigham Young brought up the rear on the 24th. See Figure 12-2 for a map of their entire trek.

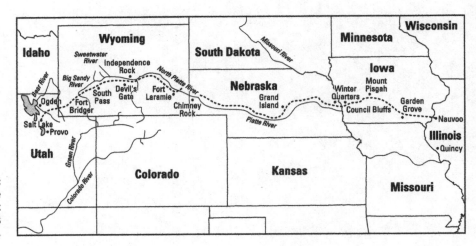

FIGURE 12-2: Map of the Mormon trek from Illinois to Utah.

Keep 'em coming: The Perpetual Emigrating Fund

After the initial trek from Illinois, converts to Mormonism in the United States, Canada, and Europe continued to emigrate to join the main body of the Church in Utah. To help aid European Mormons, Brigham Young established the *Perpetual Emigrating Fund (PEF)* in 1849, a revolving fund that paid expenses for about 50,000 converts as they bought sea passage, crossed the plains, and settled in Utah.

This fund wasn't a free lunch; it was an interest-free loan. The idea behind the PEF was that emigrants would pay back the money as soon as they became established in their new home, replenishing the fund so other families could borrow for their journeys. The LDS church had to discontinue the program in 1887 when the federal government froze the Church's assets in an attempt to stop polygamy; see Chapter 13 for the story of that trial.

Today, the Church's Perpetual *Education* Fund is modeled on the old emigration program. Through this revolving fund, young Latter-day Saints in designated needy nations can receive loans from the Church to get college or vocational educations in their homelands. Since it was established in 2001, the Perpetual Education Fund has helped more than 90,000 applicants.

Chapter **13**

Building the Kingdom in Utah

When Brigham Young indicated that Salt Lake City was the place for the Latter-day Saints, some of them felt a little disappointed — the land seemed so stark and, well, ugly. It wasn't a full-on desert, but it wasn't exactly an oasis, either. Building a prosperous society amidst the mountains took all the Mormons' characteristic commitment to organization and hard work, and they hoped that this time their enemies would leave them alone. However, Mormon conflicts with the outside world took a turn for the worse in Utah. What's more, the clash was sometimes their own fault.

Before the Mormons left the Midwest, the practice of polygamy was rumored, but they hid it. After 1852, they practiced it openly in Utah — which didn't go down well with many non-Mormons. In addition, the Mormons made it clear that they had no intention of separating church and state. To make matters worse, the Latter-day Saints stained their own history by instigating one of American history's worst-ever civilian massacres: the Mountain Meadows Massacre of 1857.

In this chapter, we celebrate this period of Mormon history by pointing out the courage of the Mormon pioneers in settling the West and taming the frontier, but we also look at the darker side of the early Utah story. In addition, we explore how the Church made the transition from the 19th to the 20th centuries, from a polygamous fringe movement at odds with the government to a bulwark of traditional values and American patriotism.

Building Zion

When the first company of Mormons arrived in the Salt Lake Valley in July 1847, they took a quick break to thank the Lord for their safe passage and to consecrate the new land to him. Less than two hours after they arrived, they got to work plowing and irrigating the land. Because this place was going to be their new homeland, the Mormons weren't seeking just to survive but to honor God with a flourishing settlement.

The Mormons named their new region *Deseret*, a word from the Book of Mormon that means "honeybee." (Today, you see the symbol of a beehive everywhere in the Mormon world, from the pulpit in the Salt Lake Tabernacle to the logo for the Church's Humanitarian Relief program.) The busy-bee Mormons chose this term because it summed up their labor of building Salt Lake City and sending representatives to establish other Mormon towns throughout the West.

Settling the Salt Lake Valley

The Mormons' first task was to create Salt Lake City, which became the Church headquarters and, after Utah became a U.S. territory in 1850, eventually the region's government headquarters as well.

Laying out the city

Visitors to Salt Lake City today are sometimes surprised by the layout and organization of the downtown area. The place is so clean, so darn *orderly*. Imagine how visitors in the late 19th century felt when they discovered the city's broad streets (wide enough to turn a wagon completely around without backing up the oxen) and temple-in-progress.

Within days of the Mormons' arrival in Salt Lake City, Brigham Young set aside a grade-A spot for building a temple. (Although they got an early start, they didn't exactly rush to get the job done: The Salt Lake Temple took a full 40 years to build, and Brigham didn't live to see the end result.) The temple lot, now part of a five-block downtown area called *Temple Square*, was the hub for the entire city.

The Mormons aligned their streets to compass directions and numbered them based on their distance from the temple — and this system still remains in place. For example, if you stand at the corner of 500 South and 200 East, you're five blocks south and two blocks east of the temple. All the city streets radiate from the temple like shuttle probes from a mother ship; getting lost is nearly impossible, though one of the authors of this book has managed it.

Other Mormon settlements used similar patterns and numbering systems. You can often tell exactly where modern-style suburban development began in Utah communities just by noting where the streets start to get names and run in something other than straight lines.

Taming the frontier

Because Salt Lake City was so far away from suppliers in the East (1,000 miles) and California (700 miles), the Latter-day Saints had to be self-sufficient from the get-go. The land and its accompanying critters didn't make their job easy. That first winter of 1847–48, the Mormons rationed their flour carefully to get them through the cold months, and their sacrifice paid off, because no one died of starvation that first winter. (Compare their situation to the poor Pilgrims, who lost half the *Mayflower* company in the first year. Ouch.)

But hard times were just ahead. In May 1848, the Mormons suffered a serious setback when a whole mess of crickets (we're talking a plague of Old Testament proportions) destroyed their newly planted crops. The desperate Mormons tried to kill the invaders with brooms and sticks but to no avail.

What happened next filled the Mormons with faith. Before all the crops were devoured, flocks of seagulls gobbled up the crickets. Some of the crops were saved, and the Mormons didn't starve. Not surprisingly, the seagull is now Utah's state bird, and Temple Square features a lovely monument to the fowl tale. Some cynics point out that seagulls aren't exactly strangers to the Salt Lake area, so their presence in 1848 is no big shocker. Others note that if the Mormons had eaten the high-protein insects themselves, as people do in many parts of the world, they would've come out even better. Although Mormons have exaggerated the miraculous aspects of this story over the years, the seagull remains a symbol for Mormons of God's provision in difficult times.

Living alongside Native Americans

The Mormons were the first permanent Euro-American settlers in Utah, but they were by no means the only people there. Native American tribes had occupied the region for centuries, and the Mormons who settled in Utah had to learn to negotiate with them.

On the one hand, Mormons treated Native Americans more fairly than other white groups did at the time. They had several reasons for doing so:

>> **Early Mormon theology said that Native Americans were descendants of the Lamanites in the Book of Mormon.** In other words, they were considered part of the house of Israel. (For more on the Lamanites in the Book of Mormon, see Chapter 9.)

>> **They faced a common aggressor: the U.S. government.** As the old adage goes, the enemy of one's enemy is one's friend.

>> **Brigham Young, ever the practical leader, thought it was better to feed them than to fight them.** In some cases, Mormon families adopted Native American orphans into their homes to raise and educate.

However, Mormons were sometimes guilty of the same racist attitudes toward Native Americans that characterized other white people of the 19th century. And some battles did occur between Mormons and Native Americans, most notably the seven-year Black Hawk War. Although Mormons had a mixed record in dealing with Native Americans, they were generally peaceable neighbors. Today, many Native Americans are members of The Church of Jesus Christ of Latter-day Saints, and the Church has missionaries and congregations on many reservations throughout the western United States.

Movin' on out: Settling the Jell-O Belt

When pioneers arrived in Utah, most of them thought they could settle down with the other Latter-day Saints and start prospering. But for some, this idea was only a dream. Over the next three decades after the 1847 arrival, President Brigham Young, concerned that the Mormons needed to stake their claim on the surrounding territories so they could have a healthy bit of elbow room, directed some families to pack their bags yet again.

In all, the Mormons founded nearly 100 communities in their first decade in the West and more than 500 throughout the 19th century. One of the first and most successful distant communities was St. George, Utah, just north of the modern-day border with Arizona. Attracted to its mild southern climate, Brigham used St. George as a winter home, and many Latter-day Saint senior citizens still winter or retire there.

Other Mormon colonies included

>> Cardston, Alberta, Canada, named for the Card family of Mormon settlers

- » Carson City and Las Vegas, Nevada
- » San Bernardino, California
- » Snowflake, Arizona, founded by Mormon families whose last names, believe it or not, were Snow and Flake

Some Mormons claim that Mormons *founded* Las Vegas, but they're wrong. Someone else discovered the place about ten years before the first Mormons got there. The Mormons were, however, the first European Americans to *settle* in Las Vegas. They did so in the mid-1850s, though they couldn't make a go of it and left after a couple of years. Although the LDS effort was short-lived, the early Mormon presence in Las Vegas is an ironically delightful historical twist, considering that Las Vegas is now known for gambling, drinking, and other decidedly un-Mormon activities. Today, even the Mormon temple in Las Vegas has slot machines in the lobby. (We're just *kidding*.)

Mormon colonization stretched from Utah to all its surrounding territories and was strongest in Nevada, southern Idaho, western Wyoming, eastern Washington, Colorado, and northern Arizona. Today, this core area is called the *Mormon culture region* by demographers and the *Jell-O Belt* by many affectionate Latter-day Saints, because Mormons have a high per-capita consumption rate of that wobbly treat. In Utah, Mormonism is the number-one religion in terms of believers, and in several surrounding states it takes second or third. A smattering of Mormon-heavy communities also shows up in Nevada, California, Washington, New Mexico, and western Canadian provinces such as Alberta, British Columbia, and Saskatchewan.

Conflicts with the Outside World

When the Latter-day Saints arrived in the Salt Lake Valley in 1847, they had reason to hope they'd forever escaped conflict with the American government. At the time, Mexico owned the territory that eventually became known as Utah, and that government was more than willing to leave the Mormons alone. However, only months later, Mexico lost its war with the United States and had to hand over all its lands in the West, including Utah. The Mormons found themselves right back in the thick of American controversy.

Today, people often think of Latter-day Saints as flag-waving, staunch Republican supporters of the U.S. government. (The extensive presence of Latter-day Saints in military leadership, the CIA, and the FBI demonstrates pretty clearly that the United States has no lingering concerns about their patriotism.) But in the

19th century, people saw Mormons as fugitives from the long arm of the law. Their stubborn practice of polygamy, as well as their determination to merge church and state in the Rocky Mountains, made the Mormons a top public enemy.

The Utah War and the Mormon Reformation

Utah became a U.S. territory in 1850 with Brigham Young as its governor. Before long, the federal government expressed grave concern about the "Mormon problem." Two basic issues were at stake:

>> **The Mormons acknowledged in 1852 that they practiced polygamy, or plural marriage.** This topic had long been grist for the rumor mill, but the Latter-day Saints had always publicly denied it. After they let the cat out of the bag, the nation cried foul. The 1856 Republican National Convention denounced polygamy as one of the "twin relics of barbarism" that afflicted the national conscience (the other was slavery). For more on the doctrine of plural marriage and why Mormons practiced it, see the section on polygamy later in this chapter.

>> **U.S. government officials worried that the Mormons were trying to establish a *theocracy*, or a merging of religion and government.** As a natural outgrowth of its role in promoting and coordinating economic development in Utah, the Church owned prominent businesses and held a stake in many of the industrial enterprises of the region: mines, sugar refineries, textile mills, and the like. Even more concerningly, it virtually controlled local politics and the judicial bench.

Anticipating war

The tensions between Mormons and the government erupted in 1857–58. When the federal government sent troops to Utah because Brigham Young wouldn't surrender his title as governor to a non-Mormon federal appointee, the so-called Utah War got underway. *War* is actually a bloodier name than the event deserves, because no one was killed — in fact, no one even fired any shots — during the smoldering conflict. But the fact that the government was willing to send the largest peacetime army in the nation's history all the way out to Utah shows how concerned it was about the Mormon question.

To the Mormons, the government's interference appeared to be a rehashing of the same old story that had always ended so badly for the Latter-day Saints in Ohio, Illinois, and Missouri. They saw it as the first strike in renewed persecutions and government attempts to force them to give up their beliefs and way of life.

The lingering image of the Utah War isn't bloodshed but Brigham Young's attempt to prevent it. Rather than risk the lives of any Latter-day Saints when the army arrived, Brigham evacuated 30,000 people from Salt Lake City so that the soldiers arrived at a ghost town. With military combat avoided, the people of Salt Lake returned peacefully to their homes.

Reacting with a reformation

In 1856, when the Mormons realized that the government was sending an army that could destroy them, no one could've predicted the peaceful and uneventful outcome of the controversy. Some Mormons saw the intrusion as a sign of the last days and believed that they were about to see the obliteration of their beloved Salt Lake City.

With this fear in mind, they entered into a brief period of their history (1856–57) known as the *Mormon Reformation*. To prepare themselves spiritually for the end, they prayed more fervently, met more frequently, and performed round-the-clock ordinances in the Endowment House (the building that substituted for a temple while the temple was under construction). They also made a dizzying number of plural marriages, with some men marrying several women on the same day.

The Mormon Reformation was a time of deep, and even bizarre, fervor in Latter-day Saint history and played an important part in understanding the religion's greatest tragedy: the Mountain Meadows Massacre.

The Mountain Meadows Massacre

Although the 1850s Utah War was bloodless, Mormon history in the 1850s wasn't. The government may not have traded bullets with the Mormons, but many of the Latter-day Saints suspected that civilians in emigrant trains crossing the Utah Territory were in league with the invading army. For this and other complex reasons, a group of Mormons made a large-scale attack on an emigrant train in September 1857. Interestingly enough, the worst of the bloodshed happened on September 11, a day that almost 150 years later similarly became associated with the violence that can stem from religious fanaticism.

The massacre occurred about 200 miles south of Salt Lake City, when a group of men, women, and children passed through southern Utah on their way to settle in California. Some accounts claim that Native Americans initiated the attack and that the Mormons joined in later; others claim that the Mormons planned and executed the whole affair. The latter explanation seems more credible to most historians. At the end of the day, more than 120 men, women, and older children were dead. Young children, the oldest of whom was 6, were left alive, and many were temporarily adopted into the families of local Latter-day Saints before being returned to their homes in Missouri and Arkansas.

Questioning the motive

Why would this group of Mormons, who'd been on the receiving end of violence and persecution themselves, carry out such an unforgivable atrocity? Historians have identified several possible motives for the attack. Some or all of these reasons may help to explain it, though nothing can excuse it. No one will ever know for certain exactly what happened and why, even though a new book on the massacre shows up nearly every year, it seems.

» The Mormons, who were expecting an army of 2,500 soldiers to attack them any day, were swept up in a feverish, warlike mentality and believed they stood alone against the world. The emigrant party arrived in Utah at a very bad time.

» The emigrant group was from Missouri and northern Arkansas, and historical evidence suggests that they may have taunted the Mormons with boasts of being among the wildcats who drove Mormons from Missouri 20 years earlier. The massacre may have been a misguided attempt at Mormon justice for past wrongs, especially the much smaller massacre at Haun's Mill, where some Mormon children died.

» One popular history suggests that the Mormons may have committed the massacre because the people of southern Utah were poor and coveted the emigrant party's wealth and livestock. (This theory doesn't satisfactorily explain, though, why the attack happened to this *particular* party at this *particular* time when other emigrants passed through the region without incident.)

Reacting to the event

We'll probably never know the reason, or reasons, for the attack. The questions remain: How much did Brigham Young know, and when did he know it? Did he order the assault, or did the southern Mormons take matters into their own hands? Apparently, when Brigham found out what the southern settlers planned, he immediately sent a messenger ordering them to allow the emigrants to safely pass through. However, they acted before they received his message.

Unfortunately, the Church — caught up with the impending Utah War and anxious not to give the federal government any reason to attack — chose to cover up the evidence of the massacre for years, blaming local Native Americans even when Mormon involvement was obvious. Gradually, the Church claimed at least some responsibility, but only one man, a local Mormon leader named John D. Lee, was ever tried and executed for the crime.

In 1999, the Mountain Meadows Association, made up of the descendants of the known victims and criminals of the attack, reburied the remains of some of the victims, which were disturbed during construction of a memorial. In his dedicatory remarks, LDS church president Gordon B. Hinckley promised the descendants that the Church would always treat the two and a half acres as hallowed ground, "a sacred monument to honor all those who fell."

Polygamy: A Divine Principle (But an Outdated Practice)

Today, outsiders sometimes ask Latter-day Saints — often in jest, occasionally in concern — whether they practice polygamy. (The LDS response is usually to roll the eyes and recite for the thousandth time that the Latter-day Saints haven't practiced polygamy for over a century and that anyone who practices it today is excommunicated, yada yada yada.) Although — we'll just say it once more to clear the air — *the Latter-day Saints haven't practiced earthly polygamy for over a century,* Mormonism is forever associated in the public mind with patriarchal polygamy.

In this section, we take a critical look at polygamy, explaining who practiced it and why and exploring the consequences that the Latter-day Saints experienced for doing so.

Who practiced polygamy, and why?

Modern folks aren't the only ones who feel uncomfortable about the idea of polygamy. When Joseph Smith first explained the doctrine of plural marriage to Brigham Young in the early 1840s, Brigham felt repulsed by it. Like Brigham, most of the early Latter-day Saints didn't instantly warm to the idea, but they gradually came to believe it was God's will.

Finding out who was involved

Although in recent years the Church has downplayed the importance of plural marriage to 19th-century Saints in order to keep the current stance clear (today's Church doesn't allow the practice . . . did we mention that?), history shows that polygamy was an extremely important aspect of Mormonism in the 19th century.

Modern LDS apologists have stated that as few as 2 to 4 percent of Latter-day Saints were involved in polygamy in the 19th century, a figure that professional historians know is far too low. Most historians place the figure at anywhere between 20 and 50 percent, depending on the time and place. Rates of polygamous marriages varied at different points throughout the second half of the 19th century in Mormon settlements. The 1850s saw many plural marriages, but the rate seems to have declined afterward due to government persecution and changing social standards. The numbers also varied based on geography; some towns embraced polygamy more than others.

REMEMBER

Whatever the statistic, polygamy touched almost all Mormon families, whether they practiced it themselves or not. Almost all their leaders practiced it, and those leaders preached sermons on its importance to rank-and-file Mormons in conference after conference. So, despite the understandable de-emphasis on polygamy in official Church publications today, polygamy is a fact of Mormon history, and it deserves to be recognized and understood as a historical and religious phenomenon.

Hearing the defense

Why did the Latter-day Saints practice polygamy, especially when this deviation from what was considered "normal" or moral behavior so angered America's citizens and government? Here are some reasons Latter-day Saints often bring up, both theological and social:

>> **God told us to do it. Period.** Most modern Latter-day Saints believe that although they may not understand why, the Lord chose to institute plural marriage for a brief period in the 19th century as the Church was becoming established. The 19th-century Latter-day Saints felt that they were practicing plural marriage in strict obedience to God's will and that the practice was divinely inspired. In fact, Mormon scripture still acknowledges polygamy as a divine *principle* that applies in heaven, though it's no longer in *practice* on the earth (see Doctrine and Covenants 132).

>> **It was part of the "restitution of all things."** Mormons saw their practice of polygamy as similar to that of the patriarchs Abraham, Isaac, and Jacob. They believe that their latter-day church includes, as predicted in the Bible, the "restitution of all things, which God hath spoken by the mouth of all his holy prophets since the world began" (Acts 3:21). That includes Old Testament polygamy.

>> **It brought the Latter-day Saints together.** Polygamy made the Mormons more cohesive as a people and gave them a distinct identity. Some plural wives were family members even before marriage (two sisters marrying the same man, for example), and the bonds of marriage expanded family

networks. Also, the increased persecution caused by polygamy helped the Mormons bond together even more closely as a people.

>> **It raised up a mighty generation.** Many Mormons believe that one reason the Lord sanctioned polygamy for a time may have been to help the struggling Latter-day Saints raise up a "righteous seed" of second- and third-generation Mormons to build the kingdom. Because of polygamy, Mormon families in the 19th century were better able to obey the Lord's commandment to "be fruitful and multiply," sometimes having two or three times as many children as they may have had with only one child bearer. What's more, polygamy attached women and children to men who had made a strong commitment to the Church, because those men were the most likely to enter into plural marriage.

WOMEN IN POLYGAMY

Although some people today imagine the women of 19th-century Utah to be downtrodden slaves, barefoot and perpetually pregnant, the reality is much more complex. Many Mormon women of the period argued that they were far from being oppressed by polygamy — they were actually liberated by it.

- Some Mormon women said that because their relations with their "sister-wives" (women also married to their husband) were close, they enjoyed a mutual extended family that gave them emotional as well as practical support. And hey, who can argue with sharing free housework and childcare?

- Mormon women, whose polygamous husbands were often away visiting their other families or serving extended unpaid missions, often had to fend for themselves. Some washed laundry, farmed, or took in boarders. Other plural wives were doctors, midwives, shopkeepers, newspaper editors, and teachers. Overall, plural wives were quite independent.

- Mormon women gained the right to vote 50 years before women were allowed to nationally. Also, they could obtain divorces much more easily, in case polygamy made them unhappy.

Although some Mormon women felt burdened by polygamy — keeping jealousy at bay and not giving in to resentment were certainly difficult — large numbers of female Latter-day Saints considered living "the principle" to be a privilege. Strong women who believed in the nobility of their cause didn't appreciate being described as oppressed or delusional. According to customs of the time, first wives sometimes initiated the discussions about bringing a new wife into the family and typically had to approve of the new marriage.

Busting a few myths about 19th-century polygamy

Several enduring myths are still bandied about as people try to explain polygamy (or explain it away):

>> **"Mormons practiced polygamy because women on the frontier far outnumbered men, and plural marriage gave every woman a chance to have a husband."** In actuality, men sometimes outnumbered women, especially in the early years of Mormon settlement. Some towns had three times as many unmarried men as women. In this marriage market of swinging Mormon singles, women had the pick of the litter.

>> **"Polygamy took care of older women and spinsters so they had a chance to get married."** The truth is that most plural wives were younger than the first wife, so they weren't exactly spinsters rescued by polygamy. This idea was especially true in the 1850s, though as the decades passed, convincing young women to enter into plural marriage got tougher.

>> **"Polygamous men lived in harems and had about 20 wives each."** Although a few prominent Church leaders like Brigham Young did have wives numbering into the double digits (and coauthor Christopher Kimball Bigelow's great-great-great-grandfather Heber C. Kimball, a right-hand apostle to both Joseph Smith and Brigham Young, married over 40 women), this situation was far from the norm. Most men who entered into polygamy took only one or two additional wives. If the family could afford it, each wife had her own home or apartment.

>> **"Polygamy was all about sex."** Not really. In fact, some of the plural marriages contracted in Utah were for *eternity only*, meaning that the wife would be on the man's rolls in heaven, but they would have no earthly rolls in the hay. In eternity-only marriages, conjugal relations weren't permitted, and the wife usually supported herself. In marriages for both time and eternity, the couple could enjoy conjugal relations, but the husband was bound to support his wives and any children they had.

Government pressure to end polygamy

After the Mormons' announcement of plural marriage in 1852 kindled the nation's anger, the U.S. government engaged in a vigorous tug-of-war with the Mormons in Salt Lake City. For nearly 40 years, the government applied as much political and social pressure as possible to get the Mormons to abandon the hated practice. Congress created antipolygamy legislation that gradually tightened the noose around the Church.

In 1887, Congress passed the Edmunds–Tucker Act in a final attempt to drive the nail in the coffin of polygamy. This act accomplished three things:

>> It *disfranchised* (took the vote away from) all Utah's women and polygamous men.

>> It froze all the Church's assets in excess of $50,000, basically bankrupting the Church and crippling its missionary efforts.

>> It declared all children of plural marriages to be illegitimate in the eyes of the government.

When the Supreme Court declared that this law was constitutional, the Mormons knew that continuing plural marriage could result in the government closing down their temples and threatening the very survival of the Church. Faced with this terrible situation, President Wilford Woodruff issued a manifesto in 1890 announcing the end of plural marriage. Although the manifesto is included in every Latter-day Saint's collection of scriptures as part of the Doctrine and Covenants (D&C), they refer to it as an official declaration rather than a revelation, and God isn't mentioned in it at all (see Chapter 10 for more on this document).

The legacy of polygamy

Needless to say, the modern Church has gone to great lengths to distance itself from its polygamous past. A few Mormons believe that the mainstream Church will one day restore polygamy again to the earth. Many Mormons assume that heaven's top tier will include polygamy (see Chapters 2 and 15), and although Church leaders haven't explicitly mentioned this idea in General Conference or taught it in years, older teaching supports this view.

In fact, the legacy of polygamy is still visible in the way the Church performs eternal sealings of couples. In cases of divorce, for example, a woman must obtain a cancellation of a previous sealing if she wants to be married again in the temple. A man, however, can apply for clearance to remarry in the temple without canceling the previous sealing. In effect, he can be sealed to two or more women for eternity while being legally married to only one at a time in this life. Similar conditions apply to widows and widowers who want to remarry. (See Chapter 7 for more details on the complexities of eternal marriage.)

Polygamy's other major legacy is the tens of thousands of fundamentalist Mormons who still practice it today. These folks are the subjects of endless fascination and media attention. The LDS church doesn't recognize the fundamentalists as legitimate Latter-day Saints, but some fundamentalists regard themselves as such because they share much of the same culture, doctrine, and history. In general, fundamentalists feel that President Woodruff led the mainstream Church into *apostasy*, or falling away from God when he suspended the practice of polygamy in 1890, so they've revived polygamy and other 19th-century Mormon practices. However, the LDS church excommunicates any unrepentant participants.

Mormonism in Transition

After the Mormons finally cried "uncle" with the 1890 manifesto, life in Utah started more closely resembling life elsewhere in the United States. Church leaders emerged from hiding and from prison, and the federal government stopped interfering in Church affairs. Although more than a decade passed before a true non-polygamous culture emerged, the Church began moving full steam ahead to separate church and state (at least on the surface) and gain statehood for Utah.

Pledging allegiance to the flag

Two events in 1893 seemed to signal that better days lay ahead for the Mormons. At the Chicago World's Fair held that year, the Salt Lake Tabernacle Choir won second prize, resulting in positive publicity for the Church. Even more important, the Church finally finished building the Salt Lake Temple after 40 years of problem-plagued construction. With its thick granite walls and iconic six-spire design, the temple symbolized the faith's determination to stay put in Utah while spreading its influence throughout the world.

With a new constitution banning polygamy and guaranteeing the separation of church and state, Utah finally gained admittance to the union in 1896, after six earlier attempts and almost 50 years after Brigham Young first started campaigning for it. Arid, remote Utah wasn't the Church's first choice for a homeland — to find out what was, see Chapter 11 — but now the Church could operate from a secure, safe base under the protective umbrella of the United States, toward which Latter-day Saints started developing deeper loyalty.

Facing some lingering problems

As things settled down at home, the Church redoubled its worldwide missionary efforts, but with one major change in emphasis: The Church now urged new converts to build up congregations in their home countries rather than gather in Utah. As a result, the flow of converts into Utah became a trickle (a good thing because most of the region's best land was already taken).

Even after Utah became a state, however, the Latter-day Saints still faced some challenges. Federal prosecution of polygamy had caused considerable economic trouble for the Church, and it was saddled with debt. By reemphasizing the payment of tithes (see Chapter 16), President Lorenzo Snow put the Church back on sound financial footing. By 1907 the Church had paid all its creditors.

In addition, polygamy continued sending out aftershocks. In 1898, when Utah elected an LDS U.S. Representative who'd married plural wives *before* the manifesto, more than 7 million Americans signed a petition against him, and he was refused his seat. In 1903, when Utah elected a high-ranking LDS apostle to the U.S. Senate, the Senate commenced an investigation, prompting the Church to issue the *Second Manifesto* to crack down on more than 200 plural marriages that had taken place since 1890, some with the covert blessing of the First Presidency. The apostle, who was monogamous, managed to keep his Senate seat, but the media muckraked the Latter-day Saints well into the 20th century, often with outright fabrications.

Gathering strength for a worldwide boom

Overall, the first half of the 20th century was a time for the Church to lie relatively low, consolidate and refine its methods and messages, and gather strength for the growth boom that began shortly after World War II. (For more details about the modern Church's explosion in membership all over the earth, see Chapter 14.)

As the 20th century progressed, the LDS church took deliberate steps to overcome its bad public image. Several trends helped the process:

>> **The Church started appealing to tourists, particularly by promoting Temple Square in Salt Lake City.** By 1905, this site was drawing 200,000 annual visitors, and it soon became one of America's most-visited destinations west of the Mississippi (see Chapter 8 for more on Temple Square). In addition, the Church established visitors' centers at historic Mormon sites around the country, and the Mormon Tabernacle Choir performed for audiences throughout the nation.

>> **The Church reached out to the media.** At first, it focused on rebutting false information and providing sympathetic portrayals of its controversial history. By the 1920s, Mormonism was getting more favorable press coverage, with President Heber J. Grant appearing on the cover of *Time* magazine. In time, even Hollywood came around, most notably with the Mormon-friendly movie *Brigham Young*, released in the 1940s.

>> **During the Depression years of the 1930s, the Church gained admiring national attention for its extensive welfare program.** This program helped members survive the dismal economy and allowed many of them to get off the government dole. Latter-day Saints became known for taking care of their own. (For more information on the Mormon welfare program, see Chapter 8.)

>> **The Church stepped up its evangelistic efforts by shifting the work from older, married men to younger, single missionaries, including women.** The missionary force grew from fewer than 900 annually in 1900 to more than 2,000 by 1940. In addition, the Church made improvements in missionary training and resources. As a result, Church membership mushroomed from about 268,000 in 1900 to almost 1 million by 1945 — but the real exponential growth was yet to come.

>> **Many Latter-day Saints started seeking education and jobs in other parts of the nation, especially California.** This change allowed more Americans to witness firsthand that Latter-day Saints weren't weird but could be as conventionally middle class as anyone. As the Church constructed meetinghouses and temples around the nation and started building them overseas, the faith's visibility and respectability increased.

>> **Although 19th-century Mormons fled the United States because the government failed to protect their rights, 20th-century Latter-day Saints became highly patriotic.** Numerous Church members rose to prominence in America's political, business, and professional spheres, and the Latter-day Saints did their share — and sometimes more — to support the United States in wars and other efforts.

TIP

If you're interested in a highly readable narrative of LDS history from 1820–2020, check out the Church's recently published four-volume series called *Saints: The Story of the Church of Jesus Christ in the Latter Days.* For more details, visit www.churchofjesuschrist.org/learn/history/saints.

4

Mormonism Today

You see a snapshot of Mormon life today, spending a day in the life of a missionary and finding out about the growing pains that naturally go along with the Church's rapid expansion. We also clue you in on some of the hot-button issues in Mormonism, from race and the priesthood to women's roles and Mormon views on homosexuality.

Then you look at some daily, weekly, and monthly Mormon disciplines, from the spiritual (prayer, scripture study, fasting, and keeping the Sabbath) to the temporal (food storage, tithing, and emergency preparedness). You discover why Mormons believe that doing these things makes them more devoted followers of Jesus Christ, even if they have to make certain sacrifices. Finally, you dive into Mormon culture, including film, music, and literature.

Chapter **14**

Called to Serve: Missionaries and International Growth

Upon hearing the word *Mormon*, many people instantly envision two wholesome-looking young men or women walking or bicycling through the neighborhood wearing the telltale black missionary badges. These missionaries are the main means by which the LDS church fulfills its sacred mandate to spread the restored gospel and church of Jesus Christ throughout the earth. As we explore in this chapter, missionary service is a huge part of Mormon culture.

Largely because of this dynamic force of about 68,000 — at this writing — full-time teaching missionaries, the LDS church has grown remarkably fast since World War II. In the past 75 years, Mormonism has mushroomed from 1 million members in 1950 to over 17 million in 2024. Much of this growth has occurred in far-flung places, with more than half the Church's total membership now living outside the United States, in more than 165 nations and territories. As we show you in this chapter, these membership statistics don't tell the whole story of how many members are actually active participants in the LDS church, but they indicate Mormonism's reach into many nations and cultures.

Missionaries of All Shapes and Sizes

At the age of 3, Latter-day Saint boys and girls begin learning a song titled "I Hope They Call Me on a Mission." However, the song is really aimed mostly at the boys, who make up about three-quarters of the total missionary force. Missionary service is practically encoded into the DNA of Mormon-born males, and it's considered a priesthood duty. Young women are welcome to serve missions, but Church leaders say they should feel no obligation to do so. On the other hand, Church leaders increasingly encourage senior Latter-day Saint couples and singles to serve missions if they don't have any dependent children and their health and finances allow it. After all, older folks provide maturity and wisdom that the youngsters can't match.

Citing the rigors and demands of missionary life, the Church sets high qualifications for missionary service, particularly for the boys. Increasingly, leaders are weeding out young people who sow their wild oats and then try to repent or who aren't prepared to succeed on a full-time proselytizing mission, including for health reasons. The Church expects missionaries to demonstrate real faith and a genuine desire to serve instead of going on a mission to meet social expectations, to try to convert *themselves* to Mormonism, to please girlfriends who will marry only a returned missionary, or to get the new car their parents promised if they serve a mission. Those who are worthy to serve a mission but who suffer from physical or emotional problems often volunteer in local positions rather than in full-time, faraway missions.

As the teen years progress, parents and youth advisors help Latter-day Saint youths prepare for their missions. This preparation includes not only religious knowledge and belief but also practical skills, such as:

>> Saving and budgeting money

>> Speaking in public and teaching individuals of all ages

>> Working hard and getting along with others

>> Laundering, mending, and ironing their clothes

>> Preparing nutritious meals and doing basic housework

Boy wonders

For over a century, a mission has been Mormonism's rite of passage into adulthood for young men, almost like a two-year tithing on the first 20 years of life. Many begin serving soon after high school graduation, while others work or attend college before serving. A male can sign up for a mission as early as 18 and as late as age 24 — after that, he's expected to stay home and evangelize the single gals until he finds one who's willing to become his wife and have babies. The mission window for men opens again starting at age 40 when single men can apply to go on a full-time mission.

Every qualified, able young man is expected to serve, and the social pressure is enormous. Not going — or going but leaving or getting sent home early — can make a young man feel like a second-class Latter-day Saint for years afterward. Whether or not a missionary wins many converts, the experience is considered essential preparation for future Church service and leadership.

Girl power

Some Latter-day Saints used to joke that women went on missions only if they couldn't get married. In recent years, however, increasing numbers of young women have chosen to serve missions before getting married. These "sister missionaries" must wait until they're 19 to leave, which means they need to find something else to do for a year or so after high school, but they don't have age limits like the men do — even a 30-year-old woman can go on a mission if she's still single.

Although young men serve for two years and generally stick to finding and teaching prospective converts, young women serve for 18 months and may receive special assignments, such as staffing a Church visitors' center or helping disadvantaged people improve their health and hygiene. However, female missionaries can also be extremely effective in their evangelizing. Male missionaries typically baptize their own converts, but female missionaries can't because Mormon women don't hold the priesthood. Instead, the male missionaries or a local priesthood holder does it for them (for more on the priesthood, see Chapter 4).

Silver is golden

With today's prosperity and longevity, many Latter-day Saint couples and singles find themselves with plenty of money and energy still left after they retire. Serving from home or abroad, senior missionaries focus their efforts on helping the Church and its existing members. In particular, the Church has discovered that senior missionaries provide a valuable leadership role in less-developed parts of the Church. Requests for senior missionaries have become more frequent and urgent in recent years, and it's becoming common for willing, able seniors to serve multiple missions during their "retirement" years.

Senior missionaries can choose from among several kinds of missionary assignments and locations, although most volunteer to go wherever they're needed. Depending on their background and skills, they may work in a temple, gather family history data, teach in a Church educational program, serve as agricultural specialists, work as medical doctors or nurses, help people find employment, or fulfill other humanitarian roles. Senior missionaries have more flexibility in determining their length of service, and they don't have to follow the same strict schedule and rules as the young men and women (see "Living the Missionary Life," later in this chapter).

Hail to the chief

Although being a missionary is hard work, probably the most challenging assignment is to preside over one of the Church's 300-plus missions worldwide as a *mission president*. While foot-soldier missionaries volunteer to serve when they're ready, the Church calls mission presidents at its own discretion, often surprising a couple in the middle of their careers.

Can you imagine being responsible for a hundred or two 19-year-old boys, plus several dozen women and couples, for a period of three years? Not only must you constantly train, motivate, organize, and discipline these people in the often-discouraging work of preaching LDS Christianity to a largely indifferent — if not outright hostile — world, but you must also deal with the missionaries' mistakes, problems, illnesses, crises, complaints, conflicts, sins, and special requests. In addition, you must work closely with both the Church's local leaders and its General Authorities, including the highest-ranking apostles (see Chapter 8).

Sound fun? Add another factor: If you accept the calling of mission president and you're still a working man, you have to leave your job and forgo earning a salary for three years beyond the modest living allowance that the Church provides. If you and your wife still have children at home, you have to uproot them to live somewhere else, possibly somewhere quite foreign. We don't know how the Church identifies which men — couples, really, because the mission president's wife is usually involved in the day-to-day running of the mission — to call, but we know that Latter-day Saints generally admire these couples.

Enlisting in God's Army

A few months before the desired departure time, a Latter-day Saint begins filling out the missionary application, which requires medical and dental exams and worthiness interviews with local Church leaders. In applying to serve a mission, young missionaries don't get to choose where they'll go and what language they'll speak. What's more, they have to pay all their own expenses, except airfare to and from the mission field, which the Church covers.

After the missionary's stake president (see Chapter 6) sends the application to Church headquarters, it takes just a few weeks to process it. Because a missionary may be assigned anywhere in the world, anticipation runs high for receiving that all-important call online from Salt Lake City. Before the missionary opens it, family and friends typically gather round.

Embracing the calling

Receiving a call to Wyoming when you were hoping to go to Hong Kong — or vice versa — can be a little challenging. However, Latter-day Saints believe that each mission call is divinely inspired. Nevertheless, the number of calls issued each year — well over 30,000 — undoubtedly results in some bureaucratic randomness. Reports say that top-level apostles review all the calls and correct any that don't feel right.

Some Latter-day Saints believe that a person's mission call was determined in the premortal life (for more about the Mormon concept of premortality, see Chapter 2). Faith-promoting stories circulate about the missionary who, while diligently knocking on doors, meets someone who seems instantly, uncannily familiar. The common explanation for such déjà vu is that in the premortal life, the missionary promised this person that during mortality, the missionary would find and teach them the truth. This widespread folk belief not only helps missionaries accept their callings but also motivates them to work hard so they don't break their promise to find that special someone.

Financing the mission

Ideally, missionaries pay their own clothing and living expenses with money that they save up beforehand. Missionaries used to cover their own costs directly, an idea that was fabulous if you went to Guatemala but not so great if you went to Tokyo. Now the Church centralizes and equalizes missionary finances, with each missionary paying the same monthly amount no matter where in the world they serve. At the time of this writing, the monthly U.S. amount to support a missionary is $500, which totals $12,000 for a young man serving two years and $9,000 for a young woman serving 18 months.

If the missionary hasn't saved enough to pay for his or her entire mission, the parents help out. If the parents can't afford it, the local congregation pitches in. If the local congregation can't swing it, Church headquarters contributes funds under certain circumstances.

Missionary boot camp

After giving a "farewell" talk in church, missionaries start their training. Many missionaries begin their training online at home and then continue at one of several *missionary training centers* around the world, which are commonly known as *MTCs*. Depending on the circumstances, some missionaries may do all their training from home or all of it at an MTC. The Church maintains an especially large MTC adjacent to Brigham Young University in Provo, Utah, where several thousand missionaries can undergo spiritual boot camp at the same time.

At the Provo MTC, English-speaking missionaries spend a few weeks in intensive study and preparation, and foreign-speaking missionaries spend even longer. The Mormon approach to mastering languages is so effective that government agencies and companies have adopted some of the methods. However, Mormons would attribute their success at least partly to the spiritual gift of tongues, as described in the Bible's New Testament. (For more on spiritual gifts, see Chapter 3.)

The MTC is known as a place of emotional highs and lows, where some missionaries nearly burst with enthusiasm for converting the world, while others deflate with homesickness or lack of faith. In this spiritual pressure cooker, missionaries who've attempted to hide earlier sins tend to come clean, sometimes resulting in their being sent back home temporarily — or permanently.

Living the Missionary Life

SCRIPTURE

A missionary's guiding purpose is to bring people to Christ through baptism. Latter-day Saints take very seriously the Savior's biblical "great commission": "Go ye therefore, and teach all nations, baptizing them in the name of the Father, and of the Son, and of the Holy Ghost: teaching them to observe all things whatsoever I have commanded you" (Matthew 28:19–20). Although Latter-day Saints respect many of the teachings and practices of other Christian faiths, they don't recognize other Christian baptisms as eternally valid (to find out why, see Chapter 4).

How many convert baptisms does the typical missionary achieve? It varies widely from place to place. It's not uncommon for a missionary to baptize dozens in South America and *none* in Europe. Approximately 251,000 converts joined the Church in 2023, making the annual worldwide average about seven or eight converts per missionary pair.

This section looks at how missionaries gain converts and what rules missionaries must follow. (By the way, for an entertaining, somewhat realistic peek into Mormon missionary life, we recommend two independent movies: *God's Army* and *The Best Two Years*. For a more horrific, R-rated take, check out *Heretic*, if you dare.)

Finding and teaching

Before missionaries can baptize someone, they have to find that person and teach the gospel to that person. Missionaries work in pairs all day and evening in three basic activities: finding people to teach, teaching them, and working with local members.

Making initial contacts

In most missions, the task of finding people to teach takes the majority of the missionaries' time and energy. They have several ways of doing it, including the following:

>> **Following up on referrals:** Some missionaries are given the assignment to visit people who've requested information at a Church visitors' center or who've responded to a Church advertisement, often for a free book or video. The most productive referrals come through local members whose friends have agreed to visit with the missionaries, often in the members' homes.

TIP

Anyone can request a visit from their local Mormon missionaries at www.churchofjesuschrist.org/comeuntochrist.

>> **Street contacting:** Missionaries often hang out in public areas and try to strike up conversations with passersby. Parks, shopping centers, and public transportation are good places for this method. Sometimes, the missionaries set up a display.

>> **Tracting:** If this word has an air of self-torture about it, that's fitting. Knocking on doors is called *tracting* because missionaries used to hand out religious tracts, although they rarely do so anymore. Most doors go unanswered, and most answered doors result in rejection, a slam, or even verbal abuse. When missionaries are invited inside a house, it's often by a lonely elderly or unemployed person or by someone who wants to debate religion. Still, tracting yields converts more often than haystacks yield needles.

Teaching people the gospel

When someone agrees to hear the Mormon message, that person becomes what the missionaries call an *investigator*. The missionaries' job is to teach the investigator a set of basic gospel principles over the course of several flexible visits. Missionaries used to recite memorized scripts, but today the Church encourages them to use their own words and rely on the guidance of the Holy Ghost.

Applying a technique called the *commitment pattern*, missionaries prepare their investigators, invite them to make commitments and follow up to resolve any concerns.

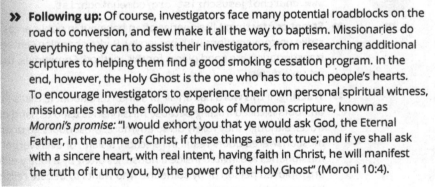

>> **Preparing:** The main way missionaries prepare investigators is to help them feel the influence of the Holy Ghost. During their teaching, they frequently bear solemn, earnest personal testimony that the principles are true. Other ways to help investigators feel the Holy Ghost include praying with them, singing a hymn with them, reading the scriptures aloud together, telling about personal spiritual experiences, and performing acts of service for them. Missionaries often say something like, "Do you feel a warm, good feeling right now? That's the Holy Ghost, testifying to you that what we're saying is true." (For more on the Holy Ghost, see Chapter 3.)

>> **Inviting:** As they teach the gospel, missionaries often pause to ask investigators what they're thinking or feeling. When the time seems right, the missionaries ask the investigator to make certain commitments that move the investigator closer to baptism. The commitments include reading selected passages from the Book of Mormon, praying to know if the gospel is true, attending the local Mormon congregation, and quitting the use of tobacco or coffee. If it feels right, the missionaries will ask the investigator to commit to a baptismal date (for more on Mormon baptism, see Chapter 6).

SCRIPTURE

>> **Following up:** Of course, investigators face many potential roadblocks on the road to conversion, and few make it all the way to baptism. Missionaries do everything they can to assist their investigators, from researching additional scriptures to helping them find a good smoking cessation program. In the end, however, the Holy Ghost is the one who has to touch people's hearts. To encourage investigators to experience their own personal spiritual witness, missionaries share the following Book of Mormon scripture, known as *Moroni's promise:* "I would exhort you that ye would ask God, the Eternal Father, in the name of Christ, if these things are not true; and if ye shall ask with a sincere heart, with real intent, having faith in Christ, he will manifest the truth of it unto you, by the power of the Holy Ghost" (Moroni 10:4).

Working with local Church members

A big part of missionary life involves teamwork with the local Latter-day Saints, who provide the missionaries with moral support, give referrals of people to teach, and help welcome new converts into the Church. (Perhaps most important, local members often provide home-cooked meals for the missionaries. When left to their own devices, the young men in particular tend to overdose on ramen noodles or macaroni and cheese, a.k.a. the yellow death.)

When missionaries don't have teaching appointments in the evening, they usually spend that time visiting local members and giving them short gospel presentations. If the members are active churchgoers, the missionaries ask them if they have any friends or family members who may be willing to hear the gospel. If the members aren't currently active in the faith, the missionaries encourage them to start attending church again. In working with members, missionaries often use the same commitment pattern described in the preceding section (prepare, invite, and follow up). In fact, lots of returned missionaries continue using that pattern in their marriages and careers.

REMEMBER

Church members play a vital role in conversion because after a convert is baptized, the missionaries move on, and the convert becomes the responsibility of the local congregation. All too often, that transition isn't successful. Although the new convert has usually developed a close personal relationship with the missionaries, he or she often hasn't bonded with anyone in the local congregation. For this reason, when a promising convert makes it beyond the first few missionary lessons, the missionaries often start bringing along local members to the teaching appointments, and they try to get the potential convert involved in the local Mormon social scene.

The LDS church continually urges Mormons to share the gospel with their friends and neighbors, help retain new converts, and reach out to reactivate members who've fallen away. Members are encouraged to hand out copies of the Book of Mormon and other Church publications, including handy little pass-along cards that offer a free LDS scripture book or video. The Church asks them to invite people into their homes to watch Church videos and, if possible, arrange for them to meet the missionaries. Although the rejection rate is still high, member referrals result in much more success than cold-calling techniques do.

Following the rules

Succeeding as a missionary requires many strong qualities. A missionary must be patient, loving, persistent, and articulate. However, the Mormon missionary program seems to emphasize one virtue above all others: obedience. Over and over again, Church leaders tell missionaries that in order to effectively teach and convert people, they must follow the Holy Ghost's promptings, but they won't be able to feel the Holy Ghost unless they obey all the mission rules and regulations.

WHEN YOU HEAR THE KNOCK

Eventually, almost everybody in the world will encounter Mormon missionaries. Most people feel either irritated or apathetic toward them, but some feel curiosity or even compassion.

If you decide to invite the missionaries into your home, here are some suggestions to help the missionaries stay the course:

- If you're the opposite sex of the visiting missionaries and you're home alone or with children only, invite them to come back when an additional adult will be present.

- Turn off your screens and other distractions.

- Don't smoke, drink alcohol, or use profanity in front of the missionaries. Offering them a refreshment is okay, but don't be like the guy in Melbourne, Australia, who got arrested for feeding marijuana-laced brownies to the missionaries!

- Be frank with them about your intentions and motivations. If you're willing to hear their message, say so. But if you just want to let them take a break or get to know them a little, be clear about that. If the weather is uncomfortably cold or hot, they'll especially appreciate it.

- If you must know their first names, go ahead and ask. But continue addressing them as Elder or Sister So-and-So, as indicated on their name badges. Feel free to ask about their hometowns and other small-talk stuff.

- If you invite the missionaries over for a meal, have it ready when they arrive because they're not allowed to stay for more than an hour.

So, what are the mission rules? Most of them are spelled out in a small, white booklet that missionaries are supposed to carry at all times. In addition, individual mission presidents make their own rules, which can sometimes seem arbitrary: coauthor Christopher Bigelow had one mission president who prohibited yellow neckties and asked missionaries not to use mousse in their hair. Because the mission president can't be everywhere at once, missionaries supervise each other by means of an organized system of zones and districts.

Following is an overview of the most significant rules that missionaries must follow:

>> **A missionary *always* stays with a companion.** For many people, this rule turns out to be the most difficult aspect of serving a mission. The only time a missionary can be alone is in the bathroom — and not for too long. This policy is mainly to protect missionaries from falling into sin or danger.

>> **Missionaries strive to follow a daily schedule.** They arise early, spend time in personal and companionship gospel study, and then work all day and evening, with one-hour breaks for lunch and dinner. Frankly, many missionaries struggle against wasting time by idling in the apartment, going shopping or sightseeing, hanging out too long at members' homes, and so on.

>> **To stay spiritually pure, missionaries don't watch TV or movies, keep up with the news, or listen to secular music.** The only reading material allowed is the scriptures, the Church magazines, and a handful of approved Church-published books. Missionaries can use social media but only for missionary work.

>> **One day each week, missionaries take a preparation day, or P-day.** They use this time to shop for groceries, wash their clothes, clean their apartments, fix their bicycles, contact their families, and run personal errands. If they have time left over, they can play mission-approved sports or visit nearby tourist attractions.

>> **Missionaries wear formal proselytizing clothes.** Exceptions include playing sports on P-day and performing service projects requiring grubby clothes — but they still wear missionary badges even then. In recent years, missionary clothing rules have loosened. Women can now wear dress slacks. In some missions, men can wear blue dress shirts instead of white and go without a suitcoat or tie.

>> **Missionaries keep their distance.** Shaking hands is the most physical contact they can have with the opposite gender and with children, and an additional adult of their own gender must be present when they meet with a single person of the opposite gender.

>> **Missionaries don't date.** If a missionary gets romantically involved with someone, the missionary is usually transferred far away, possibly even to another mission. If a missionary has sex, they're usually excommunicated and sent home, hopefully to repent and eventually get rebaptized. (For more on LDS sexual standards, see Chapter 16.)

Rapid Growth: Mormonism Around the World

After lying relatively low through the Great Depression and World War II, the Church launched an unprecedented worldwide growth binge, which continues (although at a slowing pace) to this day. The Church poured tremendous resources into opening diplomatic relationships with individual nations, sending out more missionaries than ever, constructing meetinghouses and temples all over the globe, and providing local leadership support and resources to help the Church take root wherever it was planted. Table 14-1 illustrates how much the Church has grown since 1950 after missionary efforts were kicked into high gear.

TABLE 14-1 ## Church Growth, 1950 to 2023

	1950	1990	2023
Total membership	About 1 million	7.3 million	17.3 million
Number of full-time teaching missionaries	6,000	40,000	68,000
Number of *stakes* (local clusters of congregations)	180	1,700	3,565
Number of temples	8	44	186 (with 55 more under construction and 94 in planning stages)

Religions change tremendously as they grow, and the LDS church is no exception. Consider how much it had changed since the pioneer days (see Chapter 13) when Mormons were clannish, Euro-American, and polygamous. Today, they're multinational, multicultural, and most decidedly monogamous. Who knows what changes are in store for the next century, as Mormonism increasingly takes its place as a bona fide world religion?

So far in its rapid growth, several challenges have emerged, along with new Church programs and efforts to resolve those problems.

Retaining members

One of the most serious issues facing the Church at home and abroad is that of *retention*, or keeping new members active in the Church after they're baptized. In some parts of the world, baptism rates are very high, but converts may not remain active in the Church because they don't know local members, they have cultural concerns about being involved in an American-based church, or they simply don't yet understand the level of commitment expected of Latter-day Saints.

In the United States and Canada, the average rate of weekly attendance at *sacrament meeting* (see Chapter 6) is often thought to hover around 50 percent of members. But elsewhere in the world, attendance rates may be far lower, around 20 to 30 percent. This may reflect members' difficulties in traveling to meetings that are far away when they don't have cars or reliable public transportation.

The Church takes retention very seriously, striving to ensure that all new converts have three basic things:

>> A friend in the Church to answer questions and nurture them in the faith

>> A *calling* (an assignment or job to do in the local congregation; see Chapter 6)

>> Training in the scriptures and Church teachings through ongoing classes and resources

Being sensitive to cultural differences

In the 19th century, Mormon missionaries encouraged converts abroad to gather in Ohio, Missouri, Nauvoo, or Utah — wherever Church headquarters was located at the time. Although this gave way to the bloom-where-you're-planted strategy that characterized the 20th century, it's sometimes still a struggle for Mormon converts abroad to remain true to their own culture and heritage while being involved in a church that people often perceive as being very American.

As the LDS church has expanded into many lands and cultures, it's made strides in celebrating the local heritage of its members. Although the core teachings of the Church remain the same everywhere, its cultural expression can vary from place to place. For example, music is one area where American missionaries and Church members are learning to be more flexible with local customs in Latin America, Africa, and elsewhere. (Somehow, the staid organ music typical of American sacrament meetings just doesn't translate.)

One issue that crops up as the Church expands into many nations is the importance of training strong leaders who are native to those lands. When the Church relies too heavily on short-term missionaries to lead congregations, the congregations have no continuity of leadership, and the rising generation isn't prepared to assume those roles in the future. As you see in the next section, the Church has implemented several policies to address this issue.

Strengthening the worldwide Church

In addition to providing more inclusive leadership from headquarters, some of the Church's current strategies for improving retention and promoting native leadership include

>> **The Perpetual Education Fund:** The Church believes that its most promising asset is its young people all around the world. Through the Perpetual

Education Fund, which we also discuss in Chapters 8 and 12, many young Mormons in underdeveloped countries can get an education through a revolving loan program. The Church believes that when young people can get an education and achieve financial stability, they're freed for greater Church activity and receive more blessings of the gospel.

>> **Native missionaries:** In recent years, the Church has placed a greater emphasis on training missionaries who are native to the land (or at least to the language) where they're serving. For retention purposes, the immediate benefit is that native peoples don't dismiss Mormonism simply as an American church, but it also has the long-term effect of preparing excellent native leadership for the years to come. Today's missionaries make tomorrow's local leaders.

>> **Temple construction:** Temple building has greatly accelerated around the world. Locating temples closer to where members live increases the Church's visibility around the world and strengthens the individual members, who can make temple attendance a regular part of their spiritual life rather than a once-in-a-lifetime pilgrimage (for more on the temple, see Chapter 7).

Whereas a hundred years ago Mormonism was largely an American and European faith, most of today's growth is happening in Africa, Asia, and Latin America. In fact, the Church has been cutting back its missionary force in Europe and elsewhere due to a lack of results, and the convert growth rate in the United States is lower than it used to be. Clearly, the stage is set for the further growth of Mormonism in other key areas.

Chapter **15**

Hot-Button Issues for Latter-day Saints

L ike any human organization, The Church of Jesus Christ of Latter-day Saints has its share of gray areas, internal contradictions, flip-flops, zigzags, and conflicts that, for some members, require patience and faith to negotiate — especially now that everything's so transparent online. Many of the challenges result from this young religion's dynamic, evolving nature, which leaves some people wanting to return to earlier ways, some struggling to reconcile the past with the present, and some trying to speed up the process of change.

This chapter looks at key areas where Latter-day Saints and outside observers experience the most disagreement, skepticism, or lack of resolution. Since 2013, the Church has been releasing unusually frank, nuanced, scholarship-supported position papers on controversial subjects, giving them what the Church considers their proper context. These important articles have become known (rather blandly) as the "Gospel Topics Essays," and you can find them all at www.churchofjesus christ.org/study/manual/gospel-topics-essays. At this writing, there are 14 of these essays, and we'll briefly go over each one, also acknowledging some of the pushback. The Church hasn't issued a Gospel Topics Essay on LGBTQ+ issues, but this chapter on controversies wouldn't be complete without a discussion of this topic, so we include it too.

Are Latter-day Saints Christian?

The first Gospel Topics essay, titled "Are 'Mormons' Christian?", doesn't leave any room for suspense: "Members of The Church of Jesus Christ of Latter-day Saints unequivocally affirm themselves to be Christians." This essay addresses three common arguments for why Latter-day Saints are not Christians:

>> **The LDS church does "not accept the creeds, confessions, and formulations of post–New Testament Christianity."** Why? Because the Church believes those later changes were "a grave error." Instead, the Church adheres to what it considers to be original Christian views.

>> **The LDS church is not connected to a branch of Christianity, such as Catholicism, Eastern Orthodoxy, or Protestantism.** Correct, the Church is not an outgrowth of any previous Christian church. "This is the 'restored,' not a 'reformed,' church of Jesus Christ," the essay says.

>> **The LDS church accepts books other than the Bible as scripture.** Yes, but the Bible never claimed to be the sole source of God's word. Besides, other Christian churches accept extra-biblical sources as well — for example, those post–New Testament "creeds, confessions, and formulations" mentioned earlier. (See Chapters 9 and 10 for more on Mormon scripture.)

This Gospel Topics essay concludes by asserting that a Christian is simply someone "who sincerely loves, worships, and follows Christ." However, many mainstream Christians still have some questions about LDS claims to Christianity, such as:

>> The New Testament warns of people preaching "another Jesus" (2 Corinthians 11:4). So, which Jesus do the Latter-day Saints worship? Is it really the one found in the Bible?

>> How can Latter-day Saints consider themselves Christian when they have historically rejected the idea of being saved by Jesus' grace alone? (Ephesians 2:8–9)

>> Why are Latter-day Saints so intent on being called Christian when they consider mainstream Christianity to be in a state of apostasy?

For more about LDS views on Jesus Christ, see Chapters 3 and 19.

Becoming Like Our Heavenly Parents

This Gospel Topics essay, titled "Becoming Like God," immediately nails down the relationship between God and mortals: Mortals are literally children of God. "Just as a child can develop the attributes of his or her parents over time, the divine nature that humans inherit can be developed to become like their Heavenly Father's." In other words, Latter-day Saints believe in deification — that they can eventually become gods themselves.

So, why is this topic covered in a Gospel Topics essay? Partly because Mormonism presents itself as a monotheistic religion — believing in just one God. But if God's children can become gods too, then doesn't that make Mormonism a polytheistic religion? The essay rejects that descriptor, saying that God's children will always worship only him. However, the essay doesn't talk about the next logical step: Is there a "heavenly grandfather" — our God's god? Are there other gods who may be siblings to our God? And so on.

REMEMBER

The essay points out that most of Christianity calls God the Eternal Father but believes it only metaphorically. They do not believe, as Latter-day Saints do, that God was once human and had to progress to attain his level of holiness. Rather, today's Christian God has always been God and has always been holy — otherwise, he wouldn't be God. This essay uses early Christian writings to support the Mormon concept of God, so check it out. (For more on humans becoming like our Heavenly Parents, see Chapters 2, 3, and 19.)

DNA Science versus the Book of Mormon

As you read in Chapter 9, the Book of Mormon is billed as a history of ancient civilizations on the American continent. At the beginning of the Book of Mormon, Lehi and his large family, including many grown children with their spouses, migrate from Jerusalem to America and start to multiply, and the book covers more than a thousand years of their turbulent history. The two main groups are the Lamanites and the Nephites. By the end of the book, the Lamanites have destroyed the Nephites.

For more than 150 years, the official interpretation of the Book of Mormon was that the Lamanites' descendants — Native Americans — were of Hebrew descent and, therefore, part of the House of Israel. In fact, the first missionaries deployed by Joseph Smith visited some nearby Native American tribes to start the "gathering of Israel." From the 1920s to 2007, the Book of Mormon's introduction page stated that the Lamanites were the "principal ancestors" of the Native Americans.

This belief augmented the Church's missionary efforts in Central America, South America, and Polynesia (where some Lamanites are believed to have immigrated), with many converts in those areas being taught that they had Lamanite heritage.

So, it was a shock to many Latter-day Saints when DNA studies showed that Native Americans had overwhelmingly East Asian DNA. It seemed to strike at the very foundations of not only the Book of Mormon but also the identity of many Latter-day Saints.

In 2007, the Book of Mormon's introduction was softened to say that the Lamanites were only "among the ancestors" of Native Americans. But as DNA study continues, Middle Eastern DNA remains elusive in Native American populations. Titled "Book of Mormon and DNA Studies," this Gospel Topics essay addresses the problem by declaring that "DNA studies cannot be used decisively to either affirm or reject the historical authenticity of the Book of Mormon." It uses the concepts of *founder effect*, *population bottlenecks*, and *genetic drift* to show how Middle Eastern DNA could "remain undetected" in Native American populations. (We'll leave it to you to learn more about those DNA-science terms if you're interested.)

SCRIPTURE

In the end, this Gospel Topics essay deems DNA studies to be irrelevant to the Book of Mormon's value because "the primary purpose of the Book of Mormon is more spiritual than historical." The essay quotes Moroni 10:3–5: If you sincerely study the Book of Mormon with faith and prayer, God "will manifest the truth of it unto you, by the power of the Holy Ghost."

Getting Seer-Stoned

Much of the Book of Mormon's miraculous nature — and its tendency to trigger skepticism — arises from its modern-day origin story (which we cover in Chapter 9). Titled "Book of Mormon Translation," this Gospel Topics essay states that Joseph Smith "had very little formal education and was incapable of writing a book on his own, let alone translating an ancient book written from an unknown language." And yet his wife Emma said that Joseph "would dictate to me for hour after hour, and . . . after interruptions, he would at once begin where he had left off," not even needing to reread what he'd most recently dictated.

This Gospel Topics essay stands firmly behind the miraculous nature of the Book of Mormon's translation. So, why did the Church deem this essay necessary? For many decades, the Church produced dignified images featuring Joseph Smith studying the golden plates while his scribe sat close by, quill to paper. But then historians started rediscovering descriptions of Joseph's main dictation method: putting his face in his hat and staring at a glowing "seer stone" that, as a boy, he'd used to lead people through the night in pursuit of buried treasure. This image is awkward enough that it was lampooned on *South Park*, the animated sit-com created by the same guys who did the Mormon send-up musical *The Book of Mormon*. Some Latter-day Saints started wondering what else the Church had been hiding about the translation history. The seer stone also brought up the startling fact that Joseph was deeply involved in his era's folk magic.

Instead of beating around the bush, this Gospel Topics essay talks plainly about Joseph's use of the hat and stone in his translation process and about his involvement in folk magic. But it doesn't deeply address a much stickier question: How did the Book of Mormon translation process actually happen?

This isn't just an academic question. It connects with the most serious questions about whether the Book of Mormon documents an actual civilization. The main difficulties are in the Book of Mormon's anachronisms, such as the presence of horses, wheeled transportation, barley, and steel. The book also quotes extensively from parts of Isaiah in the Old Testament that, according to most Bible scholars, were written after Lehi's family would have left Jerusalem.

Two main theories exist for how Joseph Smith translated the Book of Mormon:

>> He simply read off the words shown to him by the seer stone.

>> He was given concepts by revelation that he then had to render into language.

The testimonies of Joseph's scribes seem to uphold the first theory, but the second theory later became popular as it helped account for the Book of Mormon's anachronisms. If Joseph was rendering concepts into English words, then of course his own experiences, conceptions, and worldview would bleed into it.

The Gospel Topics essay sticks solidly to the first theory, leaving the anachronisms unaddressed. As in the "Book of Mormon and DNA Studies" essay, this essay encourages readers to pray for a testimony of the Book of Mormon's truthfulness.

One Vision, Several Versions

Joseph Smith's First Vision (described in Chapter 4) has become a central pillar of Mormonism. It's one of the first things missionaries tell the people they teach. It's often used as proof of the Mormon concept that God the Father and Jesus Christ are two separate beings. But most importantly, it establishes Joseph Smith as a prophet.

The odd thing is that most early Mormon converts didn't hear about the First Vision. In fact, we don't have any evidence of it until 1832, twelve years after it reportedly happened, when Joseph wrote about it in an unpublished autobiography. He talked about it again to a visitor in 1835, and a scribe recorded this account in Joseph's journal. But it wasn't until 1842, 22 years after the vision reportedly took place, that an official description was published.

These time lapses between the vision and Joseph's reports have led critics to charge that Joseph concocted the vision to bolster his authority as a prophet. As further evidence of the concoction, they point out that there are significant differences among the four versions Joseph gave of the vision. For example, in the first account, Joseph describes only one heavenly being appearing to him. In the second, he describes two beings along with "many angels." In the third, the angels are not mentioned.

The Gospel Topics essay on this controversy is titled "First Vision Accounts." That the Church published this essay at all means that many Latter-day Saints were unpleasantly surprised by these multiple accounts and the differences among them. Though the essay points out that the Church previously published articles and books on the different versions, the news apparently didn't make it to much of today's Church membership.

The essay offers several ways to read the various First Vision accounts as evidence of Joseph Smith's "increasing insight" into his experience of the vision. It points out that the versions were produced in different circumstances that likely affected how Joseph related his story. The essay also suggests that when Joseph wrote in the first version, "the Lord opened the heavens upon me and I saw the Lord," the first *Lord* was referring to God the Father and the second *Lord* was referring to Jesus Christ, thus getting the two heavenly beings into the first account.

As in many of these essays, the reader is pointed toward prayer as the final arbiter of truth: "Knowing the truth of Joseph Smith's testimony requires each earnest seeker of truth to study the record and then exercise sufficient faith in Christ to ask God in sincere, humble prayer whether the record is true."

Women and the Priesthood

For most of Christian history, priesthood and leadership roles have been restricted to men. Only in the late-20th and early-21st centuries have some denominations started ordaining women. In 2015, a grassroots Mormon activist movement called Ordain Women arose, and within two years the Church released a Gospel Topics essay titled "Joseph Smith's Teachings about Priesthood, Temple, and Women."

In the LDS church, it's true that women hold the top leadership positions of three "auxiliary" organizations: Relief Society, Young Women, and Primary (see Chapter 6). This Gospel Topics essay points out that, in most churches, one would have to be ordained to the priesthood to carry out such responsibilities. But it's also true that no matter how high in the chain of command a woman can serve, there will always be a male priesthood holder above her. She may, for example, set an auxiliary organization's budget, but a man will have to approve it.

At both the local and global levels, the Church's top councils consist entirely of men. Many other aspects of the LDS priesthood are also restricted only to men, such as performing ordinances and giving blessings of comfort and healing. Early in Church history, women could give healing blessings, but that practice slowly eroded until the Church rescinded it in 1926.

Some scholars have argued that, in the early days of the Church, Joseph Smith made statements showing that he intended to ordain women to the priesthood. The Church's Gospel Topics essay says that, yes, Joseph did intend to ordain women to the priesthood but not to specific priesthood *offices*, which can only be held by men. The priesthood authority that Joseph gave to women can be used only in the temple endowment ceremony (see Chapter 7), during which women can perform certain ordinances for other women. Further, the essay says that Joseph set up the priesthood organization so that women could fulfill priesthood duties, but only those delegated to them by male priesthood holders.

While the essay explains why Joseph Smith's statements do not imply that women should be ordained to priesthood offices, it uses a footnote to answer the next question on people's minds: "Why can't women be ordained to priesthood offices now, considering that our church has continuing revelation?" In answer, the Church quotes an apostle: "The Lord has directed that only men will be ordained to offices in the priesthood. . . . Presiding authorities 'are not free to alter [this] divinely decreed pattern.'" In other words, women can't be ordained to priesthood offices because God says so.

The essay concludes by emphasizing the "interdependence of men and women in accomplishing God's work through His power." For more about the Mormon priesthood, see Chapter 4.

What About Heavenly Mother?

As Chapter 3 points out, Mormonism's unique theology says that not only does Heavenly Father have a tangible body, but he is also sexed. This is a far cry from most Christian theologies, which conceive of God as a being without "body, parts, or passions." As we saw in this chapter's "Becoming Like Our Heavenly Parents" section, Mormonism considers humans to be literal children of God. Put these two concepts together, and it stands to reason that there must be a Heavenly Mother as well as a Heavenly Father.

Titled "Mother in Heaven," this Gospel Topics essay affirms that the concept of Heavenly Mother is "a cherished and distinctive belief among Latter-day Saints." However, it has been a very quiet belief. In official LDS discourse, references to Heavenly Father likely outnumber references to Heavenly Mother by half a million to one. For many decades, there's been a taboo in the Church against talking about Heavenly Mother or addressing her in prayer. In fact, people have been excommunicated for speaking and writing publicly about her.

This essay is the first really substantive statement from the official Church on Heavenly Mother. The most important thing it does is clearly establish Heavenly Mother as a doctrine, officially pulling her further into mainstream LDS discourse. This has been met with enthusiasm in many quarters. For many Mormon women (and men), the idea of having a Heavenly Mother is a powerful one.

But it is precisely concerns about that power that may have led the Church to publish the essay in the first place. In the second-to-last paragraph, the essay says explicitly that Latter-day Saints "do not pray to Heavenly Mother." Why would the Church double down on this? Possibly because praying to Heavenly Mother would make Mormonism appear closer to polytheism, which would make it even more difficult for the Church to find acceptance in mainstream Christianity. Some writers have also posited that the Church fears that praying to Heavenly Mother might make LDS women less compliant in the Church's patriarchal power structure.

Nonetheless, this essay does seem to open the door wider for at least talking about Heavenly Mother in the Church. Questions such as "How does Heavenly Mother fit into the godhead?" can now be more safely addressed. And LDS women can now more openly explore how Heavenly Mother might be spiritually interacting with them here in mortality and what it might mean to become a Heavenly Mother themselves in the eternities.

Crimes of Violence

It's been said that if horror is the pop-culture genre most identified with Catholicism and comedy with Judaism, then true crime has become the genre most identified with Mormonism (thanks, Netflix, Hulu, and others). It's true that the Church has its fair share of violent crime in its history, with Mormons as both victims and instigators.

In a Gospel Topics essay titled "Peace and Violence Among 19th-Century Latter-day Saints," the Church addresses historical Mormon violence from both perspectives. As victims, the early Mormons were violently ousted from several states (see Chapter 11), with their persecutors sometimes even resorting to murder and sexual assault. The Church's essay acknowledges that these difficulties stemmed partially from the fact that the Mormons were, as they described themselves, "a peculiar people." They had a unique set of beliefs and tended to quickly populate areas, which could swing political power into their hands. While this understandably alarmed the locals, it certainly didn't justify violence.

So, the Mormons trekked across the plains to live and worship in peace, making great sacrifices along the way. Pioneer stories of persecution and mass migration bring Latter-day Saints together in solidarity and inspire them to great works. However, especially after settling in Utah and environs, sometimes Mormons were the violent criminals.

"Settlers throughout the 19th century, including some Latter-day Saints, mistreated and killed Indians in numerous conflicts," says the Gospel Topics essay, "forcing them off desirable lands and onto reservations." Racism and colonialism were part of American culture during the 19th century, and the Mormons were involved in both. They believed that a massive portion of today's Western United States was their promised land, but they also believed that Native Americans were descended from the Lamanites in the Book of Mormon and, therefore, part of the House of Israel, so they tended to treat Native Americans better overall than other settlers did (see also this chapter's "Racial Rapprochement" section).

The essay also covers the infamous Mountain Meadows Massacre. In 1857, a group of Mormons, along with some local Native Americans they'd recruited, killed 120 people — men, women, and children — who were part of a wagon train passing near Cedar City, Utah. As with other violence against Mormons and perpetrated by them, the motivations for this massacre were complex — several scholarly books have been written about it. But the Gospel Topics essay boils it down by quoting a top apostle: "What was done here long ago by members of our Church represents a terrible and inexcusable departure from Christian teaching and conduct."

Puh-puh-puh . . . Polygamy

This topic is so delightful for Latter-day Saints — *not* — that the Church has given it not one but four Gospel Topics essays under the header "Plural Marriage." You can just feel the tension in the opening line of one essay: "The marriage of one man to one woman is God's standard, except at specific periods when He has declared otherwise." The overall theme of the four essays is that plural marriage was very difficult, but it also brought some blessings to the Church and its people. (See Chapter 13 for more about 19th-century Mormon polygamy.)

REMEMBER

The origins of Mormon polygamy during Joseph Smith's time are very difficult to trace, as there are no contemporary records about it. From what we can tell, Joseph Smith was the first to marry plurally, probably without the knowledge of his first wife, Emma Hale. Then, he started introducing it secretly among his closest associates. However, word about plural marriage soon leaked out, and it triggered a chain reaction that culminated in Joseph Smith's murder.

Brigham Young goes public

In 1852, Church president Brigham Young announced to the Church and the world that Mormons practiced plural marriage. He introduced it as a higher law that the most righteous Mormons should practice. Plural marriage was part of Joseph's vision of sealing the entire human family together — as well as an effective way to procreate more faithful children in the Church.

In some ways, polygamy did function as a higher law for the Latter-day Saints, as it required a great deal of sacrifice. As one Gospel Topics essay points out, God commanded polygamy but "did not give exact instructions on how to obey the commandment." No one knew how these polygamous relationships should work. What did husbands owe their wives? What did wives owe their husbands? What did they owe their sister wives? Zeal often outstripped wisdom, and this led to much hardship, both emotionally and financially.

However, this sacrifice often served to increase polygamists' commitment to the Church, and many reported intense spiritual experiences related to it. During the 50 years that plural marriage was openly practiced in Utah, some members came to appreciate the extended safety net of a large polygamous family, the supportive relationships between sister wives, the independence some wives felt from their exceptionally busy husbands, and the fact that pretty much any woman could marry and have children if she wanted to. As one essay admits, "the practice was generally based more on religious belief than on romantic love."

The Saints moved to the area that now includes Utah to get out of the United States so they could practice polygamy. However, the United States soon annexed the area. When the Edmunds-Tucker Act was passed to eliminate polygamy, polygamous Mormon men had to go into hiding lest they be arrested (and many were). Pregnant polygamous wives had to hide to avoid having to testify against their husbands. Children also worried about being forced to testify against their polygamous parents. But, as one essay points out, this pressure likely only increased Mormons' commitment to the Church.

The end of polygamy?

Soon the federal government was preparing to confiscate the Church's property unless it gave up polygamy. So, in 1890 Wilford Woodruff, third president of the Church, issued a manifesto rescinding plural marriage — but not completely. Mormon families were sent to Canada and Mexico to continue the practice. It took a lot of political pressure to force the Church to end polygamy once and for all in 1904, when it issued a second, more definitive manifesto. It still took decades to clean up the mess, however, and many "fundamentalist Mormons" still practice polygamy.

As you can imagine, the four essays repeat again and again that the LDS church does not engage in earthly polygamous marriages anymore. But polygamy is still technically part of official doctrine. A man can be sealed to more than one woman if he remarries after his wife dies or divorces him (for more on temple sealings, see Chapter 7). Some Mormon women wonder if they'll arrive in the afterlife only to find that their husband has taken on additional wives.

One quasi-official theory is that there must be polygamy in heaven because many more women than men are sufficiently righteous to get into the top tier of the *celestial kingdom* (see Chapter 2), and, therefore, multiple women will need to marry one man. Latter-day Saints can have deceased ancestors *sealed* (see Chapter 7) to all their spouses if they married more than one during mortality. The only comfort the essays offer is that, in all cases, God will eventually sort out everything.

Racial Rapprochement

From 1859–1978, the LDS church barred Black men from holding the priesthood, and Black people could not participate in temple endowment and sealing ordinances (see Chapter 7). Interestingly, Joseph Smith had been liberal in his priesthood ordination policies, ordaining at least two Black men to the priesthood, including Elijah Abel and Q. Walker Lewis. Abel also participated in temple ordinances. But in 1859, Brigham Young officially announced that the Church no longer ordained Black men.

In early Mormonism, the color of a person's skin held unique implications. In the Book of Mormon, when the Lamanites become wicked, God curses them with a "skin of blackness" specifically so that the Nephites, who have fair skin, will find them "loathsome" and not intermarry with them (2 Nephi 5:21; see Chapter 9 for more on the Book of Mormon). However, this dark skin did not mean that Lamanite-descended Native Americans and Polynesians were barred from the priesthood. But top-level Church leaders used to teach that their brown skin would lighten if they converted to the Church (the top leaders don't teach that anymore).

However, like some other Christians, Latter-day Saints believed that Africans were descended from Cain, who killed his brother Abel, as recounted in the Old Testament, and eventually must have made his way to Africa. The Church believed that God cursed Cain with black skin and that Africans inherited both his skin color and his curse. Another theory for the Church's racial ban was that people with African ancestry had been "less valiant" as spirits during the premortal "war in heaven" (see Chapter 2). Brigham Young taught that the curse would eventually be lifted, but he didn't say when or how. So, while Native Americans and Polynesians could fully lift their "curse" by joining the Church, Africans could be baptized but not enjoy priesthood or temple privileges.

According to the Church's "Race and the Priesthood" Gospel Topics essay, the ban against ordaining Black people was walked back incrementally, first when the Church started allowing Fijians and Australian Aborigines to be ordained, and then when South Africans were no longer required to trace their ancestry to see if they had any African blood. But it was not until 1978 that the ban was officially lifted. Black men can now be ordained to the priesthood, and Black people can participate in temple ordinances.

In what amounts to a highly unusual rebuke of early Church leaders, this essay explicitly rejects the theories those leaders raised about why Blacks could not be ordained to the priesthood or receive temple ordinances. The essay lays the blame squarely on Brigham Young, pretty much absolving Joseph Smith. The essay also admits that Mormonism has been influenced by the racism prevalent in American culture.

The way the Church positioned this essay likely reflects worries among top leadership that racism still exists in the Church today and that some members still cling to the old racist theories for the Black exclusion policy. The ban itself — and especially its long history — has disconcerted many Latter-day Saints, and Church leaders likely felt that being forthright about the Church's history was the best way to diffuse tensions over it.

One thing the essay does *not* do is offer an actual Church apology for the ban, which many Latter-day Saints have hoped for. But an apology may never come.

As one top LDS apostle recently said, "The Church doesn't 'seek apologies' . . . and we don't give them." If that statement makes you raise your eyebrows, you're certainly not alone.

Mummy's the Word

As we discuss in Chapter 10, in 1835, Joseph Smith acquired some Egyptian mummies with accompanying papyri that Joseph said contained sacred writings of the Biblical Abraham and Joseph (he of the many-colored coat). "Translating" these ancient writings, Joseph produced the Book of Abraham, which can be found in the Mormon scripture called the Pearl of Great Price, a collection of Joseph's canonized writings. The Book of Abraham includes some facsimiles of images contained in the papyri.

Until 2013, the Church's introduction to the Book of Abraham said that it was "a translation from some Egyptian papyri." But a straight-forward interpretation of "translation" became problematic in the 1960s when a museum in New York discovered some parts of Joseph Smith's papyri in its archives and offered them to the LDS church. Scholars found that the text on the papyri didn't match the text in the Book of Abraham at all. Earlier scholars had already pointed out that the facsimiles included in the Book of Abraham were common Egyptian funeral texts and had nothing to do with Abraham. And a translation of the Egyptian alphabet that Joseph and some associates had produced turned out to be all wrong as well.

Titled "Translation and Historicity of the Book of Abraham," this Gospel Topics essay reviews theories that have been advanced by LDS apologists to explain the disconnection. One theory is that the New York museum had only fragments of the papyri Joseph used, so Abraham's text could have been inscribed on the other parts that are still missing. The essay also points out that the Book of Abraham seems to describe some aspects of Biblical history that weren't discovered until after Joseph Smith's time.

But the essay's central argument is that Joseph's "translations" were always powered by divine revelation. "Joseph Smith did not claim to know the ancient languages of the records he was translating," the essay says. When he "translated" the Book of Mormon, he was often not even looking at the golden plates. When he was producing the inspired translation of the Bible, his translation was revealed to him rather than coming from elements within the text. Following this pattern, the essay hypothesizes that the papyri may have acted as a catalyst for a revelation that became the Book of Abraham. As the post-2013 introduction to the Book of Abraham reads, the text is an "inspired translation of the writings of Abraham."

As with many other Gospel Topics essays, this one ends by encouraging the reader to gain a testimony of the Book of Abraham's truth through spiritual means. "The truth of the book of Abraham is ultimately found through careful study of its teachings, sincere prayer, and the confirmation of the Spirit."

LDS versus LGBTQ+

The Church has not released a Gospel Topics essay on LGBTQ+ issues — rather, in 1995, it spelled out its doctrine on gender and sexuality in a one-page document titled "The Family: A Proclamation to the World," which we also discuss in Chapters 5 and 10. According to this proclamation, God recognizes and upholds only marriage between a man and a woman, and "Gender is an essential characteristic of individual premortal, mortal, and eternal identity and purpose." As of 2024, the Church considers gay sexual activity — even in a committed monogamous relationship — and gender transitioning as sins that may warrant Church membership restrictions or withdrawal.

Oddly enough, Mormon scriptures — including the Book of Mormon, the Doctrine and Covenants, and the Pearl of Great Price — say nothing about LGBTQ+ issues (see Chapters 9 and 10 for more on Mormon scriptures). In rejecting homosexual relations, Latter-day Saints rely on the same Bible passages as other Christians, which warn against homosexual lust and promiscuity but don't address anything resembling morally ethical same-sex marriage.

The Church's gay track record

Church leaders started talking publicly about homosexuality in 1952, and in 1959, two apostles were assigned to work with homosexual members. At the time, the Church followed the American Psychological Association in considering homosexuality a mental illness. Church leaders advanced theories for why someone would become homosexual, from an overbearing mother or a distant father to simple selfishness. During this time, even just identifying as homosexual could be grounds for excommunication. The Church tried to "cure" homosexuality among its members by means such as sustained fasting and prayer, heterosexual dating and marriage, and electroshock aversion therapy at Church-owned Brigham Young University.

Nowadays, the Church takes no position on the causes of homosexuality, and it doesn't support any kind of therapy for changing one's homosexuality, only for managing it. In 1995, an apostle admitted that the origins of someone's sexual feelings are complex, making room for the idea that homosexuality could have an inborn component. By 2012, high-level Church leaders were stating that homosexuality is not a choice. Today, a Latter-day Saint can publicly identify as homosexual and still participate in every aspect of the Church, including attending the temple, as long as they remain homosexually celibate.

In recent decades, the Church's strictness about gay issues has ebbed and flowed, with some jarring policy flip-flops at times. The Church campaigned vigorously against legalized same-sex marriage, but it favors equal housing and job rights for LGBTQ+ people. In 2022, the Church supported the federal Respect for Marriage Act, which defines marriage as a legal union between any two adults while also protecting religious liberty so faith groups can uphold their own marriage beliefs. Meanwhile, progressive Mormons offer theories for how homosexuality could fit into LDS theology. One observer points out that Mormonism's top heaven, the *celestial kingdom* (see Chapter 2), is divided into three sections, one of which is for heterosexually married people and the other two of which are not yet defined (see D&C 131:1–4). Might one of these sections be for righteous same-sex couples?

If full LGBTQ+ acceptance and equality in the LDS church ever come, it may still take decades. For better or worse, today's mainstream Latter-day Saints are predominantly politically conservative, and the Church often drags its feet on social progress. As gay Mormon historian D. Michael Quinn (1944–2021) discussed, it's possible that some top LDS apostles already know more about homosexual potential in God's plan but can't publicize it yet because not enough Church members — perhaps including fellow apostles — are ready to face a new reality. In a comparable situation, it took until 1978 for the Church to reverse its ban on Black members holding the priesthood and attending the temple. Members and outsiders alike put increasing pressure on the Church, and eventually, that revelation did come.

Transgender Latter-day Saints

Of course, transgenderism is a distinct issue from sexual orientation, as transgender people can be heterosexual, homosexual, or asexual. The LDS church teaches that "feelings of gender incongruence are not a measure of your faithfulness," but acting on these feelings is sinful. The Church defines gender as one's sex assigned at birth.

Transgender Latter-day Saints face their own special restrictions. Like other LGBTQ+ members, they can attend Sunday services regardless of their membership status. However, in Church classes where men and women meet separately (see Chapter 6), they can only attend the class that aligns with their birth-assigned sex. In any Church building, transgender people must either use the restroom for their birth-assigned sex or ask someone of the correct sex make sure the restroom is empty before they enter and then guard the door while they use it. Also, if a transgender member makes any move toward transitioning — including changing pronouns, dressing and grooming as the sex opposite to their birth-assigned sex, starting hormone-replacement therapy, or getting gender-confirming surgery — they're generally barred from working with Church youth and attending the temple.

Many transgender Latter-day Saints say they agree with the Church's teaching that "gender is an essential characteristic of individual premortal, mortal, and eternal identity and purpose" (for more on these concepts, see Chapter 2). Transgender people point out that, in this imperfect mortal world, sometimes biological switches don't get flipped correctly, including those that match a person's mortal body to their eternal gender. The transgender person's goal is to correct an earthly error, not change their eternal gender.

» **Following Mormon dietary regulations**

» **Donating a tenth of your income**

» **Going without food and drink once a month**

Chapter **16**

Earthly Sacrifices for Heavenly Blessings

In a distinctively Mormon hymn written during the pioneer era and still widely sung, Latter-day Saints croon, "Sacrifice brings forth the blessings of heaven." For Latter-day Saints, sacrifice is the essence of life's mortal test, because sacrificing earthly things is how people become pure and obedient enough to one day reenter Heavenly Father's presence and become like him.

Fortunately, Mormonism no longer typically requires the extreme, all-encompassing sacrifices common in 19th-century pioneer days, when persecution drove Mormons to give up their possessions and comforts, their places in society, their homes, and sometimes even their lives for faith's sake (see Chapters 11 through 13 for more on Mormon history). These days, Mormonism's most challenging sacrifices come mostly in the form of disciplined lifestyle choices that are increasingly at odds with what mainstream culture accepts and values.

The most difficult area is probably sexuality, which Latter-day Saints believe must be strictly channeled into marriage between one man and one woman. Famously, Latter-day Saints abstain from coffee, tea, tobacco, alcohol, and harmful, addictive substances (which doesn't include sugar, thank heavens). In addition, committed, temple-attending Latter-day Saints donate 10 percent of their income to the Church, and once a month, they skip two meals as an exercise in spiritual discipline and charitable giving. In this chapter, we discuss these sacrifices and why Latter-day Saints believe that making them is the road to holiness and, ultimately, heaven.

Chase and Be Chaste: The Law of Chastity

A Mormon dating website used to advertise the motto "Chase and Be Chaste," which is a pretty accurate summary of the Mormon attitude toward sexuality. Far from being a debased but necessary earthly function or even simply a gift of God to humankind, sexuality is nothing less than a divine attribute of the Heavenly Parents themselves (see Chapter 3 for a more detailed discussion of Mormon views on Heavenly Father and Heavenly Mother). Although it's not a topic that comes up much — if ever — in Mormon Sunday school today, earlier leaders taught that the eternal parents procreated human spirits through a glorified version of the same procreative act that humans use on earth.

Stated in the simplest terms, the Mormon law of chastity prohibits any sexual relations outside of lawful, heterosexual marriage. Chastity is one of the covenants that adult Latter-day Saints make in the temple (see Chapter 7 for more on the temple covenants). For Latter-day Saints, practicing chastity includes not only abstaining from sexual activity outside of marriage but also actively seeking a suitable marriage partner, because self-imposed celibacy thwarts God's designs for humankind (unless you're gay or lesbian, in which case God *does* want you to be celibate, according to current Church policy — see Chapter 15 for more on that). In fact, some early Church leaders taught that the Savior himself may have married and fathered children during his earthly life.

Understanding the purposes of sexuality

Considered from an eternal perspective, the reasons are clear why Latter-day Saints consider sex a sacred privilege that the law of chastity must govern. Latter-day Saints believe that Heavenly Father entrusted humans with sexuality not only to populate this planet but also as one of the key elements of their mortal test (for more info on the mortal test, see Chapter 2). In fact, how people conduct themselves sexually and parent any resulting offspring may be one of the most important factors in determining their eternal status. Those who live worthily and become eternally sealed to their mate in a Mormon temple can become heavenly fathers and mothers themselves, procreating spirit children and creating earthly planets to house those children during their own mortal tests.

When other Christians express concern that the Mormon concepts of God's sexuality and humankind's eternal potential are blasphemous, Latter-day Saints point to certain biblical passages for support. During his New Testament ministry, for example, Jesus Christ commanded his followers to "be ye therefore perfect, even as your Father which is in heaven is perfect" (Matthew 5:48). To Latter-day Saints, the meaning of *perfect* includes not only freedom from mistakes and blemishes but also completeness and wholeness. In fact, one dictionary definition of the word *perfect* is full sexual maturity, which is what Latter-day Saints are striving for on the eternal level, as commanded by the Savior.

Staying chaste

The law of chastity forbids any form of fornication or adultery, and the Church also warns against "anything like unto it," including dressing immodestly and viewing pornography. Some married Latter-day Saints strive never to be alone with a member of the opposite sex except family members, and some Mormon daters try to avoid intimacy beyond holding hands, hugging, and mild kissing.

Steering clear of pornography

In the Mormon view, pornography damages spirituality, weakens self-control, degrades the actors and viewers, and plants the seeds of sexual sin. Some Latter-day Saints even choose to avoid R-rated movies due to possible nudity and sex. However, the Church does not take disciplinary action against members for viewing pornography except in cases of "child pornography or intensive or compulsive use of pornography that has caused significant harm to a member's marriage or family."

Mormon leaders used to preach openly against masturbation, but the practice is rarely — if ever — publicly mentioned anymore. Instead, members are generally urged to "strive for moral cleanliness in your thoughts and behavior." In the Church's current handbook for local leaders, the only time *masturbation* appears is in the list of things for which a leader should *not* formally discipline a member. However, in private interviews, some leaders may informally counsel members about pornography and masturbation.

Maintaining modesty

In the area of modesty, the main sacrifice adult Mormons make is avoiding any clothing style that isn't compatible with the temple-issued underwear commonly known as *garments*, which cover almost the entire torso to the knee and shoulder (for more information about temple garments, see Chapter 7). Mormon youth are urged to "avoid styles that emphasize or draw inappropriate attention to your physical body."

For sports and swimming, adult Latter-day Saints remove their temple garments and don appropriate gear. Many Mormon females choose not to wear two-piece bathing suits, and Mormon girls are encouraged to avoid immodest prom dresses. In addition, many Mormons forgo body tattoos and piercings beyond one pair of earrings for women, but the Church doesn't have official proscriptions against those.

Keeping hands under control

Young Latter-day Saints are warned: "Outside of marriage between a man and a woman, it is wrong to touch the private, sacred parts of another person's body even if clothed." Church leaders urge dating adult members to follow these guidelines as well.

Of course, many Mormon couples venture into risky territory. Whether teen or adult, those who end up having premarital sex and want to repent must confess to their local bishop (see the later section "Dealing with sexual sin"). For those who stop short of fornication but feel guilty about how far they went, some Latter-day Saints would say they still need to see the bishop. However, some couples who've reached second or third base repent without the bishop's involvement.

Enjoying marital intimacy

Although Mormons view procreation as one of the primary purposes of sex, they also place a high value on its role in expressing marital love and binding couples together emotionally and spiritually. Mormon publishers put out detailed books about how to enhance sexual pleasure and compatibility, and couples enjoy wide latitude for sexual expression within marriage as long as they avoid "unholy and impure practices." Back in the 1980s, the Church tried to ban oral sex even in marriage for temple-attending members, but that didn't last long.

Receiving the blessings of chastity

All in all, Mormons see the law of chastity as the only safe, sane way to deal with sexuality, which Latter-day Saints sometimes compare to electricity. Although electricity can be a powerful, life-changing force for good when properly channeled, it can be devastating when unleashed through misuse or negligence. Mormons take pride in statistics demonstrating that they enjoy some of the world's lowest rates of sexually transmitted diseases, teen pregnancy, divorce, and other problems. Nevertheless, as Joseph Smith himself warned, sexual immorality in all its varieties is the main temptation that besets Latter-day Saints.

WHAT ABOUT BIRTH CONTROL?

Statements against birth control used to be much stronger in Mormonism, with warnings that limiting the number of children could force spirits intended for one's own family to be born into other families, perhaps even — *shudder* — a non-Mormon family. Today, nearly all forms of contraception are used by Mormons, including carefully considered surgical sterilization. The Church states, "The decision about how many children to have and when to have them is extremely personal and private. It should be left between the couple and the Lord. Church members should not judge one another in this matter."

The only form of elective birth control that LDS leaders forbid is abortion, although the Church makes rare exceptions in cases of rape, incest, and medical necessity.

REMEMBER

For Latter-day Saints, being chaste requires constant vigilance against tempting thoughts, flirtations, and entertainments. Latter-day Saints strive to continually subdue their unchaste desires and impulses. The blessings from doing so include not only peace of mind, stronger marriages and families, and freedom from the consequences of sin, but also the hope of a full and complete resurrection, including eternal procreative powers (see Chapter 2).

Dealing with sexual sin

According to the Mormon outlook, mortals who crash during their earthly test-drive of procreative powers — and fail to fully repent — will be resurrected to a lesser degree of glory that doesn't include the opportunity for eternal parenthood (see Chapter 2 for more on the afterlife). Although Mormon authorities understand that a predatory pedophile is in a completely different class from an engaged couple who has sex before their wedding ceremony — and treat such offenders very differently — the Church refers collectively to sexual sins as second only to murder in degree of seriousness. However, Latter-day Saints believe that God will forgive sexual sins upon full repentance, including stopping the sinful behavior.

Finding forgiveness for sexual mistakes

If a Latter-day Saint succumbs to sexual temptation and wants to repent, the process includes the following steps:

1. **The sinner confesses their sexual misbehavior to the local bishop during a private interview in the bishop's office, located inside the meetinghouse.**

Members who feel themselves sliding into sexual temptation are encouraged to consult with the bishop sooner than later. Sexual sin is like spiritual cancer — better to catch it early.

2. **The bishop offers support and guidance for repentance, emphasizing how the Savior's atonement applies to the sinner and can help them repent.**

3. **The bishop gives practical advice for overcoming the sin, including referring the sinner to a professional if they need extra help to overcome addictions or compulsions.**

   Repenters are expected to make lifestyle changes similar to those advisable for a recovering alcoholic in terms of avoiding places, people, situations, entertainment, thoughts, and negative emotions that lead to sin.

4. **The bishop decides if a formal *membership council* is needed to consider disciplinary action (see the next section).**

   Not only does Church discipline help motivate the sinner to access the Savior's redeeming power through repentance, but it may be needed to protect other people (such as in the case of predatory behavior) and the Church's integrity.

5. **To gain Church forgiveness, the sinner usually needs to demonstrate several months of renewed religious devotion under the bishop's supervision, including complete chastity.**

   In the case of unwed pregnancy, the Church supports an individual's prayerful decision, whether it's marriage, single parenting, or adoption. However, the Church does not condone abortion except in rare circumstances, such as rape, incest, or medical necessity. The Church doesn't facilitate adoptions, but local Church leaders can refer members to professional counseling that's "in harmony with gospel principles."

Facing the music

Although Mormon disciplinary actions aren't common occurrences, the vast majority of the punishments that do occur are triggered by unchaste behavior. Discipline varies from situation to situation, depending on the frequency of the sin, the sinner's level of responsibility, his or her degree of remorse, and other factors. In making disciplinary decisions, Mormon leaders seek inspiration, because only Heavenly Father fully knows the sinner's heart and what consequences will best foster full repentance. But the reality is that local leaders vary widely in how strictly or leniently they handle similar situations — some Latter-day Saints refer to this as "leadership roulette."

In general, the following disciplinary pattern seems to apply when a member confesses unlawful intercourse:

>> Youth usually get *informal membership restrictions* for a time, such as not speaking or praying in church, partaking of the sacrament (see Chapter 6), or attending the temple.

>> Single adults who've received their temple endowment (see Chapter 7) may receive *formal membership restrictions,* which requires approval from Church headquarters to remove.

>> Full-time missionaries and married members sometimes face full *withdrawal of membership* (formerly known as excommunication), which requires not only Church headquarters approval to reverse but also starting over again with rebaptism.

If confessed, sexual sins that stop short of intercourse may prompt informal spiritual counseling and temporary restrictions, but sex crimes such as rape, incest, and pedophilia virtually always result in membership withdrawal. The Church provides a hotline for local leaders to get legal counsel on handling allegations of sexual abuse.

As we discuss in Chapter 15, homosexuality is a charged issue for the LDS church. Mormons don't blame anybody for feeling involuntary same-sex attraction, but in the Church, sexual relations between people of the same biological sex at birth are always sinful — even if the participants are married — and can result in discipline. For members who desire, LDS bishops and therapists try to help them manage their unwanted same-sex attraction and prevent or stop homosexual activity.

Whaddya Mean, No Coffee? Living the Word of Wisdom

Many non-Mormons know very little about what their Mormon friends believe about Christ, the afterlife, or the plan of salvation. But they almost always know about the Mormon ban on certain intoxicants and stimulants!

Where did this commitment come from? Well, like many aspects of the LDS religion, the duty to avoid potentially harmful substances has its roots in revelation, in this case, a section of the Doctrine and Covenants (see Chapter 10) that Mormons call the *Word of Wisdom.* The legend surrounding its origin is that Joseph Smith and other early LDS leaders used to chew tobacco during Church meetings, spitting juices on the floor. Joseph's wife, Emma Hale Smith, was disgusted by this, and her complaints led the Prophet to ask God whether tobacco use was really appropriate for Latter-day Saints.

The Lord's response, contained in D&C section 89, covered more than just tobacco; it also warned against "strong drinks" (alcoholic) and "hot drinks" (coffee and tea). Although some Mormons understand this scripture as suggesting that all caffeine should be avoided, the Church has clarified that drinking caffeinated soda does not violate the Word of Wisdom.

REMEMBER

While committing to obey the Word of Wisdom is required for baptism, members don't get kicked out of the Church for knocking back a few. However, members who disobey the Word of Wisdom generally can't get a temple recommend (see Chapter 7). So, although nobody gets excommunicated for smoking cigarettes or doing Jell-O shots, the full blessings of Church membership are reserved for those who walk the straight and narrow path.

Interpreting the Word of Wisdom

During the 19th century, Mormons understood and enforced the Word of Wisdom in widely varying ways. Not until well into the 20th century did the Church require obeying the Word of Wisdom as a qualification for getting a temple recommend. Today, Latter-day Saints generally understand that the Word of Wisdom prohibits alcoholic beverages, tobacco in any form, coffee and tea, and — an obviously necessary modern addition — illegal drugs, recreational drugs, and misuse of prescription medications.

Of course, gray areas still exist. Some members shun anything that even looks like sin, while other temple-attending members occasionally enjoy nonintoxicating things like desserts flavored with coffee or liqueur; decaffeinated coffee and tea; nonalcoholic beer, wine, and cocktails; and foods cooked using small amounts of wine, beer, or liquor.

REMEMBER

While it's easy to get legalistic about the Word of Wisdom — and easy to spot logical flaws in its details — the spirit of the law is what really matters. Is something habit-forming, illegal, or potentially addictive? Is it known to harm health or spiritual well-being? If so, stay away from it.

(By the way, the Word of Wisdom explicitly cautions that Mormons should eat meat only sparingly and in times of winter or famine, but Church leaders don't preach about this, and most Latter-day Saints are unabashed year-round carnivores.)

Reaping Word of Wisdom benefits

Most Latter-day Saints feel that keeping the Word of Wisdom not only enhances their health but also helps them enjoy greater overall well-being. After all, in the original Word of Wisdom scripture (D&C 89), the Lord promises protection, knowledge, and wisdom to those who obey it. Plus, as one saying goes, "A little coffee may not keep you out of heaven, but a little disobedience will."

Today, the Word of Wisdom's health benefits are supported by scientific evidence. In the United States, Mormon men who are active in the Church live about seven and a half years longer than non-Mormon men, and religiously active Mormon women live about five and a half years longer than their non-Mormon peers. Active Latter-day Saints enjoy lower rates of cancers of the colon, stomach, pancreas, uterus, ovary, and prostate than non-Mormons do.

In addition to promoting robust health and longer life, the Word of Wisdom saves Latter-day Saints from addictions that are potentially very serious. Nowadays, addictive substances are more widely available than ever before. Learning to say no to small things like coffee helps prepare Latter-day Saints to say no when someone offers a drug that could ruin or end their life.

Another Word of Wisdom benefit is that it helps build Mormon unity. After the 19th-century Mormons gave up the practice of plural marriage, strict compliance in living the Word of Wisdom became another way of signifying Mormon identity. Today, keeping the Word of Wisdom helps bond the Mormon community as well as strengthen individual Latter-day Saints.

Tithing: Paying the Lord's Tax

Many Churches apply the word *tithe* to any donation, but Latter-day Saints take the word's meaning of "tenth" literally. The LDS church expects its members to give the Church a full 10 percent of their *increase*, which most people understand to mean all the personal income they receive, after business expenses but before living expenses. (When it comes to taxes, some members pay tithing on their gross income and some on their net income after tax.)

Sound hard? It is. For many families who faithfully pay tithing, the cost is one of the biggest household budget items, in some cases second only to the mortgage. For this reason, tithing is often the most difficult day-to-day commandment to obey, requiring some real spiritual and financial discipline to develop the habit and stay consistent. To get a head start, Mormon children typically start handing coin-filled tithing envelopes to the bishop before they're even baptized at age 8, while most adults pay online on a monthly or yearly basis.

Donating tithing gladly

Prophets have taught that paying tithing is a commandment essential to both full *salvation* (returning to live with God) and *exaltation* (becoming like God). While obeying this law is required to get a temple recommend (see Chapter 7), it is not required for participation in local meetinghouse activities.

By paying tithing, Latter-day Saints demonstrate their love for the Savior and devotion to his earthly kingdom. Tithing funds provide the main means for the Church to carry out its missions, but members don't get to vote on how the Church spends or invests their tithing dollars. The Church expects members to pay their tithing without grudge or reservation, and failure to do so is considered the same as robbing God. Technically, it counts as tithing only if it's paid to the Church, but some members give their tithing dollars to outside charities and still claim to be full tithe payers.

SCRIPTURE

Even in Old Testament times, people tithed. This principle was part of the *Law of Moses* (the law that governed the Israelites until Christ came), and the prophet Malachi recorded the following words, which Mormons often quote from the Bible: "Bring ye all the tithes into the storehouse, that there may be meat in mine house, and prove me now herewith, saith the Lord of hosts, if I will not open you the windows of heaven, and pour you out a blessing, that there shall not be room enough to receive it. And I will rebuke the devourer for your sakes, and he shall not destroy the fruits of your ground; neither shall your vine cast her fruit before the time" (Malachi 3:10). In other words, when God's people demonstrate their faithfulness by tithing, God responds by pouring out his blessings.

TITHING IS ONLY A WARM-UP EXERCISE

As much of a sacrifice as paying tithing is, Latter-day Saints see it as a lesser law that God gave because people couldn't live the higher *Law of Consecration*.

Revealed by God to the Prophet Joseph Smith early in the Church's history, the Law of Consecration basically meant that the Latter-day Saints should give everything they owned to God's kingdom. In practical terms, the Mormons pooled together all their wealth under a central Church authority and received only enough back to meet their reasonable needs and wants. The goal was to live together in complete harmony and abolish economic inequalities. According to scripture, some ancient groups succeeded at living this law — but for the most part, the 19th-century Latter-day Saints couldn't make it work for long.

Many prophets have taught that the principles required to live the Law of Consecration are necessary to become like God. At some point, when God feels they're ready to handle it, the Latter-day Saints expect to start fully living the Law of Consecration, which also includes devoting all their time and talents to God's kingdom. In the meantime, individuals pay tithing and strive to maintain an attitude of consecration in their minds and hearts.

Every year, the bishop invites each family to meet privately with him and declare whether they've paid a full tithing. Typically, parents and their children all attend this annual appointment together. If someone isn't paying a full tithing, the bishop can help them understand the blessings of recommitting to do so in the future.

Knowing where your tithe is going

CONTROVERSY

The Church doesn't disclose financial information, but most outsider estimates of its annual tithing income are about $7 billion. In addition, the Church runs several for-profit businesses and investments that net several hundred million more dollars annually. Now worth more than $200 billion, the Church has come under increasing pressure from both inside and outside the faith — including lawsuits and government sanctions — to disclose its finances more transparently and spend its tithing receipts in more charitable ways, instead of hoarding so much wealth.

On a worldwide basis, the Church collects and uses tithing to pay for things like the following:

>> Meetinghouse and temple construction, including land acquisition

>> Local *ward* (congregation) activities and expenses

>> Modest living allowances for full-time Church leaders (local leaders aren't paid for their volunteer efforts)

>> Salaries and facilities for a few thousand Church administrative employees

>> Family history facilities and equipment

In addition, tithing helps supplement member payments of additional donations, tuition, and fees for the following:

>> Charitable welfare efforts

>> Church publications and materials, including over 200 million copies of the Book of Mormon to date

>> Church universities, schools, and educational programs

>> Missionary efforts

CONTROVERSY

To some members' dismay, the Church has occasionally used tithing dollars to fight for conservative social values in the political arena, including opposing equal rights for women in the late 1970s or, more recently, opposing gay marriage in Alaska, Hawaii, and California.

From a practical standpoint, tithing money lends an equality to Mormonism that is missing in many other denominations. Wards with affluent members send more tithing money to Church headquarters than the ward receives in return, while wards with lower-income members send less tithing money to headquarters than the ward receives. The result is a high level of ward equality across the Church, rather than a few upscale wards with elaborate programs and many wards with meager resources.

Receiving tithing dividends

Although tithing is a test and a sacrifice, Latter-day Saints consider it the source of many blessings, both material and spiritual. Tithing may appear to lop 10 percent off the family budget, but Mormons believe the Lord compensates them with other blessings, sometimes including economic benefits.

In Mormon speeches and magazines, inspiring stories dramatize the benefits of faithfully paying tithing even when the immediate financial outlook is bleak. A typical tithing story may involve a family deciding to use its last hundred dollars to pay tithing rather than buy food. The next morning, they wake up to find bags of groceries anonymously left on the porch.

However, paying tithing is no guarantee of prosperity. Tithing doesn't cancel out foolish financial choices, and money problems can still happen to those who faithfully obey this commandment, although they exercise faith that the Lord will hasten their economic recovery.

Making the sacrifice of paying tithing has a profound effect on members' lives, binding them more closely to the religion. Sitting in a meetinghouse or temple, a tithe-paying member can take pride in having made a substantial personal investment in the beautiful facilities. In addition, obeying this commandment helps with discipline, humility, and other traits that bring a person closer to the Savior.

Fast Sunday: The Slowest Sabbath of the Month

The first Sunday of the month is likely to find some Latter-day Saints a little grumpy. Their patience with their children is at a low ebb, and they grab at the sacrament bread with a little more enthusiasm than usual. The sound of their church meetings is occasionally punctuated by prominent abdominal growling.

Yet throughout the day, they often feel the Spirit more strongly than usual. Welcome to Fast Sunday!

On monthly Fast Sundays, the main Latter-day Saint church service is devoted to the spontaneous bearing of testimonies (for more on sacrament meeting, see Chapter 6). It's open mic, and any member, including small children, can go up to the podium and tell the congregation about their beliefs and experiences and testify of the Savior.

Fast Sunday can be difficult for some people (and the Church doesn't recommend it for everyone — see the section "How and when to fast (And who shouldn't)" for more information). A full two-meal fast (about 24 hours) is tough to do; the only food or liquid that passes the lips of observant Mormons during this period is the sacrament bread and water. But fasting is one of the regular spiritual disciplines that can bring people closer to God and each other and offer new insights into spiritual questions.

Why Mormons fast

Latter-day Saints point to three basic reasons why they fast once a month, which we explain in this section.

Mastering the body

Much of life's energy is consumed with meeting physical needs and wants. You spend time earning a living to buy food; you spend time shopping for and preparing that food; you linger over that food and then wonder if maybe you also deserve some dessert. In fact, many people expend a whole lot of energy each day just thinking about food.

To Latter-day Saints, fasting offers an opportunity to step off the food treadmill for a while and think more about God, who gave us food and every other good thing. It gives Latter-day Saints the chance to both test their bodies and cleanse them. A Church leader once said that self-control over the physical body is one of the greatest achievements humans can attain, because "the greatest battle any of us shall ever fight is with self."

Helping the poor

When Latter-day Saints fast, they gain a short-term understanding of what going hungry feels like. From this experience, they grow in compassion and desire to serve others.

True to the Mormon character, members act out this compassion in a very concrete, practical way. When Church members fast, they contribute money to the Church welfare fund. The Church encourages members to donate, at a minimum, the money that their family would've spent on the two meals they skipped. The bishop of each ward decides how to apply fast offering money, which he and the Relief Society president (the woman who oversees the ward's women's organization) can discreetly use to help members in need pay for food, clothing, and shelter.

If members can afford to give more, the Church encourages them to do so. When Latter-day Saints pay a generous fast offering, they can feel good that they're helping fellow members, both locally and internationally. As we explain in Chapter 8, any money in the welfare fund that isn't needed to help Church members spills over into the humanitarian relief fund, which provides aid to people of other religions all over the world.

Growing spiritually

SCRIPTURE

The most important and lasting benefits of fasting are spiritual. Doctrine and Covenants section 59, for example, equates fasting with joy and rejoicing. (See Chapter 10 for more on the D&C, one of the four standard works of scripture in the LDS canon.) At times, this idea seems like a daunting task for Mormons — fasting is hard enough, and doing so with joy can seem impossible when your blood sugar is plummeting. But Mormons aspire to fast as the Bible says Jesus instructed, not with a sad countenance but with quiet joy (Matthew 6:16).

The key element is prayer. For Mormons, the fast begins and ends with a prayer and is often characterized by spontaneous prayers for strength in between ("Heavenly Father, please help me not to steal my toddler's Cheerios!"). On a serious note, Mormons believe that fasting makes prayer more meaningful — and prayer, in turn, gives meaning to the fast.

Here are two key spiritual benefits of fasting:

>> **Fasting helps Latter-day Saints grow closer to each other.** Because all Mormons around the world fast on the same Sunday, everyone's in the same pickle. (Oops, a food reference — amazing how many of these words pop up when people are trying not to think about food.) Fasting also has a communal element to it that happens on the local level. Sometimes, a whole ward fasts and prays on behalf of a church member who's sick or injured. Other times, the ward fasts and prays together for a particular spiritual purpose.

>> **Fasting makes Latter-day Saints feel closer to God.** In addition to the monthly fast, many Mormons fast while attending the temple. They also do extra fasts on an individual level when they're seeking inspiration about a particular issue in their lives. However, Church leaders don't recommend fasting too often or for more than 24 hours at a time.

REMEMBER

A fast becomes an acceptable sacrifice to God when humility and honest searching accompany it. Giving up food isn't enough; Mormons believe they must do so in a spirit of prayer and delight. When a fast just involves not eating, it has little spiritual benefit and actually focuses *more* attention on food. The goal is to think less about food and other worldly concerns by praying more purposefully than usual. (By the way, many people find that eating a big meal before starting a fast makes them feel hungrier during the fast than eating a smaller meal.)

How and when to fast (And who shouldn't)

The basic guideline is that Mormons abstain from food and drink for two meals, or about 24 hours, though some individuals vary in how they fast. The regular monthly fast usually begins after dinner on Saturday evening and continues until dinner on Sunday evening — well, maybe midafternoon. In addition to praying during the fast, Mormons usually begin and end the fast with a personal or family prayer that says, in essence, "Heavenly Father, I'm now beginning a fast for such-and-such a purpose" or "Heavenly Father, I'm now ending my fast and going into the kitchen to stuff my face with crackers, even though dinner is only ten minutes away."

Because the first Sundays in April and October are always churchwide General Conference, those monthly fasts typically take place on the last Sundays of March and September. A ward can also move Fast Sunday if a ward or stake conference conflicts with it. (For more information on these Church conferences, see Chapters 6 and 8.) One of the most simultaneously sinking and exhilarating feelings in Mormonism comes when a member, while munching breakfast on a Sunday morning, suddenly remembers it's Fast Sunday: "Darn, I forgot! I guess I may as well eat another piece of bacon."

In general, the following groups are exempt from the fast:

>> Pregnant and nursing women.

>> Those who are "delicate in health" or otherwise "subject to weakness," including the elderly and the sick.

>> Young children (often, Mormon kids start fasting for one meal around the time they're baptized at age 8 and graduate to two meals when they advance from Primary to Young Men or Young Women at age 12.)

The Church encourages those who can't fast to get involved as much as they can by making the day a time of prayer and meditation and by taking part in testimony meeting if they feel so inspired.

REMEMBER

President Heber J. Grant counseled Mormons to not get too hung up on the technical details of fasting. The main thing, he cautioned, is to promote the *spirit* of fasting, drawing closer to Heavenly Father and Jesus Christ.

> » Observing weekly sabbath and family home evening
>
> » Performing monthly fasts and attending temple
>
> » Ministering to fellow members by assignment

Chapter 17

Connecting with God and Each Other

Mormonism isn't just a Sunday religion. It's a 24/7 commitment to God and his people. In this chapter, we focus on how today's Latter-day Saints participate in certain daily, weekly, and monthly spiritual practices so they can grow closer together, retain the constant companionship of the Holy Ghost (see Chapter 3), and become more like their Heavenly Father.

Note: We should point out that the daily, weekly, and monthly frequencies represent the ideal. As imperfect humans, most Latter-day Saints don't keep every single Sabbath, pray on their knees every morning and evening, or fulfill their ministering assignments without fail. But most members try to do most of these things most of the time as their circumstances allow, believing that these practices contribute to their spiritual growth.

What Latter-day Saints Do Daily . . . Ideally

In the Mormon view, each day is a gift from God and represents an opportunity to grow closer to him and his Son, Jesus Christ. That belief translates into some daily practices that are designed to help Latter-day Saints nurture their relationships with God and the Savior and make them more aware of the spiritual things in everyday life.

It's been said that when Latter-day Saints want to talk to God, they pray, and when they want God to talk to them, they read the scriptures.

Talking with the Big Guy

Latter-day Saints believe strongly in making time every day for Heavenly Father. Of course, they call on God for help when they're sick, in trouble, or worried. But God isn't just a foul-weather friend; Latter-day Saints believe that if they want to have a strong relationship with him, they need to talk to him even when everything's swell. Heavenly Father loves all his children and wants to communicate with them daily.

Although the prime times for routine, formal prayer are in the morning, evening, and before meals, Latter-day Saints also zoom up prayers to God at appropriate times throughout the day, such as when asking for patience with a cranky toddler, strength to overcome temptation, or wisdom on some complex spiritual or temporal issue. There's no *wrong* time to pray.

When Mormon families gather, they say their prayers out loud, but when individuals pray, they can do so either aloud or silently. Latter-day Saints believe that God hears both kinds.

Spending a little time alone with God

Latter-day Saints pray directly to God the Father. They pray "in the name of Jesus Christ," but they don't believe that having an *intermediary* (one who stands in between the person praying and God) is necessary to access the Father. Therefore, they don't pray to Jesus Christ, Mary, or any saints (in Mormonism, the term *saint* applies to all members). Although Latter-day Saints sometimes don't feel like praying, they know that these times are when they especially need to pray so that they can maintain a close connection with their Heavenly Father and remain sensitive to his will for their lives.

As Mormon missionaries teach anyone who will listen, LDS-style prayer has four basic steps:

1. Call on Heavenly Father.

The most common opening phrase is simply "Dear Heavenly Father," but variations are okay.

2. **Thank him for blessings.**

Before getting into needs and desires, Latter-day Saints meditate on blessings and express gratitude for specific ones.

3. **Ask for blessings.**

This part of the prayer is nearly always the longest, but Latter-day Saints try not to treat God like Santa Claus. Instead, they seek to understand God's will and pray for it to come about, asking for strength to withstand temptation or meet new challenges; confessing their sins and asking for forgiveness; remembering loved ones who are ill or troubled; or praying about national or worldwide conflicts.

SCRIPTURE

4. **Close in the Savior's name.**

Every Mormon prayer ends with this basic phrase or one much like it: "In the name of Jesus Christ, amen." This practice stems from a verse in the Book of Mormon, where Jesus tells the Nephites to "always pray unto the Father in my name" (3 Nephi 18:19).

Navigating "thee" and "thou"

New converts and non-Mormons are sometimes surprised by the archaic language that English-speaking Latter-day Saints typically use for prayer. The prayers that Latter-day Saints say in public sound like King James English, and many Latter-day Saints pray this way at home, too.

REMEMBER

The key point to remember is that Latter-day Saints use the formal language to refer to God, not to other people. So it's correct to say, "Heavenly Father, we thank thee for thy blessings and ask for thy protection for our son Jared, who's leaving this week for BYU." But Latter-day Saints don't use the lofty language throughout, so "Heavenly Father, our son Jared, who tarries here before departing for college, requireth thy protection" would be over the top.

This language is sometimes tricky for new converts to get used to, and using it certainly isn't a requirement, though it's customary in the English-speaking Church. Other languages often adopt other terminology for prayer — sometimes formal, sometimes not.

Minding body language

One of the unique aspects of the Mormon approach to prayer is the emphasis on a particular body posture (see Figure 17-1). Although Latter-day Saints believe that sincere prayer can occur in any position, many choose to pray on their knees with their hands or arms folded, heads bowed, and eyes closed. (However, this wouldn't work for one of this book's coauthors, who says nearly all their personal prayers aloud while driving the car.)

FIGURE 17-1:
A Mormon family
kneels in prayer.

While Latter-day Saints often get on their knees for personal and family prayer, they don't kneel during their church or temple services. In sacrament meeting and other church meetings, the person who gives the opening or closing prayer does so standing up, and members of the congregation stay in their seats.

Getting answers to prayer

SCRIPTURE

In the Book of Mormon, the Savior tells the Nephites that whatever they ask God for in Christ's name will be given to them, provided they do so in faith and ask for something "which is right" (3 Nephi 18:20). Yeah, that last part is a bit of a catch. In other words, if they pray for something and expect Heavenly Father to come through, they'd better be praying for something righteous and in harmony with his will.

Latter-day Saints believe that when they pray, one of several outcomes typically happens:

» They immediately receive whatever they ask for, often via spiritual promptings about a decision or problem or through a fellow human who God inspires to help them.

» They eventually receive what they asked for.

» They don't seem to receive any answer at all and may later realize that what they were asking for wasn't part of God's holy plan.

Although it'd be nice if the first outcome happened more often, the last one is often more conducive to long-term spiritual growth because it teaches patience and humility.

One final note on answered prayers: Although Latter-day Saints believe that any time or place is appropriate for sincere prayer, many report receiving special inspiration when they're in a temple. Latter-day Saints can sit in the celestial room of the temple for as long as they want. In this quiet room, Latter-day Saints feel a unique connection with Heavenly Father. Maybe they sense this connection because, when they're away from the hustle and bustle of daily life, they have time to truly listen for the Spirit's voice. (For more on temples, see Chapter 7.)

Praying together as families

In addition to mealtime prayers, the Church encourages Mormon families to kneel together each day — both morning and night if possible — to give thanks for their blessings and pray for their spiritual and material needs. Many families rotate whose turn it is — including young children — to act as a voice for the prayer. Although getting everyone assembled and holding the kids' interest is a challenge, Mormon parents believe that family prayer is one of the most important tools for raising spiritual children in a secular world.

Studying scriptures

In addition to daily prayer, most Latter-day Saints strive to study at least a few scripture verses every day as individuals or families. You can flip back to Chapters 9 and 10 for more on the LDS scriptures, but for now just know that Latter-day Saints have four books (known as *the standard works*) that they regard as canonized scripture: the Bible (including the Old and New Testaments), the Book of Mormon, the Doctrine and Covenants (D&C), and the Pearl of Great Price. The Church publishes paper editions and provides the Gospel Library app for members who prefer to access scriptures electronically.

To help members stay — literally — on the same page with scripture study, the Church publishes an annual manual with a reading schedule and supplementary material, including a very handy version in the Gospel Library app. Focusing on one main volume of scripture each year, this coordinated program — currently called *Come, Follow Me* — is designed for use at both home and church by individuals, families, and classes. Because the Book of Mormon is so vital, the Church encourages members to read from it always, even in years when the main focus is on another book of scripture.

Latter-day Saints use all kinds of methods for studying the scriptures, including the following:

>> Whether on paper or using the Gospel Library app, many members highlight significant passages and make personal notes.

>> Some members read the cross-references to other scriptures and to the Bible Dictionary and the Topical Guide, two alphabetical resources included in LDS scripture editions.

>> Some read doctrinal books and articles or go online to compare their daily scripture reading with what various authorities say about a passage, helping them understand it in a wider context.

REMEMBER

One thing you don't normally see in Mormon circles is group study beyond Sunday school class, as is common in some other churches. For Latter-day Saints, the emphasis is more on individual and family scripture study, in addition to Sunday school and other formal classes. However, Latter-day Saint congregations sometimes hold evening lectures commonly known as *firesides*, presumably because they used to be held in members' living rooms; nowadays, they usually take place in a meetinghouse.

What Latter-day Saints Do Weekly . . . Ideally

Fifty-two weeks a year, Latter-day Saints are expected to keep the Sabbath day holy, including devoting some focused, gospel-oriented time to their church and families on Sunday. Although honoring the Sabbath is a commandment for Latter-day Saints, the Church leaves some room for individual interpretation of the details of observance. In addition, the Church strongly suggests that members hold a weeknight *family home evening* each week.

Observing the Sabbath

If you've ever known a Latter-day Saint, you've probably seen firsthand that they don't do some things on Sundays. They aren't as rigid about Sabbath observance as Orthodox Jews are — Latter-day Saints drive cars and turn on electric lights, for example — but they're stricter about Sabbath-keeping than most Christians nowadays. In this section, we examine why and how Latter-day Saints keep the Sabbath.

Why Latter-day Saints keep the Sabbath

In the Old Testament, God commanded the Israelites to rest from all their labors on the seventh day, as he did when he created the world. In Hebrew, the verb *shabbat* means "to cease or desist" — an important indicator of what a Sabbath ought to be like. For Latter-day Saints, as well as for Jews and other Christians, keeping the Sabbath means setting apart one day a week for spiritual renewal. Latter-day Saints "cease and desist" from the cares of the world in order to pursue holiness.

For Latter-day Saints, the rhythm of the whole week revolves around the Sabbath. They try to get their work, household chores, and shopping done by Saturday evening so that Sunday can be entirely free of worldly concerns. Most Latter-day Saints look forward to the Sabbath, seeing it as a time set aside to celebrate God and rejoice in his rich blessings.

SCRIPTURE

God commanded people to observe the Sabbath for the following two reasons:

>> **Worship:** The Old Testament is clear that the Sabbath is meant to be "a day to the Lord" (Leviticus 23:3) — in other words, it's God's day. The whole point is to honor God. Latter-day Saints keep that commandment by spending part of Sunday in church, where they learn more about God and Jesus Christ (for more on LDS church services, see Chapter 6). They also worship privately as individuals and families on Sunday, through prayer, service, and study.

>> **Rest:** Worshiping God while also taking care of life's daily worries and stresses is tough. So, in order to worship sincerely, Latter-day Saints step back from those day-to-day activities and aim for Sabbath rest. God set the pattern for this situation: After he created the world, he took a much-needed daylong vacation. He blessed the Sabbath day and made it holy (Genesis 2:3) by resting — a model that Latter-day Saints take as their example.

Don't get us wrong. Latter-day Saints believe very strongly in the value of hard work, and the Mormon work ethic is a wonder to behold. But Latter-day Saints believe that Sunday is a day for rest and that they should forgo any activity that's intended to make money or to increase their worldly productivity. One problem in Mormonism is that sometimes people do so much Church volunteer work on Sunday that they don't spend enough time with their families — but hey, at least Church work is a change of pace from earning a living.

How Latter-day Saints keep the Sabbath

Like most Christians, Latter-day Saints observe the Sabbath on Sunday, not Saturday. They regard it as a morning-to-bedtime affair rather than a day that begins at sundown on Saturday night and ends at sundown on Sunday. Some newbies are surprised to discover that Mormon temples are actually closed on Sundays to encourage members to focus on worshipping in their local meetinghouses and homes (for more on temples, see Chapter 7).

Latter-day Saints are very diverse in terms of what they do or don't do on the Sabbath. Newly married LDS couples often must reconcile their differences on this score: One may have grown up in a conservative family in which everyone stayed dressed in their Sunday best all day, while the other was reared in a more free-wheeling environment, where Sundays included listening to worldly music or playing touch football on the lawn. Our goal in this section isn't to present a one-size-fits-all approach to the Sabbath or to suggest what LDS church members should or shouldn't do on Sundays, but merely to show a range of approaches.

In general, keeping the Sabbath means doing the following:

>> **Attending church services and meetings:** As we say in the preceding section, worship is one of the two most important aspects of the Sabbath, and the communal part of that worship happens in church (see Chapter 6). In addition, some members attend additional Sunday meetings for things like managing a Church organization, coordinating service efforts, or singing in the choir.

>> **Paying extra attention to the spiritual side:** If attending church is the public, visible component of Sunday worship, then the private component involves concentrated individual attention to spiritual matters. Many Latter-day Saints see Sunday as a chance to spend a little extra time in prayer and scripture study, beyond what they do on regular days.

>> **Refraining from work:** Some Latter-day Saints, of course, have jobs that require them to work on Sunday. But Church leaders routinely emphasize that, if possible, members shouldn't do paid work on Sundays, not even at home. Many Latter-day Saints also avoid Sunday yardwork and housework beyond essentials like washing dishes or shoveling snow. Some well-organized students even manage to avoid doing homework on Sunday.

>> **Resting:** Latter-day Saints like their Sundays to be rejuvenating, and many spend at least part of the day taking it easy. At least one Mormon prophet has said that naps are an acceptable Sabbath activity, prophetic counsel that both of your coauthors keep faithfully.

>> **Not spending money:** The idea is that Sunday should be a noncommercial day that you spend thinking about spiritual things, not material concerns, and Latter-day Saints don't want to encourage businesses to hire people to work on the Sabbath. Of course, sometimes members must buy essentials on a Sunday, such as food and gas while traveling or medicine if someone gets sick.

>> **Making time for family:** Latter-day Saints run the gamut on how they strengthen their families through Sabbath observance. Some, for example, make an enormous meal and invite extended family, while others avoid intensive cooking. Some allow their children to play with neighbor kids, and others don't. Some allow TV, and some more hardcore members don't, not even the Super Bowl. Some play indoor games, but many avoid outdoor activities.

>> **Serving others:** Some Latter-day Saints do their assigned ministering on Sunday (see the section "Reaching out to others"), and some visit sick or elderly people. It's also a good day for reaching out to family members who live far away.

REMEMBER

However Mormon families choose to navigate the small stuff about Sabbath observance, the key point to remember is that Sabbath activities center on two ideas: worshiping God and resting. Latter-day Saints try to avoid *legalism*, or adhering solely to the letter of the law, by focusing instead on the spirit of the law and the purpose of the Sabbath.

Family Home Evening (Sorry, no Monday Night Football)

Sunday may be the LDS Sabbath, but Monday evenings hold nearly as much spiritual significance for Latter-day Saints. This evening is so sacred that all Mormon buildings are deserted and locked by 6 p.m., and even telephoning another family on that night is considered poor form. In communities where lots of Latter-day Saints live, they often lobby schools, sports teams, and other organizations to schedule activities on other evenings.

What's all the fuss about? Well, the LDS church expects its members to spend Monday evenings together as families. As we discuss in Chapter 5, the family has eternal potential for Latter-day Saints, and they put lots of effort into building family unity. Far more than an occasion to simply gather around the television or go on a picnic, the Church's *family home evening* program includes praying, singing, and studying the gospel together.

A typical Monday night

On many Mormon refrigerator doors, next to A+ spelling tests and soccer schedules, you find a little homemade poster listing several family home evening tasks, such as *prayer*, *song*, *lesson*, *game*, and *refreshments*. Each family member's name is written on a movable marker, and the markers are rotated from task to task each week.

In most Mormon homes, family night — as it's often called — begins right after dinner on Monday. Ideally, each family member has prepared their assignment by then, particularly those in charge of the lesson and refreshments. In the case of young children, a parent or older sibling helps them get ready. Here's how a typical family home evening goes:

>> **Prayer:** Most families begin and end the evening with prayer. Some families kneel, and others remain in their seats.

>> **Song:** Family songs often come from the Church's official songbook for children, but nonreligious songs are okay too, especially at holiday times.

>> **Lesson:** The heart of family home evening is a gospel lesson geared toward the kids. The Church publishes the *Family Home Evening Resource Book* with lesson ideas and other tips.

>> **Planning and discussion:** Many Mormon families take time during family night to discuss family plans and problems, like how to divvy up chores or whether to visit Yellowstone or Disneyland for summer vacation.

>> **Activities and refreshments:** Many families build a component of fun into the evening, such as going bowling or playing a board game. Some families do service projects for the needy as part of family night.

>> **Other traditions:** Customizing the basic family home evening program is easy. For example, each family member could briefly report the best and worst thing that happened to them during the previous week.

Although the preceding list reflects some common approaches to family home evening, each family finds what works best at different stages of life. To avoid family home *screaming*, it's important to keep the evening fun and flexible. You want the kids to look forward to it, not dread it!

Other kinds of family home evening

Of course, not everyone is available on Monday evenings, so some families set aside a different night for family home evening. New and old married couples without children at home are still encouraged to hold family home evening, and groups of singles or empty nesters sometimes meet together on Monday nights. Of course, you don't have to be Mormon to hold family home evening — many members of other faiths or no faith have adapted the model to meet their own needs.

What Latter-day Saints Do Monthly . . . Ideally

At least 12 times a year, Latter-day Saints strive to contact their assigned ministering members, skip two meals and donate to the needy, and attend the temple if one is reasonably close. Of course, Latter-day Saints can do these things more or less often than once a month, as their circumstances allow.

Reaching out to each other

At the local level, the Church organizes a unique program called *ministering*, through which each adult member is assigned to keep in personal touch with a few specific members or families in the *ward* (congregation).

SCRIPTURE

In a Mormon ward, leaders assign a pair of men to every household as its *ministering brothers*. In addition, they assign a pair of *ministering sisters* to each woman. According to the Church, "Ministering sisters and brothers represent the Lord. They also help members feel the love and support of the bishop and Relief Society or quorum leaders. They are to 'watch over' Church members and 'be with and strengthen them' (Doctrine and Covenants 20:53)." They also "discern needs and provide Christlike love, caring, and service." (For more on ward leadership, see Chapter 6.)

In addition to lending help and comfort in times of spiritual or physical need, ministering brothers and sisters build social connections and encourage Church activity and progress. They regularly touch base with their assigned members through personal visits, interactions at church, phone or video calls, texts, emails, snail-mailed cards, or social media. Latter-day Saints are known for their sweet tooths, so one common ministering technique is delivering a plate of fresh-baked dessert.

At least every quarter — and more often if needed — ministering brothers and sisters update ward leaders on how their assigned members are doing and whether certain members need additional help. The ministering program can also function as an information network and calling tree for getting messages out to the whole ward.

Like many religious duties, ministering sometimes feels a little tedious, but magical things can happen. From time to time, ministering brothers and sisters make a real impact on people's lives, such as helping a less-active family come back to church or providing a positive male role model for the son of a single mother. Through ministering, members come to know and love each other, and this unites Mormon congregations and brings them closer to Christ.

Break out the breath mints

On the first Sunday of most months, Latter-day Saints skip two meals, going without food and drink for about 24 hours. No, they're not trying to lose weight — they're trying to master their physical appetites, tune up their spiritual sensitivity, and draw closer to Heavenly Father. In addition, they donate the money they would've spent on food — and more, if they're able — to the Church's fund for supporting those in need. During sacrament meeting on *Fast Sunday*, people share spontaneous testimonies about the Savior (see Chapter 6).

Latter-day Saints consider fasting to be a commandment, and it's not effective unless coupled with focused prayer. While fasting, some Latter-day Saints keep breath mints handy, because going without food and drink takes a toll on oral freshness. Latter-day Saints can fast more often than monthly if they choose, but the Church discourages going longer than 24 hours at a time. (We discuss fasting in more detail in Chapter 16. Also, for more information about what happens to the money collected during the monthly fast, see Chapter 8 on the Church's welfare program.)

Mormon "date night"

Friday and Saturday nights are some of the busiest times at LDS temples because many couples make temple attendance a monthly date. Inside the temple, Latter-day Saints perform several different *ordinances*, or physical rituals necessary for returning to live with God and become like him. In Chapter 7, we discuss these ordinances in more detail, along with other aspects of the temple.

Here are two reasons why Latter-day Saints strive to attend the temple monthly, if not more often:

>> **Keeping spiritually in tune:** Although temple ordinances follow a set script, Latter-day Saints draw continual spiritual sustenance and eternal perspective from them. The levels of reverence and sacredness are much higher in a temple than in a public meetinghouse, so there's no other place on earth where a Latter-day Saint can feel closer to God, the Savior, and the Holy Ghost (for more on the Godhead, see Chapter 3).

>> **Helping redeem the dead:** Each time a Latter-day Saint completes another temple ordinance, they do so on behalf of someone who died without receiving their own ordinances. Latter-day Saints hope to perform temple ordinances for all their own ancestors and, ultimately, for everyone who's ever lived, so every little bit helps, even just once a month. Of course, the spirits of deceased persons choose whether to accept or reject physical ordinances performed on their behalf. (For more on Mormon beliefs regarding family history work, see Chapter 5.)

Chapter 18

In the World but Not *of* the World

Mormonism has always been a hands-on religion, and especially so when Latter-day Saints are trying to live spiritual lives in a secular world. They want to be *in* the world but not *of* it. In the New Testament, one of the letters attributed to Peter speaks of the need to become "a chosen generation, a royal priesthood, an holy nation, a peculiar people" (1 Peter 2:9). That goal is hard to reach in this day and age, but Latter-day Saints aim for it, knowing that their quest for holiness will — at the very least — make them a little bit different from their worldly peers.

In addition to the spiritual practices we explore in Chapter 17, Latter-day Saints engage in a variety of practical activities that are religious as well as temporal and cultural. In the Mormon view, faithfulness in taking care of this life's physical responsibilities is an important part of preparing for the responsibilities of eternity and developing divine attributes. For theological and practical reasons, Latter-day Saints make the habit of storing food and being prepared for emergencies. Similarly, both spiritual and financial reasons spur Latter-day Saints to stay out of debt. And partly in response to a prophet's inspired advice, they seek to make a record of their lives through journals and scrapbooks. In entertainment and the arts, Latter-day Saints have carved out a distinct subculture and also influence mainstream American culture. In this chapter, we take you through all these aspects of Mormon life.

Becoming Self-Reliant

Even people who aren't big fans of Latter-day Saints or their religion often acknowledge with grudging admiration that Latter-day Saints know how to take care of themselves and each other. To Latter-day Saints, part of being a "peculiar people" is making every effort to become independent and self-sufficient, so they don't have to depend on non-Mormons or the government for help. (For more on the LDS church's extensive private welfare system, see Chapter 8.)

In the Mormon view, becoming self-reliant has several basic components, such as

>> Being financially prepared

>> Storing enough food and supplies to weather almost any emergency

>> Always having a disaster plan in place

SCRIPTURE

Latter-day Saint scripture says that if you're prepared, you don't need to be afraid of anything (see Doctrine and Covenants 38:30; for more on the D&C, see Chapter 10).

Staying out of debt

Since the 19th century, LDS prophets have consistently emphasized two duties regarding money: Pay an honest tithe and stay out of debt. (For the scoop on tithing, see Chapter 16.) Getting out of debt — and staying there — can be tricky. People are constantly surrounded by advertisements that promise them a better life if only they'll buy this widget or that gadget. And with the easy availability of credit, it's no wonder that Latter-day Saints seem as prone as anyone else to sink into a financial quagmire. Because Latter-day Saints often have large families and ideally want the mother to stay home full time with the children, they absolutely must learn to manage their resources wisely.

Being in debt doesn't just exact a financial price. Debt also places a spiritual burden on a family because it often leads to depression, overwork, and marital tension. From Brigham Young on down, LDS leaders have taught that thrift, not material possessions, is the key to security. True happiness doesn't come from having a new car or the biggest high-def TV; in the Mormon view, it comes from having a strong relationship with God, serving others, and staying free from all forms of bondage, including financial.

SCRIPTURE

Mormon scriptures are clear about debt: In D&C 104:78, the Lord instructs his children to remain debt free, and in D&C 19:35 he equates debt with bondage. Latter-day Saints believe that God wants people to be entirely free and that human *agency* (see Chapter 2), or free will, is an essential principle of the gospel. With this idea in mind, the belief that God frowns on debt, which takes away people's freedom, makes perfect sense.

The Church recommends four basic steps for staying out of debt:

» **Live within your income.** This step is obviously the most important one. If you regularly exceed your income, spending more money than you make, debt is inevitable. You have to step off the debt treadmill and make a habit of living within your means.

» **Save for the future.** The Church encourages its members to put aside a portion of their income in retirement funds, college savings, and other investments for the future. Latter-day Saints also try to maintain an emergency fund to cover several months of living expenses in case of illness or unemployment.

» **Have adequate insurance.** Many people who get by from paycheck to paycheck are completely flattened when they have major medical bills or an unexpected death in the family. Adequate insurance — including health, life, and disability insurance — is vital to every family's financial stability. In other words, Latter-day Saints believe that God wants people to make wise provisions for possible misfortunes instead of just trusting God to make sure nothing bad happens to them.

» **Be wise about credit.** Mormon leaders would love to see Latter-day Saints borrow money only to pay for their homes and educations — assets that either appreciate in value or help people increase their income. However, many Latter-day Saints borrow money to pay for their cars and other purchases.

Getting squirrelly: Food storage

A little-known fact about Latter-day Saints is they tend to be pack rats and food hoarders. What's more, The Church of Jesus Christ of Latter-day Saints encourages this behavior, advising members to store food and supplies. Here are some reasons why:

» **A turbulent and crisis-laden history:** Having been persecuted and driven from their homes, and having survived the grueling westward trek and the travails of settling a semi-desert (see Chapters 11–13), Latter-day Saints learned to be careful with every resource. This idea is still ingrained in the Mormon mindset.

>> **Just in case the Second Coming happens sooner rather than later:** Latter-day Saints don't know when Jesus will come back (see Chapter 3). Still, being prepared can't hurt, in case society breaks down to such an extent before the Second Coming that a reliable infrastructure for food and other needs doesn't exist.

>> **To handle small or large emergencies:** It's nice to have extra supplies on hand when a blizzard causes a three-day power outage, let alone when a family breadwinner becomes disabled, sick, or unemployed.

>> **So they can help other people during *their* emergencies:** Latter-day Saints are some of the best donors of canned goods to community food banks. In tough times closer to home, a Mormon family's stored food can help their neighbors weather a weeklong storm or a difficult financial period.

>> **Because it's financially prudent:** Maintaining a large food supply allows Latter-day Saints to save money by buying items in bulk when they go on sale. In addition, by making fewer trips to the grocery store, they spend less time and energy and reduce their temptations to buy things on impulse.

Establishing a system

Ideally, Latter-day Saints aim to store a year's supply of food for their family. However, not only is this goal cost prohibitive for many, but some folks just don't have the space — imagine living in a tiny Manhattan or Tokyo apartment. It's not unusual for Latter-day Saints to store canned food under furniture or in coat closets. Some Mormon families may store enough for only a few weeks or months, but they feel that's far better than having nothing at all.

Here are three basic rules of food storage:

>> **Store what you eat.** Many people, including some Latter-day Saints, figure that if disaster ever strikes, they'll eat anything they can get their hands on, so it's okay to just store a bunch of raw wheat and dehydrated food. However, research shows otherwise. Although lots of people *say* they'd eat anything if their lives depended on it, most actually don't — when it comes right down to it, they'd rather starve than eat strange or disgusting foods. In other words, comfort food never matters more than during a catastrophe.

With this fact in mind, storing mostly foods you know your family will eat is important. A financial setback or natural disaster isn't the best situation to try that recipe for pinto-bean fudge for the very first time. If the kids devour boxed macaroni and cheese, buy a couple caseloads plus canned milk and supplement with multivitamins, in case a crisis strikes. If you can't imagine getting through a snowstorm without your particular brand of chicken noodle soup, have some to spare.

>> **Eat what you store.** Unless you're regularly eating the foods you put in food storage, they may be too old or rotten to consume when an emergency hits. Lots of Latter-day Saints think their food storage worries are over after they buy a few hundred-pound bins of wheat and dried beans. But if they never open those bins and use that food, it eventually becomes the favorite breakfast of untold varieties of critters. To prevent this dilemma, some Mormon families routinely grind their stored wheat to make bread and cereal and include some dehydrated foods in day-to-day meals. This way, everyone gets used to the different tastes.

>> **Eat the foods on a rotating basis, so you consume the oldest stuff first.** After Latter-day Saints go grocery shopping, they often date the food they've just purchased. If a can doesn't already have an expiration date on it, they use a permanent marker to write the date they bought it. Then — and this part is important — they move the new purchases to the back and push the older items to the front so the older foods are the first items available the next time Mom sends a kid to get a bottle of ketchup or a cake mix.

The Church also emphasizes home production: grinding wheat to make bread, raising vegetable gardens, dehydrating food, prepping freezer meals, and so on. Some Latter-day Saints still do their own canning, making jams, pickles, preserves, and all manner of foods that have a long shelf life.

REMEMBER

Don't forget the other basics, too: pet and baby needs, an alternate source of heat for warmth and cooking, a battery-operated radio, candles, and so on. You can find more information and helpful lists in the emergency-preparedness section at www.providentliving.org.

Getting started with food storage

TIP

Storing food doesn't have to cost a fortune or drain a family's time. One tip is to adopt the 5-5 plan: Spend an extra five minutes and five dollars a week building up food storage. At the beginning, you just buy, say, a couple jars of peanut butter and an extra box of crackers each week. Then begin adding some canned soups. After a few months, you'll have enough basics to last your family through a short-term crisis, and you can then start thinking about storing for the long term.

When you get to this second stage, take advantage of the numerous companies that sell dried and packaged food-storage products that can last 15 or even 20 years (though we suggest you skip the textured vegetable protein taco meat).

Preparing for emergencies

Newcomers to Mormonism are sometimes surprised at how much practical attention the Church gives to preparing for emergencies. At Relief Society and priesthood meetings and even in sacrament-meeting talks (see Chapter 6), members routinely emphasize the need to be prepared. *Family home evenings* (see Chapter 17) sometimes include lessons on how to give mouth-to-mouth resuscitation, behave in an earthquake or tornado, and meet up with parents in case family members are separated.

In addition to staying out of debt and storing as much food as is practical, many Latter-day Saints keep a 72-hour kit handy for each member of the family. Basically, a 72-hour kit (a.k.a. bug-out bag) should include everything a human being needs to survive for three days anywhere. (The family had better pray that an emergency doesn't stretch to 73 hours, or they're toast.)

REMEMBER

Unlike food storage, a 72-hour kit needs to be portable. Say you experience a flood and your entire town is evacuated. Or imagine that emergency officials have declared your high-rise apartment building in Los Angeles a disaster area because of a nearby earthquake. You grab your 72-hour kit and hit the road.

Many people keep their 72-hour kits in a backpack or other convenient bag. Typical items include

>> Cold, hard cash, small bills preferred

>> An extra set of warm clothes, plus an emergency blanket or sleeping bag

>> A first-aid kit

>> Meals for three days (such as military-style MREs — yummy)

>> A radio and flashlight, with extra batteries

>> Toiletries and toilet paper

>> Water for three days (the heaviest item)

Sometimes, Mormon families take a dry run at an emergency situation and practice leaving the house with their 72-hour kits. Through this experience, they figure out what works and what doesn't in their disaster plan and fine-tune accordingly. When they stop to fix a meal somewhere, for example, they may discover that their planned supper of Progresso soup doesn't work because they didn't think to bring a can opener. Practice makes perfect, and they hope that by preparing, they'll be ready should the unthinkable ever happen.

Journaling, Scrapbooking, and Other Mormon Pastimes

SCRIPTURE

Another practical way that Latter-day Saints put their religious values into daily life is by keeping records of what goes on at home and in the family. Putting it all down on paper isn't just a nice thing to do; the Book of Mormon says that record-keeping can enlarge the memory and enhance the lives of an entire people (see Alma 37:8).

Just as present-day Latter-day Saints still feel a pull toward their pioneer ancestors (see Chapter 12), future Latter-day Saints may look to the journals and scrapbooks that Latter-day Saints are making now for inspiration and information.

Keeping a record

In 1980, LDS president Spencer W. Kimball spoke about the need for Latter-day Saints to keep a journal for themselves and for their descendants. (President Kimball, at the time he was called to be the prophet, had already filled 33 black binders with his own accounts of his life, so he clearly practiced what he preached.)

Not all Latter-day Saints keep a journal, and certainly not everyone does so consistently from elementary school to the grave. Obviously, some members are naturally more gifted at writing than others and gravitate toward this kind of counsel anyway, but for others, the task is a struggle. Journaling requires a significant chunk of time for it to be an effective spiritual and mental discipline. However, most Latter-day Saints at least make the attempt at some point.

Why journal? By keeping a journal, Latter-day Saints record their hopes and dreams, their challenges and responses to obstacles. Venting and analyzing one's problems in a journal can yield peace and solutions. Some young people keep journals for their future spouses so their marriage partners can get to know the people they were as children and teenagers. Missionaries keep journals of their missionary experiences — for many Latter-day Saints, that's the only time they really succeed at journaling.

Most Latter-day Saints expect that their children or grandchildren will someday read their journals, so they try to record the experiences that they think may be helpful or interesting to later generations. They may not confess something that makes them look too bad, but they may include spiritual experiences that are too personal or sacred to share with most people.

Getting scrappy

"Crop till you drop," reads a sign posted in the window of a Utah scrapbooking store. And many Mormon women do. (*Crop*, in scrapbooking lingo, means to cut or shape a photograph.) They also embellish, emboss, stamp, create borders, write detailed captions, and spend hours searching for the perfect stickers for each page.

Like many people, Latter-day Saints have been creating photo albums since the invention of the daguerreotype. A latter-day scrapbook, however, is a whole different animal because it involves not just photos but also journaling and decorating. This pastime arose in Mormon culture and — like today's "dirty soda" trend that started in Utah — soon went mainstream. Some of scrapbooking's most visible product lines, stores, magazines, and national companies were founded by Mormon women.

Most Latter-day Saints who scrapbook do so to make a beautiful record of family life. The sky's the limit, with the only restrictions being the scrapbooker's time, creativity, and budget. And perhaps someday, future generations will look at the items preserved on acid-free paper — always use acid-free paper! — and get to know a bit about our era and its people. For tips on how to get started, pick up *Scrapbooking For Dummies* by Jeanne Wines-Reed and Joan Wines (Wiley).

Crafts and comfort food

When it comes to handicrafts and comfort food, today's Latter-day Saints — at least in the United States and Canada — tend to be very Midwestern in their tastes and traditions, with some distinctive Mormon twists.

Many Mormon women are known for their handicrafts — witness the quilt hanging in the ward's Relief Society room or the homemade floral scripture tote. Knitting, needlework, sewing, and many other handicrafts are popular. A few weeks after coauthor Jana Riess was baptized as an adult, she attended her first crafting event at her ward. One of the sisters congratulated her on having her "real" baptism into LDS womanhood — she had done a craft!

Rumor has it that whatever Latter-day Saints *can't* consume (learn about the Word of Wisdom in Chapter 16), they often make up for with voracious overeating, especially in the sugar category. Go to any Mormon potluck and you'll see an abundance of country-style cooking, such as pot roast, mashed potatoes, chocolate cake, and homemade breads. Many Latter-day Saints enjoy a dish popularly known as *funeral potatoes*, because this creamy, buttery, cheesy item often shows up at post-funeral luncheons. Many in Utah and elsewhere love a big, warm glob of honey-slathered fry bread, although for some reason they call it a scone.

Mormons are also known for loving Jell-O salad — especially the green variety — and *fry sauce,* an orange-pink combination of ketchup, mayo, and spices that's available in many Utah fast-food restaurants. For more on Mormon comfort food, pick up *The Essential Mormon Cookbook: Green Jell-O, Funeral Potatoes, and Other Secret Combinations,* by Julie Badger Jensen (Deseret Book).

Taking in a Bit of Culture

In Mormonism's 13th Article of Faith, founding prophet Joseph Smith echoes the words of the Apostle Paul: "If there is anything virtuous, lovely, or of good report or praiseworthy, we seek after these things" (for more on the Articles of Faith, see Chapter 10). Latter-day Saints pride themselves on seeking — and, to a less-successful degree, helping create — the world's most inspiring artistic entertainment and enlightenment.

Although Mormon prophets have called upon members to achieve the highest artistic goals, Mormonism has yet to cough up any Shakespeares or Michaelangelos, let alone Beatles or Spielbergs. On the other hand, they've given the world the Osmond family and best-selling fantasy author Brandon Sanderson. Perhaps Mormonism's artistic culture hasn't yet fully blossomed because too many Latter-day Saints prize creative expression more for what it *isn't* than for what it *is.* When asked their opinion about a movie or novel, many Latter-day Saints will recommend it — or not — based on how few swear words or sex scenes it has, rather than its artistic merits.

When creating their own art, many Latter-day Saints flee from anything too dark, graphic, skeptical, or frank. Nearly all Mormon art strives to be "uplifting," which often translates into self-conscious propaganda for the faith instead of striking originality, groundbreaking exploration, or cathartic honesty. At the same time, some maverick-minded artists are creating Mormon-themed works that may one day break out of the LDS cultural ghetto and gain significant audiences and critical notice. In this section, we look at some of the most interesting Mormon music, literature, drama, and film.

Lifting a chorus to the Lord

The Tabernacle Choir at Temple Square (formerly known as the Mormon Tabernacle Choir) is the 800-pound gorilla of Mormon artistic culture. Tracing its roots at least as far back as the small choir that debuted shortly after the first pioneers arrived in the Salt Lake Valley, the choir has achieved considerable worldwide fame. Since hitting its stride early in the 20th century, the Tabernacle Choir has accomplished the following:

>> Performed in many of the world's finest concert halls

>> Made more than 150 recordings and launched its own record label

>> Earned five gold and two platinum records, in addition to winning a Grammy Award

>> Anchored the nation's longest-running weekly radio program, *Music and the Spoken Word,* which reached the 95-year mark in 2024

>> Sung at numerous U.S. presidential inaugurations

Staffed by about 360 rigorously screened volunteer singers who rehearse for hours every week (see Figure 18-1), the choir functions both as an enhancer of Mormon worship and as an ambassador for the faith. Many a door-knocking Mormon missionary has gained entry into a household because the person's heart was previously touched by a choir performance, recording, or broadcast.

FIGURE 18-1: The Tabernacle Choir at Temple Square.

Living Legend/Adobe Stock Photos

A little bit rock and roll

Mirroring the rise of contemporary Christian music, the Mormon culture has spawned its own inspirational music, with notable success by artists such as Jenny

Oaks Baker, Kenneth Cope, Michael McLean, and Hillary Weeks. Mormon pop music has even sprouted LDS boy bands and rock-and-roll adaptations of classic Mormon hymns, but churches don't play this music during Mormon worship services, where generally only sedate hymns are welcome.

As with business, media, politics, academia, and sports, you can find Mormons (or Mormon-adjacent) people throughout the mainstream music world. The Osmonds are probably still the highest Mormon achievers, and another famous name is Randy Bachman of the Guess Who and Bachman-Turner Overdrive. More recently, Mormon-affiliated musicians have played major roles in bands like Arcade Fire, Imagine Dragons, The Killers, and Neon Trees. Some well-known musicians have become Mormon converts, such as Gladys Knight and New York Dolls bassist Arthur "Killer" Kane.

When it comes to Mormon attitudes toward popular music, Church authorities and motivational speakers regularly warn young Latter-day Saints against listening to "inappropriate" music. Nevertheless, Mormon youth typically listen to the same music as their non-Mormon peers, although they may avoid the more graphic and profane stuff. At youth dances held in the recreational halls of Mormon meetinghouses, DJs play mostly mainstream hits.

Mormon books

With its emphasis on education and literacy, Mormonism has given rise to its own multimillion-dollar book industry. In addition to popular historical and romance novels, Mormon publishers crank out plenty of inspirational and doctrinal nonfiction, including many books written by top Church authorities. For a flavor of what Latter-day Saints are currently reading, visit Cedar Fort (www.cedarfort.com), Covenant (www.covenant-lds.com), or Deseret Book (www.deseretbook.com).

The Mormon literati

Most Latter-day Saints don't know it, but Mormon culture includes a small internal-facing literary scene, in which edgy, highbrow books are wildly successful if they sell 1,000 copies. One of the most highly regarded literary authors is Levi Peterson, particularly for his novel *The Backslider* (Signature). Other noted internal-facing literary authors include John Bennion, Douglas Thayer, and Margaret Blair Young.

For Mormon-themed literary works, culturally liberal Latter-day Saints turn to independent publishers like Signature Books (www.signaturebooks.com) and By Common Consent Press (www.bccpress.org). For current Mormon-flavored literary stories and poems, the best sources include the journals Dialogue (www.dialoguejournal.com) and Sunstone (https://sunstone.org). In addition, the Association for Mormon Letters serves as a literary hub, including sponsoring an annual conference and putting out the online literary magazine *Irreantum* (www.associationmormonletters.org).

Literary writers with Mormon affiliations have made ripples on the national scene, including Phyllis Barber, Brian Evenson, Judith Freeman, Walter Kirn, Todd Robert Petersen, Brady Udall, and Terry Tempest Williams. In the mid-20th century, national publishers released Mormon-themed works by several authors — including Vardis Fisher, Virginia Sorensen, and Maurine Whipple — whose books are still worth seeking out today.

Bestselling Mormon authors

Numerous external-facing Latter-day Saint authors have been quite successful. Stephen R. Covey snuck some Mormon principles into his blockbuster *The 7 Habits of Highly Effective People* (Free Press). Clayton Christensen wrote influential books about his theory of disruptive innovation. Glenn Beck, Richard Paul Evans, and Jason F. Wright have authored nationally bestselling inspirational fiction.

In general, Mormons adore stuff like Harry Potter and *Lord of the Rings*, and Mormon authors have scored big in fantasy and science-fiction, including Orson Scott Card, Stephenie Meyer, and Brandon Sanderson. Card is known for his novels based on thinly veiled allegories of the Book of Mormon and Joseph Smith's life and times. Other big-selling Mormon sci-fi and fantasy authors include Tracy Hickman and Dave Wolverton, who also wrote as David Farland.

Perhaps because Mormonism's tender, PG-rated cultural sensibilities are well suited to writing for teens, several Mormon authors have succeeded with young-adult books. Notable names include Ann Cannon, Ally Condie, Chris Crowe, James Dashner, Shannon Hale, Lael Littke, Louise Plummer, and Carol Lynch Williams.

Mormon theatre

Latter-day Saints have historically been big on plays, musicals, pageants, and other forms of live drama. One of the first things the prophet Brigham Young did after the pioneers arrived in the Salt Lake Valley was establish a theater, and he even played some roles himself.

Today, while Latter-day Saints still tend to be a theatergoing people, there's not much Mormon-specific drama. Homegrown pop musicals used to be a thing—despite some iffy theology, *Saturday's Warrior* and *My Turn on Earth* made big splashes during the 1970s. On a seasonal basis, the Church holds outdoor pageants on temple grounds in Nauvoo, Illinois; Mesa, Arizona; and Chorley, England, celebrating Jesus Christ and the early Mormon pioneers. If you look hard, you can find some edgy, envelope-pushing Mormon plays, such as those by playwrights Melissa Leilani Larson and Eric Samuelsen.

Of course, Mormons have also been featured in Broadway shows. While many Latter-day Saints don't like the raunchy musical send-up of *The Book of Mormon*, some wear it as a cultural badge of honor. Gay Jewish playwright Tony Kushner included Mormon characters and themes in his award-winning *Angels in America*, which debuted on Broadway and got adapted by HBO.

Mormon cinema

The LDS church has put out lots of films, most recently an ambitious series of short Book of Mormon dramatizations that you can watch on YouTube (see Chapter 9 for more on the Book of Mormon). Church-owned Brigham Young University used to produce short moralizing films, several of which have now achieved camp status within Mormon culture (especially *Johnny Lingo* and *Cipher in the Snow*).

But the real fun didn't start until 2001, when filmmaker Richard Dutcher started doing independent Mormon-themed films, most notably *God's Army*. His unexpected critical and commercial success triggered a new cinematic movement. Things got schmalzy and cheesy pretty fast, however, and the flow of independent Mormon films has now become a trickle. If you live in a heavily Mormon area, you can still occasionally watch a new Mormon indie film at your local movie theater, some of them fairly high in quality.

As far as Mormons in Hollywood, Don Bluth and Richard Rich have made many well-known animated movies for the likes of Disney, and BYU-trained Jared Hess created a nationwide indie sensation with his coming-of-age teen comedy *Napoleon Dynamite*. Several prominent actors have Mormon backgrounds, including Amy Adams, Eliza Dushku, Aaron Eckhart, Ryan Gosling, Katherine Heigl, and Matthew Modine.

AN R-RATED CONTROVERSY

Several decades ago, an apostle warned Mormon teens not to see R-rated movies. Since then, some stricter Latter-day Saints have viewed this warning as a semi-commandment for all members, regardless of age. They believe that watching R-rated movies can dull a person's spiritual purity and sensitivity.

However, some faithful Latter-day Saints watch carefully chosen R-rated movies, and the LDS church has shown signs of acknowledging that the U.S. movie rating system isn't a reliable viewing guide, especially for members in other nations. Some Latter-day Saints have discovered that some R-rated movies are more morally edifying than some PG-13 ones, even if the *F*-word count is a little higher.

An LDS-adjacent company called VidAngel enables customers to filter out sex, violence, and profanity on streaming services, including Netflix. However, four Hollywood studios sued VidAngel, and the company isn't allowed to filter their content. But that still leaves thousands of movies and TV shows that VidAngel can filter for those who prefer to avoid "mature" content.

5
The Part of Tens

You get answers to ten frequently asked questions about Mormonism and find out about ten places to visit where you can discover more about Mormon history and belief.

> » **Reviewing Mormon beliefs about families, the Book of Mormon, and the priesthood**
>
> » **Looking at ongoing controversies about women, godhood, and polygamy**

Chapter **19**

Quick Answers to Ten Common Questions About Mormonism

Mormonism may not be the world's most unusual religion, but it's far enough off the beaten path to generate lots of questions from outside observers and people who are new to the faith. In this chapter, we address some of the most common questions Latter-day Saints typically encounter at one time or another. We cover nearly all these topics more deeply elsewhere in this book, so the answers in this chapter are the boiled-down versions.

Are Latter-day Saints Christian?

SCRIPTURE

Latter-day Saints, of course, absolutely believe that they're Christians, because they love and worship the Savior, Jesus Christ, and endeavor to follow his example in all things. To paraphrase the Book of Mormon, they talk about Christ, rejoice in Christ, preach about Christ, prophesy about Christ, and look to him alone for the forgiveness of their sins (see 2 Nephi 25:26). In what way could they not be Christian?

Well, it seems that the deciding factor depends on how you define the word *Christian*. If the word means its primary dictionary definition — "one who professes belief in the teachings of Jesus Christ" — then the answer is an absolute yes. But the people who ask this question sometimes don't think that this belief is enough. For example, they may call Latter-day Saints non-Christians because Latter-day Saints reject the concept of the Trinity as other Christian churches have traditionally defined it: that God is one ultimate being with three persons. (For more on Mormon views of God, see Chapter 3.) So if that's the litmus test, Latter-day Saints don't make the grade because they view the godhead as three separate beings who are one in purpose.

Other issues are at stake as well. For example, some people believe that Latter-day Saints can't be Christians because they've added other books to the canon of what God has revealed as scripture (the Bible). What's more, Latter-day Saints believe that revelation is still open-ended and claim that God reveals new doctrine today through his prophet. So, if the definition of *Christian* rules out any additional scriptures or revelation, once again, Latter-day Saints don't qualify.

Another point of contention centers on priesthood authority. Many different Christian churches, even when they disagree with each other over matters of doctrine, still accept each other's ordinances, such as baptism, as being essentially valid. However, Latter-day Saints believe that the priesthood was lost from the earth until God restored it through Joseph Smith. As a result, Latter-day Saints believe that other churches, no matter how much good they do, don't possess full authority from God, and converts to Mormonism must be baptized again even if they were already baptized into another Christian church. (For more on Mormon views about the priesthood and its restoration, see Chapter 4.) As you can imagine, members of some Christian churches find this view insulting.

Some Latter-day Saints use the tagline "Christian but different." In other words, Latter-day Saints consider themselves Christians, but their beliefs and practices are sometimes quite different from traditional creedal Christianity. It's helpful to think about adding "Latter-day Saint Christian" to the other kinds of Christians already out there: evangelical Protestant Christians, Eastern Orthodox Christians, Roman Catholic Christians, and on and on. Latter-day Saint Christians believe that although their doctrines may sound unusual to other Christians, their good works and spiritual sincerity reflect well on the Savior that all Christians seek to emulate. And as Christ himself said, his followers will be known by their fruits. (See Chapter 15 for more on why Latter-day Saints believe they count as Christian.)

How Can Latter-day Saints Give Up 10 Percent of Their Income?

Faithful Latter-day Saints give the Church a full 10 percent of their income (some pay 10 percent of their gross income, and others pay on their take-home amount). For many Mormon households, tithing is one of the largest monthly budget items. When Latter-day Saints face the choice between paying tithing and buying groceries, the Church expects them to exercise faith, put the Lord first, and trust in his providence, which the Church itself sometimes provides through its welfare program. (To find out more about the Mormon practice of tithing, see Chapter 16.)

Certainly, tithing sometimes causes Mormon families to miss out on luxuries that they otherwise may have enjoyed, and in some situations the sacrifice might be even greater. On the other hand, Latter-day Saints aren't generally known for being materially needy or economically underprivileged (in the United States, at least). Latter-day Saints believe that tithing helps them grow spiritually, but the real key to gladly obeying this commandment is the Mormon belief that the Lord increases one's blessings in return for supporting his kingdom. Paying tithing doesn't guarantee riches or protection from temporary setbacks, but many Mormon tithe-payers believe that, at the end of the day, they come out ahead materially as well as spiritually.

For new LDS converts, disciplining their budgetary habits to accommodate the tithe can be one of the hardest parts of coming up to speed as a Latter-day Saint. However, Church classes and magazines frequently give advice about managing finances wisely, and developing a consistent tithing habit is quite possible. For faithful Latter-day Saints, the question isn't how they can afford to pay tithing, but how they could afford *not* to pay it.

What Happens Inside an LDS Temple?

After the prophet or an apostle dedicates a Mormon temple for sacred use, only Church members who are morally and spiritually worthy can enter. Inside, they reverently participate in a number of different *ordinances,* or physical rituals necessary for returning to live with God and becoming like him. Latter-day Saints perform these ordinances not only for their own spiritual benefit, but also on behalf of those who died without receiving them. (For detailed info on temples, including how they differ from regular LDS meetinghouses, see Chapter 7.)

Although Latter-day Saints don't receive their own baptism, confirmation, and — for all worthy males — priesthood ordination inside a temple, they can perform these ordinances on behalf of the deceased only inside a temple. Living and dead people alike may receive Mormonism's higher ordinances only inside a temple: the *endowment*, a multipart ordinance that rehearses God's entire plan of salvation, and *sealing* for eternity as a couple or family.

Latter-day Saints perform their own temple ordinances only once; after that, they visit the temple to perform ordinances for the dead. In the spirit world, each deceased person's spirit can choose whether to accept or reject the ordinances that people on earth perform for them.

Why Don't Latter-day Saints Drink Alcohol or Coffee?

Like Jews, Muslims, and Hindus, Latter-day Saints have a list of substances that they're forbidden to consume if they want to remain orthodox. Sort of like Mormon kosher, the list is a cradle-to-grave program for maintaining spiritual and physical health. In a nutshell, Latter-day Saints stay away from alcohol (wine, beer, and liquor), coffee, tea, tobacco, and any drug that they can't buy over the counter or that wasn't prescribed to them by a doctor.

This guideline, called the *Word of Wisdom,* comes from the revelation that God gave to the prophet Joseph Smith in the 1830s. Interpreted slightly differently over time, this advice has held the status of commandment since the early 20th century. The Word of Wisdom is important enough now that the LDS church requires members to obey it in order to be admitted into the temple. (For more on the temple, see Chapter 7.)

Latter-day Saints believe that bodily purity and spiritual holiness are connected, and they consider the requirements of the Word of Wisdom to be easy to keep when compared with their spiritual benefit. Latter-day Saints aren't free to drink a sea breeze cocktail, for example, but they're free from addiction to alcohol or the potential for it. In addition, they're protected from the impaired judgment and bodily harm that often result from intoxicants. These freedoms are a tremendous blessing in an age of excess and dependence.

The basic guidelines of the Word of Wisdom are clear, but some of the small stuff falls into gray areas, such as decaf coffee or herbal tea. You'll find Latter-day Saints on both sides of such issues. For more information on the Word of Wisdom, see Chapter 16.

Why Do Latter-day Saints Have Such Large, Strong Families?

To Latter-day Saints, the nuclear family is an eternal principle, with husband and wife *sealed* together eternally and their children sealed to them. Therefore, when Mormon families put effort into strengthening their harmony and togetherness, they're mindful that the investment extends beyond this life. In other words, if they're going to be stuck together forever, they may as well learn to enjoy it. (For more on Mormon families, see Chapter 5.)

Although the Mormon birthrate has declined in recent years, Latter-day Saints still have larger families on average than the typical citizen. One of the main reasons is rooted in the Mormon belief that before birth, all human spirits exist in a state that Latter-day Saints call *premortality* (refer to Chapter 2). Those spirits who are currently embodied on Earth are responsible for bringing still-waiting spirits into righteous Mormon homes and shouldn't put off having children for selfish or worldly reasons. In addition, some Latter-day Saints believe they formed spiritual family relationships in the premortal state, and they don't want to leave behind any spirits who belong in their earthly family.

On the practical level, Latter-day Saints use several techniques for strengthening their families. Throughout Mormondom, families typically reserve Monday evenings for *family home evening*, which they devote to learning the gospel, discussing plans and problems, and enjoying activities together (refer to Chapter 17 for more). In addition, Mormon families ideally read scriptures and kneel in prayer together daily, and the Church constantly teaches good parenting skills and other family-enhancing principles. Latter-day Saints can divorce and even apply to cancel an eternal sealing, but the rate of divorce among temple-sealed couples is much lower than the national average.

Do Latter-day Saints Believe in the Bible or Just the Book of Mormon?

In the Mormon view, the Bible and the Book of Mormon go together like peanut butter and choc— . . . um, we mean that Latter-day Saints love both and regard them both as scripture. The Book of Mormon isn't a replacement for the Bible but a companion to it. As its subtitle says, this book is "Another Testament of

Jesus Christ," pointing readers to the Savior and further describing his role and ministry.

Mormonism's eighth Article of Faith states, "We believe the Bible to be the word of God as far as it is translated correctly; we also believe the Book of Mormon to be the word of God." Latter-day Saints look to the Bible for guidance, knowledge, teachings, and spiritual consolation. They don't, however, think that God stopped there. Although the Bible is primarily an account of God's dealings with the house of Israel in the ancient Near East, God also gave the world the Book of Mormon, a record of Israelites who fled to the Western Hemisphere. In the Mormon mind, both books flow together to tell the story of how God redeems humanity through the atoning sacrifice of Jesus Christ, and both books reveal his ultimate plan for creation.

As we explore in Chapter 9, the main event of the Book of Mormon is the appearance of the resurrected Christ in the New World. The Book of Mormon clarifies some points of doctrine that the Bible doesn't resolve, such as the proper method and reasons for baptism (2 Nephi 31; 3 Nephi 11:23–26) and the nuts and bolts of the eventual resurrection of our bodies (Alma 40). The Book of Mormon complements the Bible but doesn't compete with it. In addition, Latter-day Saints believe in other works of scripture from both ancient and modern prophets, including the Doctrine and Covenants and the Pearl of Great Price (see Chapter 10).

Do Latter-day Saints Really Believe that Humans Can Become Gods?

Nowadays, Latter-day Saints prefer to say that humans can eventually become *like* God, which sounds less presumptuous. But Latter-day Saints don't expect it to happen any time soon. It's not like LDS Sunday schools teach members how to create planets and parent billions of offspring. And it's not like Latter-day Saints will ever stop honoring and obeying their Heavenly Father, even if they become eternal parents like him.

SCRIPTURE

To Latter-day Saints, the idea that God's children can grow up to become like him makes perfect sense, even if humans are still only in the embryonic phase. Other kinds of Christians see this belief as blasphemous, but Latter-day Saints find justification right in the New Testament, where the Lord commands, "Be ye therefore perfect, even as your Father in Heaven is perfect" (Matthew 5:48). The word *perfect* means not only pure and unblemished, but also complete and whole. (For more on the nature of God, see Chapter 3.)

The best summary of this Mormon belief is a phrase that LDS Prophet Lorenzo Snow coined: "As man now is, God once was; as God is now, man may become." For Latter-day Saints, this belief is basic to understanding the purpose of life and the answers to the great questions: Where did we come from? Why are we here? Where are we going? In a nutshell, this life is a test to see who's worthy of godhood, which is attainable only by living the full gospel of Jesus Christ as offered in modern times by the LDS church. (For more about the plan of salvation, see Chapter 2; for more on humans becoming gods, see Chapter 15.)

Why Can't Women Hold Priesthood Offices?

Although Latter-day Saint women can hold some non-priesthood leadership offices in the LDS church, they are never called or ordained to hold priesthood offices, which are the exclusive province of Mormon men.

The reasons for this limitation aren't crystal clear. Most Latter-day Saints seem content to believe that God simply ordained it that way, and it's not our place to ask why what's good for the gander isn't also good for the goose. One widely held theory is that women are so innately spiritual and righteous that they don't need to fulfill priesthood leadership roles in order to grow and become more like God. But this kind of reverse sexism says that women are naturally superior to men, so many Latter-day Saints who feel the explanation is inadequate have rejected it.

While women can't hold priesthood offices, Mormonism offers some ideas that are uniquely empowering to them, such as the belief in a Heavenly Mother (see Chapters 3 and 15) and a positive view of Eve and her role in elevating humankind (see Chapter 2). To outsiders, the fact that women don't hold priesthood offices may appear limiting, but Latter-day Saints don't usually feel that way. Women can receive all the blessings of the priesthood even if they don't hold priesthood offices themselves. As one Mormon prophet put it, "In this Church, the man neither walks ahead of his wife nor behind his wife but at her side. They are coequals in this life in a great enterprise."

For a quick explanation of the meaning of priesthood to Latter-day Saints, see Chapter 4. For more about women and the priesthood, see Chapter 15.

Do Latter-day Saints Still Practice Polygamy?

No. No, no, no, no, and no. Any questions?

Seriously, Latter-day Saints are often surprised and frustrated at just how often this question comes up. The LDS church hasn't approved of earthly polygamy since 1904 (see Chapter 15), and nowadays the Church even excommunicates people who practice it. So the fact that the question never dies is kind of irritating.

In part, this persistence is due to the fact that several fringe groups with ties to old-timey Mormonism still practice polygamy and have often been featured in media and entertainment. Some of these fundamentalists claim that the LDS church has betrayed God by forbidding polygamy. The Church has distanced itself from these small but high-profile groups, urging members of the media to appreciate the distinction between polygamists and mainstream Latter-day Saints.

Some Latter-day Saints complain that in its zeal to be distinguished from contemporary polygamists, the LDS church has gone too far in the other direction, downplaying the vital role that polygamy played in its own history prior to 1904 (see Chapters 13 and 15). But who can wonder why the Church wants to avoid any confusion when people continue to mistakenly believe that Latter-day Saints still practice polygamy?

Why Do Latter-day Saints Revere Joseph Smith?

An angel told Mormonism's founding prophet that his name would "be both good and evil spoken of among all people," and that claim has certainly come to pass. Although Latter-day Saints revere Joseph Smith as a prophet, they realize that he was an imperfect mortal who made some mistakes and needed to repent of some sins. In fact, Joseph himself admitted that he was subject to the faults of human nature, although he denied committing any gross sins.

If the young Joseph was involved in some of the loopy trends of his time, such as digging for treasure and dabbling in folk magic, perhaps that idea simply demonstrates his keen imagination and openness to new things, useful attributes for an emerging prophet of God. In fact, Latter-day Saints love Joseph all the more for his vibrant, down-to-earth personality. The product of a hardscrabble rural upbringing, he was known for roughhousing with children, playing sports, and enjoying a good laugh. Regarding his practice of polygamy, Latter-day Saints don't see it as a character flaw but as his reluctant obedience to one of God's most difficult commandments.

Many anti-Mormons unjustly criticize Joseph Smith, and some observers make the mistake of thinking that Latter-day Saints worship Joseph or put him on an equal footing with the Savior. Although Latter-day Saints believe that Joseph Smith is the world's greatest prophet who ever lived, in terms of his revelatory output and contribution to humankind's potential salvation, he nevertheless remains in the same class as Moses, Abraham, Peter, and other biblical prophets. (For more on Joseph Smith, see Chapters 4, 9, 10, 11, 12, and 15.)

Chapter **20**

Ten Mormon Places to Visit

LDS church members aren't the only ones who are interested in visiting Mormon sites. Many people's first experience of Mormonism comes by either intentionally visiting or haphazardly stumbling upon a historic site that has special significance for Latter-day Saints. Going to some of the places listed in this chapter is a terrific way to find out firsthand about Mormon history and today's Church of Jesus Christ of Latter-day Saints.

In this chapter, we offer a brief overview of some of the most important sites connected with Mormon history and culture, organized in rough chronological order. Except where noted, all these places are open to the public six days a week and are free. Some Church-owned sites are also open for limited hours on Sundays. You can find current details at https://history.churchofjesuschrist.org.

Sharon, Vermont

Sharon, Vermont (also called South Royalton), the birthplace of Mormon founder Joseph Smith, is a little off the radar but well worth a visit. Here you'll see Joseph Smith's birth site, with a small stone marking the place where the Smith family home stood in 1805. A visitors' center offers a permanent exhibit telling the story of the Smith family's years in Vermont, and you can see a 38.5-foot granite monument — one foot for each year of the prophet's life — that the Church dedicated in 1905.

Plan to spend half a day in Sharon to see the Smith family sites. If you're tooling around Vermont, you can also check out Brigham Young's birthplace in Whittington in the southern part of the state. Though Brigham's house no longer stands, you can see a 12-foot granite monument to him, as well as a plaque marking the road where his birthplace once stood.

Palmyra, New York

As the site of many of Mormonism's most sacred events, Palmyra has become a Mormon tourist hot spot in recent years, especially since the Church dedicated a temple there in 2000. Among the many places to visit in and around Palmyra, some highlights include

- » **Sacred Grove and Smith Farm:** This area is thought to include the forest clearing where the teenage Joseph Smith prayed and received the First Vision in the early 1820s (for a recap, see Chapter 4). The site also includes restored buildings used by the Smith family.

- » **Hill Cumorah:** This is the place where Joseph Smith said an angel directed him to the buried golden plates from which he translated the Book of Mormon (see Chapter 9). The site includes several trails, an Angel Moroni monument, and a visitors' center.

- » **Grandin Building:** Located in downtown Palmyra, this building is where the Book of Mormon was first printed in 1830. Unlike many other historic buildings from the Church's founding days, the original Grandin is still standin', making it a particularly interesting place to see.

Kirtland, Ohio

The Mormons' first full-fledged community, located in Kirtland, near Cleveland, Ohio, has gotten a superb facelift. The Church has restored numerous buildings in the town to what they looked like in the 1830s, when more than 2,000 Mormons lived there. Some places to visit in Kirtland include

>> **The Kirtland Temple:** Shown in Chapter 11, this historic temple is open to the public, unlike other Mormon temples (see Chapter 7).

>> **The Newel K. Whitney home and store:** Located on Kirtland's main drag, this building is the original place where Mormons shopped for provisions and where, in an upper room, Joseph Smith received many of the revelations that Mormons regard as scripture. Even those people who don't share the LDS belief in continuing revelation can appreciate this meticulously kept store as a window into the American past, from the bolts of calico on the wall to the hard candy at the counter.

>> **The Kirtland Visitors' Center:** This center offers tourists historical exhibits and a short film about Kirtland in the 1830s.

Other things to see include an old Mormon schoolhouse and the homes of Sidney Rigdon and Hyrum Smith, brother of Joseph. (For more on Mormonism's Kirtland era, see Chapter 11.)

Missouri

Missouri was the site of great heartache and persecution for the Mormons — for a rehearsal of that litany of woe, read Chapter 11 — so visitors to Mormon sites in Missouri today are treated to a mostly sad story of persecution, mob violence, and exile. Many of the sites related to Mormon history are in and around Independence, the Saints' first major settlement in the state. The city is important not just to Latter-day Saints but also to several other Mormon-related denominations that still have a presence in the area. Things to see include

>> **The Community of Christ's auditorium and temple:** With about 250,000 members in more than 60 countries, the Community of Christ is the second-largest Mormon-related denomination, founded by some early Mormons who didn't follow Brigham Young to Utah. The auditorium is the faith's gathering place for their world conferences; their lovely temple, dedicated in 1994, is open to the public for tours, prayer, and worship.

>> **The LDS Visitors' Center:** This visitors' center, which is across the street from the auditorium, occupies a small portion of the land that Joseph Smith declared would be home to Christ's great temple in the Millennium (see Chapter 3). The Community of Christ and other groups own the rest of this choice parcel.

But the Independence area isn't the only place to visit in Missouri. Be sure to stop at the Liberty Jail in Liberty. Joseph was held behind bars in Liberty, so the name must've seemed a bit absurd to him. While he was in jail, though, he received some of the most beautiful revelations of the Doctrine and Covenants (D&C 121–23), which discuss how to deal with adversity and hardship. The Church has rebuilt the jail in cutaway fashion — almost like a movie set — so visitors can imagine where Joseph spent the cold winter of 1838–39.

Nauvoo and Carthage, Illinois

Nauvoo is the pinnacle of the Church's restoration efforts, welcoming approximately 350,000 visitors annually. As such, this city has become quite a tourist mecca, and Latter-day Saints with temple recommends (see Chapter 7) enjoy attending the reconstructed Nauvoo Temple, shown in Figure 20-1.

FIGURE 20-1:
The reconstructed Nauvoo Temple, dedicated in 2002.

walkingarizona/Adobe Stock Photos

Nauvoo and nearby Carthage have so much to see that we can only mention a few of the most significant places:

>> **The Nauvoo Visitors' Center:** This center is a good place to start because you get an overview of Nauvoo history from the Mormon point of view and can arm yourself with maps and brochures of nearby attractions.

>> **Joseph Smith's home and redbrick store:** This home, called the Mansion House, also functioned as an inn where the Prophet and his wife Emma housed visitors to the city. The upper floor of the store was the site of many significant events in Mormon history, including the organization of the women's Relief Society (see Chapter 6) and the introduction of the temple endowment (see Chapter 7).

>> **The Scovil bakery:** No, this place doesn't have great historical significance, but while you're learning about 1840s baking techniques you can munch on their free cookies.

>> **Cultural Hall:** This three-story building is where Mormons held lectures, concerts, dances, and plays. Besides the temple, this building is the most impressive one in Nauvoo.

>> **Carthage Jail:** Here is where Joseph and Hyrum Smith were assassinated on June 27, 1844. Visitors can see a bullet hole in the door to the second-floor room where the brothers were held.

You can also tour the homes of Brigham Young, Wilford Woodruff, Lucy Mack Smith, and Heber C. Kimball (ancestor of coauthor Christopher Kimball Bigelow); see on-site demonstrations of trades and crafts from the period; and enjoy historical performances and presentations at various sites around Nauvoo. For good reason, Nauvoo has been called the "Colonial Williamsburg of the Midwest."

Winter Quarters, Nebraska, and Council Bluffs, Iowa

Although the sites in this section are in two different states, they're both right on the border between Iowa and Nebraska. In case Missouri didn't teach you enough about the Mormons' sufferings and persecutions, just wait — there's more! The winter of 1846–47, which the Saints spent at the place they called *Winter Quarters* (the Mormons sometimes aren't very poetic about place names), was one of the most difficult periods of Mormon history. About 600 people died here from cold, hunger, and disease. Today, the site is called the *Mormon Trail Center* and is an interesting place to visit if you're in the Omaha area. Here are some things to see and do:

» **Check out the pioneer memorial and museum.** The trail center itself features a pioneer memorial, a small museum, and interactive activities for kids, such as pulling a handcart. The center also features a short film about the hardships the Mormons faced in Winter Quarters.

» **Peek around the cemetery.** The adjacent Mormon Pioneer Cemetery was the final resting place for about 325 Latter-day Saints, but the names of all 600 who died here are listed on a memorial plaque. The most memorable object is probably the arresting life-size sculpture of a Mormon couple burying their child in an open grave. Many Mormons consider this statue to be a beautiful tribute to the sacrifices and courage of the pioneers.

» **Stand in the place where Brigham Young became the LDS president.** Just on the other side of the Missouri River was the Mormon settlement in Kanesville (now Council Bluffs), Iowa, where the Church owns a log tabernacle near the site where a church building stood in 1847. This tabernacle represents the place where Brigham Young was sustained as the second president of the Church three and a half years following Joseph Smith's death. (Mormon prophetic succession is much faster nowadays; for more on Brigham Young and the challenges of this first transition of power, see Chapter 12.)

Martin's Cove, Wyoming

No east-to-west, roughly chronological road trip would be complete without a stop at Martin's Cove, the death site for some unfortunate Mormons who were part of the Martin Handcart Company of 1856. Because of their late start in heading west, this pioneer company was trapped by fall blizzards in Wyoming, and 145 of them died before help arrived.

In the late 1990s, the Church leased the land and opened it as a living-history museum, where individuals can try wheeling 150-pound handcarts on fairly challenging expeditions. (Less-hardy pioneers may want to opt out of this exercise.) The story of the hardships and miracles of these handcart pioneers is frequently repeated throughout Mormonism today.

Salt Lake City, Utah

Obviously, Salt Lake City, which has been Mormonism Central ever since the Latter-day Saints arrived in July 1847, has dozens of Mormon history sites to visit. Try to spend several days in Salt Lake City, and stay right downtown if you're not renting a car. Here are the highlights, most of them located in a five-block area known as Temple Square:

» **The Salt Lake Temple:** The temple itself isn't open to the public (sorry, Charlie), but you can walk around much of it, taking in the exterior architecture and the beautiful grounds. This six-spire temple is the pinnacle of LDS architecture and took 40 years to build.

» **The tabernacle:** Home of the world-famous Tabernacle Choir at Temple Square (see Chapter 18), this dome-shaped building resembles half an egg. The coolest part of the tabernacle is its amazing acoustical resonance; you can literally hear a whisper from one end of the building to the other. If you want, you may be able to watch a rehearsal of the Tabernacle Choir.

» **Joseph Smith Memorial Building:** Near the temple is the Joseph Smith Memorial Building, formerly a glamorous hotel that the Church now owns and uses for wedding receptions, office space, movie screenings, restaurants, and local congregational meetings. For fun, take the elevator up to the top floor and enjoy the view. Even on weekdays, you'll be amazed by the number of brides having their pictures taken on the grounds below.

» **FamilySearch Library and Church History Museum:** Located west of the temple, the library houses the world's largest collection of genealogical records (see Chapter 5), and the museum exhibits art and artifacts related to the Mormon experience.

» **Conference Center:** This center takes up an entire block just north of the temple and is open daily for free tours. The 21,000-seat building was completed in 2000; for details, see Chapter 8.

» **Beehive House:** Get a glimpse into 19th-century polygamous life by touring Brigham Young's home, the Beehive House. This national historic landmark is open for free tours and is a great window into President Young's private and public life, even though many of the guides never mention plural marriage.

TIP

After the tour, go around the corner of the building to have lunch in the Lion House Pantry, a cafeteria that offers the best of Mormon comfort food. Be sure to check your low-carb diet at the door and feast on the homemade rolls, cakes, and pies.

Provo, Utah

Unlike Salt Lake City, Provo's highlights are easy to see in a day, and the town is remarkable mostly for the fact that there are just *so ... many ... Mormons*. They're everywhere, gosh darn it. Although Salt Lake City is less than half Mormon now, Provo is one of the most Mormon cities in Utah, with a population of around 95 percent Mormon in some pockets.

The most important site in Provo is Brigham Young University (BYU), which regards itself as the Lord's university and proclaims the motto of "Enter to learn; go forth to serve." Many of the buildings are named after people and places in the Book of Mormon (Deseret Towers and Helaman Halls, for example) or individuals from LDS history. Hit the BYU Store to check out a great range of Mormon books, modest knee-length shorts, and Mormon gifts for sale. You won't find coffee for sale in the BYU student center, but by heavens, you can get all the sugar your heart desires.

Polynesian Cultural Center, Hawaii

Unlike all the other sites in this list, the Polynesian Cultural Center charges admission, and it's not a Mormon history site per se. Begun by the LDS church in 1963 to call attention to the various cultures of Polynesia, this place is the most-visited paid attraction in Hawaii, with more than 1 million visitors annually. Think of it as a very wholesome theme park, with shows, music, craft demonstrations, Polynesian foods, and entertainment (sorry, no roller coasters).

The park is staffed mainly by students from nearby BYU-Hawaii, many of whom are natives of Fiji, Tonga, Samoa, Tahiti, New Zealand, and Hawaii. Although the center isn't directly related to Mormon history, it offers a great window into the Mormon present, because it showcases some of the cultures where Mormonism has taken a strong hold. For information on the Polynesian Cultural Center, check out www.polynesia.com.

While you're in Hawaii, stop by the Laie Hawaii Temple visitors' center (most Mormon temples don't have visitors' centers, but a few do). One of the oldest LDS temples and the first outside the continental United States, the Laie Hawaii Temple was dedicated in 1919. Like the Polynesian Cultural Center, the temple is located in Laie, a Mormon-heavy town on Oahu's North Shore. Regular shuttles connect the cultural center with Waikiki and other places.

Chapter **21**

Ten Famous Latter-day Saints You've Probably Never Heard Of

There are more than 17 million Latter-day Saints in the world. In the United States, 1 in every 50 people is LDS. So, it's no surprise that plenty of famous Mormons exist. In this Internet age, it's pretty easy to find out who the current ones are, so we want to offer you something different: a list of ten famous Latter-day Saints you've probably never heard of, people whose work in politics, science, and the arts has had far-reaching effects.

Martha Hughes Cannon

Visitors to the United States Capitol in Washington, D.C., can see two statues representing Utah. One is of Brigham Young, the LDS church's second prophet and president. The other is of Martha Hughes Cannon (1857–1932). Cannon holds this esteemed place because she was the first woman in the United States to be elected to a state senate. Interestingly, she defeated her own husband for the office — her *polygamous* husband (she was wife number four of six). As a state senator, Cannon got right to work, sponsoring three successful bills in her first month. The first bill provided for the compulsory education of "deaf, dumb, and blind citizens." The second bill mandated that female employees be provided a place to sit while not serving customers. The third bill established a state board of health.

Before becoming a state senator, Cannon had already been a vocal part of the national suffragist movement (as were many Mormon women at the time), speaking at suffragist conventions with Susan B. Anthony and Elizabeth Cady Stanton. During her senate term, Cannon spoke before the U.S. House Committee on the Judiciary about the positive effects of suffrage in Utah. However, it would be another two decades before the Nineteenth Amendment was passed, and women could vote nationally.

In addition to being a politician, Cannon was also a medical doctor. She was the only female student in the medical program at the University of Pennsylvania. When she returned to Utah, she was made the resident physician of the Deseret Hospital in Salt Lake City.

Walker Lewis

During the 1840s and 1850s, the home of Walker Lewis (1798–1856) in Lowell, Massachusetts, was a stop on the Underground Railroad. To help escaping African Americans evade detection, Lewis's son Enoch gave them used clothing, and Walker cut and restyled their hair. Even before then, Lewis had been a high-profile abolitionist. He helped found the Massachusetts General Colored Association in 1829, an all-Black organization that pushed for emancipation. He was also president of the African Humane Society in Boston, which built a school and sponsored a ship for African Americans who wanted to emigrate to Liberia in West Africa.

In 1842, Lewis met a Mormon missionary, converted to the LDS church, and was ordained to the priesthood by Joseph Smith's brother William. He was only the third Black man known to hold the Mormon priesthood before the Church's ban on such ordinations (see Chapter 15 for more on that unfortunate policy, which continued until 1978). Lewis journeyed to Utah in 1851 and received his patriarchal blessing (for more on those, see Chapter 5). During his six-month stay, however, the Utah Territorial Legislature passed an act that made slavery legal in the territory, and Lewis soon returned to Massachusetts to again take up his anti-slavery work.

Floyd Gottfredson

When Floyd Gottfredson (1905–1986) started working for Walt Disney, he had never seen a Mickey Mouse cartoon. By the time he retired, he had probably drawn Mickey more than any other person alive.

Gottfredson grew up as a Latter-day Saint in the still-tiny town of Sigurd, Utah, about 180 miles south of Salt Lake City. He took some correspondence courses in drawing and eventually won second place in a nationwide cartoon contest. In 1928, he went to Los Angeles with his family, hoping to find newspaper work, but was instead hired by Walt Disney.

At first, Gottfredson did some animation, but Disney asked him to take over his daily Mickey Mouse newspaper comic strip until he could find someone else. Forty-five years later, Gottfredson retired from the strip. However, Mickey's readers had no idea that Gottfredson was the artist — and often the writer too — because all the cartoon strips were signed "Walt Disney" for branding reasons. Gottfredson also created the Phantom Blot character, who became a recurring villain in Disney comics for many years. It was only after Gottfredson's retirement that his work was publicly acknowledged.

Philo T. Farnsworth

Possibly the only place more remote than Sigurd, Utah — where Floyd Gottfredson grew up — was Manderfield, Utah. This is where Philo T. Farnsworth was born in 1906. He was one of those kids who was always taking something apart and then fixing it. When Farnsworth was 12, his family moved to Rigby, Idaho, where he fixed the farmhouse generator and converted the hand-powered washing machine into an electric one. At 14 years old, he conceived an idea that, years later, he developed into the first all-electronic television system. This invention became the basis for all broadcast and video systems that followed.

From there, Farnsworth went on to become one of the most prolific inventors in the United States. By the time of his death in 1971, he had received 300 patents, including a method of sterilizing milk using radio waves, an infrared telescope, and the precursor to today's air traffic control systems. In 1990, Utah placed a statue honoring Farnsworth in the United States Capitol, where it stood until Utah replaced it in 2024 with Martha Hughes Cannon's statue, as we discuss earlier.

John Held Jr.

When you think of a "flapper" from the 1920s, the image that comes to your mind is likely based on famous illustrations by John Held Jr. (1889–1958). Held sold his first illustration when he was nine. By the time he was 15, he was drawing for the *Salt Lake Tribune*'s sports section. In 1912, he moved to New York and, after drawing maps for the military in World War I, started illustrating covers for national magazines, including *Life*, *Vanity Fair*, and the *New Yorker*. He thought the fashions and culture of the Roaring '20s were hilarious, and he enjoyed satirizing them in his art. People embraced his portrayals, making him rich and famous.

Held lost both his money and fame when the Great Depression hit, though he continued working and teaching (including a stint at Harvard). Then, in 1953, his 1920s work was revived when *Playboy* (gasp!) published reprints in its first issue.

Held had four wives, but, because he lived after Mormon polygamy ended (see Chapters 13 and 15), he had to divorce his current wife before marrying another.

Frank E. "Ted" Moss

Every time you struggle to open a child-resistant medicine lid, you can thank Utah Senator Frank E. "Ted" Moss (1911–2003), who served from 1959–1977. In addition to sponsoring the Consumer Product Safety Act, he led the effort to set aside Capitol Reef and Arches as national parks, along with places in California, Oregon, Michigan, Wisconsin, Texas, Indiana, New York, Massachusetts, North Carolina, Washington, D.C., and Maryland. This earned him the nickname "Mr. National Park."

Perhaps Moss's Mormonism motivated him when he sponsored a law requiring cigarette companies to put warning labels on their products (see Chapter 16 to learn about the LDS health code). The law also restricted cigarettes from being advertised on television and radio. Moss took this focus on health a step further when he sponsored a series of laws that created Medicaid.

Moss was eventually defeated by another Mormon, Orrin Hatch, who claimed that Moss's 18 long years in Washington had made him lose contact with his constituents. Hatch then went on to serve in the United States Senate for a mere 42 years.

May Swenson

You've likely read a lot of poems by May Swenson (1913–1989). You just don't remember her name because you probably read them in grade school. Though Swenson never set out to write for children, her "riddling poems" have been a big hit since her book *Poems to Solve* came out in 1966. Maybe you remember the one about the visitor from outer space who thinks Earth's inhabitants are cars ("Southbound on the Freeway"). Or the one about young May cutting off a tree branch and using it as a horse, even chomping on a bit of grass herself ("The Centaur").

Swenson was born in Logan, Utah, to Swedish parents who had joined the LDS church and immigrated to the United States. When she was 23, she moved to New York explicitly to become a poet, where she worked for decades on her craft before publishing her first book. She eventually received a MacArthur Fellowship, also called the "genius grant." Mormon author Stephenie Meyer (author of the horror-romance *Twilight* series) used Swenson's poem "Question" at the beginning of her book *The Host*. Though Swenson was not an active LDS church member after she moved to New York, she published poems in some of its official magazines and maintained Mormon ties through her family.

Samuel W. Taylor

It's a classic shot: Fred MacMurray flying with his dog above the city in a car powered by "flubber" in the 1961 Disney movie *The Absent-Minded Professor*. Flubber hit the big screen again in a 1997 movie starring Robin Williams. These movies were based on a short story written by Samuel W. Taylor (1907–1997), grandson of third LDS church president John Taylor and son of apostle John W. Taylor, who was eventually excommunicated because he just couldn't let polygamy go. While Samuel Taylor was a student at Brigham Young University during Prohibition, he wrote a newspaper article about rum-running on campus. The administration asked him to reveal his sources, but he refused and got suspended. After another five suspensions, he dropped out of BYU and moved to California to become a writer.

Taylor wrote short stories, magazine articles, novels, and screenplays — some of them way more serious than anything with flubber in it. He also helped introduce Mormon history to the American public through his novel-like nonfiction books, such as *Nightfall at Nauvoo* (about the trek west) and *The Kingdom or Nothing* (a biography of his polygamous grandfather).

Esther Peterson

When Esther Peterson (1906–1997) was a young girl, she read the letters her big brother sent home during his mission in England. He described the terrible living conditions of the working poor, which Peterson said "let me know very early that all was not right in the world." Also motivated by a Mormon children's song called "Have I Done Any Good in the World Today?" Peterson dedicated her life to social causes.

Starting out teaching classes at the YWCA, Peterson soon moved up from there. She eventually worked with Eleanor Roosevelt on President John F. Kennedy's Commission on the Status of Women, became special assistant on consumer affairs to President Lyndon Johnson, and served as chair of the Consumer Affairs Council for President Jimmy Carter.

At one point, Peterson introduced the idea of nutrition labels to some food company executives. "I got into a squabble with one of the big canners who kept saying that they could not tell the consumer how much water there was in a can of beans." Drawing on her years of bottling food storage, Peterson assured them that a Mormon housewife could figure out how much water was in a bottle of beans, so they could too. It was through her efforts that packaged food now has nutrition labels.

Gladys Knight

Yeah, we know — this is a chapter on famous Mormons you *don't* know, and just about *everybody* knows singer Gladys Knight. But when someone so amazing joins our church, how can we keep from bragging?

Back during her days in Motown with the Pips, Knight surely never imagined she'd one day hear about Mormonism through the grapevine and take the midnight train to Utah. Sure enough, however, in 1997, one of her children introduced her to the faith, and she got baptized. (As far as we know, no Pips have taken the plunge yet.)

Since then, Knight has performed and recorded what some call Mormon gospel music, including gospel versions of Mormon hymns. Invited to perform at several high-profile events at Church headquarters, Knight once commented that she loved Mormon music but then added, "I just think some of it could use a little zip!" Today she lives in Las Vegas, where she leads a Mormon gospel choir.

Index

A

Aaronic Priesthood, 13, 67, 69–71, 113
Abel, Elijah, 261
Abinadi, 168
Abraham (prophet), 87, 179–180, 263–264
Abrahamic covenant, 87, 180
accountability, 22
activities
  during family home evening, 292
  stake, 116
Adam, Mormon view of, 17, 26–28
Adams, Amy (actor), 307
adultery, sealings and, 136
afterlife, phases in, 31–39
age of accountability, 106
agency, 22, 84, 174
alcohol, 314
Alma (prophet), 174
Angels in America (show), 307
animals, 38
announcements, in sacrament meetings, 101
answering spiritual questions, 175
antichrists, 174
Apocrypha, 184
apostasy, 231–232
apostates, 197
Apostle Paul, 125
Apostle Peter, 141
apostles
  about, 143–145
  in Melchizedek Priesthood, 72
  Mormonism on, 18
appearance
  for missionaries, 247
  for sacrament meetings, 100
applying for missions, 240–242
"Are 'Mormons' Christian" essay, 252

Articles of Faith, 86–87, 182–183, 303, 316
Assembly Hall, 138
Association for Mormon Letters, 306
atonement, Mormon view on, 17
authors, bestselling, 306
auxiliary leaders, women as, 145
avoiding sin of pride, 173

B

baby blessings, 109–110
Bachman, Randy (artist), 305
The Backslider (Peterson), 305
Baker, Jenny Oaks (artist), 304–305
baptisms
  about, 105–106, 120
  for the dead, 124–125
  by immersion, 186
  preparing for, 106–107
  process of, 107–108
Beck, Glenn (author), 306
"Becoming Like God" essay, 253
Beehive House, 139, 327
before-life, 20
Benson, Ezra Taft (prophet), 173
bestowing the gift of the Holy Ghost, 73
The Best Two Years (film), 243
Bible
  about, 157–158, 315–316
  additional scriptures with, 160
  King James Version (KJV), 158–160,
    178–179, 180–181
  Matthew, 180–181
  Moses, 178–179
  Smith's corrections to, 160–162
Bigelow, Chris (author), 74, 81, 213, 215, 246, 325
Bigelow, Nahum, 215
birth control, 271

O

P

About the Authors

Christopher Kimball Bigelow is the great-great-great-grandson of an original Mormon apostle and his first of 43 wives. He has authored several books related to Mormonism, including nonfiction, fiction, and memoir. His Mormon-ish literary projects have also included *Irreantum*, a literary magazine; *The Sugar Beet*, a satirical news website; and Zarahemla Books, an alternative press. He served an LDS mission to Melbourne, Australia, and worked as an editor at the LDS church's *Ensign* magazine. His degrees include a BFA in writing, literature, and publishing from Emerson College and an MA in creative writing from Brigham Young University. He has five adult offspring, and he lives with his wife in Provo, Utah. You can reach him at chrisbigelow@gmail.com.

Jana Riess, PhD, is the former Religion Book Review Editor for *Publishers Weekly* magazine and a senior columnist for Religion News Service. She is the author of many books, including *The Next Mormons: How Millennials Are Changing the LDS Church* and *Flunking Sainthood*. She holds degrees in religion from Wellesley College and Princeton Theological Seminary and a PhD in American religious history from Columbia University. She is frequently interviewed by the media on trends in religion. A convert to the LDS church, Riess has spoken at Brigham Young University Women's Conference and at other Mormon gatherings, as well as at professional conferences. Now an empty nester, she lives in Cincinnati with her husband.

Authors' Acknowledgments

We want to thank our mutual agent, Linda Roghaar, who introduced us to each other and encouraged us to collaborate on this project so long ago. We also thank Kathy Cox, our acquisitions editor, and Chrissy Guthrie, our project editor, who oversaw the first edition of this book from concept to finished product.

For this second edition, Chris would like to express appreciation to Stephen Carter, who served as technical editor and provided important expert guidance. Chris also received valuable input from Ann Bigelow, Nathan Kitchen, and the Rev. Katie Langston, and he quite enjoyed working with Katharine Dvorak, his helpful and friendly project editor.

Publisher's Acknowledgments

Executive Editor: Lindsay Berg
Managing Editor: Ajith Kumar
Project Editor: Katharine Dvorak
Technical Editor: Stephen Carter
Editorial Assistant: Shannon Kucaj

Production Editor: Tamilmani Varadharaj
Cover Image: © Alysta/Adobe Stock